P9-CDV-357

TO SERVE THE PEOPLE

John R. Johannes

To Serve the People

Congress and Constituency Service

University of Nebraska Press: Lincoln & London

Portions of the text and tables have previously been published, in different form, in John R. Johannes, "The Distribution of Casework in the U.S. Congress: An Uneven Burden," *Legislative Studies Quarterly* 4 (November 1980): 517–44; John R. Johannes, "Casework as a Technique of U.S. Congressional Oversight of the Executive," *Legislative Studies Quarterly* 4 (August 1979): 325–52; John R. Johannes and John C. McAdams, "The Congressional Incumbency Effect: Is It Casework, Policy Compatibility, or Something Else? An Examination of the 1978 Election," *American Journal of Political Science* 25 (August 1981): 512–42; John R. Johannes, "Congress, the Bureaucracy, and Casework," *Administration and Society,* forthcoming, 1984; John C. McAdams and John R. Johannes, "The 1980 House Elections: Re-examining Some Theories in a Republican Year," *Journal of Politics* 45 (February 1983): 143–62.

The paper in this book meets the guidelines for permanence and durability of the Committee on Production Guidelines for Book Longevity of the Council on Library Resources.

Library of Congress Cataloging in Publication Data

Johannes, John R., 1943–
To serve the people.

Bibliography: p.
Includes index.
1. United States. Congress. 2. Representative government and representation—United States.
I. Title. II. Title: Constituency service.
JK1071.J63 1984   328'.331'0973   83-17050
ISBN 0-8032-2561-X (alk. paper)
ISBN 0-8032-7558-7 (pbk.: alk. paper)

TO FRANCIE

CONTENTS

TABLES

Students of Congress rightfully have devoted most of their attention to the legislature's policymaking and oversight functions. Thus the literature abounds with
books and articles on leadership, committees, and roll call voting behavior. Only
in the last decade has attention seriously focused on the linkage between members of Congress and their constituents. Congressmen's representative styles and
activities have come under scrutiny, but seldom systematically. Casework—
helping constituents with their encounters with the federal bureaucracy—surely
is central to the way congressmen relate to their constituents, but for some reason
scholars virtually have ignored it. With the exception of a handful of articles
written in the 1960s, students of Congress have little detailed information about
this burgeoning function. And only with an explosion of research efforts on
congressional elections in recent years have scholars sought to explore the
theoretically interesting correlates and consequences of constituency service
work. A desire to fill the descriptive void, and to do it analytically to address those
more fundamental implications of casework, accounts for the appearance of
this book.

Actually, there is a simpler and less profound reason for the six years of effort
represented here. On a spring day in 1976, a colleague was advising a student
who wanted to do an internship in the office of a Milwaukee congressman. Not a
specialist on Congress, he asked me what readings were available to assign on the
subject of constituency service. My answer was, ''Not much.'' His rejoinder hit
home: ''Why don't you do something about it?'' Little did either of us know then
that his invitation would yield this book.

My debts for this manuscript run wide. Marquette University's Committee on

Research, the American Philosophical Society's Johnson Fund, and the Everett Dirksen Center for the Study of Congressional Leadership provided crucial funding for trips to Washington, mail questionnaires, telephone calls, and miscellaneous expenses. Some of the data used in this book were made available by the Inter-University Consortium for Political and Social Research. The data for the American National Election Studies of 1978 and 1980 were originally collected by the Center for Political Studies of the Institute for Social Research at the University of Michigan under a grant from the National Science Foundation. Neither the original collectors of the data nor the Consortium bears any responsibility for the analyses or interpretations presented here. I also owe a debt to the staff of the House Commission on Administrative Review, especially its director, Prof. Joseph Cooper. Not only did the staff collect important data and make it available, but several staff members have written thoughtfully on subjects related to constituency service. My colleagues at Marquette and elsewhere provided criticism and, most important, encouragement and stimulation. Referees for various scholarly journals forced me to think and write more clearly. In particular, I am grateful to the editors of the *Legislative Studies Quarterly*, the *American Journal of Political Science*, the *Journal of Politics*, and *Administration and Society* for permitting me to reprint sections of previously published articles. My friend and colleague John McAdams helped both with his critical eye and his statistical wizardry. I owe much to Arthur Maass, my mentor of graduate school days long gone by, for teaching me patience, persistence, and commitment to scholarship. My graduate assistants over the years — Bert de Sousa, Rich Krupa, David Kennedy, Dave Pierro, George Bach, Julie Houk, Anita Clark, Mark Morien, and Dave Kistenbroker — took a good portion of the tedious work from my shoulders, as did our loyal departmental secretaries and typists.

Needless to say, this book could not have been written without the cooperation of the hundreds of senators, representatives, congressional staffers, and department and agency officials who consented to be interviewed, responded to mail questionnaires, and/or talked with me over the phone. During the time I worked on this project, I came to admire them for their dedication, hard work, honesty, patience, and good humor. The casework system (chapters 4 and 5) is populated, with a handful of exceptions, with devoted public servants, many of whom find themselves trapped in a frustrating system not of their own making that places incredible demands on their physical, emotional, and mental health. They taught me a great deal, and I want to thank them publicly. There are too many to mention by name, but three deserve particular attention: Louise Buchanan, Barbara Means, and Mary Jane Yarrington. Each gave me extra time and provided unusual degrees of insight into and enthusiasm for a complex phenomenon. Former

Congressman Henry Reuss (D., Wis.) and his staff put up with my presence in their Washington office for two weeks in 1982 and deserve a Medal of Honor for it.

Finally, I owe the greatest debt to my sharpest critic, constant prodder, and favorite person, my wife, Francie. Not only did she keep me going when I got discouraged, but she was invaluable when it came to using the Marquette computer system to type, edit, organize, and index the manuscript. Some of her computer skills rubbed off on our daughter, Terri, who also worked to produce the final version.

This book, then, is not just about another aspect of congressional life. It is about *people* — people who give of themselves in a variety of ways. People constitute government as much as, or more than, laws, rules, or procedures. I have tried to write about people and how they behave. A number of hypotheses and theories come under scrutiny, and some fare better than others. What follows may not be the final word on casework — I hope it is not, since there is a lot left to be learned. Acknowledging the cooperation and assistance I have received, I take responsibility for errors of fact and interpretation.

John R. Johannes
Marquette University

CHAPTER 1

Introduction

What do people do when they run into problems in dealing with the federal bureaucracy? Stand in a line a little longer? Plead? Hire a lawyer? Picket? Or give up? More and more, in recent years, the answer seems to be: they write their congressman.

Scarcely a day goes by in a congressional office during which congressmen and their staffers are not confronted with constituent complaints and requests. Whether the problem is a social security check that is overdue, a soldier requesting a transfer to another base, a plea to expedite a special immigration application, or a mayor's request for assistance in applying for a sewer grant for his city, helping constituents cope with bureaucratic red tape has become big business in Congress. Along with the growth of this "constituency service" or "casework" function of the legislature come time pressures on senators and representatives, burgeoning and increasingly specialized staffs, the expansion of congressional offices in home districts and states, a concomitant growth in federal agency congressional liaison offices—and some intriguing problems, consequences, and, mostly, questions. Since the 1960s a veritable revolution of casework in Congress has occurred, in terms both of workload and Congress's ability to cope. This book examines the manifestations, causes, and consequences of the so-called ombudsman or "errand boy" role of Congress.

1.1. The Many Faces of Constituency Service

Although this is a study of one type of constituency service, namely casework, there are a host of ways in which senators and representatives tend to the needs and whims of their constituents. Nowhere, perhaps, have they been better described than in Luther Patrick's definition of a modern member of Congress:

A Congressman . . . has become an expanded messenger boy, an employment agency, getter-out of the Navy, Army, and Marines, a wardheeler, trouble shooter, law explainer, bill finder, issue translator, resolution interpreter, controversy-oil pourer, glad hand extender, business promoter, veterans affairs adjuster, ex-serviceman's champion, watchdog for the underdog, sympathizer for the upperdog, kisser of babies, recoverer of lost baggage, soberer of delegates, adjuster for traffic violations and voters straying into Washington and into the toils of the law, binder-up of broken hearts, financial wet nurse, a good samaritan, contributor to good causes — there are so many causes — cornerstone layer, public building and bridge dedicator, and ship christener.[1]

Contemporary discussions of constituency service include at least the following: obtaining federal government funds for states or congressional districts; furnishing government pamphlets to new parents, gardeners, and amateur carpenters; providing documents to scholars and students; sending flags that have flown (if only for a few seconds) over the Capitol to veterans' groups; getting tickets for special White House tours; securing hotel reservations for visitors, and seeing them when they come; allocating patronage appointments and helping constituents seeking jobs; and distributing service academy appointments — to name just a few. And such "service" activities only scratch the surface of techniques available to congressmen for bringing themselves to the attention of voters. Taped interviews or reports for local radio and television stations (prepared at nominal cost in House and Senate recording studios), newspaper columns, press releases, newsletters and questionnaires, speaking engagements, visits to the home district or state, letters of condolence or congratulation, "town meetings" and office hours in the home district, and, above all, prompt and polite responses to constituent letters and phone calls — all these might be called forms of "service" as well.

This study employs a much narrower focus, examining two particular forms of constituency service: casework and federal projects assistance (sometimes called "high-level" or "super" casework). Casework is intervention for individuals, groups, or organizations (including businesses) that have requests of, grievances against, or a need for access to federal (and occasionally state or local) government departments or agencies. "Projects" refers to assisting state and local governments in their attempts to secure federal grants from agencies that possess discretion in allocating such funds. Projects in this sense are distinguishable from traditional "pork barrel" activities, which entail crafting legislative provisions to secure federal revenue sharing, contracts, buildings, dams, bridges, or harbor dredging for districts or states.[2] Similarly, casework is distinguishable from merely filling requests for documents, providing White House tour tickets, or making military academy appointments. The essence of both casework and projects as defined here is simply the activity of senators, representatives, and their staffs to break through bureaucratic logjams to help citizens receive their "due" or help them register their complaints. It is, in short, the function of Congress as intermediary between the government and the governed — between citizens and the bureaucracy. In its most innocuous form, casework could be a follow-up phone call from a congressional office to an agency to inquire about the status of a constituent's application for some government benefit. In its extreme form, it could mean the introduction of a private bill to make an exception to a federal statute for a constituent in need.[3]

An objection can be raised: why limit the study of constituency service to casework? Why not include the whole range of activities designed to assist or satisfy constituents? The answer has both practical and theoretical components. In terms of feasibility, it would be virtually impossible to collect data on, measure, and analyze all the things congressmen do to serve constituents. More important, the focus is on casework because, by "re-presenting" constituents to executive bureaucracies, congressmen become intermediaries and linkages. The study of other "errand boy" and "home style" aspects of the job must be left to others.

1.2. The Rationale for Studying Casework

As Walter Kravitz indicated in his 1968 review of the literature on casework: "Casework has generated considerable controversy among observers and members of Congress for many years. That controversy involved not only the merits of the practice but also the facts about its nature and extent. Reliable and comprehensive information is in short supply. The available literature seldom treats the subject in any detailed or systematic fashion. . . . [T]here is little precision in our knowledge of this area of congressional activity."[4]

The reason for Kravitz's lament is that most of what is known about constituency service derives from anecdotal accounts, memoirs, journalistic treatments of congressional office activities, and simple common sense. Worse, despite growing references to casework in studies of congressional staffing, elections, oversight, and behavior, virtually no one has responded to Kravitz's call for serious — let alone systematic — study of congressional casework. The same is true for constituency service in state legislatures. Surprisingly, however, the literature on constituency service in other nations, especially those of the third world, is substantial, as is the literature on the ombudsman in various countries. Unfortunately, such studies offer few hypotheses or insights directly applicable to the United States.

This book constitutes an attempt to fill the void. Its theses are that casework has become semi-institutionalized, so that Congress now functions as the American version of the European ombudsman; that casework is an important element of the broader representative function; that this form of representation has negative consequences for Congress and the executive; but that its positive contributions outweigh the drawbacks.

Since "representation" is such a complex and catchall term, a useful alternative to use in examining some aspects of casework is "responsiveness." Legislators' responsiveness to constituents occurs in four areas: policy responsiveness (voting behavior in accord with constituents' needs or, perhaps, wishes); service responsiveness (casework, legislative mail, attentiveness to constituents); allocation responsiveness (federal projects, pork barrel, and distributive policies); and symbolic responsiveness (public satisfaction with the legislator).[5] Scholars tend to concentrate on the first and fourth dimensions, attempting to ascertain how well congressmen's roll call voting reflects constituent opinion on policy matters, how much impact constituents have on their representatives, and what sorts of role orientations legislators adopt. The second and third (and, to an extent, the fourth) of these are of concern here: how and how well do senators and representatives exhibit allocation and especially service responsiveness — and with what consequences?

If casework in fact is a linkage mechanism for re-presenting citizens to their government — if it is an important form of responsiveness — two sets of questions must be addressed. The first concerns the nature of the linkage system. Who is involved: which citizens, which legislators, what sort of congressional and agency staff personnel? What motivates people to request help, and what motivates congressmen to devote either time or staff resources to this enterprise? How is the casework operation structured? By what legislative-executive transactions are citizens' demands and grievances dealt with? Can these motives, decisions, structures, and processes be systematically explained?

The second set of questions concerns the consequences of Congress's having become the national ombudsman — or, more precisely, of each individual congressman's having become one of 535 ombudsmen for his or her constituents. These consequences concern the interrelationships among the four forms of responsiveness and the impact of casework (service responsiveness) on the institutional performance of Congress in other areas.

It has been well documented that congressmen represent their constituents' policy views reasonably well, at least when those views bear on salient issues and when those views are known to the congressmen. Congress collectively may represent American public opinion even better than it does dyadically (on a district-by-district basis).[6] What is of interest here is whether by being attentive to particularistic, nonpolicy constituent concerns congressmen lose the incentive to worry about policy responsiveness. If congressmen can win the support of constituents by tending to their requests for help and favors, will such support lead to electoral security? If so, will security lead to greater voting and policymaking leeway for the legislators? And will that leeway contribute to or detract from genuine policy responsiveness? Although the results of this research cannot directly assess the impact of casework on policy representation (or on symbolic representation), it can help to measure casework's electoral effect on voters.

The other side of the policy versus service coin has to do with the incentives that develop from citizen expectations and demands. Casework pressures on congressmen and their staffs are real. How do members react in terms of allocating their own time and that of their staffs? Does the attention given to citizen grievances excessively cut into the time and resources that might otherwise be devoted to policymaking? Was the congressman correct who several years ago complained that "I thought I was going to be Daniel Webster and I found that most of my work consisted of personal work for constituents"?[7]

Institutionally, the question can be framed bluntly: Does casework interfere with Congress's ability to perform its collective legislative and oversight tasks by diverting the attention and resources of its members and staffs? Or might it contribute positively to such duties? Looking beyond Congress, does casework interfere with the routines, integrity, or efficiency of the administrative process, thus handicapping policy implementation? How are the bureaucrats affected? Does the casework enterprise yield equitable results? If not, it would constitute a threat to symbolic representation — to citizens' trust in government and thus to government's legitimacy. Finally, can anything be done to improve the grievance-handling process? The argument throughout is that casework has created problems for Congress and for government in general, but that on balance it contributes positively to the representational and policy processes. Indeed, casework may be an indispensable mechanism for injecting the American political culture's concern with individual rights and local interests into those policy processes and for applying — concretely and beneficially — the culture's antibureaucratic values to the political system.

1.3. Methodology and Data

Casework is done primarily by congressional staffers who deal with middle- and lower-level executive branch officials. Fittingly, these men and women constitute the primary sources of data and the main focus of this study. As detailed in the appendix, the methods of data collection were mail questionnaires, personal interviews, and telephone interviews from/with congressional and executive branch personnel during 1977 and 1978. Responses that were sufficiently complete to warrant coding and storage in computerized form totaled 632: 11 senators, 37 representatives, 106 Senate staff members, 248 House aides, and 232 executive branch officials.

Since the list of questions to be asked of respondents was lengthy, and since new questions arose during various stages of the study, not all respondents were asked the same or the full range of questions. Thus, complete data were not compiled for each respondent or for each congressional office in the sample. However, at least partial data are available for the 1977–78 casework operations of 10 former senators, 27 former representatives, 75 Senate and 178 House offices, 11 departments, 8 agencies, and 3 regulatory commissions. The samples are not strictly random, but they are representative in all meaningful ways. As a check, the author used personal and telephone interviews and mail questionnaires in 1982 to collect several items of data on 137 offices, 66 of which were included in the 1977–78 sample.

Additional information comes from a 1977 survey of congressional offices undertaken by the Office of Management and Budget; the 1977–78 work of the House Commission on Administrative Review; and the 1978 and 1980 National Election Studies of the Center for Political Studies at the University of Michigan.

CHAPTER 2

Congressional and Constituent Perspectives on Casework

What are cases like? From whom do they come? How do congressmen perceive casework and why do they get involved? These are questions for which answers are all too casually offered, often leading to erroneous or at least misleading conclusions and interpretations about the "errand boy" function of Congress. This chapter examines congressmen's and citizens' perspectives on casework and surveys the sorts of cases that Congress must deal with.

2.1. Importance

Evidence accumulated over the past two decades clearly indicates that congressmen perceive constituent service as important for themselves and, to a lesser degree, for the Congress as an institution. In the early 1960s, a survey of 116 members of the House found that three-quarters agreed that congressmen should go to bat for constituents in their dealings with the executive agencies, and two-fifths of a 1971 sample gave more weight to the constituency service function than to the legislative function in describing the most important aspects of their jobs. Only one in four assigned greater weight to the legislative task.[1] And in interviews and questionnaires employed in this study with 24 former senators and representatives, more placed casework first in importance than any other function.

Such testimony may be misleading, however, and should not be taken as proof of casework's preeminent standing among congressional duties. The 24 members mentioned above, for example, rated legislative work in committee and on the floor and representing the views of their constituents nearly as important as casework; in addition, it is not always clear whether the assessments of "importance" were empirical or normative judgments. Better evidence comes from the House Commission on Administrative Review (the Obey Commission), which in 1977 collected attitudinal data from interviews with some 150 members of the House. The commission's survey asked two sorts of questions, the first pertaining to casework and projects as a duty of the House of Representatives, and the second relating to their importance for individual members. Asked what roles the House *should* play in the federal government, only 2 percent of the respondents gave first mention to the ombudsman (casework) role, compared to 72 percent citing the legislative and 10 percent the oversight functions.[2] On the second mention, the proportion of members favoring the ombudsman role jumped to 25 percent, somewhat behind the 32 percent who chose oversight. No doubt had members been afforded a third choice, casework would have been mentioned by many more respondents. Apparently, casework is judged to be an important and presumably legitimate function, but it is given a subordinate ranking in the hierarchy of important duties of Congress.

The commission also asked with what degree of importance its respondents *personally* "ought to treat" each of seventeen activities (without asking why they felt that way). Since the job of the congressman is as diverse as it is demanding, it is not surprising that 70 percent or more of the responding members rated all seventeen tasks as "very" or "fairly" important (see table 2.1). Depending on whether one uses only the "very important" or includes the "somewhat important" responses, casework ranked sixth or tenth; federal grants and projects placed eleventh. One aspect of symbolic responsiveness, "getting back to your district to keep in touch with your constituents," was rated most or second most important. "Taking time to explain what government is doing" also was highly valued. Note, however, that most of the top-rated activities were legislative and oversight tasks. Some of the most obvious forms of constituent attentiveness—meeting with constituents visiting Washington, giving speeches and making personal appearances before citizen groups, keeping in touch with local government officials, and sending newsletters to constituents—were among the activities judged relatively least significant (although still deemed very important by those surveyed). Clearly, what members believe to be the major duties of the House (legislation and oversight) also are deemed important for members personally.

What needs study is whether there are behavioral discrepancies between what members *think* is important (for the House and for themselves) and what they believe constituent and reelection—and specifically casework—pressures force them to *do*. Such questions are considered in subsequent chapters. For now, however, it is sufficient to note that casework and other forms of constituency service are seen as important, especially to members personally, but they hardly enjoy a preeminence in congressmen's collective sense of importance. Similar conclusions seem to apply to state legislators,[3] and roughly comparable results have been reported by students of legislatures in other nations, even where, for a variety of reasons, casework and constituency service receive higher marks for importance.[4]

Although one might expect otherwise, neither junior nor senior representatives in the Obey Commission's sample were disproportionately likely to mention the ombudsman role as one of the two major tasks of the House or to consider that helping constituents and securing federal funds for their districts ought to be considered "very" important for them individually. Nor did partisan differences matter with respect to individual casework. Democrats, however, did have a greater tendency than Republicans to believe that winning a "fair share" of federal largesse for their districts should be a very important concern for them. The difference might be explained by noting that Democrats tend to represent less affluent and thus more needy constituencies and that a Democratic administration controlled the executive branch at the time of the survey, thus presumably making it easier for congressional Democrats to gain access to federal grants.[5]

If the argument that congressmen overemphasize constituency service relative to legislative and oversight tasks is true—and therefore if we are witnessing a Congress increasingly populated by reelection-oriented opportunists—one would expect to find that congressmen are consistent in their views of those duties and that they dichotomize, at least mentally, the functions and duties they are to perform into "constituency" and "institutional" groupings. Thus it is instructive to ask whether members in fact divide on the basis of their general orientations towards their jobs (on the basis of their purposive "roles"). While duplicating the specific constructs used in previous studies of legislative roles is impossible, one can investigate two such orientations: institutional or policy (legislative and oversight functions) and constituency (representational functions). If there were attitudinal tensions between the two, one might expect to find representatives splitting into two clusters: one emphasizing legislative and oversight duties and downplaying the importance of constituency-related activities, and a second group stressing the value of attending to the constituency while viewing policy activities as relatively less important. Extensive analysis of the Obey Commission's data, however, reveals little evidence of such a dichotomy of orientations. Most members saw both sets of duties as important. Few viewed one type of activity as distinctly "very" important and, simultaneously, the other as relatively less important.[6]

Table 2.1: Perceived Importance of Seventeen House Functions

Function	Percentage of Members Saying Function Should Be Treated as:		
	Very Important	Fairly Important	Slightly or Not Important
Working in subcommittee to develop legislation	82	12	3
Getting back to district to stay in touch with constituents	74	21	3
Studying and doing basic research on legislation	73	21	4
Working in full committee to develop legislation	71	22	4
Debating and voting on House floor	64	26	8
Helping people in your district who have problems with government (casework)	58	26	14
Working in committee or subcommittee on oversight	56	32	11
Working with other members to build support for legislation	55	38	6
Taking time to explain to citizens what their government is doing to solve problems	53	33	10
Keeping track of how agencies administer laws	53	36	10
Making sure your district gets fair share of government money and projects	44	34	20
Taking time to gain firsthand knowledge of foreign affairs	44	30	23

continued

Table 2.1: *continued*

Function	Percentage of Members Saying Function Should Be Treated as:		
	Very Important	Fairly Important	Slightly or Not Important
Sending newsletters about activities of congress to constituents	35	35	28
Meeting with constituents visiting Washington	35	37	27
Giving speeches and personal appearances to talk to groups about matters before congress	32	40	26
Managing and administering your office	29	32	37
Staying in touch with local government officials in your district	26	44	27

SOURCE: House Commission on Administrative Review, *Final Report,* H. Doc. 95-272, vol. 2, pp. 879–82.

NOTE: For each question, 3 percent of the respondents answered "Not Sure." Percentages may not equal 100 due to rounding error. $N = 145$ or 146.

2.2. Motives

Congressmen's motives in undertaking casework are so crucial that any discussion of "importance" is suspect unless one knows *why* members believe casework and projects work to be important. If they view the importance as stemming from considerations of service, allocation, and genuine symbolic responsiveness — if they believe that constituents have a right to assistance and that rendering that assistance bolsters the legitimacy of Congress — one may applaud their sense of values. If their motives center on the possible electoral payoffs (while they judge casework to be a nuisance), a fraud of sorts is being perpetrated, especially if such judgments and motives lead to unequal treatment of requests from constituents on the basis of whether they are voters or nonvoters, supporters or opponents. Of course, from the constituent's perspective, it matters little in the short run what the motive is, provided he or she receives satisfactory treatment. In the long run, however, it would matter. Constituents might eventually discover the congressman's real goals, which could lead to cynicism. And if a constituency, collectively misled by its congressman, continued to reelect him on service or "errand boy" grounds, and if that allowed the member to misrepresent his constituents in terms of policy, a serious problem would exist.

To ask why legislators consider casework and other forms of constituency service as important as they do and to ask what rewards they get or anticipate from it may appear to be asking the obvious. Everyone "knows" that congressmen take care of constituents in order to be reelected. But the questions are more complex and the answers more subtle than what first meets the eye. Scholars investigating legislative bodies around the world find that legislators engage in constituent service for a variety of nonelectoral reasons. Perhaps the most frequently mentioned is simple constituent need, especially in third world nations where status, class, and educational inequality stand as barriers between most citizens and the executive bureaucracies that exercise control over such key commodities as food, seeds, and education.[7] Because legislators are "tribunes," who protect their constituents, writes J. Blondel, "the least influential constituents, those who are afraid to go to social workers or government offices, will tend to approach legislators for a variety of grievances and demands which could, and indeed eventually probably will, go to the 'regular channels.' "[8] Closely related to need are high "public expectations" of constituency service.[9] Public demand itself becomes a motive for service on the part of legislators — so much so that scholars have linked it to various legislative role orientations, with some identifying "errand running" as a distinctive role.[10]

Casework has been conceptualized as a power equalization mechanism. In most countries legislatures are weak vis-à-vis executives. Constituency service furnishes legislators an opportunity for exercising influence over bureaucrats, and may also contribute to enhanced personal prestige and public support for the legislator. Moreover, doing casework in such legislatures is one way — perhaps the only way — for powerless politicians to carve out a niche for themselves, and it may be a major vehicle for demonstrating competence and worthiness for promotion to higher governmental (executive) positions. Conversely, to the extent that casework has electoral consequences, members of legislatures where national partisan electoral trends are strong or where local party leaders are particularly domineering may see constituency service as a vehicle for securing independence from such forces, or even from future constituency pressures that might restrict advancement to cabinet-level duties.[11] Finally, some legislators see casework as an educational opportunity and channel for communicating valuable information which may be used in their policymaking and legislative oversight tasks.[12]

Many of these purposes and rewards hold in the American context. High on any list of motives is the expectation that constituency service will contribute to reelection, a belief held not only by members and staffs of Congress but by political scientists and journalists as well. Of thirty-nine current and former senators and representatives contacted, ten gave first mention to the electoral motivation in casework when asked why they undertook casework and what benefits they received from it. Six others mentioned it as their second or third responses. "No one will survive in Congress without good constituent service; it's that simple," said one senator.[13] According to one House member, his office is involved in casework "because it gets you votes." "Here's where you do yourself the most good politically."[14]

Asked their assessment of the proposition that "the primary reason most members of Congress perform constituency service has to do with reelection," 39 members were as likely to agree (44 percent) as to disagree (38 percent); while 297 staffers—mostly caseworkers in Washington and aides in home offices— were more in disagreement (44 percent) than agreement (32 percent). A similar survey conducted in 1977 turned up even stronger disagreement with the election motive hypothesis.[15] Younger, least experienced, and better-educated aides tended to emphasize the electoral motive more than their colleagues, suggesting either that staff orientations toward casework are evolving (toward an electoral motivation) or that a socialization process is at work, wherein experience on the job affects one's outlook.

Not just reelection, but reelection by a comfortable margin, seems to be the driving force. Congressmen want to be reelected with as much security as possible, probably as a means of gaining independence from constituents' policy preferences. Congressmen increasingly seem to want to adopt a trustee role, preferring to act on behalf of what they consider to be the national good—or the needs of their districts—rather than to follow slavishly their constituents' policy views.[16] As Fenno noted, the typical congressman "cultivates support at home, because he wants voting (and other) leeway in Washington."[17] Of 99 members and staffers surveyed, 60 agreed or strongly agreed that casework allows members policy flexibility; only 14 disagreed. Flexibility comes from being trusted and being reelected. As a junior member explained, "I can't be a real legislative honcho yet; I've got to build up some seniority."

The underlying assumption in all this is that members can "barter" service and assistance with constituents in return for favorable job evaluations and trust, which in turn lead not only to votes but to a willingness to let their representatives act as statesmen, using their best judgments to solve national problems. As will be argued later, however, this "exchange" is not always equal; nor are its terms consistently honored by the participants.

Another way to look at the reelection motive is to take the constituents' perspective. Davidson, for example, has argued that congressmen developed their staffs and services more because they believed that citizens *expected* them to run errands than because they really enjoyed doing so.[18] But just how strong are such expectations? Two means are available to measure them. One is to examine the importance that citizens assign to the casework function, especially relative to other congressional duties; presumably, the more they value the services, the more they will come to expect them. The second is to ask constituents if they believe that their congressman would help them if they needed assistance.

The Obey Commission's survey of 1,510 adult Americans asked what kinds of things respondents felt were most important for an individual congressman to do. The most frequent responses to this open-ended question (mentioned by 37 percent of respondents) fell into the category summarized as "work to solve problems in his district, help the people, respond to issues, needs, of our areas." How many of these answers refer explicitly to casework cannot be determined.[19] When the focus of the question was changed from an individual congressman to Congress itself, and when respondents were faced with eight specific functions to judge, 70 percent of the public agreed that it was "very important" for Congress to provide "people in their districts with a direct line to the Federal Government." Another 21 percent saw that role as "fairly" important. All functions were highly rated, with between 89 and 96 percent judging each to be very or fairly important.[20] Given a list of twelve activities and asked the degree of importance with which their *own* congressman "ought" to treat each, 90 percent thought it very or fairly important for their representative to help people in their district who have personal problems with the government; 94 percent believed it relatively important for their congressman to get a fair share of government money and projects for their district. Again, all twelve functions were considered important.[21] Citizens of lower social, educational, and economic status were slightly more inclined to rate constituency service as very important for Congress and for their own representative than were those of higher status.

The weakness in these data is that constituents were not forced to choose among functions; it is too easy to rate all of them as important. But the 1978 National Election Study conducted by the University of Michigan's Center for Political Studies did ask the public which of five separate functions should be the most important job of a congressman, which the second most important, and so on. Casework was ranked first by only 11 percent of the 2,304 respondents, second by 13 percent, and third by 17 percent. Over one-quarter placed it in fifth (last) place. Securing federal projects for one's district was ranked first by 15 percent, second and third by 18 percent each, and last by 17 percent of the sample. Citizens placed casework and projects one or two percentage points lower for their senators. As was true in the 1977 House commission data, there was in 1978 a notable tendency for respondents of lower socio-educational-economic status—and nonvoters—to give higher rankings to casework and projects. Using a simple ordering scheme it is easy to develop an overall ranking of the five functions. For the House, keeping in touch with constituents was deemed by far the most important function; oversight, surprisingly, placed second, followed by federal projects, legislation, and—far behind—casework. The ranking for senators was similar.

Much more indicative of the level of public expectations were the results of another question asked in the 1978 and 1980 CPS surveys: "If you had a problem that your Representative . . . could do something about, do you think (he/she) would be very helpful, somewhat helpful, or not very helpful to you?" Combining the two surveys, fully 36 percent of all respondents (excluding "it depends" and "don't know" answers) thought that their congressman would be very helpful, with half deeming theirs somewhat helpful. Only 14 percent said their representative would not be very helpful in such situations. These expectations in 1978 and 1980 were not randomly distributed. The elderly and less well-educated tended more consistently to expect their representative to be helpful, as did those who had come in contact with their congressman, who were politically active and efficacious, who exhibited low degrees of political cynicism, and who identified with the political party of their congressman.[22]

The appropriate conclusion, it seems, is that while the public does not think cases and projects are as important as legislative and oversight duties, it does value them and clearly expects that members will prove helpful if constituents have to call on them. Further, they evaluate individual congressmen quite favorably for the quality of service rendered, while criticizing the institution for its poor performance on policy matters.[23]

Congressmen understand these expectations. The House commission asked its sample of representatives what were the major kinds of jobs and duties they felt they were expected to perform as individual members of Congress. Four of five responded in terms of the constituent service role, second only to the 87 percent citing legislative and other policy-related duties.[24] Although it might be expected that junior congressmen would be most attuned to constituent casework demands, analysis of the commission's data suggests otherwise. Junior representatives were slightly less likely than their senior colleagues to mention the constituency service role when asked what is expected of them. Interestingly, members' own assessments of the importance—to them—of casework and projects were basically unrelated to the expectations they felt. Were they positively correlated one could argue that service responsiveness was genuinely operative. Were they negatively linked, one would suspect a tension at work—between perceived expectations and a sense of what members ought to be doing. Neither was the case.

Underpinning public expectations for service—and very apparent to most members of Congress—is the simple fact of need, which often is coupled with a sense of constituent powerlessness and the sort of "status inequality" mentioned above. *Congressmen care about their constituents*. In the words of a former senator, "If congressmen don't do it, nobody will; there's a lot of people out there who need help." One House staffer said of his boss: "Congressman——is a populist and has a soft spot in his heart for a schmuck getting screwed."

Surprisingly, in offices where electoral benefits are of no concern, casework remains a high priority. Said one aide: "Look, the senator's retiring next year, everyone knows that. Yet we work just as hard as ever, and he wants it that way, to take care of constituents." In another Senate office, a caseworker insisted that, vote-wise, "the senator doesn't need it, but he sees it as a real service he can provide—a service he wants to do. We're proud of our casework." And even in offices where casework carries negative connotations, there is empathy: "The senator sees it as a burden that shouldn't have to be done, but with a huge, confusing bureaucracy, it becomes necessary. People need an outside source of leverage." Interestingly, in a couple of offices where casework carried high emotional value, the congressmen themselves had begun their careers as staffers specializing in, or at least often handling, casework.

Closely tied to these motivations is an antibureaucratic feeling best summed up by a former plains state Republican senator: "If there weren't 535 people in Washington to come to the rescue of the average citizen, only God knows what more lashes those bureaucrats would lay on the backs of people. Why, those people in the agencies make life impossible." A freshman representative from the same state explained: "Given a bureaucracy that isn't very responsive and can't use discretion when needed, problems develop and citizens have legitimate complaints. Someone has to help them through the maze of the bureaucracy." And by coming to the rescue of the average citizen, congressmen can and do exert power over the executive. A few congressional offices go further. "We hate bureaucrats—we really do," said the AA (administrative assistant) to a very conservative Republican, who himself confirmed the feeling moments later.

Another constantly mentioned impulse is to "make the government work" and to correct injustice. Said one congressman: "Government is supposed to be the servant of the people; our job is to iron out the bugs." According to another, casework is needed to "get the bureaucracy to do what it should do. After all, this government is supposed to be a democracy of the people, and though it's basically organized and run democratically, sometimes it's run like a monarchy." References to casework as a type of symbolic responsiveness were common, as members lamented the danger of popular alienation from and cynicism about government. As a former Republican senator put it: "It is one method, perhaps the best method, of keeping people involved; without it they would deal only with the bureaucracy, and frustration and alienation would grow." A former midwestern Democratic representative mixed some metaphors in his description: "Casework instills confidence; it keeps the fabric of the society loose and supple — not so tightly stretched that it'll tear. It has to be done to keep the country's confidence in government. People need that connection. The congressman is the ball bearing that keeps things moving. He's the last link people have with their government."

Suggesting a possible linkage between casework and policy functions, several members mentioned that casework is a valuable means of feedback — a way not only of keeping track of what executive agencies are doing but also of staying in touch with people and their problems. A midwestern Republican congressman believed that: "Most congressmen don't live a normal life. We don't stand in line and fight bureaucrats. Casework is a link, a fragile bridge, back to the real world. Maybe through casework congressmen can develop empathy with the problems people have. This sort of pressure from constituents is good — and it is felt."

Of all the motives and rewards that senators and representatives associate with casework, personal satisfaction was ranked first by more respondents than was any other. "My greatest satisfaction comes from helping others," commented one representative. Another insisted that "it gives me a good feeling to know I can help." One former member of the House put it more colorfully: "There are few satisfactions in that zoo, so the only way to feel good was to do casework. Sometimes I could be in heat over some legislative issue, but so frustrated that I'd go to my staff and say, 'Give me a case to work on.' It was the only satisfaction I could get much of the time." And when the occasional "thank-you" letters come in, said one congressman, "I get a real thrill." A few respondents added that casework provided an opportunity to teach constituents how government works and, more important, to influence their opinions.

Allied to the sense of gratification and satisfaction is a sense of duty: "I saw it as part of my oath of office." For a few members, of course, a beleaguered sense of duty is the only (or primary) reason they do casework. The 4 percent who told the Obey Commission that casework ought to be "not at all important" really do exist. Some members and staffers believe casework to be little more than a pain in the neck.

In the United States, therefore, as in legislatures around the world, the motivations for and satisfactions from doing casework are varied. No one motive can explain the effort expended on cases and projects. To deny the electoral incentive is foolish, but to emphasize it to the virtual exclusion of others is no less so. Casework simply is perceived as an important and legitimate function resting upon a variety of motives. As one staffer put it, "You can't separate out or isolate any motives. It's a piece of whole cloth."

2.3. Types of Cases

Casework includes "particularized benefits" that individuals, organized groups, and state and local governmental units seek from the federal government through the intervention of their senators and representatives. Most "cases" come from individuals—about 80 percent of the requests received by congressional offices, according to staff estimates—although occasionally businesses, organizations, and other groups may seek help.

Individuals' cases fall into four categories. The first includes simple status checks ("When will my application be processed?"). The second consists of requests for services or preferments (favorable or expeditious treatment on, say, a passport application). Most of the cases in these two categories, which probably constitute the bulk of all cases, are what Hill terms "offensive"—the citizen is seeking something from the government.[25] A third group includes requests or demands for explanations of why a decision was made or a benefit reduced or denied. The last type concerns grievances or complaints against government bureaucracies because of unfair, inefficient, or malfeasant treatment—Hill's "defensive" cases. Here are the classic complaints about citizens' receiving discourteous or insulting treatment or having to cope with excessively lengthy lines, red tape, and the bureaucratic "runaround." Obviously, these categories are not mutually exclusive, since pleas of "I've been robbed" are likely to be accompanied by complaints about impersonal treatment from bureaucrats and requests for special action.[26]

Projects, or "high-level casework," as they sometimes are called, come from local and state government units: county boards, housing authorities, sewage commissions, schools, library systems, redevelopment commissions, and so on. In 1977–78, and in 1981–82, these constituted about one-tenth of all incoming cases. They are more common, proportionately, in the Senate than in the House.[27]

Constituents ask help from Congress on virtually everything. For example, one midwestern Republican senator's office found that in one six-month period it received case and project inquiries concerning sixty-six departments, agencies, and private organizations ranging from ACTION, the Administrative Office of the U.S. Courts, the American Battle Monuments Commission, Blue Cross, and the Boy Scouts to the Smithsonian Institution, the U.S. Information Agency, Uniroyal, Inc., the Veterans Administration, Western Union Telegraph, and the White House. Clearly, however, some government agencies and programs are more commonly the objects of requests and complaints than others. According to the Obey Commission, the most common case assistance sought by the public concerned social security and pension claims (11 percent of respondents), military problems (10 percent), and jobs (9 percent).[28] Congressional respondents in this study were asked to name the agencies and programs concerning which they received the most cases. Although nineteen agencies (with twenty-five programs) were mentioned, five dominated, accounting for three-quarters of all mentions.

These five agencies directly affect great numbers of people and often exercise a good deal of discretionary decision-making power. The most frequently cited program—fully one-quarter of all mentions—was the social security system (including Medicare): typical cases concerned late checks, problems with establishing and maintaining eligibility, and complaints about bureaucratic snafus in general. Next in frequency of mention was the Veterans Administration: cases here usually involved disputes over VA decisions concerning the extent and causes (service-related or not) of disabilities; denials or underpayment of benefits; refusal or inability to admit veterans to VA hospitals or to provide certain kinds of services and care; and canceled insurance policies. In third place came military problems: people wanting to enlist who could not qualify; servicemen seeking emergency discharges or transfers; allegations of mistreatment by a company commander or drill sergeant, or of deception by a recruiter who promised a specialty or assignment which was not subsequently made available; medical care problems for families; and changes in discharge status from dishonorable to honorable.

In the case of the Defense Department many requests fall into the "project" category: companies seeking help in getting contracts for weapons production or base facility services. In some areas of the country, where bases or defense industries are common, such contracts are crucial to the local economy and, according to conventional wisdom, the electoral fortunes of incumbents. Said Cong. Daniel Flood (D., Pa.): "Jobs, jobs, jobs. That's what that is all about."[29]

Fourth most frequently mentioned was the Justice Department, particularly the Immigration and Naturalization Service (INS), the Bureau of Prisons, and the

Law Enforcement Assistance Administration. The Department of Labor—especially the Occupational Safety and Health Administration (OSHA), the Office of Workers' Compensation Programs (OWCP), and the Black Lung and unemployment divisions—placed fifth.

The INS has considerable discretion in immigration matters, and it is heavily worked and relatively understaffed. Thus complaints pour into congressional offices from friends, families, and potential employers: "What's taking so long?" "Why was so-and-so denied immigration?" "Please stop this deportation proceeding." Federal prisoners write congressmen about prison conditions; businessmen complain to Congress about OSHA's rules and inspections; coal miners seek compensation for black lung disease (and complain loudly over eligibility decisions and payments); and workers "scream bloody murder" over the alleged inability of OWCP to process claims, render fair decisions, and mail checks on time.

Taxes and the IRS, naturally, are the objects of a good number of complaints about refunds, rulings, and audits. Small businessmen avail themselves of congressional office help, but House and Senate offices treat such requests delicately; they do not want to assist larger, well-to-do companies that are less in need of what amounts to free legal advice on taxes.

Housing programs were cited by a number of members and staffers. Local housing authorities and private businesses seek help in applying for Urban Renewal, Model Cities, and Urban Development Action grants and for federal housing subsidies. In these and similar situations, the congressional offices may merely point applicants towards the appropriate federal executive offices or bureaus; or they may become integrally involved with the planning and writing of grant proposals, as well as with keeping track of the proposals' progress through the bureaucratic decision-making process. One rural midwestern Democrat described his situation: "Big cities have their own grant-writing specialists, but not the little communities in my district; so my office serves as a federal grantsman. We plan and coordinate a lot of grant applications." Individual owners and tenants in federally assisted housing projects also write frequently, protesting HUD decisions (or those of the local housing authorities) concerning admission, rent levels, or evictions, and complaining of living conditions.

The Office of Personnel Management (formerly the Civil Service Commission) comes in for frequent constituent attention concerning promotions, working conditions, and retirements in the federal government. The State Department's Passport Office, somewhat like the INS, processes a good number of cases with discretion. Decisions on the acceptability of passport photos, to cite one seemingly trivial but persistent example, coupled with the usual reams of paperwork lead to complaints and requests for expedited treatment. A common complaint heard from congressional caseworkers concerns the constituent who wants to take a trip next week but has not yet applied for a passport—and wants the congressman to help take care of the problem. In September, 1981, the Detroit Passport Office was closed, forcing the Chicago office to handle all applications from several midwestern states. The result was total chaos, leading one of Sen. Robert Kasten's (R., Wis.) caseworkers to drive to Chicago and launch a veritable attack on the files—many still in cartons—to get passports for his constituents. [30]

The Small Business Administration makes, or refuses to make, loans based on relatively well-defined financial eligibility criteria. Many constituents do not understand those criteria, and others fail to present adequate documentation to show that they are in fact eligible. Still others know that they are not, but believe that they merit an exception. The Commerce Department's Economic Development Administration was created to assist depressed areas of the country. Senators and representatives commonly are asked for help in obtaining SBA loans and EDA grants. Similar involvement is routine, in the area of pollution control, with the Environmental Protection Agency. Another common EPA-related case, naturally, is a dispute between the agency and a company over pollution emissions and enforcement of EPA regulations.

Although most casework involves trying to get positive action from the executive, some is negative in nature: trying to stop the Army Corps of Engineers from dumping wastes, preventing the termination of Amtrack routes, trying to stop freeway construction, and the perennial battles to avoid the closing of military bases. Not all cases and projects requests and complaints are directed against federal agencies. Whether deliberately or out of ignorance, constituents contact congressional offices on state and local government problems such as road repair, garbage collection, police protection, clogged sewers, drivers' licenses, and school board decisions. And a few cases concern citizen grievances against businesses, schools, or private organizations. One House staffer said that nearly one-quarter of the cases coming to his district office dealt with the private sector (gas bills, mortgage payments, defective products). Another aide in Washington said that she felt like a consumer protection advocate, interceding with department stores, automobile dealers, and other companies on behalf of aggrieved constituents. Normally, congressional offices advise citizens to contact state or local consumer agencies or pass the inquiries along to local governments, but some—two out of five, according to one study—make a practice of handling cases that properly should be directed to state and local governments. [31]

The types of cases received vary considerably from time to time, region to region, and even district to district. To a degree, each office seems to have a unique clientele with its own problems. The staffs of senators and representatives from Florida, southern California, Arizona, and other areas where there are a number of retirement communities, for example, report that they deal mostly with social security cases. Representives from coal mining regions are beseiged with black lung claims, while those from districts near Washington receive an unusually high number of civil service problems. Many coastal states and Texas have high proportions of immigration cases, while midwesterners confront a good number of agricultural problems. Districts where military bases are located tend to be swamped with military cases (even though, strictly speaking, relatively few of the servicemen and servicewomen on those bases are residents of those districts), while western congressmen deal disproportionately with cases concerning the Interior Department, particularly land management and Indian Affairs. Congressmen respond to these differences by developing, via their staffs, knowledge of specific programs and of executive branch contact points.

Cases vary according to the calendar and according to events. A bad turn for the economy coincides with a rise in unemployment compensation and other job-related cases, just as the end of the Vietnam War caused a shift from military to veterans' cases, and recent legislation requiring periodic reanalysis of Social Security disability status, coupled with the Reagan administration's strict enforcement, triggered an explosion of Social Security cases. The onset of the school year brings contacts by veterans seeking educational benefits, just as June and July bring disproportionate numbers of complaints concerning tax refunds. Requests for assistance in obtaining federal funds and projects tend to fluctuate according to the schedule by which such funds are released, and a surge in social security requests accompanies each increase in benefits. One HUD official claimed that, near election time, when congressmen are out on the hustings meeting their constituents, her office case load doubles. During summer, case loads tend to dwindle, but winter often brings a sharp rise. Perhaps the best predictor of the pace of casework activity is the lunar cycle: the "full moon" theory carries the status of gospel truth on Capitol Hill.

Every congressional caseworker can recite stories of interesting and unusual — even bizarre — cases: the Soviet seaman who jumped ship and would have been forced to return but for a congressman's intervention; the constituent whose invention was spurned by the Air Force in favor of a more costly but apparently lower quality substitute manufactured by a corporate giant; an elderly constituent whose electricity was restored to working order only after a congressional aide spent an afternoon calling electricians in nearby communities; and the enterprising factory worker in Illinois who, in order to save money, bought a bus and drove himself and some thirty other workers across state lines to their place of employment in Indiana, but who needed an ICC permit to do so — and got it only through the efforts of his congressman.[32] Then there was the man who was supposed to receive periodic checks from OWCP, but did not. When he sought an explanation, he received none. So he called his congressman, whose staff cleared up the matter. It seems that the government check had been mailed to another person with the same name, and the agency would not issue a new check to the man who was supposed to get it until the other man returned his. The weirdest case uncovered in the course of interviewing for this book was described by the staffer who handled it:

One of our constituents was visiting Mexico and suddenly disappeared. Her family contacted us to see what we could do. We went through the usual procedures and turned up nothing. We contacted Mexican officials. Nothing. So I personally flew down to the Mexican town where she was last seen and did my own investigation. Still nothing. Someone persuaded me to go see one of those fortunetellers — one of those psychics. And damned if she didn't put me on the right track. We finally found the woman's body — she had died in a car accident with no one around. If it hadn't happened to me, I wouldn't believe it.

Tales of tear-jerkers are common. An adopted daughter of a serviceman was not allowed entry to the United States. An aide told of a foreign-born woman, eight months pregnant, who was traumatized by a deportation notice, even though she had married an American citizen. An army liaison officer recounted a case he received concerning a young soldier stationed in Guam who had a letter from the family doctor to the effect that both parents were dying. The army denied the soldier's request to return to a base near his parents. His mother died. Then he asked again to move nearer his home, but was turned down. He finally wrote to the congressman, who contacted the liaison officer. "Just as we succeeded in getting him his transfer," the officer said, "the kid's father died." Almost every caseworker has helped elderly people so poor that they were forced to eat pet food. For a host of reasons, often through their own fault, they were not receiving their Social Security checks. A veteran caseworker recalled this episode:

There was this airman in Alaska who was scheduled to have brain surgery. The House Armed Services Committee had told the Air Force that, in case they needed to send servicemen to Air Force hospitals, they were not to overfly a base with a hospital — that they were to send the man to the nearest Air Force hospital. So they were going to send this boy to Seattle, rather than to Lackland [Texas], which has the biggest Air Force hospital. The problem was that, for him, it was important to be sent to Texas. First, because his wife lived in San Antonio; second, because of the medical talent and capabilities there; and third, the fellow would probably be flown home to Texas after the surgery to recuperate.

She winked and said: "I won that one. He went to Texas for the operation." How many lives have been saved by conscientious casework is uncertain; but if caseworkers and accounts by former congressmen can be believed, there have been many such instances.

If caseworkers deal with serious and heart-rending cases, they also get their share of comic relief. Several aides in one office enjoyed telling the tale of the constituent who wanted the senator to intercede for his son with the president of the state university's board of regents. It seems that the young man received a "C" in a political science course and had lost his appeal. Pleas for changes in roommates have also been received by congressional offices. A military liaison officer remembered receiving a call from a congressman attempting to get a young soldier thrown into jail because he was dating the daughter of a friend of the congressman.

When it comes to federal projects and funds, all offices can tell stories about how they obtained — or protected — millions of dollars in grants and loans for various businesses and local governments. Some glory in lesser accomplishments. Senator (then Representative) Charles Grassley (R., Iowa) took credit for stopping a cutoff of HEW funds for a library in Rudd, Iowa. Until Grassley intervened, the library had been scheduled to lose federal aid because it had no access facility for people in wheelchairs — however, no one in the town of 429 residents used a wheelchair.[33] Most project work, like casework, is routine: writing letters of support, providing information to localities and businesses, arranging introductions, making inquiries, and sometimes actually writing grant proposals. An interesting and somewhat unusual example, not involving federal money, was described by a former Democratic member of the House: "We had seven rat-infested buildings in this one city in my district, and no one would do anything about it. So we got involved to get the community to move to clear them away. We found a person who owned a stone quarry to let us dump the rubble there; we enlisted the national guard to provide a bulldozer, and got local citizens to supply the manpower to knock the buildings down. And we got a local construction company to supply the trucks to carry the stuff to the quarry."

This sort of community activity is common, especially for staffs located in district offices; and a search through the literature, especially memoirs, will uncover dozens of examples of this sort, and of all other types, of cases and projects.

2.4. Sources of Casework Requests

Unlike other forms of political participation, citizen-initiated contacts with their governments in the United States have received relatively little scholarly attention. The primary focus of most studies has been on local government, and when national surveys ask about contacts, they seldom distinguish between types or purposes. Representative findings, for example, have shown that about one-quarter of the public have at some time written to their U.S. senators and a third to their representatives; that 20 percent of the public have at some point initiated contact with local officials about some issue or problem and 18 percent with state or national officials; and that 58 percent have at one time or another utilized some specific government service.[34] According to the Obey Commission's survey, still fewer people have sought help on specific problems from their legislators in Washington. Nine percent of the respondents indicated that they, personally, had "requested . . . help or assistance from a member of Congress or his staff," and another 6 percent said that someone in their family had done so—a total of 15 percent.[35] The 1978 CPS study likewise found that 15 percent of respondents or members of their families had contacted their congressmen: 6 percent to express an opinion, 5 percent to seek information, and 7 percent to request help on a problem (these groups overlap, and therefore the totals exceed 15 percent). In 1980 comparable figures were a total of 14 percent making contact, with 5 percent expressing opinions, 5 percent seeking information, and 8 percent asking for help.

Who are these people? If particularized demand-making (casework requests) resembles other types of citizen contacts, it is not randomly distributed across the population. Several explanations of such contact have received attention. One acknowledges the propensity of middle- and upper-class (higher socioeconomic status) individuals to have positive civic orientations, to be aware that government can solve problems, and thus to be more active in politics. Such people also have a greater sense of efficacy and would believe that complaining to legislators would work.[36] It is not surprising to find that better-educated, wealthier citizens write their congressmen more often than do others. And thus one might expect casework requests to come most frequently from upper socioeconomic groups. An alternative view is that particularized demands would come from the people who most need help, namely, those less well-off economically and socially—thus the hypothesis that the poor, various minorities, blue-collar workers, the unemployed, and the least well-educated would dominate casework requests.[37] Moreover, as noted above, citizens of lower socioeconomic status have a slightly more positive view of casework. These two contradictory models have been blended to produce a third, which argues that those in the middle of the "social well-being" spectrum would produce the most particularized demands.[38]

The Obey Commission data and the 1978 and 1980 CPS surveys can be used to test these models, but the limited number of respondents who had ever made contact — let alone sought concrete help on a problem — presents difficulties, as does the fact that there are some coding ambiguities in the commission's report.[39] Thus many cases had to be excluded from the following analysis.

Table 2.2 presents bivariate statistics describing the relationships between a large number of potentially important factors and: (1) case requests from the Obey Commission data, as defined above; (2) case requests from the 1978 and 1980 CPS studies; and (3) contacts for the purpose of expressing an opinion, also from the CPS surveys. This latter form of contacting is included to highlight some of the differences between it and case requests. Contact in each instance was coded as no or yes.

No strong correlations appear in the table. Nor, upon inspection of the data, is there evidence of any curvilinear relationships. Requesting casework assistance essentially is unrelated to demographic characteristics; but for making contact to express opinions, there are slightly more robust — though still not strong absolutely — and consistent relationships, indicating a small bias in the direction of white, better-educated, more affluent, white-collar, and higher social status constituents.[40] Thus, at least when trying to explain casework requests in general, none of the three theories mentioned above proves very useful. Only when respondents' requests are broken down by type of case (which the commission data permit) do some of the predicted differences begin to appear. The numbers involved are far too small for reliability, but inspection of the data reveals that a disproportionate number of those in the sample who were well-educated and of higher socioeconomic status said that they had made requests for publications and information, inquired about legislation and policy issues, and contacted their congressmen on tax and military academy matters. Those on the lower end of the education, affluence, and employment scales tended to make contacts relating to jobs, social security, and military discharges. Citizen-initiated particularized demand-making (casework) is, indeed, *particularized*. Scholars lumping various kinds of demands together in order to discover who makes them need to pay closer attention to the precise kinds of demands and requests being made. Unfortunately, the size of the sample required for such close analysis would be beyond most social scientists' reach.

Working with the data in table 2.2, and without breaking case requests down by types, one still can find some interesting, if weak, correlates of casework requests. In 1978, at least, government employees (or their families) stood out as being more likely than others to seek help from their congressmen. Such constituents are more sophisticated about government and, presumably, share a greater sense of political efficacy. Accordingly, they take advantage of congressmen's ombudsman orientations. Older citizens also tend to seek help.

Although the data do not appear in the table, respondents in eastern (particularly New England and mid-Atlantic) states and, to a lesser extent, in the north

Table 2.2: Correlates of Casework and Opinion Contacting: Summary Statistics

| | Reason for Contact with Congressman: | | | | |
| | Case Assistance | Case Assistance (CPS Data) | | Express Opinions (CPS Data) | |
Independent Variables	(Obey Data)	1978	1980	1978	1980
Demographics					
Education [a]	.03	.01	.01	.15**	.04**
Family income [b]	.01	.02	−.01	.09**	.03**
Personal income [b]	—	.01	.01	.03**	.04**
Occupation (blue/ white collar)	.05	.02	.04	.14**	.06*
Government employee (No/Yes)	—	.07*	.02	.03	.06*
Economic hardship (No/Yes) [c]	.03	−.01	−.01	−.03	−.06*
Race (black/white)	.00	.01	.01	.06**	.04
Age	—	.02*	.06**	.02**	.03**
Self-ascribed social status [d]	—	.04**	.01	.08**	.02*

continued

NOTE: Statistic is Kendall's *tau*: *p < .05; **p < .01

[a] For commission data, education is grouped as follows: less than high school, high school, more than high school. For the CPS data: grade school, high school, some college.

[b] Coded as: under $3,000; $3,000–$4,999; $5,000–$7,999; $8,000–$9,999; $10,000–$11,999; $12,000–$14,999; $15,000–$19,999; $20,000–$24,999; $25,000–$29,999; $30,000–$34,999; $35,000 and over.

[c] For commission data: respondent or head of household was unemployed or disabled. For CPS: respondent or family member had work hours reduced, had to work different shift, had pay reduced, took a job below his/her qualifications, was laid off, or was unemployed during the past year.

[d] Coded as lower, average working, working, upper working, average middle, middle, upper middle, and upper class.

Table 2.2: *continued*

	Reason for Contact with Congressman:				
	Case Assistance	Case Assistance (CPS Data)		Express Opinions (CPS Data)	
Independent Variables	(Obey Data)	1978	1980	1978	1980
Percent urban [e]	—	.02*	.01	.03*	.00
District's proximity to Washington (beyond/ within 100 miles)	—	.03	.00	.02	.01
Member Characteristics					
Member is leader (Yes/No)	—	.09**	.02	.01	.03
Member seniority [f]	—	.04**	.04**	.02	.04**
Member party (Rep/Dem)	—	.00	−.03	−.05*	−.03
Respondent Political Characteristics					
Political party [g]	.01	.02*	.02	−.06**	−.02
Congressman's party (No/Yes)	—	.08**	.06*	−.01	−.01
Perceived ideological discrepancy [h]	—	−.01	−.04	.03	.02

continued

NOTE: Statistic is Kendall's *tau*: *p < .05; **p < .01

[e] Coded as: 0–30, 31–90, and 91–100 percent of congressional district located in standard metropolitan statistical area.

[f] Coded as 0–3, 4–11, and 12 or more years. Separating extremely senior members (over 20 years) produces a somewhat stronger correlation.

[g] For commission data, coded as: strong Republican, weak Republican, Independent, weak Democrat, strong Democrat. For CPS data, coded as: strong Republican, weak Republican, Independent-Republican, Independent or Apolitical, Independent-Democrat, weak Democrat, strong Democrat.

[h] Absolute value of difference between where respondent places self and congressman on a seven-point ideological scale.

Table 2.2: *continued*

	Reason for Contact with Congressman:				
	Case Assistance	Case Assistance (CPS Data)		Express Opinions (CPS Data)	
Independent Variables	(Obey Data)	1978	1980	1978	1980
Name of congressman					
Recall (No/Yes)	.11**	.14**	—	.12**	—
Recognize (No/Yes)	—	.14**	.11*	.12**	.08**
Learned about, had contact with congress-man (No/Yes)	—	.12**	.14**	.13**	.11**
Cong. information index [i]	.09**	—	—	—	—
Cong. activity index [j]	.14**	—	—	—	—
Index of					
Political activism [k]	—	.07**	.06**	.10**	.07**
Political cynicism [l]	—	.03*	.02	.01	.00
Political efficacy [m]	—	.02	.03	.07*	.07**
Voting activity [n]	−.03	.10**	.08**	.13**	.06**

NOTE: Statistic is Kendall's *tau*: *$p < .05$; **$p < .01$

[i] Coded as: low, moderately low, moderately high, and high level of information about Congress. Index developed by House Commission on Administrative Review.

[j] Coded as: low, moderately low, moderate, moderately high, and high activity. Index developed by House Commission on Administrative Review.

[k] Coded from 0 to 7. Index includes: persuading others how to vote, attending political meetings, working for a candidate or party, wearing buttons or using bumper stickers, contributing to campaigns, belonging to political clubs, and voting in 1978 election.

[l] Coded from 5 (low cynicism) to 22 (high cynicism), this additive index is taken from the CPS "Trust in Government" items: government wastes money; trust in Washington; government run by special interests; government run by people who are not smart; government run by dishonest people.

[m] Coded from 6 (low efficacy) to 18 (high efficacy), this additive index is taken from the CPS "Political Efficacy" items: people like me have no say in government; voting is the only way to have any say; government and politics are too complex; officials don't care about people like me; congressmen lose touch with voters; and political parties are interested only in votes, not views.

[n] For the Obey data, respondents were coded as having: voted in neither 1974 nor 1976, voted in 1974 or 1976, or voted in 1974 and 1976. For CPS data, respondent did not or did vote in the 1978 or 1980 House elections.

central region were considerably more apt to request assistance, perhaps reflecting greater need (such areas have undergone severe economic strain in recent years) or a different political culture (as discussed in the next chapter). Two interrelated member characteristics correlated with casework contacting: member seniority and leadership status. Combining the 1978 and 1980 surveys, over 8 percent of the respondents whose congressmen were party or committee leaders (chairmen or ranking minority members of committees or subcommittees), compared with 5.5 percent of those with backbench representatives, requested case assistance. Well over 10 percent of those whose congressmen had served over twenty years, compared to 4.3 percent of those with members having five or fewer years of seniority, had requested help. Whether this result merely reflects the greater exposure of senior members and their increased opportunities to advertise their services over the years or actually constitutes a strategic calculation on the part of constituents that senior members have more clout (and would be more helpful) is unclear.

If the demographic hypotheses fail to account for casework requests, certain political characteristics may. "Civic orientation" and political efficacy have been found to be key explanatory factors for various forms of political participation (although, curiously, not for particularized demand-making).[41] Not surprisingly, then, constituents who could recall or recognize the names of their congressmen, those most interested and active in government and politics, those in possession of large amounts of information about Congress, and, of course, those who had come into contact with their congressmen—and thus at some time might have been encouraged to ask for help—were more likely to have requested casework assistance. So, naturally, were those who *expected* that their congressman, if asked, would be helpful. For example, 12 percent of the CPS samples in 1978 and 1980 who had met their congressmen, heard them speak at meetings, talked with staff assistants, or received mail from them had (or lived in a family that had) submitted requests for help on personal problems, versus 1.2 percent who had had no contact. Twice as many respondents in the commission's 1977 survey who had met their congressman or heard him speak as had not said that they had made requests for ombudsman services (or that someone in their family had). Of course, one must be careful here. It is possible that much of the casework requesting preceded some of the political activities (or even political attitudes) or accompanied them. Neither the CPS nor the Commission surveys distinguished as to when or how often the contacts and requests occurred. Although higher political efficacy is very weakly associated with writing to express an opinion, it is almost absolutely unrelated to casework. Surprisingly, political cynicism or mistrust is not negatively associated with casework contacting, a finding which challenges the notion that citizens "turned off" to politics would shy away from seeking help. Finally, one interesting relationship deserves mention. Although seeking help was unrelated to constituents' (or members') partisan identifications, it was linked to common party affiliations; nearly 10 percent of the 1978–80 respondents of the same party as their representatives asked for help versus about 6 percent who did not share common partisan ties.

Table 2.3 presents a PROBIT analysis of casework and opinion contacting using the most important variables in table 2.2. PROBIT allows one to examine relationships between two variables while holding the effects of others constant. It is the appropriate multivariate test to use when the dependent variable is dichotomous.[42] The equations omit several variables that one might argue should be included: recognizing one's congressman, having come into contact with him, and perceived ideological compatibility. The reason is that these could be effects of casework requesting rather than causes; or at the very least, both sets of factors (casework requests and expressions of opinion as well as these three variables) could be caused by other forces or attitudes, thus raising problems of spurious correlation. For comparison, similar equations were run to explain opinion expressing. The results confirm those discussed above. Holding other variables constant, it becomes clear that being older, living in the East and perhaps in the Midwest, working for governments (at least in 1978), having a senior representative—especially of one's own party—and being politically active lead one to request help more than would be expected in the absence of those characteristics.

2.5. Summary

The data suggest that asking for help is to a degree an activity distinct from writing to express an opinion, although neither form of contact can be very well predicted (note the small proportion of the variance in case requesting and opinion expressing explained by these equations). Perhaps what drives people to seek help is the expectation that it will be forthcoming (when that variable was included in the equations, it produced large positive coefficients), but it is impossible to prove that relationship because of the possible two-way flow of causality. Apparently seeking casework assistance from Congress, while limited to a small percentage of the citizenry, is more directly related to constituents' political awareness and activity and to the seniority of their congressmen than to personal or demographic traits. That in turn suggests that there may not be as much socioeconomic bias in this form of political participation as there is in others, such as voting, opinion

Table 2.3: Casework and Opinion Contacting

	PROBIT Maximum Likelihood Estimates			
	Dependent Variables:			
	Casework Requests		Expressions of Opinion	
Independent Variables	1978	1980	1978	1980
Demographics				
Education (years)	.026	.002	.086**	.021
Personal income	−.000	.000	.000	.000
Hardship [a]	−.038	.134	−.281**	−.333*
Age	.002	.012	.000	.008*
Percent urban	.001	−.001	.000	−.001
District proximity to Washington				
(beyond/within 100 miles)	.182	−.003	.170	.065
East	.446**	.276*	.078	−.010
Midwest	.373**	.196	.353**	−.249
Government employee	.392**	.184	.326*	.380*
Member Characteristics				
Member Seniority (years)	.028**	.033**	.003	.042**
Member Party (Dem.)	−.045	−.065	−.281**	−.041
Political Characteristics				
Same party as congressman	.309**	.156	−.025	−.088
Index of cynicism [a]	.033	.033	.035	.005
Political activism [a]	.157**	.170**	.231**	.247**
CONSTANT	3.011	3.149	3.496	2.955
(N)	(1602)	(1098)	(1602)	(1098)
Estimated R-squared	.15	.13	.23	.19

[a]See notes to table 2.2.

NOTE: All tests of significance are two-tailed tests: *$p < .05$; **$p < .01$.

expressing, involvement in political campaigns, and so on. There is, however, a regional or political-cultural bias towards the East. Perhaps the "payoffs" or benefits to citizens likewise are more equitably spread. To the extent that one is concerned with the overall service responsiveness or representativeness of the political system, this relative lack of bias is a welcome finding. Coupled with the diversity of motives that underpin congressmen's involvement in casework and the extreme variety of problems citizens complain about, it would appear that in undertaking the casework function, Congress indeed is becoming a national ombudsman serving, essentially, the entire cross section of the American public.

CHAPTER 3

The Casework Burden

3.1. Casework: The Workload

It is impossible to measure precisely the volume of congressional casework. Probably only a bare majority of offices keep somewhat accurate statistics,[1] and many of those that do define casework differently. Little wonder that previous calculations of case and project loads have varied so much and that so few systematic attempts have been made to assess casework loads. For example, casework volume in the Senate has been estimated at between 7.8 and 65 percent of all incoming mail, whereas in the House members and scholars have claimed that casework accounts for between 7.5 and over 50 percent of all letters—from a low of seven to a high of some three hundred cases per week.[2]

Three surveys during the 95th Congress provide the best estimates to date. The first, by Cain, Ferejohn, and Fiorina, found only 16 of 100 House offices with case loads exceeding 100 per week, and 56 indicated loads of fewer than 60.[3] A more comprehensive estimate of casework loads comes from the work of the House Commission on Administrative Review, which asked 131 members of the House to estimate the annual number of constituent requests for help in dealing with problems they had with the government. Responses ranged unbelievably from a low of just 20 to a high of 95,000; the mean was 11,954 and the median 7,008.[4] No wonder one House staffer was given to mutter: "I don't think people can get up in the morning without calling their congressman."

As part of this study, staff members engaged in casework were asked to estimate the number of cases and projects their offices received in an average week (see the Appendix for details). Though in no way guaranteed to be without error,

Table 3.1: Casework Loads

	Number of Cases and Projects Received Per Week: All Offices			
Type and Number of Respondents	Mean	Median	Std. Dev.	Range
Senators in 95th Congress (53)	302.4	175.3	335.3	12–2000
Representatives in 95th Congress (155)	115.2	100.2	78.8	10–465
Representatives in 95th Congress (131)	229.5	134.8	284.9	0.39–1827
Representatives in 97th Congress Individual cases (120)	94.7	69.8	72.2	4–400
Representatives in 97th Congress Federal projects (101)	10.3	4.9	15.9	0–98
Former representatives (22)	90.6	50.0	94.1	6–333

SOURCE: Except for the third item, which was taken from the House Commission on Administrative Review, *Final Report,* 95th Cong., 1st sess., 1977, H. Doc. 95-272, p. 890, data are from the author's interviews and questionnaires.

the findings, along with the Obey data, are presented in table 3.1. During the 95th Congress, the average weekly case and project load for senators was 302, with a median of 175. The representatives in the sample received an average of 115 cases (with a median of about 100). The annual workload therefore exceeded 4 million cases. These figures are a little below the Obey Commission's calculations but higher than most previous estimates.[5] Preliminary analysis of the data from part of the 1982 sample indicates a reduction in case loads — an average of about 95 per week (with a median of only 70).

Senators obviously bear heavier case loads than do members of the House, but not dramatically so. Constituents probably feel closer to their congressmen than to their senators, and thus write the former proportionately more than the latter. Representatives also are more "present" and visible to their constituents in many cases than are senators. And many senators simply are less inclined to emphasize casework. As one administrative assistant to a large state midwestern Republican put it, "On casework, we defer to the congressmen. We figure that they should take the lead; we do it, of course, but it's more a matter for them." Typically, aides on both sides felt that casework was more important to members of the lower chamber.

Several questions leap from the data in table 3.1. What causes the heavy case-work loads; have they risen over the years; and if so, why? What accounts for the great variance in casework loads evidenced by the large standard deviations and ranges; why do some members bear heavier burdens than others?

Although case loads appear to have dropped between the 95th and 97th Congresses, it is clear that recent levels far surpass those of the 1960s and early 1970s. And for many individual members, the workload continues to expand. (One eastern senator's annual case load, for example, jumped 80 percent from 1977 to 1979.) First-class incoming mail to the Senate approximately doubled between 1973 and 1978; and in the House, the total amount of mail received via the U.S. Postal Service alone rose from 22.3 million pieces in 1970 to 39.2 million in 1977.[6] While casework constitutes only a small proportion of such mail, if that proportion came at all close to remaining constant over the years, the absolute number of incoming complaints and requests must have shot up dramatically. And these figures cover only the Washington offices of congressmen. Better evidence comes from 193 members and aides surveyed in 1977 and 1978. Of these, 138 reported increases in case loads over the previous decade, while only one person thought casework had diminished. The others reported no change. Reports of increasing case volume came disproportionately from high education districts, perhaps indicating that they have only recently been as affected as others by government programs and/or have become less reluctant to register specific complaints. Interestingly, case loads have been rising worldwide, but they apparently have not reached elsewhere the levels found in the United States.[7] Reasons for the growth, and indeed reasons for casework itself, were offered by two dozen members and over one hundred staffers. They fall into three categories: government-related, citizen-related, and congressmen-related. Of some interest are the differences between member and staff replies. Half of the former but fewer than one-third of their aides placed the blame on the government (which, arguably, they "controlled"). In reverse proportions they were inclined to emphasize what congressmen themselves have done to stimulate case requests.

Congressmen always have had a need to engage in casework, but the explosion of government programs since the New Deal, and especially during the "Great Society" years of the 1960s, has generated more laws, more and more complex regulations, more and larger bureaucracies, more paperwork, and thus more problems for citizens and local governments trying to deal with Washington. One need not accept Fiorina's suggestion that the expansion of government is the result of a friendly conspiracy between congressmen and bureaucrats to "drum up" business to appreciate its impact.[8] Federal spending mushroomed from under $4 billion in 1930 to about $750 billion in fiscal 1983; federal civilian employees in the 1970s numbered nearly five times the federal workforce of 1930 and thirty times that of 1900. The number of pages in the *Federal Register,* most of them devoted to regulations, jumped from just over 2,000 in 1931 to over 83,500 in 1980. Some 1,600 different federal grants in over 400 programs for state and local governments were available in the late 1970s — so that 16 percent of the fiscal 1980 federal budget flowed to state and local governments, constituting one-quarter of their expenditures. Aid to state and local governments increased sevenfold between 1959 and 1975. As the former chairman of an influential House committee put it: "The federal government has projected itself into every aspect of life, from cradle to grave; so people naturally go to Washington to solve their problems." If, by 1982, the volume of cases had ceased its growth, it may be precisely because the numbers of government programs and new recipients of federal assistance—and thus occasions for cases and projects—have stopped expanding.

The bureaucracy itself was singled out as a prime cause of rising casework loads. As one student explained: "Constituents' complaints and inquiries—the source of interference cases—arise because centralized administration of the law is by nature inflexible and impersonal, and because bureaucrats and constituents, not to speak of congressmen, are human and therefore capable of laziness, stupidity, arrogance, and dishonesty, and all the other ills of men."[9] Whether— as members and staffers claimed in interviews—"there is a natural inclination for bureaucrats to be lazy," "some times they just don't understand the law," "bureaucrats are dictators," "illiterates," and "cowards," or "just not doing their jobs," or whether the size and complexity of government mean that "our people need government and it just doesn't work for them," the performance of executive personnel was seen as a major cause of rising case loads. Not all members or staffs were so critical; many sympathized with the bureaucrats' plight. Understanding and even empathy characterized most congressional personnel when talking about such agencies as Social Security, Immigration, and Workers' Compensation, where new legislation, understaffing, and constant backlogs led to delays, inefficiencies, and sometimes discourtesies. In some cases, bureaucrats have contributed purposefully and directly to the casework problem. It is not uncommon for civil servants, frustrated by statutory and regulatory limitations on their ability to render the service they wish, overtly to refer constituents to their congressmen in hopes of generating pressure on their agencies or getting legislation enacted to change statutory provisions. For example, an Army ROTC recruit explained that, as part of the commander's welcome address, ROTC students were told to "write your congressman" if problems arose that couldn't be handled administratively. Apparently such behavior is common. One midwestern senator's caseworker described the efforts of a local Social Security office to raise a policy issue with Washington. The office was unable, as she put it, "to get through. So the office contacted me in hopes that I would be able to. I was. In our state, the local bureaucrats know the senator's staffers." The staffs of two other senators and two representatives volunteered similar tales.

A second set of reasons for the growth in casework concerns the citizenry itself. Never renowned for their knowledge of or concern for government, Americans nonetheless have a finely tuned sense of self-interest in public affairs. Thus, as government programs and benefits proliferate, people pay attention. More important, events of the last twenty years, such as the legislature's involvement in Vietnam, Watergate, and clashes with presidents, just to name a few, may have heightened the public's general awareness of Congress. The media and private organizations interested in distributing government money and benefits to their clients and supporters exacerbate the situation. In short, there may be greater cognizance of both Congress and, in a general sort of way, available government programs. Baffled by the size and complexity of the federal executive establishment, citizens seem less and less inclined to accept passively the decisions of government bureaucrats and more and more likely to turn to the one highly visible source of help: their congressmen.

According to staffers, since the early 1960s ever-rising numbers of constituents—especially those in lower socioeconomic groups—have turned to their congressmen first, *before making contact with agencies*. Said one aide: "The people in our district simply don't know what to do or who to turn to. They're helpless. So they come to us." Community organizations and local governments (especially in rural areas) also go to their congressmen before applying to agencies for grants. Many congressional offices encourage this. "On grant applications," said an aide to one senator, "we want to be in on the ground floor. Often, by the time local governments come to us, they've missed a deadline or made errors in their applications. Then it's too late for us to do anything about it except to show them their mistakes." Especially for smaller government units, congressional offices do everything, including identifying available grants (perhaps their most important task); contacting local officials; introducing them to executive branch administrators who will decide the grants; keeping them posted; and, more and more, actually writing the proposals. One senior aide to a New England representative saw herself as a "circuit rider"—I visit all the towns in our district and try to establish relationships. We see ourselves as community builders."

Somewhat less flattering to the American public were explanations of rising case loads based on references to the selfish side of human nature: "Everyone has his hand out for government money, and they ask the congressmen because they're too lazy or too dumb.'' ''People are jealous; they see someone getting a benefit and they want some freebies for themselves.''

Other members and aides saw the increasingly heavy casework loads as rooted in the peculiarities of their constituencies. One New York district, explained the AA, has fallen on hard economic times. The only salvation is government help for individuals, businesses, and localities. Districts with booming retirement communities and areas with new (or canceled) defense bases or changing immigration patterns similarly have experienced rising casework demands. Some staffers stressed that the growth of casework was like a snowball tumbling down a hill: ''Our predecessor established a tradition of service, and *our* constituents demand it.''[10]

One constituency trait that may explain the rise in case and project loads is the greater sophistication of some state and local governments in seeking grants. Many congressional offices indicated that their largest percentage increase in cases in the early 1970s was caused by governmental units trying to get federal funds. A growing number of states have opened their own liaison offices in Washington, giving them closer contacts not only with departments and agencies but also with their representatives and senators. Credit for some of that sophistication belongs to congressmen and their staffs. Asked her thoughts in 1982 about the greatest changes since she was interviewed in 1977, a particularly astute House casework supervisor replied that there had been a ''drastic difference in constituent attitudes about themselves.'' Local government officials, especially, have ''developed an ability to figure things out. We've taught them how to help themselves and how to tap our resources.''

3.2. Soliciting Cases

Members and staffs of Congress themselves constitute a third cause of expanding casework. One senator has gone so far as to write a book on how citizens and local governments can ask Congress for help.[11] Almost all congressional offices— certainly more today than fifteen years ago—bend every effort to make themselves visible and accessible, to encourage constituents to bring their problems to their congressmen, and to develop reputations for successful case and project operations.[12] As one staffer wrote: ''Our three offices handle a tremendous amount of casework which we found exceeds other offices we checked. This we attribute to the high visibility of the congressman. He spends every weekend in the district, and he is often here on week nights.''

Senators and representatives have a number of "entrepreneurial" devices available for "hustling" cases. The physical presence of the member among his constituents—to attend city or county council meetings, hold well-publicized office hours, participate in "town meetings" or "open forums," or attend picnics, fairs, and dinners—triggers peoples' complaints and requests. When congressmen themselves cannot attend, they send their field representatives. Normally, advance mailings are sent to residents of the "target area" to let them know the times and exact locations. Such notices usually include invitations to constituents to "bring along any problems you might be having with the government." Based on evidence from the survey of offices in 1982, three-quarters of the members of the House sought cases at town meetings or open forums, and 54 percent did so when holding temporary office hours throughout their districts.

"We were very conscious of our obligation to make me and my staff as available as possible to constituents when I'd go back to the district," explained one former midwestern Republican representative. "We'd spend whole days seeing as many as thirty-five or forty people." Such devotion to constituents has become the norm. Any caseworker can recount, usually with mixed emotions, the Monday morning ritual wherein the congressman returns to the Washington office from a visit to the district and empties his pockets of dozens of scraps of paper, each of which contains the name and address of a constituent along with hastily scribbled notes about some difficulty the person is experiencing with a federal agency. Congressmen do not take the duty (or opportunity) of visiting constituents lightly. The Obey Commission's survey found that 95 percent of the members thought that getting back to the district to keep in touch with constituents was "very" or "fairly" important; and 67 percent said they spent a "great deal" of time doing it.[13] As long ago as 1973, members of the House averaged thirty-five trips home per year; by 1978 one study found that nearly half of the offices in the House reported at least weekly trips home by the congressmen.[14]

Careful resource allocation—opening or increasing the number of permanent offices in the home district or state—is another technique for bringing casework services to, and soliciting casework from, one's constituents. In 1982, for instance, the *Congressional Staff Directory* listed eighty-three senators who had at least two district offices, including forty-four with four or more. Sixty-one percent of all representatives had at least two home offices; nearly a third had three or more. The availability of such access contributes directly to citizens' propensity to take their problems to their legislators. As one aide to a prominent Texas representative said: "The biggest thing we've noticed is a sharp increase in walk-in business in our district office." And no wonder: staffers in such offices frequently spare no effort in outreach programs designed to drum up casework.

Mobile offices — vans outfitted with couches, chairs, and tables and driven to varying locations in the state or district — have enabled members and aides to bring casework services to constituents living far from permanent office locations. Some, such as one used by Cong. Thomas Downey (D., N.Y.), provide auxiliary services such as heart and blood pressure testing. A 1978 count put the number of members using such vans at eighty-two, an increase of one-third over 1976. Said Cong. John M. Slack (D., W.Va.): "My district is spread out. I represent 14 counties. I don't want to slight any of those towns by choosing one to put another district office in."[15] In 1982, 16 percent of the members studied used mobile offices.

Innovative uses of the telephone have contributed to the rising case loads. A few members solicit collect or toll-free calls from constituents on a special 800 number "hot line."[16] Numerous congressmen hooked into FTS (the Federal Telecommunications System), thus sharply reducing the costs, and increasing the frequency, of telephone exchanges with constituents. And virtually all senators and representatives have purchased WATS telephone lines for their Washington and state offices. Unsolicited calls by members and staffs to constituents, including the question, "Are you having any problems we can help you with?" were not unheard of, with no fewer than five reporting such activity in 1982.

Perhaps the most popular device for advertising and soliciting casework is the newsletter. The vast majority of senators and representatives mail such letters either to their entire constituencies (members of the House are allowed to use the franking privilege on letters addressed merely to "postal patron" six times per year, while senators must have names and addresses) or to select audiences (the aged, veterans, teachers, and so on). In addition to discussing pending legislation, the congressman's recent votes, and his positions on current issues, newsletters tabulate and often illustrate the congressman's efforts at helping constituents; emphasize past successes for both individual constituents and grant-seeking local governments and businesses; and, of course, issue the invitation to "contact me if you have any problems." Only rarely do they make clear the limits on Congress's ability actually to solve problems. In 1982, 85 percent of the members used this technique.

Some enterprising senators and representatives have gone one step further in an effort to assist localities in applying for federal aid. Former Senator Gaylord Nelson (D., Wis.), for example, published a monthly "Federal Projects Memorandum" which listed available grants and recent agency notices concerning funding, along with *Federal Register* citations, a checklist to be used in ordering more information from the senator's office, and a list of recent grants "won" by Wisconsin governments.

Similarly, many members include casework solicitations in the questionnaires and opinion polls they periodically mail to constituents. Some use weekly television or radio shows, newspaper columns, public service announcements, matchbook covers, brochures explaining federal programs and benefits, and even billboards and notices posted in supermarkets for the same purpose. Others have periodic dinners with business and local government leaders or have created voluntary citizen advisory groups, whose purpose, among other things, is to contact citizens and refer them and their problems to the congressmen. One midwestern Democratic senator, for example, had a forty-person committee, while a New York representative established a "Business Assistance Council" to help him identify companies and localities eligible for federal aid. A border state Republican representative enlisted as field representatives a group of volunteers who, according to his aide, "are gas station operators, retirees, photographers, and so on. Their job is to help people contact us."

To gain some perspective on how widespread is the use of such devices, members and staffs were asked to indicate how many of the devices their offices used explicitly to solicit casework. Table 3.2 provides the breakdown, which, if anything, underestimates the actual situation. Three-quarters of the senators and 85 percent of the representatives in 1977–78 used at least one device.[17] By 1982, all but 3 percent of the House did so. Indeed, there seemed to be an across-the-board surge in casework "hustling."

Which senators and representatives exert the greatest efforts—as measured by these techniques—to generate casework? The literature on constituency service in other lands and studies of other forms of congressional constituency attentiveness have identified a number of factors that are or might be associated with serving constituents' needs. These fall into two broad categories: member-related and constituency-related. The first includes a congressman's electoral situation and seniority.[18] Newly elected members seeking to establish their reputations back home and those whose seats are not very safe would seem most likely to do their utmost—to use the most devices—to stimulate case and projects requests. Institutional constraints also might be at work. Since party leaders and committee and subcommittee chairmen and ranking minority members bear greater responsibilities and are busier than others, one would expect them to be less interested in encouraging casework. Such, at least, seems the case in Britain.[19] Finally, congressmen's partisan and policy orientations might be relevant.

Perhaps certain traits help explain why some representatives simply have stronger commitments to stimulating case requests. Among factors previously used, with mixed results, to explain positive approaches to constituents are:

Table 3.2: Number of Devices Used to Solicit Casework

Number of Devices	Former Represen- tatives	Senators 95th Congress	Representatives	
			95th Congress	97th Congress
None	14%	26%	15%	3%
One	29	26	27	8
Two	14	24	26	14
Three or more	19	17	28	76
General (unspecified) affirmative	24	7	5	NA
	100	100	101	101
(N)	(21)	(46)	(162)	(143)

SOURCE: Author's interviews and questionnaires,—specifically, responses by members and staffs to the following question in 1977–78: "Does (did) your office use any devices or techniques to solicit cases from constituents or to encourage constituents to bring their problems to you for help? Which ones?" A list of devices was presented in checklist form. It included the open-ended option of "other." In 1982 the question was: "Does your senator/representative or his/her staff do anything to solicit cases from constituents (to encourage them to request help or to apply for federal grants and projects)?" A list of six items was presented in checklist form.

NOTE: Percentages may not add to 100 due to rounding errors.

ideology, extremism, partisanship, political ambition, role orientations, peer group influence, and attitudes toward the efficacy and deleterious effects of casework.[20] Unfortunately, not all of these factors can be taken into account given the available data. But for those that can be, the hypotheses are straightforward: those representatives and senators deemed most likely to employ the most devices to stimulate case requests are liberals rather than conservatives (conservative congressmen are more likely to have a principled aversion to encouraging people to make any more demands on government than they already do) and Republicans more than Democrats (after taking ideology into account, Republicans as the "party out of power" in 1977–78 would have less of an identification with the incumbent administration and would be less hesitant to complain about "Democratic" bureaucratic snafus). Members oriented toward legislative activism presumably would be less engaged in casework stimulation. Two measures of an activist orientation are available. The first is the number of bills and resolutions introduced in 1977 (taken from the *Digest of General Public Bills and Resolutions*); the second is the frequency of floor appearances in the House and Senate, rather crudely measured by counting the number of entries in the index to the *Congressional Record* under the heading "Remarks By." If the assumption can be made that these variables do measure activism (sponsoring legislation is quite easy, and "remarks" can be inserted into the *Record* without the member's having to appear in the chamber), and if senators and representatives who introduce bills speak frequently on the floor are what Payne calls "program type" congressmen (more concerned with policy than election results),[21] bear heavier institutional responsibilities, or are particularly oriented toward the "inventor" or "ritualist" roles,[22] these variables should correlate negatively with soliciting cases. But if such activism is merely another form of currying favor with constituents (paying off key interest groups, "advertising" or "credit-claiming"), they would correlate positively.

The second set of factors represents the needs and traditions of one's constituency. Implicit here is an assumption that congressmen *react* to their constituencies. The expectations are that poor and ill-educated districts have a greater objective need for casework, but, due to a low sense of political efficacy, would have to be stimulated to ask for help. As one aide to a congressman from a poor, rural district explained: "Many of our constituents are afraid to contact us, or just don't know how. So we take our service to them." Thus a negative relationship would be anticipated. Likewise, congressmen from eastern states are predicted to undertake greater casework solicitation efforts for two reasons. First, the East has undergone considerable economic upheaval in recent years, which, added to the general problems of urban decay, pollution, and so on, render it in need of federal assistance. Second, most of that region is characterized by what Elazar has called the individualistic political culture, wherein "politicians must rise by providing the governmental services demanded of them . . .; mutual obligations rooted in personal relationships" are crucial; and "politicians are interested in office as a means of controlling the distribution of rewards of government rather than as a means of exercising governmental powers for programmatic ends." Not surprisingly, it is in the East that the urban political party machine, with its patronage and service-oriented ethos, developed. Such a culture ought to produce congressmen especially oriented toward casework and a citizenry that expects and demands constituency service. One might also expect casework outreach efforts in the South and perhaps border states, where not only is there considerable poverty and general need, but also the "traditionalistic" political culture holds sway. That culture is paternalistic and elitist. Bureaucracy is an evil to be avoided because it interferes with the "informal, interpersonal relationships'' that lie at the root of the political system.[23] In the Midwest and especially the West, where the moralistic culture tends to hold sway and where need may be less acute, one expects fewer efforts to hustle cases.

To test the hypotheses, ordinary least squares regression analysis was employed. This technique allows one to assess the independent effects of one variable on another, while holding constant the effects of other factors. The dependent variable is the number of devices used in 1978 to stimulate casework, coded as 0, 1, 2, or 3 or more. Note that electoral margin in the House is measured by the average percentage of the vote captured by the incumbent or the candidate of the incumbent's party in the four previous elections (1970–76). Using this measure eliminates some of the stochastic error that would occur by using only the 1976 election results and captures any ''permanent threat'' that might overhang any congressman or district. (A separate set of regressions was run using only the 1976 vote, and it produced no major differences.) Ideology is measured by the conservative coalition support scores, as computed by *Congressional Quarterly*. Median education and income data are taken from the 1970 census.[24] Dummy variables were created for party, leadership status, and each of the regions. For the House, a second equation is presented in which the regional factors and member seniority (which correlates strong with leadership status) are omitted. Table 3.3 presents the regression coefficients.

The first thing to note is that neither the House nor the Senate models explain much of the variance, suggesting that decisions to ''hustle'' cases are highly idiosyncratic, depending on subjective member and staff attitudes and practices.

Members' electoral situations and institutional positions prove to be useful predictors of the extent of entrepreneurial activities. Juniors and backbenchers engage in casework ''hustling'' in the House. (Inclusion of both seniority and leadership causes the former to lose its predictive power due to multicollinearity between the two variables. Separately, however, they both correlate significantly with the number of devices used.) In the Senate, seniority matters. The landslide election year of 1964 proves to be somewhat of a turning point. House members elected before 1964 were only half as likely to be active in casework solicitation as those elected since. In the Senate, pre-1964 members were even less energetic. Thus a ''cohort'' effect seems to be at work: a ''new breed'' of member has replaced older members and brought with them a new service style.

Electoral margin presents some problems of interpretation. In the House, especially when the effects of seniority and region are removed, as in equation 2, the electoral trend in a member's district correlates negatively with the effort expended on casework stimulation. But the effect is extremely weak.[25] One problem here could be simultaneous causality. Low election margins could cause

Table 3.3: Casework Solicitation in 1977–78: A Multivariate Model

Independent Variables	House (1) B	(1) Beta	House (2) B	(2) Beta	Senate B	Senate Beta
Member-related factors						
Electoral trend	−.010	−.127	−.012**	−.162	−.035	−.274
Seniority (years)	−.010	−.065	—	—	−.077**	−.438
Leadership status	−.541***	−.256	−.677***	−.320	—	—
Conservatism score	−.010**	−.285	−.011**	−.300	−.010	−.287
Party (Republican)	.722**	−.328	.774***	.352	.099	.045
Activism						
Bills	−.002*	−.191	−.002	−.145	−.006	−.211
Floor	.001	.029	.001	.037	.008*	.392
Constituency Needs and Demands						
Median income	.000	.035	.000	.095	.000	−.007
Median education	−.164	−.117	−.337**	−.240	−.548	−.283
East	.553**	.226	—	—	−.248	−.069
South	.344	.119	—	—	−.402	−.123
Border	.727*	.153	—	—	−1.287**	−.473
Midwest	.272	.112	—	—	−.709*	−.299
CONSTANT	5.282		7.449		11.548	
(N)	(132)		(132)		(39)	
R-squared	.20		.16		.33	
Adj. R-squared	.11		.11		.02	

NOTES: *Beta* = Standardized Regression Coefficient. For the House, electoral trend = the average percentage of the vote won by the incumbent or the incumbent's party, 1970–76; for the Senate, the percentage of the vote won by the incumbent in his last election.

A two-tailed test of significance is used for the activism measure: *p < .10; **p < .05; ***p < .01.

a member to do more to stimulate case requests, whereas engaging in such efforts could win votes. A negative relationship in one direction may be canceled, at least partly, by a positive one in the other direction. Lacking data over a period of time, there is no easy way to solve this problem. More confusing yet, if one uses a dummy variable set equal to 1 if the most recent vote (1976) was below the 1970–74 average, the analysis suggests that such "unsafe" or electorally deteriorating members did *less* to stimulate cases in 1977–78 than did their more secure colleagues. In the Senate, the sign for electoral margin is in the expected direction, and the magnitude of the coefficient is substantial, but it is not statistically different from zero. A simpler analysis, however, shows stark differences. While no senator who won his last election with 55 percent or less of the vote refrained entirely from casework solicitation, nearly half of the "safe" senators claimed to use no solicitation devices whatsoever.

The relationship between measures of member partisan and policy characteristics (and role orientation), on the one hand, and the number of devices used to stimulate cases, on the other, prove quite important for the House. Both ideology and party are predicted independently to affect casework hustling. Consistent with the hypothesis, House (and perhaps Senate) liberals seem to do more than conservatives. House Republicans, moreover, were more likely to solicit cases.[26] Fully 22 percent of Democrats, compared to only 6 percent of Republicans, said they did nothing to solicit case requests.

In the Senate, floor appearances are positively related to casework outreach efforts, while in the lower chamber neither activism measure makes a noticeable difference, perhaps attesting to the notion that legislative involvement (independent of leadership duties) and concern for casework are not incompatible. Such was the suggestion in the previous chapter, when only congressmen's attitudes were explored. Conversely, if the introduction of bills and frequent floor appearances are not measures of legislative activism but instead represent tendencies to engage in credit-claiming, advertising, or position-taking in order to curry favor with constituents or interest groups within the constituency, the finding of no consistently positive relationship suggests that the casework function as measured here is pursued independently of other means of gaining attention and popularity back home. And if that is the case, it may suggest that doing casework is valued as something more than a means of ingratiating oneself with the voters.

Few measures of constituency need and demands have strong effects on casework stimulation. As expected, the signs for the education variables are negative (lower education districts and states appear to be "hustled" harder),[27] and removing the regional factor in equation (2) renders the educational effect much more clear. On the other hand, some regional variables have independent effects.

Being from eastern and border states significantly and substantially inclines representatives to seek out cases via multiple devices.

Firm conclusions are difficult to draw. In the House, electoral insecurity (albeit very weakly), regional characteristics, and member-related traits such as leadership status (or seniority), party, activism, and ideology help most in explaining entrepreneurial activities. It does *not* seem to be the case that electoral pressures dominate these decisions. Except for the regional considerations, the signs of the Senate coefficients are in the same direction as those for the House, suggesting that many of the same basic factors underlie decisions to hustle cases for both senators and representatives. The weakness of the Senate equation may be due to the small number of cases in the sample relative to the statistical demands of the model. Or it may derive from the intuitively plausible reason that senators, being somewhat more free from constituency demands than are representatives, simply may be more idiosyncratic in their approach to casework.

In both chambers, some members deliberately avoided encouragement of casework altogether. Fully one-quarter of senators and 15 percent of representatives in 1977 and 1978, but only 3 percent in 1982, apparently did nothing by way of outreach efforts. Asked if his office did anything to solicit cases, one aide responded: ''Solicit cases? Hell no; we have too much work already.'' One former congressman commented that he advised his successor not to go all out right away, and especially not to use a mobile van, as he had done: ''I told him that if he got too many cases, his staff wouldn't be able to handle it. Then constituents would get mad at him. Better if he waits until his staff is well organized and has developed its own procedures.'' Several other offices indicated that soliciting cases tends to bring in weak ones that cannot be satisfactorily resolved—leading to ill will. A Texas congressman did nothing to stimulate requests because his constituents would not stand for it—they even objected to being mailed a questionnaire. A number of members abandoned the idea of mobile offices between 1977 and 1982 for another reason: they feared that their constituents would not comprehend the use of gas-guzzling vans in times of gasoline shortages. At least one office wanted to take cases only if a clear injustice had been done—hardly an incentive to solicit more. And while most offices are diligent in encouraging local communities to apply for federal grants, some take the opposite position altogether. According to an administrative assistant to Cong. Robert E. Badham (R., Calif.), ''The congressman doesn't like grant programs. He doesn't like to spend money.'' Another aide explained that ''we don't tell people that money is available. It's not our business. Our business is to react to whatever is going on, not to initiate. As for writing people about this and that, we don't try. Too many of the poor buggers are seeking grants and don't get them anyway.''[28]

3.3. The Distribution of Casework Loads

Why do some members of Congress bear greater casework burdens than others? How does one explain the demand for casework services? No single model exists to account for the variations on case loads, but it is clear that the starting points for any explanation are constituency ("demand side") and member ("supply side") characteristics. A five-part model seems appropriate. For any given senator or congressman, casework workload can be conceptualized as the product of: (1) objective constituency needs; (2) the constituency's expectations of casework services; (3) the constituency's ability and inclination to express those needs; (4) the congressman's perceived receptivity and attractiveness to constituents—in short, his or her "casework salience"; and (5) overt attempts to stimulate casework. While these factors are analytically distinct, they are in reality interconnected and not easily or unambiguously operationalized. Thus selection of measures to test the effects of the variables on casework loads poses the same sort of problems alluded to in the previous section.

Constituency Need. The difficulty in selecting measures of need is that cases arise out of many different circumstances and come from different constituents, ranging from the elderly pensioner to the well-to-do businessman. A first and obvious variable is population. Other things being equal, the more constituents, the greater the potential demand, and thus the heavier the case load. Since House districts are basically equivalent in size, the focus here is limited to the Senate.

Second, since much casework involves social security and other pension programs and since the elderly are slightly more likely to seek help from Congress, it is logical to expect that constituencies marked by high concentrations of the elderly (those over sixty-five years of age) would generate greater numbers of cases. Third, although on the individual constituent level income and occupational status do not help much to distinguish between case requesters and non-requesters, on an aggregate district-by-district basis, such characteristics might prove important. Lower income constituencies have greater need for congressional intervention, and therefore state and district median income levels should be negatively associated with casework loads.

A final measure of need concerns economic developments nationwide. The migration of population and industry from the North to the South and West has left older regions of the country (primarily the East and upper Midwest) with deteriorating economic bases and relatively heavy unemployment. Such areas are likely to seek government help and, specifically, congressional intervention in pursuit of grants, projects, and—for individuals—personal government benefits. Thus casework loads in the East and, probably, Midwest should exceed those in other regions of the country. Recall that the analysis at the individual level in chapter 2 found easterners and midwesterners disproportionately more likely to seek help.

Ability and Inclination to Request Help. Objective ability and willingness to contact congressmen for assistance is a product of intrinsic and circumstantial factors. The former refers to citizen-specific attributes, and the two measures used here are median years of education and the percentage of government workers (federal, state, and local) in the district or state.

Although well-educated states and districts may have less objective need for ''basic'' congressional casework intervention and may be less prone to see government as relevant for such matters as retirement benefits and unemployment problems, and although the analysis in chapter 2 revealed virtually no relationship between education and casework requesting, it is possible that, in the aggregate, better-educated districts would be more skillful and, probably, energetic in communicating their views and their wants when in need. Even the smallest individual-level relationships could, when summed across districts, lead to greater demands on representatives. Said one caseworker, who works for a rural southern representative: ''Many of our constituents are illiterate, and most of the rest would be intimidated by government bureaucrats. . . . Without us, they'd be in big trouble.''

Government bureaucrats themselves tend to make demands on their congressmen and senators. As one caseworker for a Maryland representative put it: ''There are a lot of civil servants in our district, and they know what a congressman can do. They write us, and the word gets around.'' In addition, large concentrations of government employees in states and districts indicate large, or many, state and local governments and/or a substantial federal presence—both of which would generate unusually heavy case demands.

Circumstantial factors contributing to the propensity to request case help include proximity to Washington and population density. States and House districts closer to Washington (within one hundred miles) would seem likely to produce heavier casework requests because access to Congress is easier and because members from such districts tend to make more trips home and see more constituents face to face. One office of a Maryland representative, for example, indicated a weekly load of two thousand letters and fifteen hundred phone calls in 1977. Urban dwellers generally have easier access to their congressmen, if only because more residents can live near or travel to congressional district offices and/or more residents can meet with their congressmen more easily at any one time.

Constituency Expectations and Traditions. For various reasons, some constituencies might develop greater expectations of service than others: those in regions where traditions of service have developed from "old-time" party systems, those whose political cultures stress service and oppose bureaucracies, and those whose incumbent congressmen have nurtured the expectations of high-volume, high-quality service. As one aide put it, "———— [the congressman] has so many ties to people in this district, and everyone calls us. We have a good reputation for service." Commented another: "News spreads when customers are satisfied. For example, we get letters that begin, 'you helped a friend of mine, and I have this problem. . . . ' "

The best way to proxy these considerations is to focus on regional differences. Members from the East should be under the greatest pressure. Those from the South and border states should—other things being equal—also receive somewhat heavier than normal loads. Midwesterners are hard to predict. As mentioned previously, some midwestern states are undergoing the same economic deterioration as the East; on the other hand, much of the Midwest is characterized by the moralistic culture, which would tend to diminish constituent service. Only in the West, with its booming development and moralistic culture, are distinctly lighter case loads anticipated.

Members who have established traditions of and reputations for quality constituency service ought to receive more requests than those who have not. Lacking time series data or measures of district-by-district casework traditions, this hypothesis is impossible to test. Individual staff estimates of success rates are available as a proxy for such traditions and reputations on the assumption that, if casework is successful, it will attract new "customers." Unfortunately, these estimates could not be grouped on an office-by-office basis; moreover, success rates could be affected *by* case loads: the lighter the load, the greater the attention that can be given to each case and, perhaps, the higher the success. At any rate, there was no correlation between these success rates and case loads.

These factors, then, constitute the "demand" side of casework. The "supply" side consists of two sets of variables.

Member Salience: Receptivity, Visibility, and Attractiveness. Although some commentators have insisted that newly elected members are inordinately swamped with case requests,[29] evidence of the last chapter and common sense argue that seniority (and the visibility it brings) should lead to heavier case loads, as should leadership status. Legislative activism, which might draw favorable press or interest-group attention, also could enhance visibility and draw more cases. Finally, partisan affiliation may affect case loads.[30] Although members of the party in power (Democrats, in 1977–78) are obliged to conduct legislative business and apparently do less to solicit cases, constituents—whatever their party—of Democratic senators and representatives might reason that *their* congressmen can be more helpful because they "control" government. Thus Democrats would receive more cases than Republicans. Another variable that might enhance member visibility is legislative activism (bills and appearances), which in turn might draw favorable press or interest-group attention.

Member Stimulation of Casework. Stimulation, presumably, is a rational undertaking. Thus the expectation is that casework loads will be positively correlated with the number of devices used to solicit cases.[31]

Table 3.4 presents the tests of the model. Two regression equations are presented for the House, one containing all elements of the model and another omitting regional variables and member leadership status (which is highly correlated with seniority). For the Senate, the full model equation generates confusing results, pointing to weakness in the data. Thus a simplified equation was estimated, eliminating the variables that bear no bivariate relationship to case load or are strongly intercorrelated.

For the House, the constituency need variables are unrelated to case loads, with the possible exception of income (in the second equation). Surprisingly, the data suggest, albeit very weakly, that when other factors are controlled wealthier districts may generate more cases.[32] Income levels are associated with the *sources* of case requests: congressmen representing poorer districts—those most in need of federal grants and projects—tend to receive greater proportions of their casework from state and local governments than do those from more affluent districts. For the upper chamber, representing larger states does bring more cases; and the coefficient for the age variable is positive (but not statistically significant), hinting at a possible relationship.

"Constituency ability" factors help to explain case loads. In the House, representing well-educated districts decreases case loads (note especially equation 2), while representing urban districts and having large numbers of government employees in one's district bring additional requests. That there is no relationship in the Senate may suggest that those most politically sophisticated constituents know that the best service can be found in the House. Both factors also are related to the sources of cases: in rural areas and areas where heavy proportions of the workforce are employed by governments, congressmen receive greater percentages of their cases from state and local governments. Conversely, in urban areas and those lacking large numbers of bureaucrats, cases tend to come more frequently from individual constituents. Although proximity to Washington correlates positively with case loads in a bivariate test, when other variables (most important, percentage of government employees and region) are controlled, the effect disappears.

Table 3.4: Congressional Case Loads in 1977–78: A Multivariate Analysis

Independent Variables	House (1) B	House (1) Beta	House (2) B	House (2) Beta	Senate B	Senate Beta
Constituency Need						
Population (1000s)	—	—	—	—	.016*	.225
Percent over 65	1.796	.056	2.685	.084	39.007	.224
Median income	.006	.163	.009*	.228	—	—
Constituency Ability						
Median yrs. educ.	−15.951	−.154	−30.979**	−.300	50.399	.100
Govt. employees	2.657*	.142	3.269**	.175	3.541	.035
Proximity to Wash.						
(within 100 miles)	−40.356	−.138	−19.358	−.066	—	—
Percent urban						
(SMSA)	.363	.145	.307	.123	—	—
Expectations						
East	47.148**	.270	—	—	−156.981	−.150
Midwest	−5.213	−.030	—	—	—	—
South	15.286	.079	—	—	—	—
Border	84.791**	.251	—	—	—	—
Member Salience						
Democrat	−9.688	−.057	−7.727	−.046	97.537	.145
Seniority (years)	3.618***	.308	3.365***	.286	2.732	.055
Activism (bills)	−.055	−.067	−.011	−.014	—	—
Activism (floor)	−.063	−.032	.034	.017	1.470*	.340
Leadership	−1.656	−.011	—	—	—	—
Stimulation Efforts						
Number of devices	9.517	.126	13.440**	.178	−8.112	−.027
CONSTANT	121.340		260.073		1035.251	
(*N*)	(122)		(122)		(36)	
R-squared	.26		.18		.28	
Adj. *R*-squared	.14		.10		.03	

NOTE: *Beta* = Standardized regression coefficient: *p* < .10; **p* < .05; ***p* < .01.

The "expectations" component, as measured here, is not as pure as would be desired, since regional dummy variables proxy not only political culture and traditions of service but also certain aspects of need and access. Nonetheless, as predicted, representing the East and border states does lead to heavier loads; and the sign on the coefficient for the South likewise is positive. As expected, case loads in the West were lighter for both chambers. Comparing urban congressmen from the East to all their colleagues produces sharp differences: these members were nearly three times as likely to bear very heavy (over 120 cases per week) loads.

Only one measure of member salience, seniority, clearly affects case loads in the House. All else being equal, each additional year of seniority adds over three cases per week. Analysis of the Obey Commission data corroborates this finding. Although Senate seniority is unrelated to case loads, the more senior senators become, the smaller is the proportion of cases emanating from individual constituents as opposed to local and state government units. It may be that once they are in office for several years, senators institutionalize their working relationships with governmental offices in their states—or vice versa—in order to facilitate attempts to secure federal funds, while paying proportionately less attention to individuals. Leadership status does not bear any strong relationship to workloads, especially when seniority is controlled. Nor do party affiliations. The data on case loads from the House Commission, likewise, reveal no partisan differences whatsoever. Measures of legislative activism were unrelated to case load burdens, but floor activism seems to generate more requests from Senate constituents. One explanation is that, whereas seniority (and the familiarity and publicity attendant thereon) distinguishes representatives in terms of visibility to constituents, all senators are relatively visible. But the ones who are *most* active, and most often make the headlines, are the ones who become most familiar. In districts and states marked by low education levels, this "visibility" factor is more strongly related to case loads, which is precisely what would be expected.

Another aspect of member salience is worth noting. Interviews with members and staffs suggest that certain peculiarly visible senators and congressmen attract disproportionately large numbers of cases from outside their states and districts. Former presidential candidates, popular black legislators, members known for their dedication to certain causes (pro- or anti-military, prison reform, tax reform), or congressmen singled out by interest groups (such as the ACLU) for their beliefs or positions are said to receive heavier than normal numbers of grievances and requests from particular groups of people.

Overt attempts to stimulate cases seem to bear fruit in the House, but the correlations are not terribly strong. Only in the simplified House equation does the coefficient reach the standard level of significance. Nor, comparing the standardized coefficients in the equations, does casework hustling appear to be nearly as important as constituent education, member seniority, and even constituent income levels. Thus, although juniors do more to solicit cases, and although solicitations apparently have an effect, it is still the more visible seniors who receive the most cases. Moreover, how one solicits cases may be crucial. Caution is advised, however; due to the limits of the data (the maximum number of devices coded was three), one cannot assess this variable's impact with certainty. The effect undoubtedly is greater.

The most effective of all solicitation devices seems to be the mobile office. "Every time the mobile office goes out," volunteered one aide, "it comes back with dozens of cases." A resumption of aggressive constituency attentiveness after years of neglect may also trigger an avalanche of cases. Cong. Henry Reuss (D., Wis.), for example, had for many years spent relatively little time and effort on constituency service. In 1976 he received his first serious electoral challenge—his first in years. The result was a turnaround: he increased the number of aides assigned to his Milwaukee office, opened a second (part-time) office, made more frequent public appearances, got involved in various community projects, worked diligently to secure a new federal building, and even held an open-invitation picnic for constituents. The result was a quadrupling of casework in his main district office and a doubling in Washington.[33]

3.4. Summary

Casework burdens on Congress are heavy and, at least until 1981 or so, appeared to be growing. Although senators bear heavier loads, theirs are not proportionately as great as congressmen's. Factors accounting for the upsurge in casework include the expansion of government at all levels, an ever more demanding citizenry, and entrepreneurial efforts by senators and representatives to stimulate requests.

Certain member characteristics explain House casework "hustling," with juniors, liberals, Republicans, and (perhaps) electorally marginal members apparently the most active. Eastern congressmen are more likely to utilize multiple devices than are others. In the Senate, casework stimulation seems to be more idiosyncratic.

The burden of casework is not spread evenly among members of Congress. In the House, a combination of constituency factors (eastern and border state, political traditions and expectations, lower education levels, urban areas, and concentrations of government employees) and, above all else, congressmen's seniority, along with overt stimulation efforts, account for heavier case loads. To a very large extent, therefore, congressmen are at the mercy of their constituents; they simply must respond to demands, and these demands seem to be heavily influenced by traditions and political culture.

Barring sharp retrenchments in government programs, it is doubtful that case loads will drop significantly in the future. Were they to continue the growth of the 1960s and 1970s, Congress would run the risk of severe overload, perhaps leading to demands for greater staffs. As discussed in the next chapters, staffing currently seems adequate and well structured to handle existing workloads.

CHAPTER 4

Congressional and Executive Participants in the Casework Process

Senators and representatives themselves devote relatively little time to cases and projects, turning over these duties to certain of their staff assistants. Such staffs have developed fixed routines and informal rules for dealing with constituent requests, trying to be as expeditious and successful as possible to project a positive image to constituents without interfering with other important functions. On the executive side, recent years have witnessed a similar evolution toward casework specialization. Both sets of staff structures have achieved a level of permanency and have encouraged the routinization of the casework process. This chapter examines the congressional and executive staffs, while the next looks at the process. The arguments, simply, are that casework has become an independent, largely bureaucratized, and semi-institutionalized enterprise that now is stable and predictable; that institutionalization affects the attitudes and behavior of the participants; and that these developments have policy and political consequences.

4.1. An Organizational-Systems Perspective on Staffing

Students of private and public organizations have noted that when organizations have to cope with or capitalize on their environments in order to survive and to advance organizational goals, they develop structures whose special tasks are interaction with the environment: representing the organization, receiving and processing incoming information, and conducting transactions. These "boundary-spanning" structures stand as a midway point between the core of the organization and the environmental forces that threaten survival and provide resources.[1]

An organization's boundary-spanning structure is both outward and inward looking, and its members occupy a somewhat awkward position, straddling, as it were, two worlds. Accordingly, boundary-spanning agents may develop a role-set quite different from, and both complementary and hostile to, that held by members of the organizational core. Boundary-spanners must deal with outsiders, often in innovative ways, while remaining accountable to the organization of which they are a part.

The situation is inherently delicate and stressful for these intermediaries. Two particularly stressful conditions are the "fault-responsibility dilemma" and representational ambiguity. The former occurs when the organizational and environmental actors are in conflict, placing the boundary-spanners at the center of controversy, often with diverse expectations and pressures. If the organizational core or the environmental participants perceive that they have not been well served, the blame may fall to the go-betweens. Representational ambiguity refers to the need to serve two masters without having full control over the powers and tools needed to do so. These stressful conditions often require the recruitment and training of, and efforts to retain, certain types of people for boundary-spanning slots. Sometimes occupants of such positions develop a particular set of attitudes toward their jobs. And emotional rewards — pats on the back, meetings with the organization's leaders, and clear-cut "victories" — frequently are needed.

Both Congress and the executive branch interact with two environmental actors: the public and each other. Something like boundary-spanning structures and agents have evolved in both institutions to cope with these needs. Each department or agency, for example, has an office of public or press relations, fully staffed with professionals. Similarly, most congressional offices have press specialists. The focus of attention here, however, is on two special groups of boundary-spanning agents. In the Congress, the congressional caseworkers (including those who work on projects) deal routinely with individual, group, corporate, or governmental constituents, processing their requests as expeditiously as possible. At the same time, another relevant environmental force is the executive branch, whose cooperation the case and projects staffers require to bring about favorable results for the constituents. On the executive side, all agencies, and, of course, the White House itself, have developed and institutionalized congressional relations or "legislative liaison" staffs. Both sets of staffs, congressional caseworkers and agency liaison officials, come close to fitting the definition of boundary-spanning roles. The correspondence is not perfect, for in the executive there are numerous program-level (service-delivery) bureaucrats who also fall into boundary-spanning positions when they serve their clientele and deal with Congress. Army recruiters and base commanders, clerks in Social Security or Veterans Administration offices, and Small Business Administration functionaries—to name just a few—interact with the public on behalf of their core organizations; and they, or their offices, frequently come directly into contact with congressional caseworkers and other aides. And on the congressional side: "It is the staff, and more especially the press aides, field representatives and caseworkers, who form the boundary-spanning structures that buffer the technical core (incumbent), smooth out environmental disturbances, reduce uncertainty, and tend to the input-output functions," entering into daily exchanges with constituents and with the executive on behalf of the congressmen for whom they work.[2]

Both sets of boundary-spanning agents—congressional caseworkers (and other aides who regularly attend to cases and projects) and agency liaison officials (along with program or service-delivery officials who routinely deal with congressional inquiries)—can be conceptualized as part of an overall system of legislative-executive-constituent interaction, as pictured in figure 4.1. Within congressional offices are the policy-making core and the constituency service specialists; within each department or agency, there likewise are the core (the policy-makers and the program-implementation and service-delivery staffs) and the liaison teams. This system is characterized by the familiar inputs (supports and demands), outputs, and concern for system maintenance, with appropriate transactions occuring between the units. These attributes exist at two levels. At the macro level, congressional offices want to remain in existence and to accomplish certain policy goals. That requires, at the very least, electoral support, which is believed to be enhanced by efficient and effective processing of incoming demands and requests. The congressional output includes (1) giving the appearance of careful and diligent attentiveness to constituent problems and requests—that is, *symbolic* output—and (2) actually winning favorable decisions from the agencies: symbolic and service responsiveness, in short. Another form of casework output for congressional offices is policy-related: new ideas or incentives for legislation and/or oversight of executive behavior. Agencies seek legislative and appropriations support from Congress. It is widely believed that by handling casework and other congressional demands, agencies will ingratiate themselves with senators, representatives, and their staffs. The exchange is simple and forthright. Finally, agencies are in business to serve their clientele, and thus complaints from the Hill are a source of information for their operations. It also is an input demand upon them for action. Agencies believe that their well-

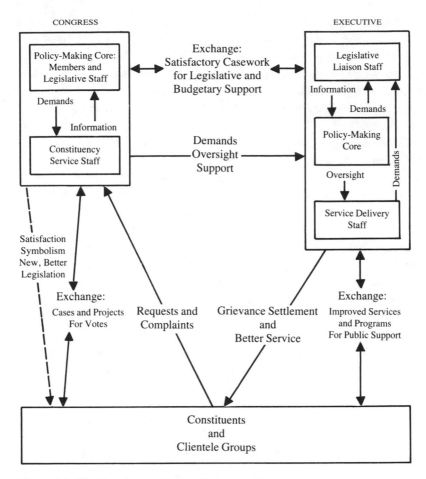

Figure 4.1. The Constituency Service System

being is secured to the extent that they keep both clients and Congress happy. If agencies process constituent and congressional casework input effectively, one form of output is likely to be an improvement in agency programs or operations due to correcting weaknesses turned up in congressional complaints. Such improvements benefit the agencies, their clientele, and, indirectly, Congress. In carrying out these functions, congressional offices need each other. Thus the interaction is one of exchange rather than compliance or pressure.

At the micro level, looking at the boundary-spanning agents, casework operations have become almost "institutionalized." That is, casework has become relatively well bounded, complex, and autonomous; it functions according to well-defined procedures and generates its own norms; and it is able to adapt to its environment and to technological innovations.[3] Caseworkers—and here are included other staffers who regularly, if only on a part-time basis, handle casework—are bombarded with demands from constituents and also from the core of their offices—the members, administrative assistants, and legislative assistants who expect them, in effect, to "keep the constituents off our backs" and, in many cases, to "keep us posted about problems our constituents are having." Thus caseworkers, collectively as well as individually in each office, can be pictured as a subsystem of the congressional office system, which itself is a subunit of the larger system in figure 4.1. In the executive branch, liaison operatives also constitute subsystems, meeting the demands of the policy-making core for continued good relations with Congress and, sometimes, the demands from the service-delivery and program staffs for information on how well programs are working. When liaison teams are working properly, they can provide (as subsystem output) internal oversight information and advice to agency policy-makers and can smooth the ruffles raised among program and service-delivery operatives by pesky congressional aides. As in Congress, this simple systems analysis is not "pure," of course, since many service-delivery bureaucrats directly receive contacts from congressional staffs and interact with them to solve constituent problems. In so doing, of course, they are acting primarily in boundary-spanning roles, but not exclusively.

Looking, finally, at the linkage between congressional staffs who routinely deal with cases and projects and agency liaison staffs (and others engaged in liaison-type activities), there is the temptation to categorize it as a unique subsystem. Certainly the patterns and norms of interaction, as well as the separate staffs themselves, have become institutionalized, with shared goals and norms. System maintenance and goal achievement dominate the agenda: How can both sides profit from the interchange? How do caseworkers and liaison bureaucrats keep the system working in the face of mounting demands from constituents, heavy expectations for success (from congressional office cores) and / or greater protection from congressional intrusion into administrative operations and prerogatives (from agency colleagues or superiors)? What threats jeopardize the system? What becomes clear is that the casework interaction occurring in thousands of locations daily does have rules and norms of behavior which serve to mitigate controversy while fostering satisfactory goal achievement on both sides.

4.2. Congressional Casework Staffs

For the past thirty years, staff positions in Congress have become increasingly specialized. A typical senator's office in Washington today includes a personal or executive secretary, an administrative assistant, an office manager, several legislative assistants, up to a half-dozen legislative correspondents, a press secretary, several secretary-receptionists, perhaps a computer terminal operator, a contingent of case and projects specialists, and miscellaneous aides.

Many home state field offices are microcosms of the Washington offices, while others are manned by one or two generalists. In the House, where each member is limited to eighteen full-time aides plus up to four part-time, substitute, or unpaid staffers (compared to the Senate, where staff sizes and allowances are based on state population and approach one hundred assistants for some senators who can afford to supplement their official staff budgets), the division of labor among aides is not as precise. But considerable similarities exist.

The number of caseworkers and projects specialists grew rapidly in the 1960s and 1970s, but it is difficult to know precisely how many such staffers there are in Congress, how much staff effort is expended on constituency service, or exactly where (in Washington or in home offices) such staffs are located and where casework operations are conducted. Not all senators and representatives clearly designate caseworkers by title; in numerous offices, particularly those in home states and districts, various staff members—sometimes all of them—try their hand at casework. And a good many offices utilize volunteers and student interns to handle mundane cases.

The House Commission on Administrative Review in 1977 surveyed administrative assistants in 143 House offices, asking for the number of casework, project work, and secretarial staff "involved in the substantive disposition of casework." The final tally showed an average of 4.2 out of a total staff complement of 15.7 (27 percent). By contrast, about 14 percent of personal office staff strength was devoted to legislative research.[4] The questionnaires and interview schedules employed in this study in 1977–78 asked for the number of staff who "regularly engage in constituency service (case and project) operations" and for the number of "caseworkers" per se. The 1982 survey asked for the number of aides regularly engaged in casework and for the number regularly engaged in handling projects, and then separately for the number of case and projects specialists. The results, with the Obey Commission data, are presented in table 4.1.

On average, senators in 1978 had nearly 5 designated caseworkers, most of whom were (and are) located in field offices, and a total of about 10 aides altogether who regularly were engaged in casework or project efforts. Similarly, a typical member of the House in the 95th Congress had 3.5 caseworkers, with about 7 aides regularly working on cases and projects. The 1982 data are not directly comparable, since they separate individual casework from grants and projects, but they do suggest a slight overall growth in the allocation of staff to casework.

When deciding where their casework operations should be located, congressmen face three choices: do it all in Washington, do it all back home, or divide the workload between Washington and district or state offices. The trend in recent years has been to shift casework staffs and operations more and more to field offices. In 1960, for example, only 14 percent of all congressional personnel office staff, according to the *Congressional Staff Directory,* were stationed in state or district offices. According to the 1979 *Staff Directory,* 39 and 31 percent of all Senate and House staffs, respectively, were located in the field. Calculations from the 1977–78 data in table 4.1 show that about half of Senate and House caseworkers and two-thirds of all aides "regularly engaged" in case and project work operated out of home offices. By 1982, three-quarters of the House staffers regularly handling cases and half of those who dealt with projects were based in the districts. An even higher proportion of casework specialists (85 percent) were based in home offices. The conventional wisdom that state and district offices are essentially—but not exclusively—oriented toward constituency service appears to be accurate.

The proportion of casework substantively handled in field offices also can be calculated from information provided by congressional offices. During the 95th Congress, an average of 63 percent of all casework and projects was done in home offices. (By the 97th Congress, the figure rose to about 75 percent for individual casework; a third of all federal grants and projects were processed in district offices.) Still, one-fourth of the senators in the sample and one-sixth of the representatives in both Congresses did virtually no casework (under 20 percent) there.

Are congressmen's constituency service resource allocation decisions consistent? Are they systematically determined? If so, do those factors point to genuine service responsiveness or to opportunism—or neither?

Table 4.1: Size and Location of Casework and Project Staffs

Casework/Projects Staffs per Member	Mean	Median	Range	(n)[a]
Senate: 95th Congress				
Total staff "regularly engaged in cases and projects"	10.0	9.2	2–35	(42)
(in Washington)	(3.3)	(2.3)	(0–20)	(47)
(home offices)	(7.2)	(5.7)	(0–30)	(50)
Total number of "caseworkers"	4.8	4.3	(0–11)	(30)
(in Washington)	(2.1)	(1.4)	(0–10)	(40)
(home offices)	(3.4)	(3.3)	(0–11)	(36)
House: 95th Congress				
Total staff "regularly engaged in cases and projects"	6.9	6.6	1–18	(144)
(in Washington)	(2.4)	(1.9)	(0–15)	(150)
(home offices)	(4.5)	(4.4)	(0–11)	(162)
Total number of "caseworkers"	3.5	3.3	0–9	(75)
(in Washington)	(1.2)	(0.9)	(0–9)	(117)
(home offices)	(2.3)	(2.2)	(0–7)	(96)
Total casework staff (Obey Commission)	4.2	3.9	0–12	(142)
(in Washington)	(1.2)	(1.0)	(0–5)	(143)
(home offices)	(3.0)	(2.9)	(0–9)	(143)
House: 97th Congress				
Total staff "regularly engaged in cases"	5.4	4.9	1–16	(136)
(in Washington)	(1.3)	(0.8)	(0–8)	(137)
(home offices)	(4.1)	(3.9)	(0–8)	(140)
Total number of "caseworkers" [b]	3.6	3.2	0–8	(129)
(in Washington)	(0.6)	(0.3)	(0–4)	(131)
(home offices)	(3.1)	(3.0)	(0–8)	(132)
Total staff "regularly engaged in grants and projects	2.7	1.8	0–11	(132)
(in Washington)	(1.4)	(1.2)	(0–7)	(134)
(home offices)	(1.2)	(0.9)	(0–8)	(129)
Total number of projects specialists [b]	0.4	0.3	0–2	(124)
(in Washington)	(0.2)	(0.2)	(0–1)	(126)
(home offices)	(0.2)	(0.1)	(0–2)	(130)

SOURCES: Author's interviews and questionnaires and data gathered in House Commission on Administrative Review, *Final Report,* 95th Cong., 1st sess., 1977, H. Doc. 95-272, pp. 1025–27.

[a] The number of offices for which both Washington and home office staff size could be determined is lower than the number for which one or the other could be; thus total staff may not equal home plus Washington staff.

[b] Those who spend three-fourths or more of their time on casework or projects.

Using 1978 casework staff size and location of casework operations as dependent variables, it is possible to test several theories that purport to explain how and why congressmen allocate their staffs. The first theory, as discussed in chapter 3, is based on the "electoral incentive."[5] In order to overcome precarious electoral situations, congressmen might emphasize casework by allocating larger proportions of their staffs to such work or by locating casework operations and staffs back home in their districts. Seniority constitutes a second explanation, but precisely what it is about seniority that makes the difference is unclear. Junior members, being new and insecure, might believe that they have to demonstrate to constituents their concern for district and state problems. Life-cycle effects may be at work: junior members simply have fewer institutional obligations, and seniors more; thus as seniority increased, members would be less interested in casework and, accordingly, would devote fewer staff resources to it. (On the other hand, they might seek to compensate for their institutional involvement; see below.) The best guess — supported by other work on perquisite use — is that there is a general cohort effect. Congressmen of recent vintage, as a group, may be more dedicated to constituency service, whereas old-timers simply constitute a different breed, never, as a group, having got used to doing constituency work back home or to having large staffs available for cases and projects. This seemed to be the case with respect to casework solicitation. Regardless of the reason, one would expect junior members to allocate greater resources to constituency service.

A third theory incorporates calculations no less rational than, yet different from, the electoral explanation. Constituency needs, expectations, and demands might influence congressmen's allocational decisions. The hypotheses are that case loads and population would correlate positively with all measures of congressmen's casework activities, and that constituency income and education would be negatively related to them. Certainly many of the findings in chapters 2 and 3 would suggest as much. Considerations of political culture and legislator-constituent interaction also suggest that congressmen from the East would have larger casework-related staffs and would locate them in home offices. Senators and representatives whose constituencies were farthest from Washington (in the West) might be more tempted to decentralize casework operations. Finally, density of population might affect decisions to allocate casework and case-related staffs in home offices. It would not be rational to locate aides in one or two field offices unless they were accessible to large numbers of constituents. Thus urban districts should experience considerable decentralization of casework.

A fourth explanation for casework activity concerns institutional obligations and legislative orientations. Although party and committee leaders probably are too busy to devote their own time to casework, they usually are advantaged by having additional staffs for legislative purposes and thus could be expected to allocate greater portions of their own staffs to constituency matters. If it were not for the fact that many leaders were "old-timers," and thus not used to moving staffs away from Washington, one might expect them to decentralize casework operations to their districts.

Legislative activists—those who introduce and cosponsor large numbers of bills—also might be inclined to compensate for their activism by allocating large numbers of aides to casework, or at least by moving them to home offices to keep constituent problems from interfering with "more important" legislative tasks in Washington. One midwestern Republican, for instance, differentiated his personal goals from those of his office: "Personally, I see my job as legislating for the nation, currently in the energy area; but my *office* deals with the folks back home." Even if introducing legislation is merely one element, along with constituency service, in a carefully planned strategy of appeasing interest groups and attracting attention, a positive relationship to casework staffs and decentralization would be anticipated.

Finally, one should not discount personal and attitudinal factors, however difficult they are to measure. One variable that might prove useful would be ideology. Conservatives, arguably, might be more inclined to keep casework operations in Washington.

Table 4.2 presents ordinary least squares regression equations for the House and Senate that incorporate these variables in predicting staff sizes and decentralization of casework to home offices. (State population is highly collinear with casework loads and with the percentage of urban residents in a state, and thus it has been omitted from the Senate equations. When included, its coefficient is trivial. Similarly, constituency education was not included, both because it correlates moderately with income and because, when included, it contributes nothing to the results.)

Although a simple bivariate test shows that prior electoral margin correlates negatively (as predicted) with the size of casework staffs and the percentage of casework done at home, when controls are imposed in the regressions those relationships disappear, pointing to a virtual lack of any independent effect of marginal electoral trend on these resource allocation decisions.[6] (The signs, however, do remain negative.) The one exception occurs when the 1976 election results or a dummy to represent a drop in the 1976 vote from the 1970–74 average, rather than the 1970–76 trend, are used to predict decentralization of casework in the House. The resulting coefficients are negative, moderately strong, and statistically significant. The implication is that, to the extent that electoral troubles do cause congressmen to move casework operations back home, it is only the most recent electoral scare that does so. Congressmen from perennially

Table 4.2: Casework Staffing Decisions, 95th Congress

	House		Senate	
Independent Variables	Total Casework Staff	Percent Casework at Home	Total Casework Staff	Percent Casework at Home
Electoral trend	−.006 [−.028]	−.129 [−.057]	−.073 [−.104]	−.087 [−.022]
Seniority (years)	−.113** [−.244]	−1.094*** [−.229]	−.162 [−.137]	−2.827*** [−.521]
Conservatism	.005 [.049]	−.214** [−.196]	−.061* [−.301]	−.231 [−.182]
Legislative activism	−.001 [−.025]	.030 [.087]	.051** [.318]	.155 [.169]
Leadership	1.011* [.163]	−1.349 [−.021]	— 	—
Constituent income	−.0003* [−.193]	.0001 [.006]	−.0008 [−.165]	−.001 [−.055]
Percent urban	—	.305** [.298]	—	.362* [.231]
East	.786 [.108]	17.206** [.226]	−7.300* [−.289]	−19.381 [−.158]
South	−.839 [−.101]	14.537** [.172]	1.231 [.070]	−.689 [−.007]
Midwest	−1.454* [−.203]	5.911 [.077]	−4.177 [−.302]	−9.492 [−.107]
West	−.308 [−.038]	11.246 [.128]	1.135 [0.71]	−.702 [−.008]
Casework load	.008** [.217]	−.035 [−.083]	.006** [.334]	.016 [.135]
CONSTANT	9.738	55.034	5.640	82.112
(N)	(116)	(136)	(37)	(51)
R-squared	.19	.35	.41	.39
Adj. R-squared	.10	.29	.18	.22

NOTE: Standardized regression coefficents (betas) in brackets: * $p < .10$; ** $p < .01$

marginal (but not noticeably deteriorating) districts do not appear to believe that putting case and projects staffers back in the district is worth the effort. As many studies have noted, members' "home styles" tend not to change over their careers. Seniority has a negative effect across the board: the less senior, the larger the casework staffs and the greater the tendency to assign case and projects operations to field offices.

Measures of constituency needs, demands, and expectations help account for casework activities. Case loads and staff sizes remain quite strongly related in both chambers; congressmen do respond to demands by reallocating staff resources. Interestingly, when the number of House caseworkers per se (rather than the number of aides regularly working on cases and projects) is examined, there is no relationship between workload and the number of caseworkers, attesting to the fact that members' freedom to increase the number of full-time casework *specialists* is limited and that offices inundated by heavy case loads must assign other aides, at least part-time, to help out. Such reallocations might hurt junior members especially, since seniors tend to be committee and subcommittee chairmen who can use committee staff for legislative—and some constituency—work. By contrast, when Senate caseworkers are examined, there is a clear positive correlation between the number of cases and the number of caseworkers, attesting to senators' greater flexibility to adjust the number of casework specialists to meet changing demands. Case loads, finally, do not have any effect on the proportion of casework handled in field offices.[7]

In the House, constituency income levels are inversely related to size of casework staffs but quite unrelated to decentralization of casework operations, even when casework loads are controlled. As expected, one of the strongest predictors of casework decentralization in both House and Senate is the percentage of the district's population living in urban areas.

Regional considerations also matter, but somewhat differently between the two chambers. In the House, something about the East and South seems to compel congressmen to decentralize much of their casework activity (although only one-quarter of southern congressmen do all their casework in home offices—the least for any region). Midwestern representatives and senators tend to have smaller case-and projects-related staffs. Since decisions to do one's casework in district offices might result from expectations generated by the practices of others in one's state delegation, it is not surprising that some rather pronounced state patterns exist. In eight of fourteen states in the sample having four or more representatives for whom data were available, all or virtually all the members did either all or none of their casework back home; in eight of thirteen, both senators used similar strategies.

Institutional positions of leadership in the House have a clear and powerful effect on the size of casework staffs. The regression equations suggest that, other things being equal, leaders have one more person doing casework than do non-leaders. Legislative activism in the House and Senate has the expected positive bivariate association with all measures of staffing allocation, but in the lower chamber these linkages disappear when other variables are controlled. Senate activists, however, allocate more staff to do casework. Given the greater flexibility in Senate staffing and senators' greater ease of access to staff help (virtually all have some committee-related aides at their disposal), such a positive correlation should not be surprising. Ideology, finally, is linked to casework activity, with liberals decentralizing casework and, in the Senate, having larger casework staffs.

The equations, clearly, do not explain all that much, suggesting that many decisions on casework staffing are idiosyncratic or are affected by factors not accounted for here. Indeed, interviews turned up a wide variety of reasons for putting casework in home districts.[8] Perhaps the most commonly heard is the problem caused by the ''workload – staff size – office space squeeze'' in Washington.[9] As one first-term Republican senator put it: ''When I was elected, I had the smallest Senate office: we just didn't have room for (caseworkers) so we moved them back home. Plus, it's cheaper there.'' Some members simply want to get constituent service out of the hair of the Washington staff. Moreover, the increasingly decentralized structure of federal departments and agencies made home-office casework very attractive. Since federal regional and area offices throughout the country usually make the decisions that cause constituents' problems, receive the congressmen's appeals, and are in possession of the records bearing on the cases, it is logical to locate caseworkers nearby. Indeed, it is common for federal agencies and congressional home offices to be in the same buildings, facilitating the interchange needed to expedite constituent complaints and requests.

Another frequently heard reason concerns representation. An eastern senator wrote that: ''I also feel that there is a real advantage to having local staff who are proficient in various areas and are able to meet face-to-face with a constituent or group of constituents on short notice. The fact that the staff live in the community that they serve also allows them to be not only more sensitive to their problems, but also more on top of local issues and concerns.'' Getting close to constituents, presumably, is a way of making a better impression on them. Then, too, having caseworkers in the district increases the volume of walk-in cases. Both may translate, eventually, into good will.

Similarly, ''members sometimes choose to allocate their resources to home in ways that deliberately sharpen the contrast between themselves and other members, past and present, with whom they will be compared.''[10] Thus, for example,

Michigan's two senators in the 95th Congress exhibited quite different staffing patterns. Veteran Republican Senator Robert Griffin—until 1976–77—did very little case and project work in his Michigan offices, which remained sparsely staffed. Freshman Democratic Senator Donald Riegle, on the other hand, had seven fully staffed offices in the state, and did most of the casework there. Griffin did shift casework to the state during the 95th Congress, but apparently it did not impress the voters, who replaced him in the 1978 election.

A final reason for decentralizing was offered by another Republican senator's administrative assistant: "Well, we had these three offices back in the state, and the people there didn't have much to do. Besides, we're pretty cramped here in Washington, so we thought, 'why not let those people back home take on the casework?'—so we did." Not all congressmen followed clear strategies. "There's no rational reason," said one administrative assistant, "why we do half the casework at home and half here."

Making the move to district offices possible and attractive is the increasingly easy communication between Washington and those offices via WATS lines, high-speed telephone copiers, and, in some offices, computer connections which can send letters and documents to Washington to allow high-ranking aides (or specialists on federal projects) to begin work on selected problems almost as soon as they are brought to home offices.

Although most offices seem happy with having relegated casework to home offices, there remain some cogent arguments against, and difficulties with, decentralization. Some offices felt that agencies' legislative liaison staffs were the best place to begin work on constituent complaints, often because they had found it particularly difficult to deal with regional or area federal agency offices. A surprisingly large number of congressional offices indicated either that they would not do casework in the field or had tried but returned the operations to the Hill because of incompetence back home. "We switched it back here," explained the administrative assistant to a senior southern senator, "due to personnel reasons—they just weren't very good back in the state office."

Complaints about possible time lags were common. "The problem," said one caseworker, "is that if we did it back there, a constituent would write to us here; we'd have to send the letter to the district office; they'd begin to process it and probably have to contact an agency office here in Washington. Then they'd get it straightened out and send the draft letter here for the boss to read and sign—my God, the whole process might take an extra month."

Concerns over coordination, supervision, member knowledge, involvement, and control haunt some congressmen, leading them to keep everything in Washington. A former Republican representative, for example, said, "I simply wanted to know what was going on, and if casework were done back in the district, I wouldn't be able to." The fears of losing contact and control, the problems of coordination, and the attendant problem of staff morale are real. Several Washington aides had no idea how much casework was done in their district offices, or even that it was done there at all; and home and Washington aides sometimes disagreed on how casework operations worked. More than one Washington caseworker was unaware that field units were engaged in outreach efforts. One district aide bemoaned her fate, complaining that the congressman she worked for "doesn't have the vaguest idea of what we're doing here. Washington only knows *that* we're here — not what we do. Sometimes it's very irritating."

The extent of these problems is not overwhelming. Only 1 percent of the Obey Commission's sample of members voluntarily complained about the problem of controlling and coordinating district staff, but 12 percent responded to a closed-end question by saying that coordinating staffs was a major irritant while another 42 percent called it a minor one. Administrative assistants in the commission's sample responded in very similar fashion. Offices that handled a greater proportion of casework in the district were more likely to complain about coordination.[11]

Most offices take precautions to avoid the coordination and morale problems. Some periodically bring field staffs to the Capitol or send Washington aides to the district. Some designate one or two Capitol Hill staffers to serve as state operations coordinators, to keep in constant contact with and to supervise home office functions. Still others place one or more high-ranking staff members back home in charge of state and district offices, assuring close supervision and instilling a sense of importance in home-based aides. Usually, the mere expression of concern by the members or top Washington aides keeps home staffers happy and hard working.

A final reason for not decentralizing, paradoxically, is the same as for doing so: impressing constituents. "When I call constituents," one Washington caseworker explained, "they are so impressed and excited to be talking to someone calling from Washington that you really don't need to do anything more."

When casework is shared between home and Washington offices, a question of the division of labor inevitably arises. At the one extreme, where all work is done in Washington, district offices serve as "intake" agents and casework entrepreneurs, channeling case and project requests to Washington. At the other extreme, case mail coming to Capitol Hill must be shipped back to the state or district for handling. For all other cases, a *modus vivendi* must be worked out. A common decision rule is that if a case can be handled in the field (if it is "easy," if it is a complaint against a state or local government unit, or if the appropriate executive agency office is nearby), it should be; but if it requires action at a higher level, raises policy or important political questions, or merely is "tough," it goes to Washington. Another widely used practice is to distinguish between individual cases, which are handled in district or state offices if possible, and federal projects, which are done in Washington. Still other offices deal with particular kinds of cases in Washington, leaving the rest for home staffs. For instance, several offices assign social security to field offices while retaining military, civil service, and immigration cases in Washington. One reason for that particular split is that the military services and the Office of Personnel Management have liaison officers on the Hill, ready for instant consultation. Moreover, immigration cases sometimes necessitate the introduction of private bills, and legislators prefer to keep such situations under close control. Some reasons are less profound. One western senator's chief caseworker explained that his office was doing immigration work in Washington for only one reason: the immigration casework specialist back home had quit. A House office's immigration specialist wanted to live in her home town, so immigration cases were handled there. And a southern senator did everything back home except military cases because the caseworker who had handled military matters for over ten years for the senator simply wanted to live in Washington. Several aides said that such decisions were made by happenstance.

When a senator or congressman has several home offices, the workload must be parceled out among them. Three patterns exist. First, the member chooses one of the home offices to do the bulk of the work, leaving to the others the intake function. Senator S. I. Hayakawa (R., Cal.), for example, did most of his casework in San Francisco. Second, each of several offices handles whatever case it gets — basically along a geographical division of labor. Senator Riegle's Michigan operations worked that way. Third, some members assign to each of their field offices certain types of cases. Senator Tower of Texas and former Senator Griffin of Michigan used this method. And, naturally, a few members of Congress mix all three patterns.

Despite the heavy case loads, staffing for casework today seems adequate. In identifying the major problems facing the congressional casework enterprise, a mere 15 percent of members and staffs pointed to understaffing and overwork. Obey Commission surveys corroborated this finding. Asked by the Commission "What are the things which bother you the most (in doing your job) — what are the things which really frustrate you?" a mere 13 percent of the representatives responded in terms of inadequate staffing, with a third of that percentage specifically pointing to casework staff. Only 20 percent of the administrative assistants said they had too few caseworkers.[12] Aides to mid-seniority members (three to five terms) were most likely to complain. The reason could be that freshmen devote large staffs to casework because they believe it will help secure reelection (uppermost in their minds and thus unlikely to trigger a serious complaint), whereas the most senior members have settled into a static and probably comfortable staffing pattern. Mid-seniority members often are policy entrepreneurs — members pushing policy initiatives — and thus in need of more legislative staff support. They are very busy, and most likely feel pressured by legislative, oversight, and constituency matters. Hence their tendency to complain.

4.3. Congressional Casework Staff Characteristics

If the notion of a boundary-spanning function is appropriate for understanding congressional casework, one would expect that staffers who deal in cases and projects would share and value particular attributes. Conversely, given the generally higher priority assigned to the policymaking functions of Congress, one also would expect that caseworkers, as a group, would rank below administrative and legislative aides in terms of age, prestige, education, and salary. Survey data indicate that this combination of characteristics well describes the situation. Caseworkers, in effect, rank near the bottom of the ladder.

Caseworkers are among the youngest staffers on the Hill. Half of the Washington-based staffers who worked on cases and projects regularly were under 30 years of age. This compares to 41 percent of all House employees and to 19 percent of Senate and 46 percent of House professional staffers.[13] Only 11 percent of case and projects workers on the Hill were over 50. Their average age of 33 in 1977 compared to 38.6 for Senate and 42 for House professionals in 1971–72. As a rule, the more senior the senator or congressman, the older the casework staff.

In the field offices the picture is somewhat different, with the average age of 113 aides who regularly handled cases and projects rising to 38.4. Only one-quarter were under 30, with 17 percent exceeding 50. The difference between home and Washington staffs suggests that there is a propensity for members to employ older, often generalist, aides in home offices. Many members also rely on volunteers and student interns, who did not show up in the survey.

Women dominate the casework enterprise, accounting for about 55 percent of Senate and 63 percent of House aides regularly involved in cases and projects. The figures for Washington staffs are much higher than for home staffs, especially if one considers only those whose jobs are strictly defined as "caseworker."

According to the Obey Commission, 92 percent of House caseworkers are women—more than in any other job category except "clerical."[14] An examination of the *Congressional Staff Directory,* on the other hand, indicates that in "projects specialist" positions, the proportions of men and women are about equal. According to the surveys used here, in home offices a good deal of all constituency service work is handled by men—the older generalists mentioned above.

Overrepresentation of women may have something to do with the supply of and demand for jobs and workers at the relatively low salary range (a 1982 average of $20,271 for Washington caseworkers and $16,679 for those in home offices)[15] into which caseworkers fall. Or it could be related to the views held by senators, representatives, and AAs—and caseworkers themselves—about the characteristics that make good caseworkers, such as patience, persistence, politeness, and an ability to exude concern for constituents. It is likely that women are perceived as possessing these traits in greater measure than are men, thus enabling them to interact successfully with constituents and agency personnel.

Congressional employees are well educated. Constituency service aides seem to fit the overall pattern, although their levels of education are markedly lower than administrative and legislative assistants. One-third of all House staffers, as well as 40 percent of House and 62 percent of Senate professional staffers, had graduate degrees or had done some graduate work, compared to 22 percent of aides in Washington (31 percent of those in home offices) who regularly dealt with cases and projects.

Of 198 caseworkers in the Obey Commission sample, 56 percent had Hill experience—a higher percentage than for any of the other six job categories save office managers—and 28 percent had their last two jobs in Congress. Experience *in case and project work* varied greatly, but Washington-based case and project staffs were considerably more experienced *in their specialty* than were their colleagues in home offices. The former averaged almost nine years while the mean number of years doing casework for the latter was about five. Despite these relatively high levels of experience, there is considerable turnover in casework positions. The Commission found that half of all caseworkers had staff tenure of two years or less, while only 18 percent had been in their positions for over five years. The apparent inconsistency between experience and turnover can be explained. For many aides, case and projects work is a steppingstone to better jobs in Congress: a way station between an entry-level clerical and, perhaps, a legislative assistant's job. For many others, it is a "job in Washington"—good for a couple of years until other life-cycle factors lead them to seek permanent positions elsewhere and to ''settle down'' to a career. Thus turnover is high and tenure low. However, a sizable minority of perennial case aides—unlike, for example, AAs—appear to remain in Washington when their bosses leave Congress. Their experience in casework is sought after, and they seem to like the job. These experienced caseworkers form a core of experts whose names and skills are well known in agency legislative liaison offices and who enjoy a modicum of ''fame'' and prestige on the Hill. A number of AAs and executive branch officials interviewed, for example, commented on one caseworker: ''She's really good—used to work for Senator————, you know.'' Said one Veterans Administration congressional liaison officer: ''Yes, some are real 'pros.' They can pick out the wheat from the chaff. Take Rita in Congressman ————'s office.'' Clearly, among such aides, almost all of whom are women, a discernible permanent casework career has developed even though they may serve several congressmen over the years. Meanwhile, a majority of caseworkers are younger and leave their staff positions, and casework, at a fairly high rate.[16]

Turnover of caseworkers can be a problem, but apparently not as big a problem as turnover in office supervisors, legislative assistants, and personal secretaries.[17] If the loss of a good caseworker—or any other aide who handles cases—is not a catastrophe, it does cause headaches until a replacement develops the requisite skills, knowledge, and contacts in departments and agencies that are essential for this boundary-spanning role. The relatively short casework careers of most staffers mean that, as new congressmen replace incumbents who retire or are defeated, they confront inevitable delays in setting up smooth case and project operations and routines. That may explain why a good number of incoming congressmen seek to hire one or more of their predecessors' aides.

Formal training programs for caseworkers are rare. Fewer than one-third of staff members said they were given some written guidelines. Most learned by following the examples of colleagues or by the ''sink or swim'' method. Nearly one-fifth mentioned attending agency-sponsored seminars and training programs. Such programs and publications for caseworkers and projects specialists have proliferated in recent years, reflecting the growth in casework and the perception on the part of agencies that improved communication with caseworkers and better casework skills will serve agency, as well as congressional, interests. Various congressional organizations, such as the Democratic Study Group and National Republican Congressional Committee, have published booklets and held seminars for new caseworkers and projects staffs. Those who attended the meetings found them profitable. These staffers, of course, utilize a variety of aids in conducting their business: the *Catalogue of Federal Domestic Assistance;* the FAPRS (Federal Assistance Program Retrieval System) and

GRANTS computer programs; and several governmental and privately published lists and phone directories.

Not surprisingly, three-quarters of the staff members who handle cases and projects believed that they know their states and districts, and the members for whom they work, ''very well.'' Only one in five admitted to (or was judged by members and AAs to possess) ''slight'' knowledge. As one would expect, House staffers felt closer than Senate aides to both the constituencies and their members, as did home-based aides relative to those in Washington.

Congressional casework staffers exhibit considerable variety in their attitudes toward their jobs. As boundary-spanning agents, they sometimes feel tension in serving their two clients, congressmen (and AAs) and constituents, while maintaining good relations with agency officials. Most—especially caseworker specialists and aides located in home offices—are strongly committed and enthusiastic about the casework enterprise, and many become deeply involved, often above and beyond the call of duty. ''I really get tied up in casework,'' said one veteran. Such zeal can backfire, of course, allowing emotions to overcome prudence and professionalism or leading to burnout.[18] Others take a neutral, dispassionate view: ''It's a job.'' ''I tolerate it,'' adds another, ''but I'm not particularly drawn to it.'' About one in ten seemed noticeably negative. Boredom from excessive routine is an occupational hazard: ''After fifteen years of this, I'm bored out of my skull.'' Staff morale can suffer from the frustration of working for a congressman who does not care about casework: ''I have a hard time getting through to the Washington office,'' said one field representative; ''many days they don't seem to care about us or know what we're doing.'' Caseworkers like their jobs, but a majority had no intention of making casework a career.

When case and projects workers were asked why casework was important to them and what sort of rewards they got from it, by far the most common response dealt with public service: staff members enjoy helping people, and the job gives them a sense of personal satisfaction. ''Those are real people out there,'' stressed one aide. Another said that there were a number of days when she just felt like crying over the plight of a constituent, but that she felt ''like a million bucks'' when she could help someone in need. Making government work, keeping it responsive, and correcting its injustices drew mention: ''It's a shame we have to do this, but ordinary people can't get decent treatment from their government.'' Over 90 percent believed casework to be a vital aspect of the congressman's representational duty.

While caseworkers tend to be an empathetic and extraordinarily people-oriented lot, many (especially the less experienced and less well-educated ones) have little patience with their clients. When invited to identify the major headaches they face, caseworkers named constituents in numbers second only to bureaucrats. They complained that "people are getting demanding and belligerent; they think the whole world owes them something"; that "constituents appear to be dumb animals at times—they can't tell the difference between federal, state, and local governments"; and that "they want you to solve problems they've created and which aren't necessarily government problems."

Several aides also objected to what they took to be an unrealistic view of congressmen. Moaned one staffer: "They think he's a miracle worker. And when we don't produce they get nasty. We often have to spell out exactly what can and what cannot and what should not be expected."[19]

A commonly mentioned headache concerns the chronic complainer or "pest." Every office seems to have one or two constituents who make contact with great regularity. One veteran House caseworker complained that "we have to spend a great deal of time with problem cases who are mostly psychos. . . . There appear to be a great many people who feel they need the support of a congressional office and think up reasons to call us to ask about their cases, and then chat about the elections, rent control, how crooked judges are, and other vital issues!" Other caseworkers were upset that constituents often fail to provide adequate information when they file their cases, thereby necessitating lengthy correspondence or several phone calls. And, of course, there are instances of outright lying.

Many of these criticisms hold not only for individual cases but for projects and grants as well. "My God," exclaimed one Senate grants expert, "you wouldn't believe how I've got to hold their hands sometimes. I wind up writing the whole proposal." On the other hand, several offices reported that in the past seven or eight years, they had noticed improvements in the quality and detail of constituent requests, particularly on grant applications. This reflects increased sophistication on the part of state and local governments and a genuine learning experience provided to those governments by the congressional staff. Constituents who bring lawyers into their appeals, and of course the lawyers themselves, come in for special criticism. Frequently, lawyers handling constituents' legal problems (especially immigration cases) write, or have the constituents write, their congressmen in order to get the congressional staffs to undertake the investigations necessary to resolve the troubles. The lawyers then take the credit—and the legal fees—without letting the client know who did the work. No wonder many caseworkers become downright livid when discussing the legal profession.

Electoral rewards were cited by a tenth of the aides, while restoring faith in government and ending citizen cynicism, generating feedback on how programs were working, the sheer joy of solving problems, and teaching individual constituents and local government officials about their eligibility for various programs and benefits each received occasional mention. Undoubtedly, the exercise of some power stimulates many staffers, although none volunteered that reason.[20] "Sticking it to the bureaucrats," to quote one aide, also was an occasional response—one that might have been expected with greater frequency, given the somewhat suspicious and negative view many caseworkers hold of federal bureaucrats. Typical of such an attitude is this comment from a House staffer:

I feel constituent services done by a congressional office are most assuredly valuable in that a person with a bureaucratic problem, or most any problem, does not get pigeon-holed in one of those red tape slots, or fall through the cracks when departmental minions refuse to accept responsibility of action in helping another human being. In my three years of pushing, shoving, wheedling, cajoling, and tersely ordering cooperation from myriad civil servants and departmental functionaries, I can describe them with one generalization—*marshmallows*.

One attitude that pervades most offices is the belief that their casework service is unique in style and quality. Each office's case and project staff believes that it serves the constituency faster, more efficiently, more intensely, more politely, and with greater success than any other.

Several questions were included in interviews and questionnaires to get a better picture of what staffers think of their work relative to other congressional duties. The results, not surprisingly, are that most think that casework is the most important function on Capitol Hill, but there were some differences, with casework and projects staffs dividing roughly as follows: younger, better-educated, and less experienced aides deemed legislation and oversight to be relatively important, while older, less educated but more experienced caseworkers tend to view representation and casework as more crucial. Is this an instance of youthful, policy-oriented exuberance versus some sort of socialization process? Or is it self-selection, with casework-oriented staffers the ones who opt for a career of helping constituents fight the bureaucracy? Several scenarios are suggested for the younger, policy-oriented aides. On the one hand, they might work on cases for a few years and then either move up to more prestigious staff jobs or simply leave. On the other hand, if they stay, they could become the "burned-out" caseworkers whose hearts are not in their jobs. Alternatively, if they do not become socialized totally to casework and do retain their policy or oversight orientations, they might be inclined to meld these interests with casework, thereby using case and project experiences as input to legislation and oversight.

What makes a good caseworker? Easily the most important trait (cited by 100 of the 181 respondents) was judged to be empathy and sensitivity to constituents. "Sometimes I just bleed for these people who need help," said one caseworker, "and it makes me work harder." Virtually all staffers gave the impression that they did sympathize with the constituents whose problems they were handling. A knowledge of executive agencies and programs ranked second. Knowing what the laws and regulations allow and keeping abreast of current developments save time and effort, and they can translate into results. (More than one instance was related of a case or project worker winning a benefit because he or she knew of legal changes before the agency liaison office did.) For projects staffers, especially, awareness of what agencies are looking for in grant applications is essential. Tied with knowledge of the executive were patience and perseverance. "You need the patience of Job," claimed one House caseworker. "Doggedness," added another, "is what's needed." (Tenacity, indeed, is cited in several "how-to-do-it" manuals used in some offices.) The ability to listen— "good ears and a strong shoulder"—and the ability to "read between the lines to see their perspectives" and to communicate were cited by a sixth of the respondents, with 15 percent mentioning dedication, hard work, and ambition. Another large group deemed intelligence to be important: "a good heart and a good head," said one caseworker. As one cynic put it, a good caseworker is "someone who is intelligent enough to solve a problem but dumb enough to listen to people bitch and whine." Interestingly, experience was cited by only one in nine members and staffers. Other responses identified such traits as "diplomacy, perception, and speed"; "the ability to break through a constituent's reticence or fuzziness, interpret what he or she wants and needs, and rephrase it so as to make an impact on the appropriate agency"; having a good knowledge of and having been active in the local community; the appearance of impartiality coupled with determination to help the constituent; having special skills or attributes appropriate to the constituency (e.g., being black, Hispanic, or bilingual); being sympathetic to department and agency bureaucrats and being nice to them; "judgment"; "good follow-through"; being "self-directed" (a trait not universally admired by administrative assistants); and being "stubborn." Since caseworker staffs are deathly afraid of being "taken in" or "conned," a desirable trait is to be able to see through false claims and complaints. "It's an art, not a science," insisted one House caseworker of several years' experience. Another staffer stressed resourcefulness and ingenuity, while summing up what all seemed to be saying:

Resourcefulness above all. Then persuasiveness and fairness are important, relative to the agencies—and patience relative to the constituent. The big step in doing casework is knowing where to call with the constituent's question or problem. About 70 percent of the time this step is fairly clear-cut. It's the other 30 percent of the time that resourcefulness is required to give the constituent the best and fullest answer possible. An average caseworker may just pass along information from a Congressional Liaison (in an executive agency) that there is a regulation blocking the constituent from getting what he wants.

. . . The above par caseworker may bring that person and the agency regulation markers together to sensitize the agency to the problem and keep an eye open for public comment periods, nearby hearings, committee oversight activities to pass along the public's gripes to when the agency or Congress is most in a position and climate to make changes.

As for persuasiveness and fairness, if you are reasonable with your contacts they are more willing to extend themselves for your cases that have merit. A good caseworker must have patience; some constituents cry, some yell, some threaten, but you have to wade through these emotions as there is usually a very valid problem underneath, often veiled in nonsense, but there is something you can work on.

These traits are not randomly distributed among caseworkers. While any attempt to describe specific role types would be premature, and any attempt to assess how many aides fall into each type impossible, there do seem to be three different case and project roles, each marked by somewhat different traits and each raising different boundary-agent problems. The first is the "ombudsman," who sees his or her function primarily in terms of helping the constituent—the "little guy." Such aides describe themselves as, and seem to value other case-workers who are, sensitive, understanding, willing and able to read between the lines, and so on. They seem to identify more with the constituent than with their offices, an attitude not always cherished by their bosses. They realize their need to get along with agency administrators and act accordingly. A second type is the "promoter" or "agent-politician," who defines the job as helping the senator or congressman win reelection. As one veteran caseworker put it, "I campaign for him from nine to five every day." Such aides are oriented toward efficiency, speed, and quantity in contacting constituents, and toward publicity; and they are afraid of "being had" by constituents. Executive officials seldom appreciate them. The third type is the "adversary" or "St. George," whose task in life seems to be to pursue and slay the dragons of inefficiency, injustice, and arro-gance in executive agencies. These staffers value different traits, such as dogged-ness and perseverance. They may or may not find support from their offices' "core" staff members. The three role types seem to cut across all age and experi-ence groups.

4.4. Staff Structure

Two attributes of institutionalization are specialization of function and the de-velopment of fixed structures. Both are evident in casework operations, although the situation is hardly simple. As casework became a fixture of congressional life, more and more senators and representatives assigned cases to specialists, just as they had done for other functions. These casework aides were, and remain, either subject matter specialists—with specific jurisdictions such as military, immigration, or social security cases—or generalists, who divide the work in an ad hoc fashion, such as alphabetically, geographically, or on a first come-first served basis. This pattern is especially pronounced in the Senate, where staff specialization is a necessity. A growing number of House offices in Washington follow a second pattern, wherein all but administrative assistants and secretaries are assigned to policy areas and are entrusted with everything (legislation, oversight, projects, cases, correspondence, publicity) in their jurisdictions. Fox and Hammond have termed these aides "multi-specialists" or "non-exclusive generalists."[21] A third pattern combines the first two: cases are done *both* by caseworkers *and* by other aides (AAs, LAs, personal secretaries, and even press assistants). Fox and Hammond, for example, found that 41 percent of the Senate personal office staff professionals they studied engaged in casework at least daily, while 18 percent did so hourly.[22]

It is difficult to generalize about staff structures because the congressmen have different casework structures on the Hill and at home. By 1982, for example, only one-third of the congressmen in the sample had casework specialists in Washington; they either had moved casework back to their districts or had adopted the second, "multi-specialist" pattern mentioned above. On the other hand, nine of ten members had "caseworkers" (or other less formally designated casework specialists) in district offices, where the first or third casework staffing patterns were followed. Simple organization theory would suggest that environmental pressures (case loads and perhaps regional patterns of expectations and traditions) would affect office structure. To a small extent they did. Eastern senators in the 1977–78 sample tended to have specialist casework staffing arrangements, while midwestern senators tended to rely more on other staffing patterns. The general rule seemed to be that the more casework was done at home, the less likely were Washington offices, and the more likely home offices, to use caseworkers and casework specialists as such; and the heavier the case load in a given office (Washington or the field), the greater the tendency to specialize.

One other factor may be at work to explain the 1980s trend away from designating aides as caseworkers in Washington. The rise of women's rights sentiment may be undercutting women's willingness to take and remain in jobs in the lower salary and prestige categories. Coupled with the dull routine of much casework, these changing attitudes are leading to an alteration in staff structures that appeared to have solidified a decade earlier.

Quite a few congressmen use their personal secretaries for casework, especially when the cases are delicate or involve friends or locally important constituents, or when the secretaries have experience in handling cases. Administrative assistants routinely get involved in casework, usually in a supervisory capacity on behalf of their senators or congressmen. They ordinarily read much or most of the incoming and outgoing mail, and frequently sign letters for their bosses. Caseworkers are instructed to take unusual or sensitive cases to the AAs. As one caseworker said: "He will get involved if it's a friend of the boss or a VIP—or if it's that little old lady who runs to the press when we don't respond right away; we're paranoid about her." More administrative assistants than would be expected claim to enjoy dealing with occasional cases.

At least a half-dozen chairmen or high-ranking members in the sample habitually borrowed committee or subcommittee staffs for cases and, perhaps more commonly, for project applications that fell under their committees' jurisdictions. Technically, the use of committee aides for personal office work is not permitted, but apparently it is a widespread practice—and not only for casework.[23] In defense of the practice it must be noted that such members tend to receive disproportionately large case loads and that often only committee aides have the required expertise on a given subject.

A few committees have reputations for doing casework for members. The Veterans and Small Business committees, like some other "service" or "watchdog" committees, have "encouraged all the members of Congress to refer constituent complaints and other departmental business falling within their respective spheres to them, and their staff justified their existence largely by the amount of casework they performed."[24] Other congressional groups, such as the Black Caucus, provide occasional staff help to members for casework.

Just how much casework committee staffs do for members is impossible to measure. Kofmehl estimated that casework took up 10 to 15 percent of their time, but Vinyard believed it was much more for such committees as the Small Business panels.[25] The only data of recent vintage are provided by Fox and Hammond, whose surveys of committees showed that over one-quarter of Senate committee aides reported working on projects at least daily and about 15 percent said they did so on cases. Another quarter indicated that they virtually never handled projects, and about half made that claim for cases.[26]

Staff structures for federal projects and grants differ somewhat from those for individual cases. Despite a steady growth in the use of specialists, in 1977–78 only 41 percent of reporting Senate offices and 28 percent of House offices utilized grantsmen.[27] By 1982, 35 percent of House offices reported having projects specialists. The difference between House and Senate is explained by staff size and the larger constituencies of senators. Even among Senate offices in the sample, those with the largest staffs and the heaviest project loads were the ones who employed projects specialists. Where there are no projects specialists, the work falls to the Washington-based legislative assistants and administrative assistants, especially when individual casework is performed in field offices. Common, too, was a pattern of involving AAs in big, important, and visible projects, while allowing grants specialists full control over routine grant applications.[28]

Decisions concerning staff structures are not neutral; trade-offs abound, with structures following relative office priorities. Having specialists enhances expertise — perhaps improving the quality of performance — and contributes to smooth office operations. On the other hand, involving other staffers may have virtues. When integrated into the duties of, for example, legislative assistants, case and projects work can contribute to other functions. Conversely, it can be relegated to secondary status by aides pursuing "more important" work. Assigning caseworkers other responsibilities relieves the boredom and may improve their casework efforts: "It helps," said one caseworker, "to handle legislative correspondence to know what legislation is pending so we can handle the cases better." One AA said that, despite benefits from specialization, he did not want to use specialists for cases and projects because everyone on the staff "ought to have an overview of the office's operations." With such an attitude, it is easier to develop and train staffers, grooming them for more responsible positions. Even when there are caseworkers, many House offices prefer generalists to specialists. "What happens if, say, the caseworker who specializes in social security or military affairs gets sick or quits?" asked one AA. "If you have that sort of division of labor, you're in a pickle."

Involving administrative assistants, secretaries, and other aides in casework and projects allows members to take advantage of particular skills and interests. In one House office, the member's personal secretary does military cases because "she's an expert at it." A former Republican member had his AA handle projects because "she knows this city [Washington] and the district like the back of her hand — she's amazing." The one drawback, however, is that caseworkers can pass the buck when they know the AA is ready and willing to help out. Said one aide, "We don't want the responsibility [for tough cases] so we send a draft of our letters to the AA."

Two additional structural characteristics of casework operations are worth noting. Both have consequences in terms of the utility of casework for policy-making. The first is that, whatever the particular casework structure, caseworkers (and, to a lesser extent, projects workers) tend to work alone, with relatively little supervision from members, AAs, or office managers. Autonomy seems somewhat greater in the Senate and in field offices. Such independence is characteristic of institutionalized functions. Seventy percent of 205 respondents indicated that caseworkers in their offices enjoyed high degrees of independence in their work; only 10 percent said they had little or no autonomy. This is in sharp contrast to the situation in Britain, where MPs grant little independence to their secretaries in casework.[29] Asked about independence, one aide said, "Yes, we are, but occasionally he'll [the member] read our answers and say 'This isn't good enough—I want more.'" One AA was wary: "No, I don't think they should be independent; I like to keep them under close supervision." Most of his counterparts, as well as senators and representatives, who try to keep close tabs on casework do so by reading outgoing mail, by receiving weekly or monthly summaries, and/or by insisting that any contacts with high-ranking agency officials be cleared in advance. One former senator recounted an instance wherein his caseworker was so frustrated that she wrote an exceptionally mean and abrasive letter to an agency and routinely checked with the boss before sending it. "I read it and looked at her and said, 'You're not going to send this out, are you?' She rather sheepishly replied, "No, I guess not.' So she went back and rewrote it. You've got to be careful."

Far more common is the practice of trying to maintain overall control (especially on big cases and projects) while letting the caseworkers do what they think best with regard to details. "We try to hire bright and sensible people," explained one administrative assistant, "and give them their heads."

The second structure-related point is the widespread disinclination to pool case and project efforts with other offices, and the accompanying lack of interoffice casework communication. Of 254 responding members and staffs, 22 percent said they and their offices *never* "pool casework or federal projects data or efforts with other congressional offices in their state delegations," and another 29 percent said they did so "rarely." Only 6 percent indicated that such cooperation occurred "often." Senate offices, naturally, claimed more often than those in the lower chamber to coordinate their constituent services. Decisions to cooperate with other offices appear to be quite random. Among House delegations represented in the sample, those from Connecticut, Indiana, Kansas, Mississippi, Oklahoma, Texas, and Wisconsin indicated greater than average tendencies to collaborate on cases and projects, but the differences were not large. In the Senate, interoffice cooperation seemed most frequent for senators from Florida, Kentucky, Michigan, New Mexico, Oklahoma, and South Dakota.

Reasons for the lack of collaboration are not hard to find. Members and their aides believe that the political credit linked to constituency service would be lost if efforts were pooled. Various partisan and interoffice rivalries, especially between House and Senate, also interfere with cooperative efforts. Representatives are notoriously resentful of the publicity advantages of senators, and they tend to consider them negligent when it comes to taking care of constituents. Said one House aide: "Of those constituents who write to both our office and the senators' offices, most write back to us and say that ours was the only response — senators don't do anything anyhow.'' One Republican House office head remarked that his office takes great pride in beating the staff of that state's Democratic senator. ''It's like a big game,'' he explained, ''we love to beat him.'' He added that one positive result of the rivalry was better service for the constituents. An aide to a Massachusetts Democrat complained that his state's senators were constantly grabbing all the credit for projects, even when he — the House member or his staff — did all the work. ''Brooke and Kennedy get the headlines; we fight in the trenches.''

A third factor is that few aides felt that they had the time to set up cooperative arrangements or even to consult another office in the state delegation. ''It would be nice,'' explained one caseworker, ''but it's just too time-consuming. We'd never get our work done.'' Perhaps it is this congeries of reasons that explains why experienced case and project workers more often reported at least ''occasional'' cooperation than did less seasoned caseworkers. The former tend to be a more professional group, somewhat less concerned about the problems listed here. Besides, their very expertise, familiarity with other caseworkers, and sense of security *enable* them to take advantage of their friendships and connections in other offices. Finally, casework aides tend to be outward-looking, as befits boundary-spanning agents. Thus inward-looking activity and orientations (cooperation) receive low priority relative to the basic job. In short, the caseworker's role orientation itself may detract from cooperation.

When contact with other offices does occur, it is as often a matter of necessity as of choice. On individual cases, an aide in one office sometimes will contact a caseworker in another office ''if we know that they have some expertise on this kind of problem.'' Such a reputation, of course, does not spread widely or rapidly, if only because of the lack of routine collaboration and interaction — again a reason why veteran aides cooperate and coordinate more. Location, especially in state or district offices, also matters. If senators' and congressmen's field offices are in the same building, cooperation is more likely — but not inevitable.

Sometimes, when the same type of case reoccurs time and again in congressmen's offices, staffs will get together to discuss legislative solutions. Another cause of interoffice contact on cases and projects is the receipt of the same case by several offices. Such multiple appeals for help are common. Respondents estimated that one of four cases they received were also sent to offices of other members (twice as often in the Senate as the House). In addition, about one in twenty cases sent to home offices are said to turn up also in Washington. Caseworkers expressed some annoyance at constituents who ''shotgun'' their problems to congressional offices (especially when they give no indication that they are doing it), but most said it presented no great problem. It might actually help:

"Sometimes it's a fail-safe system; when we find out that Senator ———'s people also wrote the agency, we assume that we might as well pursue the case ourselves if we expect anything to get done. His people just don't care that much." Still, one wonders how many hours are wasted by such multiple contacts.

The one exception to the rule of noncooperation occurs in the area of federal projects assistance, and then it is only a partial exception. State delegations frequently work together on major projects of benefit to an entire state or substantial portions thereof. In the late 1970s there were signs of a trend toward such interoffice partnerships. Former Senators McGovern and Abourezk of South Dakota shared eight field offices (although each senator was separately represented in each location); Oklahoma Senators Bartlett and Bellmon had begun to do likewise, as had Tennessee's Baker and Brock; and several other senators were discussing the possibility. Perhaps the model of such arrangements was the New Mexico Congressional Delegation's Projects Office. Located on Capitol Hill, established in 1976, funded by both senators' and two congressmen's staffing allowances, and run at the outset by John Cordova, the office's primary function, in Cordova's words, was "to make sure a grant application is not lost in the shuffle. . . . We compare our task to that of a reference library. . . . Our task is not so much to go out and do the basic research but to know where information is, to put New Mexicans in touch with the right people and the right information." Members of that delegation (and most others) believe that added clout can be had by joining forces. Said Congressman Manuel Lujan, "Let's face it, when an agency sees a letter signed by all four of us it will lend more weight than if we signed individually." The office also handled considerable amounts of individual casework. A major benefit of the joint operation was to cut down on time and paperwork.[30] Problems of funding plague such operations, since House and Senate rules differ on joint employees, combined WATS lines, and so on.

4.5. Executive Casework Staffs

How executive departments and agencies handle congressional case and project inquiries—"congressionals," in bureaucratic language—depends on their organizational structure. Two dimensions of structure are determinative. The first concerns *where* case and projects inquiries are handled. Some departments do the bulk of their casework in Washington. At the other extreme are agencies which handle congressional inquiries in regional or local/area offices. Most agencies have mixed patterns.

The second structural dimension has to do with the degree of policy centralization agencies seek to impose on the casework process. All major departments and agencies, and many of their subdivisions, have "congressional relations" or "legislative affairs" offices. Those boundary-spanning structures establish and maintain good relationships with Congress, looking toward advantageous legislative and budgetary decisions from the Hill. Naturally, such comity and cooperation include prompt, efficient, and (if possible) favorable servicing of case and project inquiries.[31] In most congressional relations units, special offices or staff specialists do nothing more than process congressionals. One assistant secretary of the Interior, for example, estimated that 75 percent of the time of his congressional relations office was taken up dealing with complaints from "people who have run afoul of the bureaucracy."[32]

The roles of such staffs vary in emphasis. Typifying one form of involvement are the military services, whose liaison units not only receive requests and complaints from congressional offices, parcel them out to appropriate levels for draft responses, and pass judgment on most such responses *before* they are sent to the Hill, but also keep detailed records on the cases and on the liaison personnel who handle the congressionals in Washington and in the field. At least three-quarters of all cases flow through the Pentagon liaison offices. Like the Veterans Administration and the Office of Personnel Management, the three military services have representatives of their liaison units physically located on the Hill, in the Rayburn Building on the House side, and in the Russell Senate Office Building. (The Defense Department itself has a separate Legislative Affairs unit in the Pentagon, but it generally does not involve itself in casework, leaving that duty to the individual services.) The services assign their "action officers" by states, so that all congressionals from a given state or region will be handled by one officer, thus facilitating familiarity with congressional staffs. HUD's Washington office works the same way. Other departments prefer to organize their contact officials by function, in order to emphasize subject matter expertise.

The most common practice of central liaison units is to serve primarily intake and clearance functions, channeling the case and project inquiries to the appropriate operating and program units and clearing their replies. Alternately, some agencies or divisions of agencies encourage or at least tolerate the congressional practice of making contact directly with the agency's operating units. Those units formulate replies and send them directly to the inquiring congressional office, with copies to the liaison unit in Washington or to regional offices. The Department of Labor seemed to function this way. The Commerce, Agriculture, and Interior departments were even less structured. Their central liaison units did little more than receive congressionals and pass them on.

For the larger departments and agencies, each regional office has its own liaison officer who performs for that region the same function that the Washington liaison office furnishes for the agency as a whole. At the local level, too, the administrative head tries to monitor all congressionals, either personally or through a close assistant.

There are advantages and disadvantages to centralization. Clearly, the more centralized the structure, the greater the ability of policymakers to control and coordinate the process, watching for political and policy implications. As one military liaison chief put it, ''Everything returns here because we want to get an overview of the problems to identify them, and we want to put the operation under a civilian assistant secretary.'' A Justice Department unit official stressed the value of having all case and project communications with Congress flow through the hands of responsible policy-level administrators, both to catch politically sensitive cases and, he claimed, to insulate decisions on grants (which are made on technical grounds by career bureaucrats) from congressional pressures. Moreover, when all congressionals are channeled through a single office, duplicate inquiries can be caught. A Veterans Administration official in Washington saw three advantages:

First, being located here on the Hill, we get to know the caseworkers in the congressional offices. Our field office people can't possibly do that. Second, our regional offices may write to the congressman in response to a congressional, but we get a copy and review them. If the response isn't any good, we'll call the local office and complain—the congressman may never know. We encourage congressmen to deal with local offices, but ''if you don't get a good response, come to us.'' Third, we can save our local offices a lot of work—we can shortstop an awful lot. We refine cases and translate them, answering many ourselves and pointing out the parameters to the congressional caseworkers.

Decentralizing casework has its advantages as well. One Agriculture Department official summed up the reasons as follows: ''Why decentralize? Because the guys who wrote the rules and regs or made the original decision know the problems far better than we do and can spot recurring problems raised by cases.'' If any one decision rule applies, it is that congressionals are processed wherever the records are located and the decision-making authority lies, unless the case is particularly delicate or important. What all this means is that although each agency has its specialists in dealing with Congress, there are other executives who, at least occasionally and often regularly, deal with congressional staffs as boundary agents. And in many instances, especially at the local level, the linkages between them are stronger than are those between congressional offices and the congressional relations offices in the agencies. Disagreements between the center and periphery on both substance and process (and often politics) thus are common.

The size of executive casework establishments is substantial, as is the cost of running them. A General Accounting Office report indicated that in 1982, twenty agencies with eighty-two offices had 1,060 employees working in congressional relations offices at a cost of about $18 million.[33] And that probably understates the situation. The precise size and budgets are not available, largely because departments and agencies lump various functions together in their congressional liaison and public relations activities, often assign congressionals to operating divisions, and prefer not to make them public. Moreover, the casework bureaucracy has grown in recent years. In 1965, for example, the army budgeted $893,729 for its congressional liaison operations. By 1975 the comparable figure was $1.8 million. A sample of figures gathered by Sen. Patrick Leahy (D., Vt.) for legislative liaison and congressional relations offices *in Washington* appears in table 4.3. The casework volume data in some instances are based on broader agency definitions and estimates than those used here. Under the column headed "Office Budget" are a variety of figures, ranging from salaries only to total office budgets, part or most of which may not actually be used for cases and projects. Similarly, the number of staff is a total figure for the office—not all of these people work full time on cases. Still, it does not require precise measurement to conclude that legislative liaison operations in general, and casework correspondence in particular, constitute big business in downtown Washington and throughout the country.

It would be natural to expect administrators to exhibit rather negative attitudes toward casework, and thereby to differ somewhat from legislators and their staffs,[34] but the federal executives interviewed and surveyed as part of this research, ranging from GS-6 to GS-18 and located at all levels of the bureaucracy, exhibited a surprisingly favorable view of casework.[35] Under 6 percent of 217 administrators agreed with the proposition that "members of Congress should not intervene on behalf of their constituents." Most of those interviewed saw casework as essential to the governmental system. Typical were such comments as:

It's hard for people to know where to go with their problems; they get the run-around. Their congressmen are there to represent them.

It shouldn't be used for political purposes, of course, but it is democracy at work; we advertise the right to our airmen.

We consider responding to congressionals part of our normal operations. It is a convenient and desirable recourse for our clients when they have been frustrated by our sometimes cumbersome system.

Table 4.3: The Executive Casework Bureaucracy

Agency (Cong. Rels. Office unless Otherwise Indicated)	Casework Volume per Month	Number of Staff	Office Budget (FY 1975 or 1976)
Air Force	4,000 written	18 action officers 11 support	$800,000
Army	8,750 at Hill offices	19 on Hill (12 at Pentagon) [a]	$327,378 for Hill office
Navy	2,150 at Hill offices	13 on Hill	$249,000 for Hill offices
Agriculture Dept. (22 offices)	From secretary's office—4,267; Others—2,620	17.3 full-time equiv. [b]	$231,466 (salaries) [b]
Commerce Dept. Office of Ombudsman NOAA	732 160	6 full-time ———	$465,000 ———
Consumer Product Safety Commission	130	4 @ ⅔-time	$137,000
Fed. Trade Commission (Corresp. Section)	2,500	23 man-years	$299,633 (ent. office)
NASA	630	28 (Legis. Aff) 6 pt.-time in Inquiries Div.	$583,699
FCC	670	1 full-time	$13,250 (salary)
Dept. Labor (Cong. liaison)	9,000	Approx. 12	$293,000
Veteran's Admin.	6,600 on Hill	14 on Hill	$250,000
SEC (Investors' Service Branch)	546	9 pt.-time	$86,576
Dept. Trans. FAA (Info. Office)	100 cases 478 other	3 casework 8 total	$183,357 salary
Nat'l Highway Safety	1,800	5	$60,000

continued

Table 4.3: *continued*

Agency (Cong. Rels. Office unless Otherwise Indicated)	Casework Volume per Month	Number of Staff	Office Budget (FY 1975 or 1976)
Urban Mass Trans.	1,100	9	$172,800
Fed. Highway Admin. (Off. Publ. Affairs)	50, plus public inquiries	8 total	$244,271 (incl. public inquiries
HUD	7,400	————	$635,000
Selective Service	537	3	$64,636 (salaries)
ACTION	167	8	$168,300
Appalachian Regional Commission	20	2	$46,986
SBA	1,850	5	$115,954
Treasury (incl. IRS)	2,000	4	$270,000
EPA	1,600	40	$868,000 (Off. of Legis.)
Farm Credit Admin.	330	4	$271,808
Fed. Energy Admin.	5,000	46	$565,000
State Dept.	397	4	$639,700
Postal Service	9,000	24	————
FPC (Off. Genl. Counsel)	379	10 full-time 3 pt.-time	$231,000
Railroad Retire- ment Board	360	4	$1,079,419
Civil Aeronautics Board	250	6	$118,900
EEOC	360	9	$146,100
Energy Research and Dev. Admin.	1,350	16	$358,000

SOURCE: Data compiled by office of Sen. Patrick Leahy (D., Vt.).

NOTE: These data apply to Washington offices only.

[a] Author's estimate.

[b] Calculated from Senator Leahy's data.

Others were more neutral ("Doing casework," said one independent agency liaison official, "is part of our overhead") or cynical: "It's very important, especially the 'ritualist' meeting between the congressmen, the constituent, and our agency, where we go and explain apologetically why we couldn't fund their community. In a way, we're in the public relations business, with Congress and its constituents as *our* constituents."

Such comments were in the minority. When executive officials were asked how serious they believed congressmen were in pursuing cases and projects for their constituencies, only 15 percent insisted that most members were merely playing politics or "just going through the motions." Said one: "They don't give a good goddamn about how the case turns out; all they want is action— fast." Conversely, one in five thought that virtually all congressmen were serious and half said that most were. According to one administrator: "Casework is the life-blood of Congress—most are really concerned with helping people. There are a lot of really conscientious people up there." Another called congressmen "pretty damned decent" and thought that most had a sense of "moral responsibility" to their constituents.

Not surprisingly, however, two-thirds of administrators believed that congressmen's primary motives for doing casework are electoral. Said one: "It's window dressing for constituents; a politician must make himself useful." The second most frequently mentioned motive was "just part of the job," followed by "humanitarian reasons." Legislative, oversight, and educational motives were much less frequently cited.

Despite a generally favorable view of casework, administrators complained frequently about constituents, especially for not knowing what they are entitled to or for raising worthless cases. As one immigration official explained: "Our backlog triggers a lot of letters. The vast majority of cases are impatient people asking for the status of an application within two weeks of their filing it; but our backlog is three to six months." Particularly galling are constituents who, as one administrator expressed it, "are seeking to exert political pressure, won't accept our answer the first time, or are looking for a job but just cannot compete." Agency personnel strongly object to constituents who, they feel, could have handled their problems through normal agency channels. "They don't need to go through Congress; a congressional inquiry is also from our constituent, and often it will have been answered already if the constituent contacted us at the same time he contacted his congressman."

The literature on boundary-spanning agents predicts that congressional liaison bureaucrats, given their two constituencies, would have mixed orientations and loyalties. Interviews with some two dozen liaison specialists in Washington and a half-dozen in regional offices seemed to support the theory. Said one Justice Department civil servant: "We are the go-betweens; we're an early warning system to the agency of Congress's concerns. We represent Congress to [the agency]." An HEW political appointee voiced almost identical sentiments, adding that "bureaucrats have no idea of what it's like on the Hill—we've got a foot in each camp." A military officer put it this way: "We see ourselves as advocates of Congress for the Department. It's difficult for the military to understand the importance of cases to a congressman, so our job is to interpret that to the various units of the [service]." One Labor Department liaison officer was blunt: "My mind is more attuned to Congress—I serve my constituents there. I identify with politicians."

This double orientation naturally creates tensions and is fraught with problems. The liaison agent must keep a balanced perspective lest he or she be seen as having sold out the agency to Congress or as not being sympathetic with the agency's own mission. As one military officer put it: "There is a danger of working here too long: you get too connected to Congress."

This "congressman in disguise" orientation of agency liaison personnel is but one of four role orientations administrators seem to take with respect to casework. A second is the "executive ombudsman"—one who wants to help the agency's clients even if they raise their problems via a congressional inquiry. At the risk of overgeneralizing from a very small sample, it can nevertheless be noted that these officials seem to be located in agencies specializing in direct service to citizens: the Veterans Administration, HUD, Social Security, and so on. As one local VA administrator put it: "Our concern is primarily with the effect on the patient, the congressman's constituent, if delays occur. We want to investigate the complaint and relieve the patient's concern or correct any error immediately." Quite a few indicated that congressional inquiries have triggered searches that resulted in finding benefits to which clients were entitled but which they were not getting. An appointed departmental official explained: "We really want to help the citizen. My job is to be a caseworker. I don't like it when a claim or application is hung up—there may be some guy out there who really needs help. We want to help. But government is so big, and the process takes time to get a case taken care of."

A third role type is the "politician," whose efforts at handling cases and projects are motivated primarily by a desire to improve relations between the agency and Congress in order to "grease the skids" for legislative or budgetary requests. "A big part of my job," said an independent regulatory commission official, "is keeping congressmen happy." Said another: "Our rules require a forty-eight–hour notice to the congressman before announcing a grant. If the decision is favorable, I keep track. I haven't had to yet, but I might want to use them someday.''

Finally, there is the ''defender,'' who views congressional intervention as a headache and an illegitimate intrusion into the bureaucratic world. Few liaison specialists adopt this view, but it is prevalent among program administrators. Naturally, many bureaucrats adopt several of these roles, alternating according to their moods or situations.

4.6. Summary

Congressional and executive casework staffs are large, growing in size, and increasingly institutionalized and decentralized. In making staffing allocation decisions, congressmen follow rational criteria—to enhance their visibility, to respond to constituent needs, and to compensate for having to direct their own attention to policy-related matters. Seniority and regional traditions or expectations also influence these decisions. Contrary to conventional wisdom, there is no evidence that a purely rational vote-maximizing strategy drives such decisions.

Most caseworkers are young, female, and not terribly well paid or trained. They share a generally positive view toward their jobs and their constituent clients, and they go about their work with a considerable independence. On the executive side, there is a surprisingly positive attitude toward casework, especially on the part of legislative liaison specialists. The two groups of participants share many of the same views.[36] Structurally and attitudinally, the casework enterprises in both branches of government are well integrated. The system linking the two branches can be jeopardized by a breakdown in the generally favorable attitudes toward casework that characterize each side and by a failure to honor the unwritten rules that are examined in the next chapter.

CHAPTER 5

The Casework Process

Because the vast majority of cases and projects are routine and relatively unimportant, many observers share the view that casework is little more than an administrative chore. There is a good deal of truth in such a view, of course; but it overlooks the world of politics that underpins the casework enterprise. As would be expected, this increasingly institutionalized political subsystem has spawned a rather complete set of ''rules of the game'' which tend to stabilize relationships between constituents, legislative staff, and executive branch administrators.

5.1. Congressional-Constituency Relations

Most cases arriving in Washington come through the mail; a few are phoned in; and, of course, congressmen returning from their districts bring constituents' problems back with them. Projects requests are more likely to be presented over the phone or in person by local government officials, many of whom arrive in town with application in hand, seeking reviews by congressional staffers and letters of endorsement and recommendation.

In district and state offices, the mode of constituent contact is varied, with about one-third (Senate) to one-half (House) of all individual cases phoned in. Walk-in cases are common. When state and district offices do not themselves handle casework, the usual procedure is to write up a ''case report'' which is forwarded to the Washington (or other field) office for processing. Cases from constituents of other senators or congressmen are sent to those offices with letters to the constituents explaining the situation—a practice known as ''congressional courtesy.''

A cardinal rule in congressional offices is to acknowledge the receipt of cases as soon as possible, usually within twenty-four hours, expressing the congressman's concern and willingness to be of assistance. Many letters of acknowledgment must request data (social security numbers, agency references) and documents (proof of age or citizenship, copies of correspondence) to supplement the information contained in the constituents' original inquiries. Since the enactment of the Federal Privacy Act of 1974, federal agencies are forbidden to release any information regarding individuals without written authorization. Thus staffers must ask constituents for such permission. The process of collecting the requisite information and documents from constituents in complex cases can go on for months, sometimes necessitating face-to-face interactions between staff members and the citizens. Perhaps the requisite follow-ups explain why so many caseworkers express a preference for personal or telephone contacts. Another reason concerns the emotional and political impact of a phone call: "People really want to hear a warm, friendly voice from their congressman's office," explained one aide.

Details of office record-keeping procedures vary, but the basics are the same. For each inquiry that cannot be handled on the spot a file is opened and — in many offices — the case logged in on a casework report sheet. Some offices keep two or even three sets of files, by agency, by constituent name, and by date. Each file folder includes all documentation pertinent to the case and in many offices includes a "Casework Action Memo," which provides at a glance the basic information on the constituent and records all actions taken on the case. A small but growing number of offices use computerized record-keeping systems. For federal projects some files become voluminous.

Most case and projects workers are afraid that cases may "fall through the cracks" in department or agency offices. Therefore, they usually seek to render as much assistance to constituents as possible, even to the point of urging those who have become discouraged to persist and to provide more, and newer, information. A common practice is to utilize some sort of "tickler" system to remind the caseworkers to make sure that the constituent has followed up on the caseworker's earlier communications and to check periodically with the agency on the status of a case. A few disdain such techniques ("I don't use a tickler system," bragged one House aide, "and I never lose more than one case a year"), and a handful of others simply believe that the problems belong to the constituents. Said one aide, "I wait for the constituents to write back. If they don't, too bad."

Most offices follow a set pattern of behavior concerning case and project contacts. A manual of casework operations prepared by several House caseworkers for the National Republican Congressional Committee summarizes it well:

Organize; set up an accurate filing system; be courteous and honest; make sure the constituent has taken the necessary preliminary actions; secure the constituent's written authorization; obtain as much information as possible from him or her; acknowledge each communication; provide a monthly status report to the constituent; don't lose files, guarantee positive results, or needlessly refer the constituent to someone else; don't try to memorize information—write it down; and don't handle cases for people living outside the congressman's district.[1]

In addition to following these recommendations, the better caseworkers go ''an extra mile'' for constituents, examining their case requests or problems for nonobvious implications. Frequently, someone complaining about inadequate social security or veterans' benefits can be helped by referrals to other government programs.

For federal projects, staff assistants are equally solicitous of constituents' interests. Since most projects workers deal with clients who are reasonably sophisticated politically (but who often harbor inflated expectations of obtaining federal funds), they are particularly concerned with projecting an image of going ''all-out.'' As one ''how-to-do-it'' manual explains:

It's important to keep in mind that your success rate in obtaining Federal financial assistance is not likely to be very high, no matter how hard you work or how effective you are. Funds are just too scarce, and competition is too severe. But winning isn't everything. Most constituents and communities are very appreciative of your efforts on their behalf. If they feel you really went to bat for them, they won't blame you if the application is denied. They might bad mouth the agency, but they're likely to sing your praises. That will occur, however, only if they have the distinct impression that you tried your hardest. Impressions like that aren't born out of thin air. You have to create them. And creating them does take hard work.[2]

Good project workers are also firm in rejecting unreasonable requests. It serves no one's interests to try to arrange a meeting between the chairman of a local library board and the secretary of the Department of Education. More than one staffer expressed reservations about accompanying a constituent personally on a visit to an agency. ''It creates false expectations,'' explained a Senate projects specialist. ''Besides, it's a waste of time.''

5.2. Congressional Procedures

While most case and project work amounts to little more than paper shuffling, a good deal goes beyond. Getting satisfactory results for constituents is not automatic. On controversial cases and grants, there develops a whole world of political interchange, with the participants, their powers, and their techniques of persuasion reasonably well defined by the casework "system" described at the beginning of chapter 4. Basically, the politics can be understood in terms of a simple exchange theory:[3] each participant—constituent, congressional office, agency liaison staff, and agency operating division—has something the others want. Bargaining, albeit implicit, underpins the casework enterprise. The politics thus blends advocacy and an adversary relationship with a need and desire to cooperate, often evolving into a "team" effort on behalf of clientele.

On receipt of a case, the congressional caseworker must make two tactical decisions: whom to contact and how. A caseworker can begin with the agency's Washington congressional relations office, can go to the Washington program-level office that deals with the problem in question, or can address the inquiry to the regional or local office from which the case originated. A majority of congressional case and project workers rely on agency liaison offices at least some of the time, but there are differences among caseworkers. Aides located in the field were four times more likely than their colleagues on the Hill to utilize regional and local agency offices, while Washington-based staffs relied more heavily on agency liaison offices. Physical proximity of congressional to executive staffers seems to be important in determining contact patterns, which in turn may account for the close relationships established in the casework process. Aides to junior congressmen and senators tend to make their contacts at local offices more than do aides to senior members, and this pattern holds across all groupings (House versus Senate, home versus Washington). One reason may be that caseworkers serving senior members realize that the position, fame, or "clout" of their employers translates more readily into cooperation and helpfulness in Washington than in local offices, where bureaucrats tend to be less aware and respectful of Washington power relationships.

Staffers give several reasons for choosing to contact liaison offices, not the least of which is that many agencies want it that way and try to steer all inquiries to their congressional relations specialists. Moreover, many caseworkers just do not know where to go on a given problem. "If the source of the decision is unknown," explained one caseworker, "I go to liaison." Indeed, 29 percent of those questioned indicated that they contact congressional relations offices solely in order to discover the name and phone number of the appropriate official.

Others—nearly half of those responding—prefer that the liaison office handle the case completely. Not only does this save the caseworker time and effort, but it sometimes serves as a double-check on the lower-level bureaucrats who prepare the answer: "We let liaison do everything," said a Senate aide, "let *them* catch sloppy agency responses to our inquiries." A few caseworkers indicated that, for military cases, they always work through liaison, both because military liaison units are of high quality and because they fear that, should they contact military base commanders directly, there might be retaliation against the servicemen.

Going directly to the program level or to a regional or local office, while a bit more work initially, has the advantage of putting the caseworker directly in touch with people having responsibility over the case in question, and it allows for the development of interpersonal relationships. It also avoids what many perceive to be a lack of responsiveness from some congressional relations units: "I go direct to district offices when I can," explained one caseworker, "the congressional liaison offices are becoming big bureaucracies." Another elaborated:

This depends to a great extent on the particular agency. From the beginning I have always gone directly to the specific commanding officers in military cases. Due to my background in staff work with the United States Army, I can almost always determine whether a case has merit based on my conversation with the COs. I also find out that they are much more willing to be reasonable when they realize that no one will be coming down from above with reports to be written. Civil Service is quite different. Due to the complexity of their system it is easier to have the congressional liaison handle the work in finding out why "Mrs. Jones isn't getting her pension." Social Security was a problem until we obtained phone numbers that allowed us to dial directly into the New York and Baltimore central offices. This solves problems with Social Security quite rapidly.

Still other aides are under special instructions. One Senate veteran reported that "Senator ——— wants our letters to go directly to department heads, but I cheat on him. It wouldn't do any good, and might cause delays, if we did what he says." And a few caseworkers in home offices have a standing practice of sending all but the most trivial cases to the chief administrator of a given agency's regional office.

Caseworkers also must decide on the means of contacting agencies: telephone, letter, or buckslip—a preprinted form asking an agency to examine the constituent's letter, take appropriate action, and advise the congressman of the outcome. Each has advantages and disadvantages. The phone usually is quicker, although one House staffer (who seemed to view his role as "dumping" cases on the executive) argued that "a letter is faster; we can type letters and send them off and let the agency worry about it faster than we could call.'' Many caseworkers also complain about the difficulty in getting through to some agencies (such as INS in Washington). Telephoning has other virtues: it allows the aide personal contact with the agency and helps to develop a ''feel'' for the administrators and their problems; it may make it harder for an administrator to say no; unlike a letter, a phone call cannot be lost; it provides flexibility and encourages the discussion of alternatives; and, as is sometimes desirable, it leaves no record. Moreover, explained another aide, ''we always use the phone when the constituent is sitting here at the desk—it makes a good impression.''

Buckslips are used for routine cases that spark little interest. Some caseworkers use them for all military cases. In other offices, buckslips are taboo: ''We never use them, because [the congressman] wants something more formal that he can sign.'' Letters allow for better, more precise questions and for more detailed record-keeping, and they also help protect against possible legal problems arising under the privacy act. Most caseworkers report using all three forms of contact, depending on circumstances. As one put it: ''Buckslips for routine inquiries and referrals, letters to prod or seek quick action, phone calls to chastise.''

Older, veteran caseworkers are much more apt to employ all three means of contact than are their younger, less experienced colleagues. With experience comes the knowledge that different forms of contact are appropriate for different cases, that they transmit different messages concerning importance and urgency, and that they trigger different responses from administrators. As one administrator described the situation: ''If I get a buckslip, we send a short response. If it's a letter, our answer is more detailed. A phone call from the congressman, of course, gets the most attention.'' That may be why nearly 40 percent of the congressmen and staffers surveyed thought that telephone contacts are the most effective method of dealing with agencies. Best of all is personal contact; but even more than phoning agencies, personal visits are very difficult to arrange.

5.3. Agency Procedures

Processing of congressionals in all but the smallest agency offices is highly routinized. In a typical Washington liaison office, an inquiry is logged in by a secretary and passed to the appropriate administrator, who decides whether the case can be handled immediately with available information or must be sent to a program unit in Washington or to the field for study. Meanwhile, the inquiry is acknowledged. (Agency congressional relations offices insist on rapid turnaround of congressionals, with some agencies mandating a preliminary response to congressmen within twenty-four hours of receipt. Operating divisions and local offices similarly try to respond quickly—often within forty-eight to seventy-two hours.) That office reopens the file, checks the previous decision against any new information turned up by the congressional office, and reaches a decision—usually that the original decision was correct. A letter to the congressman is drafted, explaining the reason for upholding the earlier decision (or why the case has not yet been decided). The letter is checked by a superior and sent to the congressman, with copies to the Congressional Relations Office and other appropriate offices; or the draft is sent to the regional administrator, the unit's Washington head, or the agency's congressional liaison chief for a final check and signature. That official then sends the letter to the Hill or, paradoxically, back to the field office of the congressman who initiated the inquiry. Naturally, some cases and projects become more involved, necessitating intra-agency discussions and negotiations, occasionally at high levels, and meetings with constituents and congressmen or their staffs. Accordingly, the process takes time. For the army, for example, the average case took 26 days to settle. Cong. Joseph Fisher's (D., Va.) staff indicated that in 1977 his cases averaged 32.3 days from receipt to settlement. His Immigration and Naturalization Office cases took the longest; 61 days.[4] Some cases drag on almost interminably, with instances of over a year's delay not uncommon.

5.4. Rules of the Game: Congress

Congressional staff members pursue several partially conflicting objectives as they process cases and projects. For each case and project handled the caseworker seeks, above all, a speedy and clear answer from the bureaucracy. Second, if the case has merit the caseworker wants a favorable decision, which may require the expenditure of considerable time and energy on the part of the executive branch administrators, who have other things to worry about. Both goals suggest the possibility of an all-out effort for each legitimate case—pushing, pressuring, and perhaps threatening. But a long-term goal is to maintain a balanced, favorable, and, preferably, friendly relationship with one's executive counterparts: "system maintenance," in more theoretical terms. Such a system must be constructed and propped up with care. In short, today's case, if mishandled, may jeopardize tomorrow's, but failing to press today's may also anger the constituent and thus ill serve the congressman. This strategic situation dictates a set of decision rules for everyone involved, and with those rules come the correlative tactics. Not all follow the rules, of course, but it appears that the veterans and more successful newcomers do.

Rule 1: Get to know agency personnel. Almost all experienced caseworkers agree that getting to know agency liaison personnel and appropriate program-level administrators is a key to fast, successful service. As one caseworker put it: "You build up a series of relationships. Liaison people are generally good; the bad ones you don't ask for—you go to someone else. You nurture the contacts." Various means of getting to know agency personnel and of developing sound working relationships exist. Many aides gladly accept agency invitations, or arrange to invite themselves, to visit the agency's offices in order to meet their executive contacts face to face and demonstrate their interest. Staff turnover in Congress therefore presents a double problem. Not only do new caseworkers not know where to look for help, but the lack of time-tested linkages between the two sets of staffers makes the entire process more difficult.

Rule 2: Cultivate your contacts—politely. The caseworker must be polite, courteous, and diplomatic, even while formally maintaining the upper hand (insisting, for example, that if a meeting must be held on a case, it will be held on congressional turf). A bit of advice heard time and time again is "honey will catch more flies than vinegar; the secret is to go out of your way to be understanding and nice." Above all, issuing threats or exerting pressure is taboo. Although all the players know that members of Congress can take retribution against uncooperative agencies—a congressional staffer will sometimes remind administrators that the congressman could vote against an agency's appropriation bill or will, as one bureaucrat put it, "express the attitude that if we don't comply life will become difficult"—most realize that threatening and carrying out sanctions can be a two-edged sword. Not only do such threats violate congressional standards of conduct, but agencies can get even: cooperation may deteriorate; cases may get lost or responses delayed; project applications may be severely scrutinized and grant announcements not sent to the congressmen and senators involved; constituents may be offended; and so on.

"You can't and shouldn't lean on them," said a typical caseworker. "Even if you did, it wouldn't do any good." A veteran House staffer explained: "We can't threaten. Occasionally we wheedle and sometimes cajole, but we can't threaten. To do so would be to burn our bridges, and we need to build bridges, not burn them, to our agency contacts." Not all agree, however. One aide boasted that "I raise hell if their answer isn't any good." A western congressman related this episode: "Some of the farmers in our district were prevented by the EPA from using DDT on their peas. I got so mad that I threatened to go down there and commit physical violence. So they held a midnight meeting and changed their minds."

Bureaucrats generally agree that caseworkers are decent and do not casually issue threats. Fifty-five percent of agency officials surveyed believed that all congressional caseworkers are courteous, and another 42 percent thought that most are. Few executives experience congressional pressure. Fully 61 percent of 177 administrators said they had never been subjected to pressure from Congress to resolve a case in a particular way. Two percent felt leaned on in less than one case in a hundred, while a third indicated pressure in fewer than 10 percent of all cases. When pressure and discourtesy come, they usually are due more to frustration with the inevitable delays and complexities than to attempts to determine the outcomes of cases or projects. Agency administrators know that one of the best ways to avoid harassment is to reduce backlogs, respond promptly, and, for many projects, deny requests early.[5] An Economic Development Administration liaison officer, for example, was emphatic that "pressure is relatively rare; congressmen tend not to throw their weight around. They're very leery about sticking their necks out these days." According to a Labor Department executive: "We get a few screamers, about three or four a week, but I don't mind if they've gotten the runaround. It's just rage. Some even tell me they spent half an hour working up their anger. Then they calm down and we have a good laugh about it."

Certain types of caseworkers, and a handful of readily identifiable congressional offices, seem to provoke the ire of the bureaucracy the most. A military officer felt that "most are courteous, but there are exceptions—individual personalities who are impressed with their own power—mostly young staffers on the Hill." A Justice Department administrator pointed to the culprits: "Usually summer interns and young staff people cause the problems. Power goes to their heads. And some old warhorses on congressional staffs are troublesome. Also there are some abusive congressmen, like ———, who encourage their staffs to be abusive. Others, like Proxmire, have staffers who are tough but polite. Some just are better."

Cultivating contacts goes well beyond being polite and not threatening sanctions. Administrators are courted, flattered, flirted with, and massaged. A personal touch is indispensable. "There's a lot of stroking," commented one Senate aide, "and a little bit of emotional involvement as well." Said another: "They'll take care of us if we treat them nicely." One increasingly common technique is to write unsolicited letters of commendation for particularly helpful bureaucrats. Several congressmen go further, occasionally taking unusually helpful agency liaison people out to lunch. The dual motives behind these pleasantries were described by a House caseworker: "We do it because we want to thank the guy; but of course there's a selfish motive: the next time I call he's anxious to help." The head of a New England Republican congressman's district office summed it up this way:

We try to stay away from liaison offices because we're second-class citizens there—it's a patronage position—so we really go out of our way to cultivate contacts within an agency. My favorite would be some little GS-6 deep inside of some bureaucracy who really gets a thrill out of talking to me and being flattered. I don't know what she thinks, but she enjoys getting a call direct. We cultivate those contacts. I'll thank her, tell her I owe her another drink. She'll say, "Anytime I can help, just call." Yeah, it's a whole different world. Donkeys and elephants don't matter.

The important question is whether or not these tactics pay off. Do flattery and cultivation work, or are they merely some sort of egotistical puffery on the part of pseudopoliticians? Administrators were asked whether the approach taken by the congressional staff members affects how they handle the congressional inquiries. About 30 percent of those responding admitted that it did, at least sometimes. "If I like a caseworker," one liaison official confessed, "I'll hustle more for her." Officials' comments indicated a variety of behavior patterns. On the one hand, there is a clear tendency not to respond favorably to the "desk-pounders." "We won't bend over backwards for the belligerent ones," said a Transportation Department official. An administrator who deals with federal grants explained that "some are obnoxious, and I politely kowtow and then set their applications and inquiries aside. Some congressmen deliberately hire abusive aides so that they—the members—can appear polite and generous while avoiding having to take and dish out the crap."

Conversely, a few administrators act more quickly for pushy caseworkers: "Obnoxious caseworkers are handled quickly just to get 'em off our back." An Agriculture Department officer in the Midwest said: "Sure, I'm more congenial to the nice ones. But sometimes I go out of the way to explain more carefully to caseworkers who are obnoxious, hoping to make friends next time."

One administrator pointed to a form of retaliation: "There are some pretty snarly people up there, but most are decent. If we get too much trouble, I'll go direct to the AA or to the member." And a high-ranking military officer elaborated on a familiar theme: "Look, I'm a senior officer, and no twenty-two-year-old snot is going to put me down. Most caseworkers realize that the person they're working with is decent and needs to be trusted. I may have to get tough with them and put them in their place, but usually they settle down and we can proceed. If they're unreasonable, we may give them a hard time and be less cooperative." And since the caseworkers need executive cooperation to do their job, most do behave. The exchange, in short, is conducted on gentlemanly grounds.

Rule 3: Be helpful. Common sense dictates that congressional caseworkers, to the extent possible, should assist administrators. The best caseworkers will go the extra mile to provide ample documentation for complex cases, screen out and not send to the executive branch cases that are trivial or can just as easily be settled by the caseworker, and signal when a case is purely routine or especially urgent. Good case and projects staffers will not take up the time of busy administrators by demanding personal attention when less dramatic modes of communication will suffice.

Of course, it is not always possible to follow these rules of thumb. Some congressmen insist that all cases be sent to the executive branch, if only to impress constituents. Moreover, busy caseworkers may not have the time to be as careful as they like. Administrators notice these failings. Asked to name the biggest problems they face in handling cases, one-third of the respondents focused on Congress. In particular, administrators complained about uninformed caseworkers, duplication of inquiries by several offices, insufficient information or inadequate documentation, a failure to screen out weak cases, repetitive inquiries from the same caseworker, ambiguity, and the like. All cause delays and difficulties and disrupt relationships. A sensitivity to these complaints distinguishes the best caseworkers from the rest. As one bureaucrat griped: "A lot of caseworkers ask for stupid things and repeat the same call or letter, even when I've told them I can't help or that I've referred the problem directly to a [program-level] person." Added a VA official: "We get lots of garbage; congressmen's offices don't screen the mail. For example, a veteran writes to his congressman on a non-VA matter, and the congressional office just automatically sends it to us. There's a lot of 'just get it over to the agency' type of thinking." A Labor Department official groused about receiving the same letter every month from one congressman whose constituent kept asking about a five dollar medical bill. The problem is that different caseworkers adjust differently to the tension between the political imperative of servicing and satisfying all constituents and the casework norm of rendering reasonable assistance to the agency operatives they are trying to cultivate. Moreover, there are a number of congressional staffers who just do not care or who believe that agency liaison offices exist to cope with *all* constituent complaints. It might be the case, therefore, that the very existence of congressional relations offices and their willingness to accommodate congressional offices contributes to the problem.

Having to "break in" new caseworkers presents a problem for some executives, since "they require so much more explaining." So do vague referrals from Congress: "Sometimes I can't tell if they're serious and really want action, or merely want a form letter." Congressmen and caseworkers who are afraid to tell the constituents the bad news are not appreciated in agencies. One complained that "they know the answer is no but don't have the guts to tell them."

Rule 4: Be reasonable and don't ask for the impossible. Most cases and projects are routine. Accordingly, caseworkers' inquiries are eminently reasonable. As John Fitzpatrick, the AA to Cong. Tom Harkin (D., Iowa), described his office's position on grants: "We'll intervene if it looks like the bureaucracy is doing something wrong or is not making decisions in a timely fashion or something went wrong. We don't intervene to say give a grant to this town or that individual."[6] Sometimes, however, more is sought.

Congressmen and their staffers were asked whether they had ever asked agencies to break, bend, or stretch laws or regulations. One-quarter of the thirty-six senators and representatives and one-third of the staffers replied in the affirmative, while the others answered no. Of interest is the difference between Washington and home-based staffs: two-thirds of the former but only one-fifth of the latter indicated that they had asked for such action. Proximity to "power," perhaps, emboldens the staffs. So, it appears, does ideological extremism: aides to the most liberal and most conservative members were more likely to have replied affirmatively.

These answers must be evaluated in light of what is meant by "bending" or "stretching." In a technical sense, any request to reconsider a decision on behalf of a constituent amounts to bending the rules. But beyond that, commented one aide: "We don't ask them to bend or break rules or violate laws, but we do ask them to go back and take another look; and if, under the rules and regs, they can do it, we ask them to reconsider the case." A second caseworker explained: "A major part of our job is to uncover information not previously considered or mistaken. We don't pressure or demand; we just ask, 'if at all possible.' Then we accept their decision." According to a former senator: "We do not have the authority, nor do we attempt to alter agency decisions. We see our purpose as assisting the constituent in correcting errors involving the *handling* of their case, not the *adjudication* of it."

Efforts to get administrators to stretch the rules occur during serious situations. "Once in a great while, and then it's an exception," said a district office manager. "Especially in the past year or two we've had a few such cases with the elderly, and it really makes you cry. Really tragic cases—destitute people who need help. In a case like that we'll say, 'dammit, bend your rules.'" Another common explanation was that such requests are made only when the caseworker knows that there is flexibility in a rule: "Sometimes we will ask for an exception or for a stretching of the reg—when we know they have discretion. But not 'break' a law. It's okay to ask, 'Please see what can be done.' In a close case, our intervention may tip the scale."

Those who said they did not ask for special treatment and exceptions gave several reasons, often centering on the ethical question. "We're probably too squeamish on the ethics of the situation," expounded one House caseworker. A former chairman of a powerful House committee pronounced that, "no, it would be wrong to do so." "We ask for reconsideration only on the case's merit—I repeat, merit," wrote a former member of the House.

If ethical considerations fail to deter, the fears of generating adverse publicity and damaging existing linkages to agency officials serve quite well as constraints. All seek to avoid accusations of tampering with justice. A House caseworker thought that to gain a reputation for asking for favors from the military would absolutely ruin her boss, who already had a reputation as a critic of the Pentagon. Aides to committee and subcommittee chairs must be doubly careful, since the members do not wish to appear to be abusing their power. An executive liaison official who previously worked for a middle western Republican recalled: "No. When I worked for——— and he became the ranking minority member of the subcommittee, I became very careful of what we did and what we asked for when making an inquiry. My congressman deliberately exercised restraint."

To check whether these responses might be merely self-serving rationalizations, the same question was put to administrators: "How often, if ever, have congressional offices asked you to violate a law, violate an agency rule or regulation, bend or stretch rules or regulations, or make exceptions for constituents?" The results are seen in table 5.1. Few respondents said that they had been asked to

Table 5.1: Frequency of Congressional Requests for
Special Treatment, as Reported by Executive Agency Officials

	Type of Request			
Frequency	Violate a Law	Violate a Rule or Regulation	Bend or Stretch a Rule or Regulation	Make an Exception for a Constituent
Never	93%	83%	57%	63%
Once or twice	4	7	13	9
Occasionally	2	6	22	17
Frequently	1	2	4	6
Yes, unspecified	1	2	4	5
(N)	(189)	(199)	(202)	(205)

SOURCE: Author's survey and interviews.

break statutory provisions or departmental / agency rules or regulations. Of those who did, most indicated that when congressional caseworkers make such requests, they generally do not realize that what they are asking for is actually off-limits. "They just don't know the regulations and our programs. There's no deliberate attempt to pressure illegally. Usually, it's an honest mistake." Administrators point to overly zealous caseworkers, not congressmen, for going beyond the limits of propriety, but insist that few aides press their claims unreasonably. "When you put it back to them bluntly what they are suggesting," pointed out an SBA official, "the suggestion is quickly withdrawn."

Far more bureaucrats are asked to bend or stretch rules and make exceptions than are asked to break them, but the approach is cautious ("Yes, we are asked, but the request usually is safely phrased so as not to look like it"). Such requests tend to arise when the situation is or seems to be an emergency and / or the agency possesses substantial discretion. A Passport Office official partially disagreed: "While congressional inquiries have never asked me outright to violate a law, they have knowingly insisted that an exception be made after clear explanation that such an action would be a violation of law. This was especially true in my many years of work overseas. There were frequent occasions."

Another was more blunt: "Many staffers are just stupid and try to use their clout to get us to take actions we can't legally take. They just don't understand what, how, and why we do what we do." "What burns me," raged a lower-level bureaucrat, "are congressmen who ask for things we just cannot do and they know it."

A distinction that needs to be made concerns the types of cases. Regular individual casework simply is not likely to draw the intense involvement and "pressure" that is found in the promotion of federal projects applications. The individual cases about which congressmen get worked up are likely also to evoke bureaucratic sympathy. But on occasion congressmen and senators might lean rather hard on administrators in order to secure funds for their districts or to alter executive branch policy. Cong. Trent Lott (R., Miss.), for example, was described as having hounded the Justice Department so many times and on such a wide variety of subjects that some employees there called him "our pen pal." One source at Justice estimated that the Mississippi conservative sent them a letter every other day.[7]

Tennessee Senators Howard Baker and James Sasser, along with several representatives from their state, were accused by an HEW official of exerting pressure to force him to award federal education funds to a Tennessee college despite his insistence that the school was not eligible.[8] And Cong. John H. Murphy (D., N.Y.), chairman of the House Merchant Marine and Fisheries Committee, pressed the Navy so hard to settle cost overrun claims in favor of Todd Shipyards (located in his district) that the Navy almost decided to refer the case to the Justice Department. Murphy was quoted as saying that the shipbuilding company merely "brought the matter of its suit against the Navy to my attention."[9] The only scholarly study of this phenomenon found that congressmen themselves believe that somewhere between "a few" and "many" members engaged in pressuring the government to make undeserved grants to universities in their districts, and that "many" subcommittee chairmen would urge regulatory agencies to disallow a common carrier's petition to drop a stop in their districts. The former practice was judged unethical; on the latter, members were divided.[10]

Rule 5: When necessary, invoke higher authority. Sometimes caseworkers simply cannot obtain the cooperation or specific results they expect and deem just. In such cases, they may invoke the help of their administrative assistants or the members. A tougher letter or a personal phone call ensues. Case and projects workers located in field offices may ask their Washington offices to intervene. Although instances of personal intervention in cases and projects fill the pages of the biographies and memoirs of former senators and congressmen, there is a tendency for members *not* to get involved. On the one hand, many fear earning a bad reputation for favoritism or throwing their weight around (often unsuccessfully); on the other hand, members are too busy and have little time for this activity. Said one aide: "The Senator doesn't want to—and actually is afraid to—get involved in most of these cases, especially any having to do with legal matters or federal adjudicatory situations." "I hate to bother him," explained a House staffer, "he's too busy with his committee work." A Republican congressman thought that "you shouldn't get personally involved very often—save it for when it's absolutely needed." The Washington offices of activist senators who have chosen to do casework in their state offices prefer not to be bothered with casework. One home-based caseworker said that it was a cardinal rule in her office not to call Washington: "I remember the first time I did it; I called the legislative assistant to get an explanation of a law. He chewed my ear off: 'Don't ever call me again.' I didn't."

Another technique employed by some case and projects workers is to call upon the staffs of appropriate committees and subcommittees, and occasionally upon the personal office staffs of key committee members, to help move recalcitrant agencies. Although the most frequent use of committees is to get information, some aides do seek the added clout of committee connections in dealing with an unresponsive agency. Such use of committees seems most common when the congressman or senator whose staff is handling the case sits on the relevant committee or has close ties to another member who does, or when the administration is in the hands of the opposite party and is believed not to be responsive to its opponents.

110

Lastly, members' offices team up on some projects (and on occasional individual cases) to enhance prospects of success or to share expertise on a particular problem. State delegations band together to support federal projects benefiting their whole state, of course, but such cooperation sometimes concerns more particularized benefits affecting only one or two districts. In such cases, there is a tendency to seek out fellow members of the state delegation who sit on the appropriate committees or to contact a known power, such as a party leader. One of the senators from a New England state explained that each senator "carries the ball in his committee—we work closely to try to eliminate duplication." John A. Ferejohn's study of pork-barrel politics found similar results. He quotes a Massachusetts Democrat: "If you are having trouble with an agency, you can have him [Speaker McCormack] call over and that has more effect than if any one of the rest of us called, and he has been very helpful on constituency matters."[11] There is, in short, a widespread belief that agencies listen more carefully to well-positioned members than to the rank and file. The next chapter discusses this possibility at some length.

Rule 6: If you must, try again at higher levels. Although all but a few cases are handled by single exchanges between congressional offices and agencies at relatively low levels in their respective hierarchies, there are times when the congressional staffers and/or members cannot get satisfaction. The rules of the game allow and even encourage them to go back a second time and take the case to higher administrative levels. As one Senate aide said: "Ninety percent of the time we just pass the agency response on to the constituent. But 10 percent of the agency responses aren't automatically returned with a decent answer. If I see a response that isn't ringing true or smells wrong—if I sense it—I'll tell the constituent that the answer isn't right and I'll go back to the agency. Then the agency will be more responsive." Many of these return engagements are directed to supervisors. In an even smaller number of cases, appeals are taken all the way to the top. Forty-four percent of 109 members and staffers indicated that they had at least once taken cases as high as the White House, with another 46 percent having bucked them to a department secretary or agency head. Tenacity, in short, is a virtue—within reason. As one congressional office's *Procedure Manual* states: "When you do [go over the head of your agency contact], it is generally advisable to let your counterpart know you are going to do this and make it clear that you are in no way blaming him or her. In most cases the problem is simply that the person you are talking to doesn't have the power or authority to do what you want done. . . . If you don't [inform him or her] you are going to have a disgruntled counterpart, who will take it out on you in future cases."

Administrators take a mixed view of appeals. On the one hand, they resent what they take to be uncalled-for repeat requests and appeals taken over their heads for unjustified reasons, and they tend to see most such appeals in that light. On the other hand, as one explained, ''sometimes we disagree with the congressman and tell him that if he doesn't like our ruling, he should go over our heads to the regional office.'' A Small Business Administration official saw certain benefits in such appeals:

Appeals are made, especially in areas of interpretation. We may interpret a rule one way, and the congressional office doesn't like it. So the congressman goes over our head and asks the SBA Administrator in Washington to interpret it differently. If he does, that then becomes the definitive interpretation, which helps us in similar cases in the future. For example, there was a farmer who wanted to open a farm implement store and asked for a loan. But his farming business was large enough to remove him from the realm of ''small business.'' So he wrote to the congressman, who contacted us. We said no, and told him that the only way we can make the loan is if the rule was changed. So the congressman talked to the SBA head, who changed the rule itself.

The ultimate in pushing a case is to introduce a private bill for the relief of the constituent. There is a time-honored tradition of introducing legislation to exempt relatives of constituents from immigration quotas and restrictions and to compensate constituents for damages caused by government activities. The recent Vietnam war, for instance, led to a number of bills providing benefits to prisoners of war. Introducing a private bill has the effect of placing a freeze on routine deportation notices to people who have overstayed their visas or entered the country illegally, and thus sponsors are commonly sought. One former congressman told the story of a building in his district owned by the General Services Administration but run by a private manager. The building, which housed government records, burned to the ground due to negligence and fire code violations by the manager. Thirty local fire departments took part in putting out the flames. ''And my office got the federal government to reimburse them, though it took a private bill to do it.'' Another case involved property damage caused by construction of a missile base. The government agency involved admitted causing the damage but insisted that the farmer (on whose land the base was being built) take his case to court. The man's senator introduced a private bill instead.

For several reasons, most members shy away from private bills. First, they raise hopes that are dashed when, as is the case more often than not, the bills fail. Second, they have the effect of tying up normal executive processing of cases. Third, such actions are too dramatic, offend agencies, and thus needlessly dissipate good will. Fourth, senators and congressmen know that in many an immigration case, some lawyer is collecting a generous fee for his work in asking the member to introduce the legislation. That irks both members and their staffs.

5.5. Rules of the Game: The Executive

Administrators follow a set of rules that complement those on the Hill. They know that case and project interventions are part and parcel of congressional life and that they will not cease. Thus, they exhibit the basically cooperative attitudes described in the previous chapter. In addition, bureaucrats see adverse consequences from not cooperating. The executive officials in the sample were asked whether any adverse effects are seen as "resulting from a lack of careful treatment of 'congressionals.'" The most frequently cited (21 percent of responses) consequence was that the agency would receive poor publicity or a bad image. Said one military liaison officer: "Lack of careful treatment does create a pressure situation and presents a very unprofessional image of the service." "It could," said one bureaucrat, "undermine the agency's integrity." Eighteen percent answered that poor cooperation meant that the case would be taken over their heads or that the congressman would become personally involved. Another 6 percent feared that the agency would be called to account at hearings. One in ten cited the possible loss of votes on agency requests for legislation or appropriations, or a generally deteriorated relationship: "There would be more legislative intervention in administration, and organization, and some cuts in appropriations," wrote an Interior Department official. An additional 6 percent mentioned that their superiors would be displeased. The remaining answers were varied. A couple indicated that poor service only makes for more work with follow-up inquiries. Naturally, higher-ranking administrators were more apt to cite bad publicity and a poor agency image than were lower-level officials, but they, as well as liaison officers, were less likely to believe that Congress would punish their agencies at appropriations time.

In short, bureaucrats are aware that sloppy handling of cases can hurt, but they do not seem excessively worried. Either they believe that their work is always good (which most seem to do) or they are convinced that there will be little retribution. Part of the former explanation is accounted for by assiduous attention to three basic rules.

Rule 1: Take care of the caseworkers. Legislative liaison officials stress the importance of getting along with congressional staffs and of being as helpful as possible. Speaking of his dealings with congressional aides, one regional EPA congressional relations specialist expressed confidence: "I have an easy relationship with them. We talk freely. I go to Washington and meet them. When you have face-to-face contact, things go better. When I meet with them, business picks up and they call me." And being called is precisely what the liaison officers want. Most of them definitely do not want congressional staffs to bypass the liaison units to pester lower-level bureaucrats directly. Thus rule number one is oriented toward maintaining the system of caseworker-liaison interchange.

Liaison officials not only seek familiarity with congressional staffs but also want to inform them about agency activities, regulations, and procedures, both to enable them to avoid inquiries and to help them ask more intelligent questions when they must write or call. As one local HUD administrator put it: "Nothing but the greatest relationship. We had one briefing and will do it again to teach the staff and the congressmen about our program. Our first was successful. Fifteen caseworkers attended. Now, in the future, when they get a complaint from a constituent, they'll be knowledgeable enough to answer."

Most agencies now conduct seminars, meetings, and tours, both in Washington and around the country, for the same purposes, and a number of them furnish written guidelines and handbooks describing their operations and including names and phone numbers. A Washington-based liaison official exemplified the executive branch efforts: "We go out of our way. On community grants we give the congressman the full dope on why cities won or lost, and what the priority ordering was among applications. We conduct our 'dog and pony' show, at the congressman's preferred location, to show cities how to apply."

Other services provided by liaison operatives include making sure questions sent to their agencies are in fact answered, interpreting to congressional staffs what lower-level administrators are saying, stirring those administrators into action, and rewriting their sometimes antagonistic or inscrutable letters to Congress. Said a congressional relations chief: "Half of my job is impressing the people in this agency with the importance and utility of 'congressionals.' " Others complained about delays, red tape, and losing cases sent down to program-level bureaucrats. A liaison specialist in a regional office fired this volley at his peers: "The problem is getting the staff to handle cases in a timely fashion. There's the pass-the-buck syndrome—the tendency to send paper down to the supervisors rather than call and write up the correct response then and there. There's also a tendency to respond defensively without answering the question. To avoid that, I read all the correspondence to and from the individual; if he doesn't answer properly I'll make him do it over. Then there's the problem of illiteracy; some of these people have no writing skills." Conversely, lower-level bureaucrats, especially those in area offices, become upset at the difficulty in getting answers from headquarters on policy questions, and several objected to what they thought was unnecessary pressure from their bosses or liaison specialists.

Liaison officers find themselves in a precarious position. Although many view the bureaucracy with suspicion, unless they themselves possess a good deal of expertise, they must rely on the bureaucrats below. And if they are to maintain their relationships with those administrators, they cannot intervene on their own initiative or too often challenge administrative decisions, even if they have the time and inclination to do so. Explained one Washington liaison head: "When we get a case and send it down and get an answer, we just have to assume the guy writing the letter downstairs is telling the truth. If we get a second letter from Congress, [my assistant] or I will give it a closer look, personally, at times. We check it out with the district offices or program office here." Not all congressional relations staffs are able to do so, however. Still, some are quite assertive and demanding. One boasted that "our people in the field know we can get them transferred to a lousy office if they don't cooperate with Congress. And I'd do it, too, because I know Congress and how important it is to keep them happy." No wonder a number of the very low-level bureaucrats in district offices were afraid that congressional offices would report poor treatment and uncooperative behavior to their superiors.

Finally, a number of liaison officials provide caseworkers and, especially, members and AAs with assessments of the performance of their case and project operations. Several administrators pointed out instances in which they had to tell congressmen that they were being ill-served by staffers. Conversely, one caseworker mentioned that executive offices sometimes called her to check up on their subordinates as well.

Rule 2: Handle cases quickly and fairly. Liaison personnel and most program-level bureaucrats know that congressional offices want, above all, fast action on their inquiries. Therefore, they insist on rapid turnaround time and immediate acknowledgment of letters; and they seek to reassure their counterparts that they are doing all that they can as rapidly as possible. During 1977, to take an exceptional example, the Social Security Administration was sending out six hundred mailgrams per month assuring congressmen that their inquiries on behalf of constituents were being faithfully attended to.[12]

A discussion of the fairness and equity of casework is provided in chapter 6, but it should be noted here that the dominant practice in departments and agencies is to honor the bureaucratic norms of universalism and equity by treating all comparable cases the same way, with no favoritism—at least with respect to the substantive disposition of the cases. As one INS official observed, "No, if you start giving preference, you'll be getting requests from all of them. You've got to cover yourself; make sure that if you make an exception, the facts justify it."

Rule 3: Know how to say no. Most congressional casework challenges to administrative decisions have to be turned down. Thus it is imperative that denials be as painless and polite as possible, to avoid needlessly ruining agency-caseworker relationships, to prevent caseworkers from appealing, and to prevent (in the cases of federal grants and projects) congressional-citizen coalitions from forming. Accordingly, agencies must persuade congressional staffs that their procedures are fair and impartial, so that when rejections come, they are accepted as valid.

Although the normal rivalries and distrust between branches of government might suggest a rather negative view by Congress of the executive's cooperation on cases and projects, it appears that cooperation is quite good. Congressional respondents were asked to rate executive cooperation with casework and federal projects efforts. Of 311 who responded, 9 percent thought cooperation was always good, 64 percent deemed it "usually" good, and 8 percent termed it "fair." Only 5 respondents complained that the service they got was poor." The responses were remarkably consistent across all categories of respondents: senators, representatives, administrative assistants, and caseworkers, both in Washington and at home. Typical of responses was that of a Senate aide: "I really think that the people in the agencies try to be fair." A House caseworker described an exceptional example of cooperation: "I was trying to locate someone whose dad was dying, and I called the IRS. The person told me she couldn't release any information on the man's whereabouts, but that if I asked the right questions, she would say yes or no."

Many of those who found cooperation to be wanting—and nearly half of all congressmen and staffers cited the bureaucracy as the biggest headache they have in assisting constituents—cited delays or sloppy responses. "They're too slow." "The worst problems are the bureaucrats, who are afraid to do their job and to stick their necks out and make a decision." A problem occurs "when there's bad communication with an agency and the people there don't know what they're doing." "You just can't get the information you need."[13] Several indicated that cooperation was fine if the right contacts had been established: "Once you find the right person, cooperation is good. But getting to that person is time-consuming. You get the bureaucratic runaround. One guy passes you to another, and you can't get hold of him. It may take five or six calls."

Clearly, some agencies have better reputations for helpfulness than do others. Respondents in 1977–78 were asked to name the most and the least cooperative agencies. The combined data are presented in table 5.2.

By far the most helpful agencies, in the eyes of congressmen and staffs, are the Veterans Administration, the three military services, the Social Security Administration, and—up to 1981 at least—the State Department's Passport Office. Three factors may account for their popularity: they are older and more experienced; they tend to be highly client-oriented and seek aggressively to deliver

Table 5.2: Most and Least Cooperative Executive Agencies

Department or Agency	Number of Times Most Cooperative	Mentioned as Least Cooperative
Veterans Admin.	44	3
Military Services	27	6
Social Security	48	12
State (Passport Office)	9	1
Commerce	3	1
Postal Service	1	0
FEA / Energy	1	0
Small Business Admin.	2	2
Civil Service Comm.	4	5
Agriculture	4	5
Interior	2	3
IRS	8	9
HUD	5	9
HEW (all but Social Security)	5	12
EPA	0	2
Immigration and Naturalization	5	29
Labor	1	56

SOURCE: Author's questionnaires and interviews: based on responses of 12 former members of Congress and 103 staffers during the 95th Congress to the question: "Are some agencies more/less cooperative than others? Which?"

benefits; and two of them (the military and the VA) have highly developed, thoroughly professional, and extremely centralized liaison teams, *located on the Hill*, that are unusually solicitous of congressional caseworkers. Conversely, the least popular agency was the Department of Labor, charged with administering the Workers' Compensation, Black Lung, Pension Guarantee, and Occupational Safety and Health programs—all of which seem to cause inordinately high levels of confusion, delay, and appeals. These programs are somewhat newer and more controversial.[14]

In addition to the very common complaint that certain agencies are hard to reach (due to high workloads relative to their complaint-handling abilities), several were singled out as being unusually careless or arrogant. As one aide said:

"HUD is bad—they're giving us erroneous data that we pass along. INS is horrible but it's understandable, given their workload." Another explained: "The Labor Department is sloppy. I once had to make sixteen calls to get a response. It's a problem of attitude—they don't care."

Once a case inquiry has been satisfactorily answered by a department or agency, or once project grants have been allocated, the final task is to inform the constituent. Usually, a letter is prepared for the member's signature, but there are exceptions. The first is the tendency of some offices to use the "good news/bad news" rule, which holds that if the result of the case is favorable to the constituent, the congressional office informs the constituent. For important or highly visible cases, many federal projects, or cases that have piqued the member's interest, the senator or representative may personally phone the constituent. When an agency has rejected a case, some congressional offices have the bad news sent directly from the agency, or at least forward the agency's letter to the constituent with an apologetic cover letter. Good news letters invariably express the congressman's happiness and willingness to help in the future. Bad news letters express sorrow, and they, too, invite future inquiries.

On project applications, congressional offices tend to want to communicate directly with the applicant before the agency does, especially if the news is favorable. All agencies have at least an informal rule that requires that a senator or congressman involved in a project application be informed before the grant is made public, thus allowing the member to make the announcement and, presumably, take the credit. A forty-eight-hour advance notice is typical.

Finally, in some offices caseworkers are allowed and encouraged to identify themselves to the constituent and correspond under their own names. Even in such offices, however, the final letter informing the constituent of the disposition of the case often comes over the member's signature.

5.6. Summary

Both congressional and executive branch offices have developed standard operating procedures for handling cases and projects. In recent years, the executive agencies, especially, have formalized and centralized their processing capabilities.

Successful casework goes beyond merely following routines. The strategic premises of both sides have inclined them to develop decision rules vis à vis constituents and each other. Central to those rules are the imperatives of going all out for constituents—or at least appearing to do so—and of being reasonable and helpful with each other. When each side deals openly and forthrightly with the other, both benefit. In such circumstances, appeals by caseworkers over the heads of their executive counterparts are accepted without bitterness, as are refusals by agencies to reverse previous rulings. Thus the system's equilibrium is maintained, allowing for smooth exchange relationships in the future. Congressmen benefit from the appearance of responsiveness, while agency administrators can adhere to norms of universalism, neutrality, and equity.

CHAPTER 6

Casework: An Equitable
Redress of Grievances?

The following three chapters turn explicitly to an evaluation of congressional casework and its consequences. Chapter 7 examines casework in terms of its relevance for the policymaking duties of Congress, while chapter 8 focuses on the electoral and symbolic effects. This chapter asks whether "running interference" for constituents is a fair, equitable, and ethical undertaking that produces benefits for all eligible citizens. To the extent that factors other than the inherent merit of a citizen's complaint determine the outcome of his case, the growing ombudsman function poses a threat to the integrity of the political process and to citizens' faith in government. Service responsiveness could undermine genuine symbolic responsiveness.

Among the standard criticisms of the casework process are charges that it is unfair, uneven, and preferential; that some people receive help and others do not; and that legitimate grievances go unanswered while meritless requests are granted. Congressmen, their staffs, and administrators, on the whole, do not concur in these judgments. Asked if they thought that "congressional casework for constituents is unfair in that it affords preferential treatment to some citizens," fewer than one out of five Washington caseworkers, the same proportion of agency administrators, and one out of twenty congressmen and home-based staffers agreed. The typical congressional response was: "Unfair? How can anyone say that—everyone is free to write their congressman." But of course not everyone does. What is meant is that there are no barriers to asking for and receiving help; and the analysis in chapter 2 of who in fact seeks assistance seems to support this view. Still, there are reservations, as indicated by an Immigration and Naturalization Service official: "Sure it's unfair. We don't get a bunch of poor old Mexicans here. The aliens who are asking congressmen for help have connections and money. A lot of big companies bring in foreigners for training or for exchange, and those companies know what to do and whom to see.''

Fairness and equity, of course, go well beyond what can be revealed by the answers to this one question. (One might, indeed, discount totally the testimony of participants.) Specifically, inequity and challenges to the standard bureaucratic norms of universalism and affective neutrality[1] can stem from activities of constituents, congressmen and their staffs, and administrators. There are, basically, four problems: constituents can present cases that are without merit; congressional offices can pass them along and have administrators support the claims; worse, congressmen and staffs may accord preferential treatment to some constituents, even to the point of illegitimately pressuring executive agencies; and, for whatever reason, administrators can engage in overt favoritism of one sort or another.

6.1. The Validity of Cases

The first potential source of inequity concerns the inherent legitimacy of the requests and grievances citizens bring to their congressmen. As Mississippi Congressman Frank E. Smith wrote: ''Some of the requests are unreasonable; some of them are downright outrageous; some of them concern matters which have already been rightly disapproved at every executive level and on which the decision could not properly be reversed no matter how many congressmen intervened or how often the problem was reconsidered.''[2] There is no way to obtain an objective assessment of the quality of incoming cases, but members and aides were asked to estimate the percentage of cases lacking substantive merit. Their judgment was that approximately one in five cases proved to be meritless (using the median reduces the proportion to one in seven). Bureaucrats, by contrast, were more skeptical, claiming that fully half were without merit. Where one stands on casework, apparently, depends on where one sits.

Staffers had no difficulty recalling examples of worthless cases: refusals to pay income taxes, civil servants complaining that they hadn't been promoted, unreasonable or illegitimate disability claims for veterans or social security benefits, attempts to reverse dishonorable military discharges—even complaints about having been sent to jail for committing crimes. One caseworker recounted the story of a soldier who wanted to keep ten dogs in his quarters against clear army rules; another told of the family seeking permission to bury three of its members in one veterans' cemetery grave; and a third told of a constituent trying to gain admission to a housing project after being refused on the grounds of documented cases of vandalism and refusal to pay rents at another project.

Many, perhaps most, of the meritless cases arise out of ignorance. Constituents do not know what they are and are not entitled to. Of course, less flattering interpretations exist. One former aide to a midwestern Republican senator wrote that meritless cases were often raised by people who were lonely, by political supporters who felt the senator "owed them a favor," and by "social parasites and outright liars." Apparently deception sometimes constitutes a serious problem. One such case involved a miner who, after twenty-five years of digging coal, was entitled to—and claimed—black lung benefits. The only catch was that he had not actually been digging coal for the required twenty-five years—and he knew it. Phony injury claims for veterans benefits and similar falsehoods abound. For the most part, however, the attitudes of caseworkers seemed to be that outright, deliberate lying was relatively rare. "Most people don't really lie," said one aide; "they just see their side of the question" and thus do not tell the caseworkers the whole story. Most agency respondents also took a benign view of invalid cases, stressing "close-call" claims, constituent—or caseworker—ignorance, or "human breakdown."

Another reason given for finding cases to be without merit is that many people—the average estimate was 50 percent—do not exhaust all bureaucratic channels of redress before contacting their congressmen. As one aide put it: "Exhaust their bureaucratic remedies? Heck no. They just fire away at us." Equal proportions of agency officials put failures to exhaust available remedies at "most," "half," and "few" complaining constituents.

Among the meritless cases are a number of "crackpot" cases, people "looking for a shoulder to cry on," "pests," "malingerers," and the simply obnoxious people who "cannot take no for an answer." The tactics employed in these cases often are interesting. It is not uncommon for offices to receive letters beginning, "I voted for you last time and I always have." Such attempts to invoke sympathy—constituents sometimes claim to be relatives or school chums—usually can be picked out without difficulty. One amusing story involved a southern congressman who received a letter one day that informed him: "I always voted Democratic and I think you're doing a fine job. I'll vote Democratic next time, too." The problem was that this congressman was a Republican. The administrative assistant broke out in laughter. "And do you know what? Someone in another [Democratic] office showed me a letter from the same man with the same comment about voting Republican." But in virtually all of these cases, the aides insisted that they worked just as hard as they would with any other one.

Some constituents become insistent. Especially in district and state offices, where people can walk in and confront staffers at their desks, the situation can become dangerous. A good number of such aides told of being verbally, and occasionally physically, assaulted by irate constituents. One midwestern Democratic congressman had a "panic button" installed in each staffer's desk so that, with a touch, the building's security personnel could be summoned.

Cases lacking merit would pose no difficulties were it not for the possibility that congressmen might spring into action with uncritical zeal, determined from the outset to win for the complainant because he is a constituent, not because his case is known to be just.[3] Even allowing for some exaggeration, there is an element of truth here. Despite the acknowledged lack of merit in many cases and the failure of constituents to pursue their grievances or requests through executive branch channels, the majority of caseworkers do take the attitude that "the customer is always right," preferring to leave no room for error. One aide described a situation in which a woman wrote about a Department of Agriculture benefit she claimed she was entitled to. The caseworker had never heard of the program involved and indicated as much. When she called the department congressional liaison officer, he, too, had never heard of it. But both decided to investigate further: "And do you know what? The woman was right—she knew about the program even before Agriculture's liaison did. You just can't make any snap decisions." More dramatically, more than one catastrophe may have been prevented because some congressional caseworker or congressman took an interest in an "obviously" worthless case pressed by a dejected constituent. A House caseworker explained that "even the kooks get a response—one of them might be another Arthur Bremmer, and maybe a letter from the congressman will satisfy the guy and calm him down." Indeed, as a local HUD official recalled: "We got a congressional [inquiry] about an irate constituent. We called, and he was really upset and threatened suicide. So we called all over—the Suicide Prevention Center, a church, a hospital—to get help. A month later, the guy called and thanked me for the help."

Other aides take a more discriminating approach: "We screen all cases. If the case is garbage, we try to talk the constituent out of it." Cautious lest her boss acquire a bad reputation within the bureaucracy for pushing pointless cases, yet worried about projecting a losing image with constituents, one aide said that "verbally we attempt to point out the deficiencies in the claim and dissociate the congressman from the decision." Much depends on the staff member involved. Some are more, some less, inclined simply to process each and every case, regardless of merit.

In most offices, a distinction is made between meritless individual cases and weak or meritless grant applications. Said one aide to a midwestern Democratic senator: "We operate on the assumption that *any* government application is worthy of support. For private and nonprofit groups, we investigate first. The problem is that with grants, people don't know what's available—it's more of an information thing."

To the extent that administrators are pressured by Congress into deciding cases—even meritless ones—in favor of constituents, there is a real risk of the casework process's becoming dysfunctional. However, as will be argued later, such occurrences are extremely rare. But the danger of *accidentally* sustaining weak cases may be slightly greater. Lower-level administrators might mistakenly perceive a conciliatory or pro-Congress attitude in their superiors and lean over backward to accommodate case requests. After describing an incident in which he had to "chew out" a loan officer for careless treatment of a congressional case inquiry, an SBA administrator wondered aloud whether the officer might not be less rigorous and not hold to the agency's standards the next time a superior sent him a congressional. Another possibility is that administrative officers, out of sheer weariness, might find it easier to grant a request than to subject it to careful scrutiny.[4] Both situations seem unlikely, but they undoubtedly do happen. In either case, congressmen may use the executive officials as whipping boys—as they do when even legitimate cases are denied. The inimitable Hubert H. Humphrey (D., Minn.) expressed his fears and sympathies this way:

I cannot help but express a note of concern that administrative officers who are asked, at the request of Senators or Representatives, to do something, may later be accused of having given a special privilege or favor, when there was not such desire on the part of either the Member of Congress or the administrative officer. I have had citizens from my State come to my office. I do not have a chance to give them a political blood test or run them through a test of morals and character. If they come in as responsible citizens so far as I know, and ask me to do something for them that seems within the spirit and intent of the law, I pick up the telephone, call up the appropriate officer, and ask, in my name as a Senator of the United States, if something can be done. If those officers do not give us at least a friendly response, we are the first to criticize them. If they look into the question and try to ascertain whether or not something can be done, and later we find the constituents were unworthy or were crooks or were violating the law at least in spirit, we point at the administrative officers.[5]

A danger is that raw favoritism may exist in the casework process, leading to preferential treatment and stronger advocacy for some constituents. It is in this area that charges of conflict of interest, political influence, and even bribery arise. Democratic Congressman Daniel Flood, known for his ability to protect his Pennsylvania constituency, was charged with conspiracy, bribery, and perjury in connection with pushing for federal grants and loans for a Philadelphia hospital. In January, 1980, he resigned his seat and, a month later, pleaded guilty to a misdemeanor charge. In 1976, Cong. Robert L. F. Sikes (D., Fla.) became embroiled in a scandal when he urged state and federal officials to authorize establishment of a bank at the Pensacola Naval Air Station even though he owned stock in the bank. He replied that his actions were "normal constituent service rendered by a congressman."[6] And former Congressman Frank Clark (D., Pa.) was accused of charging constituents for helping them with passports and with putting daughters of key constituents on his House payroll.[7] Cong. Fernand J. St. Germain (D., N.J.) likewise was charged by a newspaper columnist with trying to channel inordinate amounts of federal largesse to favored constituents.[8] It has long been suspected, moreover, that some representatives allocate a disproportionate number of their military service academy appointments to the children of influential constituents, such as newspaper editors and various newspaper, television, and radio reporters.

Members and staffs were asked: "When they make requests for help, do friends of the Congressman or local VIPs receive faster or special treatment from your office?" About 40 percent answered in the affirmative, although half of them added qualifications such as "rarely" or "very seldom." A few staffers also said that they would go to extra lengths to promote cases in which the congressmen took a personal interest. Clearly, some favoritism does exist, and staffers seemed rather forthright in discussing it. "On that one I'm torn," said one aide. "Our office philosophy is that everyone should be treated equally and have the help of an ombudsman, but I know not everyone does benefit equally." "The congressman's friends, or the AA's, get better treatment," confessed another. Other caseworkers singled out "anybody with influence" and "a party or labor leader" for occasional special treatment. Two House staffers in one House office disagreed about showing favoritism toward big financial contributors: "I do," said one, "but I know for certain that she doesn't."

The nature of the preferential treatment has to do with the care and diligence with which a case is handled. It normally amounts to faster, more polite action on a case; sometimes the congressman or administrative assistant will handle it personally, or at least keep close watch over the aide to whom it was entrusted.

Certainly there does not appear to be any preference for fellow party members. Not one caseworker believed that a constituent's party affiliation matters. The typical response was that "there's no way we would discriminate on that basis—we don't know what their party is." Although many constituents volunteer their partisan affiliation to caseworkers in hopes of swaying them, such expressions of political loyalties are discounted. "It seems that everyone who writes us is a Democrat," commented the aide to a House Democrat, "and has voted for us every year since the fall of Rome." If partisan discrimination existed, one might expect to find it in the area of federal projects: a congressman might try to reward or punish a town or county in his district or state for its electoral behavior. But that really is implausible. No congressman can afford to run the risk of alienating part of his constituency by treating it less favorably than another part—or even of being accused of doing so. One ex-representative, a moderate midwestern Democrat, described how he had gone out of his way to help obtain a $3 million grant for the staunchest Republican county in his district—one that had voted against him four times.

Several reasons explain the low incidence of political favoritism. The first is that a member may not receive requests for special favors. Said a Republican congressman: "The kinds of friends I have just wouldn't ask for special favors, and my district was such that neither would most important people." One caseworker indicated that, while friends might get better treatment, in the long run there is little benefit from giving it to them: "Yeah, they'll get more polite treatment. Rather than write, I'll call the constituent. Normally friends don't write for help. But it seems that when they do, we fail to get them what they want. It's an irony of sorts. The friends we can't help, but they stay friends. Totally unknown constituents write, we help them, and we succeed—but they never say thanks."

A second reason for the lack of special treatment is that caseworkers seldom are able to recognize the names of prominent constituents and are strongly inclined to discount claims of special status. "I wouldn't know one of the party leaders if he hit me over the head with a billboard," one caseworker pronounced. "Everyone claims to be the congressman's friend," added another. One aide pointed out a general tendency of constituents to claim to be big contributors. "There's this one constituent," a House caseworker related, "who calls often for favors and reminds us of his financial support. It turned out that he contributed five dollars once. When people remind us that they're contributors, we are alert that there's something big coming down the line." It is likely that when casework is done in Washington by aides not familiar with district personalities, chances of favoring local VIPs are reduced. Conversely, decentralized and poorly supervised casework operations allow for greater freedom on the part of the staff. However, when tested, no differences in tendencies to admit to favoritism or to push cases more vigorously for friends or prominent constituents existed between aides on Capitol Hill and those back home.

Third, there is in many offices a strong ethical stand against playing favorites, and the members want to keep casework nonpolitical. "I won't tolerate favoritism in my office," said a midwestern Republican. "No," emphasized an aide; "if anything, he opposes special treatment for friends. He's very careful not to show favoritism." Members know that laws prohibit accepting payment for services rendered, and most know that Congress has issued rules and advisory opinions against preferential treatment. In 1970, for example, the House Standards of Official Conduct Committee enunciated a set of principles explicitly recognizing the right of representatives to contact agencies on behalf of constituents, but insisting that:

1. A Member's responsibility in this area is to all his constituents equally and should be pursued with diligence irrespective of political or other considerations. . . .

2. A member should make every effort to assure that representations made in his name by any staff employee conform to his instruction.[9]

The committee also advised that "direct or implied suggestion of either favoritism or reprisal in advance of, or subsequent to, action by the agency contacted is unwarranted abuse of the representative's role."

The fear of being accused of illegal or unethical conduct in today's political atmosphere is a potent deterrent. "It would be political suicide," said a western senator. "It's likely to get you in trouble," added a House aide; "besides, it would be wrong." The fear of being accused reaches its zenith on legal or quasi-legal matters, such as judicial proceedings or decisionmaking by independent regulatory commissions or government appeals boards. "We stay as far away from those as we can," remarked one staffer.

A fourth reason is that a reputation for preferential treatment would trigger a flood of "special" pleas. Every constituent would seek favorable treatment on some pretense or another. Finally, there is the increased professionalization and institutionalization of casework. Staffers take a good deal of pride in their work and do not want *their* reputations tarnished by allegations of preferential treatment. Said one caseworker: "We've always had a good reputation of serving everyone. None of us would ever yield to someone's claim to be close to the congressman. We've had no orders from above on whom to favor. If anything, anyone giving us a hard time and claiming special privilege — we would resent it." A veteran House staffer admitted that some congressmen might be inclined to do more for certain constituents, but her response typified the importance of the caseworkers' growing professionalism: "Oh, I'd think he'd [the member] *like* to expedite and push cases for his friends, but we restrain him." Asked if she favors anyone, another House aide replied that "I don't really, but I sometimes let them think they're getting extra special attention."

Unfortunately, there is no clear way to test the hypothesis linking growing professionalism, independence, and institutionalization with a decrease in casework politicization and favoritism. The data gathered on casework attitudes and behavior indicate weakly negative relationships between the age and experience of Washington staffs and their propensity to admit to favoritism. Younger and better-educated staff members (who tend to be more "political" and see casework as a nuisance) do tend slightly more than others to admit giving preferential treatment. And aides indicating the greatest degree of autonomy within their offices are less apt to admit playing favorites.

There is another kind of favoritism that has not been the object of any complaints, but nonetheless certainly is worth noting for what it says about the process and the participants. When some cases are pushed harder than others, the reason usually has less to do with whose case it is than with the sort of case. Indeed, probably the greatest single cause of "unfair" or unequal treatment is the degree to which the caseworker—or member—perceives a case to be important, interesting, or unusual. Staffers are free, within constraints imposed by the need to serve constituents promptly, to set priorities. As one House aide confessed: "It depends if I get fired up. My background in drug and alcohol policy gets me going on some cases. Or maybe the constituent does. For example, some grant applications get us fired up to work harder for them, especially behind the scenes." Another admitted: "Some constituents have the ability to make you want to do everything you can for them, and others are very demanding and inadvertently turn the caseworker off." One House staffer explained that she was prejudiced against people with weak cases. But: "You have to watch your biases. I may try harder to compensate for my own lack of charity by working harder on cases I don't believe in. Priorities? It depends on how it plays on your heartstrings. Tearjerkers go to the top."

6.2. Success in Casework

To what extent is casework inequitable because administrators cave in to congressional pressures or favor certain congressmen over others? How influential, in general, is Congress in persuading agencies to alter or reverse decisions previously made? In short, what accounts for success? And whatever the secret is—is it fair? Before examining the equity question, an overall view of casework success is in order.

Based on questionnaires and interviews asking 14 congressmen and 254 staffers what proportion of cases result in reversals of or changes in prior agency decisions, it appears that approximately 40 percent of all cases in 1977–78—using the rather narrow definition of this study—resulted in action favorable to constituents. In 1982 that figure dropped to 28 percent among 105 aides queried.[10] The difference could be due to sampling error or to a hardening of administrative attitudes on a number of cases such as social security disability claims. The estimates double when the definition of success is broadened to include speeding up decisions and/or getting clear explanations of denials. (These figures are estimates from individual respondents and reflect judgments primarily about individual and group cases; relatively few concern federal projects. Obviously, these numbers could be inflated and self-serving.) Four points deserve brief mention. First, even discounting somewhat the reported level of victories, it appears that congressional staffs may be more successful than are state legislators or European ombudsmen.[11] Second, although no comparably systematic survey was undertaken to obtain estimates from executive branch personnel, interviews downtown produced lower estimates of casework success. Third, estimates varied according to the type of case. Routine requests for exemptions from clear statutory provisions (such as social security) yield low success ratios. Finally, different groups of congressional respondents provided different estimates. Administrative assistants in the House provided the lowest estimates (28 percent), while current and former representatives offered the highest (48 percent).[12] Overall, Senate and House staffers offered very similar estimates, but there was a substantial difference between figures provided by staffs in Washington (33 percent) and those in home offices (43 percent).

Assuming that the reported success rates reflect more than mere wishful thinking or at least that the estimates were uniformly inflated by all respondents, the obvious question is: to what can these levels of success be attributed? A simple model of success can be constructed, composed of the inherent merit of the case; caseworker's age, location, and skills (with the latter measured by versatility in contacting executive agencies—i.e., whether the caseworker relied on only one contact point, such as a liaison office, or regularly used various contacts); and member seniority and party. Because of multicollinearity between the "home" and "age" variables, three equations are presented in table 6.1.

The quality of the cases themselves seems to be the most important factor. Indeed, when asked what factors they believed made for success, 38 percent of the staffers answered in terms of merit. "We win when we should," explained one veteran—"when the case has merit." Corroborating evidence comes from agency officials, who said they believed that constituents would have gotten what

Table 6.1: Casework Success in the House, 1977–78: A Multivariate Model

Independent Variables	(1) B [Beta]	(2) B [Beta]	(3) B [Beta]
Percent cases lacking merit	−.260** [−.202]	−.268** [−.208]	−.248** [−.193]
Caseworker age	.455** [.210]	.592*** [.278]	——
Caseworker versatility[a]	5.390 [.119]	4.761 [.105]	6.965** [.153]
Member seniority	−.452 [−.145]	−.607** [−.194]	−.166 [−.053]
Member party (Democrat)	−2.903 [−.059]	−2.099 [−.043]	−5.163 [−.105]
Respondent location (home office)	7.299* [.153]	——	10.614*** [.227]
(N)	(106)	(106)	(139)
R-squared	.18	.16	.15
Adj. R-squared	.12	.12	.11

NOTE: Standardized regression coefficients in brackets: * $p < .10$; **$p < .05$; ** $p < .01$.

[a] Those who use more than one executive point of contact.

was due them, even without congressional intervention. The solution merely took time, or, perhaps, a second look at the problem. As one Agriculture Department official put it, "Sure, cases are reversed, but 75 percent of the time we would have done so ourselves if we'd known about the problem." Indeed, many times the decision on behalf of the constituent was already in the pipeline. A Social Security official added that "the constituent gets our answer, routinely arrived at, and thinks that the congressman did it."

Most administrators admit that mistakes are made and that inquiries from Congress can inadvertently point them in the right direction. But, they insist, changes are not made and decisions are not overruled *because* of congressional intervention. A Federal Energy Administration (now Energy Department) liaison specialist elaborated: "Yes, but only due to a faulty interpretation of a rule by one of our people in the first place. For example, we had a case of a typical little guy in the propane gas business who was threatened with a million dollar fine for over-charging. So he got his senator into the case. That led us to ask for an independent audit or a second look by our auditor's superior. The senator asked me personally to attend the meeting, which produced a $200 fine. The original fine was a screw-up caused by some personality friction.''

Some interventions by congressional offices, while not technically reversing earlier rulings, end up providing constituents with greater benefits than they or their congressmen had hoped for. According to a VA liaison: ''We have frequent victories for congressmen. We often physically review a case here to see if some-one in the agency goofed up. And more—often in checking out one claimed benefit [that was denied] we have discovered even more for the constituent.''

Caseworker traits prove important. Age and location independently affect reported success levels, with the importance of either increased in the absence of the other. Strangely, caseworker experience, education, and self-assessed knowledge of the constituency are unrelated to success. The coefficient for case-worker versatility is positive in each model and statistically significant when age is removed.

As would be expected from the discussion in chapter 4, a number of congress-men and caseworkers, moreover, were convinced that their skills do matter. Fully one-third answering the question on the sources of success cited casework-er attributes. According to one administrative assistant: ''Some caseworkers have a special rapport and have made connections with people in the bureaucra-cy. Some are especially adroit and skillful; they really put the 'fear of God' into agency people. Sure, some 'lucky' caseworkers are extra successful.''

It makes sense that staffers who do their homework and have nurtured contacts in departments and agencies can do a better job of explaining to executive of-ficials what it is they are seeking and why the request is reasonable. They prob-ably are more persuasive in borderline instances when their bureaucratic counter-parts have discretion. And those who go out of their way for their clients—such as the one who was described by her boss as ''literally walking constituents through the local unemployment office''—ought to fare better.

There was some dispute about whether women fare better than men. Several female aides agreed with the one who claimed that ''sweetness matters a lot, especially with the VA and military, because most of that is done over the phone. There's a big advantage in being a woman.'' Other women emphatically dis-agreed. ''Ridiculous,'' answered one; ''if anything, I have to work harder be-cause I'm a woman.'' Yet another directly contradicted an earlier respondent: ''No question about it; men are better with VA and military cases.'' Perhaps the key distinction here is between success in dealing with constituents and effectiveness in working with agencies: "Sometimes yes, sometimes no, in dealing with constituents. Men want to talk to men. As far as the agencies are concerned, there's no difference."

What of the members themselves? According to a senior Republican, "Sure you have clout, but you don't have to use it; a senior person can get results where a junior member couldn't." The analysis in the table, however, fails to support his view. (Note, however, that the only statistically significant coefficient for member seniority occurs when location of the respondent is omitted. The bulk of the staffers studied were in field offices, not Washington, and it is junior members who put them there.) Perhaps the comments of a former two-term congressman seem appropriate: "On regular cases, I don't believe there would be a big difference in how an agency would act if it were Tip O'Neill calling or if I called—how could they move faster than forty-eight hours?"

That home-based staffs should report greater success rates in the late 1970s is not puzzling. One explanation might be that such aides simply estimated on the high side due to misperceptions or excessive optimism. In fact, they did seem less cynical than their colleagues in Washington. Alternatively, home offices may have dealt more often with noncontroversial cases than did Capitol Hill offices, sending the sensitive and tough ones to Washington. Finally, such aides just might have been better at their tasks than their Washington colleagues. It is generally conceded that home-based staff are more oriented toward constituency work, and certainly the pace of the job in field offices is less frantic than in Washington, allowing them more time to concentrate on their work. Home-based staffers who do case and project work tend to be older and better educated, and they profess to know their states and districts better than staffers located on the Hill. Moreover, it is highly likely that they would become well acquainted with local and perhaps regional administrators, nurturing the contacts deemed essential for productive casework. By 1982, however, there was no difference in reported success rates between Washington and district aides. Perhaps this change from five years earlier is attributable to the increased devolution of casework duties—including tough cases—onto home staffs and the increased bureaucratization, at home and on the Hill, of casework operations.

Lastly, party affiliation appears to explain nothing. If anything, Republicans fared better than Democrats in achieving high success rates under the early years of the Carter administration. This is surprising, since two-fifths of the congressmen and fully half of the staffers in the sample believed that casework cooperation (which might be different from success) varied with the political party of the administration. On the other hand, a number of senior Republican offices believed that they were getting better cooperation from the Carter people than they had from the previous two Republican administrations. Everyone praised the

Reagan administration. In all likelihood, the chances for serious, systematic discrimination or special privileges on partisan bases — except in such matters as informing the offices of fellow partisans or friendly members first on grant announcements for their districts or states — are relatively slim. Even if some agency leaders were to decide to give certain members better or worse treatment, it is far from clear that their regional and area offices would follow instructions, especially where they had worked out amicable relations with local congressional staffs.

6.3. Congressional Influence on Cases and Projects

The lack of positive relationships between member characteristics and casework success is striking. Assuming that these results are real and do not merely reflect greater modesty among aides to senior Democrats — which certainly is possible — and in the face of intuitive speculation and much conventional wisdom to the contrary, the matter deserves further examination. Two basic questions arise. First, are congressional offices able to make a difference in determining the outcome of cases and projects independent of their inherent merit? Second, if party, seniority, and general leadership status of senators and representatives do not seem to matter, which member characteristics do?

The key distinction concerning the impact Congress has on cases is that between substantive and procedural effects. Virtually all members and staffers agreed that three very real results of congressional involvement with the bureaucracy were (1) that constituents' problems were looked at more carefully; (2) that they received attention at higher levels of the agencies; and (3) that communications from departments and agencies were forthcoming much more quickly than if the constituents had persisted on their own in seeking redress. As one Small Business Administration official said, ''I'd be a liar if I said that when a call comes in we didn't give the case a little more of a 'look-see.' '' Previous studies, relying largely on impressionistic evidence, have reached the same conclusion with a unanimity rarely achieved in social science or journalistic research.[13] The only investigation based on an examination of agency records corroborated these findings. Final response times in six of seven government agencies that deal with consumer complaints were shorter for congressional inquiries than for those originating with citizen-consumers; and in three of five cases, response time was shorter for congressional than for White House – originated complaints.[14]

There are, however, a good number of exceptions, rooted either in the bureaucratic imperative of following standard operating procedures or in a broader norm of equity. One SBA administrator, for example, insisted: "When congressionals come in we do *not* speed up the action as a result of the inquiry. I ask the loan officer when he's going to get at the application; he tells me; and I forward that information to the congressman." A Labor Department official, having explained that a letter of acknowledgment goes out immediately for each congressional received, agreed: "Our responses to congressionals do not cause us to address the complaint of the congressman's constituent out of the order received. Each complaint or person who seeks service from this agency is just as entitled to service as the next person. We will not service the complaint of a person who contacts his congressional representative any quicker than we will one who does not contact his representative. Conversely, we won't delay service to anyone who does contact the congressman." The remarks of other bureaucrats suggest that it is not always the congressional contact or appeal per se that moves a case along but rather the fact of *any* serious appeal, contact, or "harassment." According to a local HUD office chief, "No—congressionals don't move a case. When we get a congressional, or any inquiry from a group or a citizen, we pull the file and take a look." These views ought not to be dismissed out of hand; several congressional staffers shared them completely.

Many executive units appear to be selective, moving quickly only on those congressional inquiries revealing genuine need or signaling an emergency. The contact from Congress focuses attention on the case, leading to a decision to deal with it at once or return it to the pile. Said a Passport Office executive: "Congressionals do raise an individual's case to the top of the pile so that an answer can be gotten back to the congressman. Then a decision is made on the urgency and the merit of the case. If it truly is an emergency, or if it's terribly worthwhile, the case will go into the priority pile." Similar comments were heard from immigration officials in several locations, one of whom was very explicit in explaining that his office once routinely put congressionals on top of the pile but has since stopped doing so unless the case is especially urgent. In short, what seems to be happening is that congressionals are processed more quickly, but: (1) in some instances it is the substance of the case alone that triggers the speed; (2) some personnel either ignore the congressional interest or consider it to be only a warning sign and an occasion—not a mandate—for swift action; and (3) the willingness to respond rapidly to congressional "commands" varies among and within agencies.

Congressional influence of a substantive nature is much more difficult to document or dismiss. Undoubtedly there are occasions in which congressional inquiries coupled with "pressure" do lead to reversals of decisions or the awarding of grants. The problems come in assessing whether or not those reversals or decisions were justified on the merits and would have occurred anyway, and in ascertaining how often such exceptions occur.

As noted in the previous chapter, congressional offices rarely ask for decisions that are not warranted. And when they do, executive administrators are not inclined to accommodate their requests. Norms of equity and universalism, not to mention potentially adverse legal and political consequences, forbid it. More important, far too many government programs are governed by rigid formulas and eligibility criteria to allow for wholesale, retail, or anything more than occasional congressional influence.[15] A number of administrators commented on how the process works:

Look, congressmen can't affect the way we make [project] allocations. There are economic formulas for everything we do. If housing projects are ranked 1, 2, 3, and so on, that's the way we fund them. You can't go 1, 2, 5, 7, 3 just because some congressman wants it. But, then, they don't ask us for such favoritism, either.

Outside pressure is not important. Congressmen are interested and will call frequently on big projects, but I've yet to see a case where political pressure mattered.

Politically it would be disastrous to be perceived as being political in giving grants. It's not congressmen but peer review groups that cause the funding. Congressmen have a right to have answers to letters quickly. They ask for meetings on behalf of constituents who want to talk about a grant or project—that's all they're asking. But no one gets anything more than a meeting.

We do keep a computer profile of how much money goes to each state and district. And we notify all congressmen of grants. We try to insulate politics from programs. We prefer to handle everything here [in the liaison office] to keep politics out of it. The Richardson rule is followed: keep congressmen's inquiries in *their* files, not in the grant files.

That there are exceptions, however, was indicated by the administrator just quoted. After a detailed explanation of why political influence never mattered, he rolled his eyes, grinned, and held up two fingers about a half-inch apart, indicating some leeway.

In an attempt to measure at least the frequency of congressional intervention, the administrators who were asked whether congressional offices had urged them to violate a law or an agency regulation, or to bend or stretch rules or make exceptions (see the previous chapter), were also asked: "Have you or your office ever done any of these things?" Although some discount has to be applied, owing to normal hesitancy to respond candidly (a hesitancy reduced by the anonymous nature of the mail questionnaires, however), only 2 of the 161 respondents admitted to having broken a law and 3 to having violated departmental or agency rules. Fourteen said that they had bent or stretched regulations, with 12 of the 14 adding "almost never" or "occasionally." Fifteen administrators said that they had made exceptions. Altogether, about one in five indicated that they had at least once taken one or more of these actions. But a good portion of these concerned extensions of time, delays, and the like—actions more of a procedural than substantive nature; and in 10 percent of the cases the frequency of action was "almost never."

Contrary to the impressions held by congressional staffers, there is no evidence that their substantive influence is greater on lower-level than higher-level administrators. It probably is true, however, that local or area office officials, especially in small offices, jump a bit faster when contacted by congressional offices.

Executives who admitted to having taken these actions offered several mitigating circumstances. Fully 43 percent said that they had the discretionary authority to make exceptions or pointed out the inherent merit of cases within the *spirit,* if not the letter, of the law or agency regulation. Another 14 percent spoke explicitly of the seriousness or urgency of the case. The following comments are typical:

Depending on the situation, we have bent rules. Usually our problems are interpretations and management discretion. We try to live within the spirit, if not the rigidity, of the law.

We will break a rule—rarely. It usually is a situation that if we made a strict interpretation of our rules, the result would be grossly unfair or there are mitigating circumstances.

Do we make exceptions? Sure. There was this little old lady who lived in the heart of a wilderness area, and her permit expired, meaning that she had to leave. So she wrote to her congressman, who contacted us and asked us to give her a lifelong permit. We should have done that in the first place.

Four administrators said that they had broken or stretched regulations for "political" reasons, or to placate irate congressmen and get them and their aides off their backs. But even then they hedged. As a military liaison chief put it: "Sometimes a congressman needs a win—but only in a close call or borderline case do I recommend that it be decided in favor of the congressman against our rules." Administrators sometimes remind congressmen that they can only make exceptions a few times and that granting a favor now precludes one in the future. Few congressmen press the matter further.

The standard tactic of administrators confronted by requests for dubious action is to refer the matter to higher authorities. A military liaison official elaborated:

Yes, they ask for exceptions, stretching, and even outright violations. But it comes in under 10 percent of the cases. We don't do it very often. For example, we'll send our chief of personnel to sit down with a congressman to talk about a case. We're willing to initiate a modification of our rules and regs—but not in this one case only. If the congressman still wants an exception made, he is free to go above my head—above the uniformed service level—to the assistant secretary or secretary to reverse our decision. But I won't. Maybe three times in the last two years it's happened.

One rather cantankerous Small Business Administration official described how he handled attempts to dictate results: "When they ask me to violate a law or regulation, I send the case to the regional office, which often leads to meetings. I recall one meeting in a congressman's office when the congressman gave an order to my superior's superior which was contrary to our rules and to my ethics. The [higher-ranking official] had to order my boss to do it because I refused. Then later, the congressman backed off and reversed his position."

Since administrators regularly buck "tough" or politically sensitive cases to higher levels, it is possible that political influence would appear, not in the actions taken by lower-level bureaucrats, but rather in decisions taken by their superiors. Such officials either could order the lower-level administrators to make certain decisions or could themselves overturn their subordinates' decisions. Indeed, five respondents admitting to having broken, bent, or made exceptions to laws or regulations claimed to have done so because of pressure from superiors triggered by congressional intervention. A local SBA administrator claimed that "there's no pressure at this end, but I know that the SBA Administrator in Washington has overruled us due to pressure from Congress." According to a Passport Office bureaucrat, "Congressional interest in certain cases prompts the Department of State in Washington to bring great pressure on its representatives to make decisions in favor of the inquiries whenever possible, often to the extent of stretching the laws."

Agency officials were asked to estimate the percentage of cases and federal projects on which decisions made at their level had been overturned or modified at higher levels as a result of "pressure" from Congress. Of 168 respondents, over 54 percent answered "none" or "never," with another 15 percent indicating that such occurrences were extremely rare ("an infinitesimal percentage," "once in my memory," or "almost never"). Fourteen percent guessed that 1 percent had been overturned. Only 10 administrators claimed that 10 percent or more of cases had been reversed. The median response was under 0.5 percent.

Obviously, congressional intervention sometimes does lead to reversals, but even in such instances the process tends to be complicated, as this account from an Agriculture Department official illustrates:

Our field representative turned down a loan. The guy went to his congressman, who raised hell. I examined the case and agreed that the facts did not warrant the loan. He called his congressman again, who went to the assistant secretary, who called the FmHA head in Washington. He contacted us and asked why we wouldn't give the loan. We prepared a thick file to document our refusal, and it was so good that it persuaded the Washington office that we were right. The FmHA Director and his staff went to a meeting with the assistant secretary and persuaded him that we were correct. Just then the assistant secretary's staff guy came in and said that we had to give the loan because he had committed the Department.

This decision became a matter of keeping a pledge that should not — and normally would not — have been given by a middle-level official without his superior's permission.

Thus there is some evidence in support of the congressional influence thesis, but it is weak. Congressional ''clout'' seems to affect high-level (projects) casework much more than individual-level casework, but even at the higher level intervention seems to occur infrequently. When agencies do bend to congressional will, giving the benefit of the doubt to constituents on whose behalf the congressional offices have interceded, the decisions to do so are taken by relatively high-level officials, usually in Washington. And it is not necessarily true that ''pressure'' was at work. But the argument for unfair congressional influence requires greater specification. Influence is likely to vary according to the member's position vis à vis the agency and to the intensity of his or her involvement.

Could it be that when senators or representatives personally make the calls or the visits an increment of influence is added to that which might be held by their staffs? Again, solid evidence is not available. Interviews with congressional personnel produce an almost unbelievable concensus that congressmen's personal actions, while speeding up the process at times, have little substantive effect independent of the merit of the cases and of what the caseworkers could achieve on their own. As one well-known former Republican senator put it: ''It doesn't take influence so much as time and merit; when you have those and can make your case, you are successful — otherwise not.'' Said the chairman of a prestigious and powerful House committee: ''Heck, if some bureaucrat knows the situation and has all the facts, and if he changed a decision just because of a phone call from me, I'd want him fired.'' A former Democratic member from the midwest described his clout as a mixture of the merit of the case, the amount of discretion held by the administrator, sound staff work, and his willingness to become seriously involved.

It depends on the parameters. If the bureaucrat is up against the wall and has no discretion, we won't have any luck. But a hard-working congressman, picking up the phone himself, ought to be able to move the average bureaucrat to the limits of his discretion. If you know what you're doing and have your facts straight, and your staff person is there with you, you can get results. For example, you can call the agency and say to the bureaucrat: ''Don't you have ten more days for this decision? Why don't you hold off and give the constituent the extra time?'' Sometimes the bureaucrat will say, ''I'd like to help you but I can't.'' So I ask what if I can call the secretary, and he'll say, ''Sure, go ahead, but I doubt if even he can help.''

In a comment similar to many others that distinguished between cases and at least certain kinds of federal projects, one member explained the nature of congressional influence as he saw it:

On projects, the congressman can be crucial. He needs to push the agency and get them out to see the situation firsthand. When I took the people from EDA to my district and showed them what an EDA grant could do, they said that they could really appreciate the need. It's so much better than just reading the grant application forms, which are so cold. The congressman can give proof or validity to the grant application by getting the agency to see the reality of it. The more the agency knows of the situation and the impact of a grant on the local level, the more they'll be aware—and the better the chances for funding.

What matters even more, probably, is the congressman's ability to stimulate sound grant applications. The member just quoted took great pride in the fact that during his term in office, his district received over twenty times more federal funding than during the last term of his predecessor. But he also explained how he and his staff grantsman ''hustled'' local governments to apply for any and all possible projects. The real question is whether the spectacular results reported by the member were due to his ability to impress agency officials or simply to the fact that his district dramatically stepped up the number of its applications. Again the query: do congressmen have influence? If so, what is it composed of? The safe bet is that most of its content can be reduced to diligence and skill in bringing meritorious cases and projects to the fore.

When a member takes action personally, it is not always to apply pressure.

Usually the goal is to impress on an administrator that the matter is, in fact, important. As one official put it: ''Some congressmen are more personally involved than others, but most of them do so fairly. George Mahon, for example, will call on a case but will say, 'I don't want anything I'm not entitled to, but take a good second look for me.''' An Agriculture Department official elaborated: ''When members do get involved, they just want to know that due process has been given—that all the facts supporting decisions have been examined. Usually the congressman doesn't know what it's all about—doesn't understand the legal problems and questions. They just want due process.''

According to executive officials, personal intervention by members does have effects. Administrators were asked whether it matters, in terms of how a congressional inquiry is handled, if the senator or representative personally makes the contact with their offices. They also were asked what sort of difference it made and were offered three choices: an effect on the substantive disposition of the case, an effect on the speed with which it was handled, and an open-ended ''other'' choice. Only 4 percent of the 205 total responses indicated *substantive* effects. Fifty-four percent said that personal intervention made or would make no difference at all! For the most part, this is because almost any inquiry from a congressional office *already* has received top priority, and having the member call could not move it along any faster. Said one INS administrator: ''No, just because the congressman calls doesn't mean we can move any faster in reviewing a case than we do when the caseworker calls. It just can't be done.'' One-third said that they would act more rapidly. Two percent indicated that the level at which the case was handled would be changed. One administrator mentioned that ''when the senator or congressman gets into a case, they don't call us. They call upstairs—we find out later. When that happens, we have to clear our responses through the assistant secretary's office.'' Several volunteered that when congressmen become personally interested, cases are handled more carefully. ''If the congressman personally calls,'' a military liaison officer pointed out, ''it tells me that he's interested. We may go over there and explain personally.'' Reply letters to such calls normally contain more elaboration.

If congressmen generally have little substantive influence over cases and only a bit more when it comes to the awarding of projects and grants, and if member seniority, general leadership status, and party seem not to matter, there remains the possibility that congressional influence is much more specific. Certainly the literature on pork-barrel politics suggests that members of the authorizing committees and Appropriations Committee subcommittees having jurisdiction over specific agencies seem to benefit most from the distribution of projects, contracts, and military bases by those agencies.[16]

However, as R. Douglas Arnold has pointed out, the situation is not quite so simple.[17] Previous studies of committee-related benefits have produced mixed results, sometimes indicating that committee members do not benefit disproportionately. Further, the studies do not clearly demonstrate whether congressmen seek committee assignments because their districts are already receiving benefits; whether congressmen's presence on key committees brings them clout to be used in "persuading" executive agencies under the committee jurisdiction to allocate projects and funding to their districts; whether bureaucrats fear the potential power of such congressmen and, according to the "law of anticipated reactions," provide disproportionate benefits without having to be asked or forced to do so; or whether the bureaucrats are in control, rewarding key members of Congress for past behavior favorable to the agencies, punishing others for infidelity and nonsupport, and enticing still others to join pro-agency coalitions in the future. In other words, congressmen may be "protectors," "promoters and traders," "invisible forces," or mere victims of bureaucratic power. Arnold's study of military base openings and closings, and water, sewer, and model cities grants concluded that bureaucrats reward key members of their supporting coalitions and consider their preferences when appropriate. Usually such congressmen are key committee and subcommittee members, but not always. Thus juniors and seniors, conservatives and liberals, and Republicans as well as Democrats could benefit disproportionately. Moreover, the allocation of government funds varies greatly by program, and some agencies have more discretion than others. As suggested earlier, many deliberately strive to separate politics from policy and program administration, including the awarding of grants.

The data on individual success rates cannot be used to test whether key congressmen receive better treatment from agencies over which their committees or subcommittees have jurisdiction. But several other survey and interview questions did explore that possibility. The first asked a subsample of congressmen and staffers: "How important, in achieving favorable decisions for constituents, is the identity and position in Congress of the Congressman? For example, does it help if he chairs a subcommittee or is a member of a key committee?" Of 150 who responded, 56 percent said "yes"; 9 percent answered "sometimes"; and 5 percent replied affirmatively for projects but not for cases. Aides to committee chairs (86 percent), followed by staffers working for subcommittee leaders (76 percent), were significantly more likely to respond affirmatively than were backbenchers' caseworkers (48 percent). Comments that "committee membership is extremely critical" seemed to come most frequently from offices of members heavily involved in military cases. But interviews suggest that most caseworkers were responding in terms not of the substantive effects but of procedural impact: speeding up cases, getting them answered more carefully, and so on.

Administrators were asked whether the identity of the senator or representative whose office is making the inquiry affects how, where, or how rapidly the inquiry is handled. And if so, what sorts of members would receive "better treatment"? Over three-quarters answered that it did not make any difference; 3 percent said it sometimes would; and 21 percent said that it did or would matter. Respondents who had formerly served on the Hill, those specializing in liaison work, and those with considerable experience in handling "congressionals" were substantially and significantly more likely to indicate that a congressman's identity did or would matter. Naturally, these are precisely the types who are more sensitive to the political ramifications of casework. Supporting Arnold's findings that members who are important to the bureaucracy in question are more likely to benefit from its largesse, 40 percent of all replies cited committee or subcommittee chairmen as likely to receive special treatment; 20 percent mentioned members of key committees; 10 percent pointed to congressmen and senators in whose districts or states their agency offices were located; 7 percent thought that favors would be extended to members who had expressed continuing interest in their agencies' programs; and 6 percent cited party leaders. Another 10 percent answered in terms of members or staffs who were particularly polite or knowledgeable about their program.

Again the important question is: what, precisely, are the benefits associated with being one of the congressmen for whom agencies are particularly solicitous? Asked to specify among the several choices offered, forty-one of the seventy-eight respondents said that for such members, the inquiries would be handled faster, and twenty-two indicated that their cases would be dealt with by higher-ranking officials. Another dozen cited generally better attention and more concern for detail. Only three indicated that inquiries from these key members were more likely to receive *substantively* different, or more favorable, decisions. As one Justice Department official explained: "We'll handle inquiries faster and keep closer touch with congressmen who are concerned or have close influence over our programs. Yes, our ears are perked up by them. There's a little pink slip for important referrals." Said an Agriculture Department executive: "When we get one from Whitten or Foley or Talmadge, we do notice and we handle it more carefully; but it wouldn't affect the quality of the decision." Added a VA official: "We're aware of who the member is. If you're going to flub up, don't do it for a member of the Appropriations Committee." And a Labor Department official described how he handles these situations: "We recognize the names of Williams and Perkins. Sometimes I remind the people downstairs that those guys up on the Hill run this department, not us. When their offices call, we respond. I'll call back before going to lunch, not after. We merely handle the case quicker. It still should be decided on its merits, but as soon as possible. On grants, we'll notify these congressmen extra quick; but we don't want to affect the application in any way.'' Favoring fellow partisans, important committee members, or, as a Transportation Department liaison person put it, ''the most interested member of the state delegation'' on grant announcements is, of course, traditional.[18] Just a little advance notice, he said, went to the Senate majority leader or the Speaker of the House.

Several administrators themselves confessed, or feigned, surprise at the relatively low level of political influence. An HEW liaison officer explained that: ''Favoritism to committee and subcommittee chairmen is not as blatant as I expected. It's pretty ethical. I haven't seen one grant that went to a congressman because of who he is. Maybe if it's a tie, or if the other congressman got one last time, maybe this time the other guy will get it. We really do try to insulate politics from programs and grants. But, sure, for the bigwigs, we try to be responsive—faster—get their letters to the top of the pile. It's faster, procedural.''

There were a handful of rather strong denials, indicating that whatever influence does exist, it does not prevail across the board. A Commerce Department liaison person provided this view: ''No: it depends on how much time I've got. I prefer to deal with amicable aides regardless of who they work for. We like to let committee members *think* that we put their inquiries on top of the pile, but I deal first with those from people I like.'' Said another liaison chief: ''Committee members are more demanding—so I do less.'' A military officer thought that ''we probably bend over backwards for critics of the [service] and for those who have hypersensitive caseworkers.''

The picture that emerges certainly is not one of special substantive influence on cases for key congressmen, but it does provide evidence that they are serviced faster, more carefully, and more deferentially than are others. However, even this degree of preference is limited. Several caseworkers for members sitting on the Education and Labor Committee of the House complained as bitterly as anyone about the ''shabby'' treatment they received from the Labor Department. A half-dozen staffers offered a surprising explanation for this apparent paradox. ''In theory,'' said one, ''agencies do respond better to members of their oversight committee; but lots of people downtown don't know who the congressional 'biggies' are.'' Said another: ''I'm amazed that the bureaucrats in the Labor Department don't even know that [my boss] is on the Labor/HEW Appropriations Subcommittee.''

Since the relationship between caseworkers and their executive contacts often is so personalized, it is not surprising that some liaison officials favor certain congressional aides. What was surprising was that in three or four offices, caseworkers insisted that because their congressmen or senators were famous and popular, they received better treatment. "They all love Senator ———," said one administrative assistant. "They fall all over us when we call." "The congresswoman is a hero to lots of bureaucrats because of her role in ———. When we call, they can't wait to help. It makes my job lots easier."

Although some members are served more expeditiously and perhaps given the benefit of the doubt more often than others, the question of precisely *why* that occurs still cannot be answered. In addition to the obvious reason—that the member has power and can help or do damage to an agency—two more subtle and complex ones emerged from interviews. First, certain congressmen and senators, *because* of their committee positions, receive more cases of a particular type, which increases the "traffic" back and forth to the agency, which in turn may solidify and routinize relationships—leading to better service overall. Second, access to or control over committee staff, coupled sometimes with the use of committee staff members to handle cases and projects, leads to more intelligent and more informed casework. Questions are better, weak cases are filtered out, and so on. A House staffer and an agency administrator provided complementary explanations of how the process works:

I get better service because [the congressman is] such a nice guy, but also because of his support for the military. We get some better service from agencies under the jurisdiction of his subcommittee . . . because we know these people and have for years: we deal with them constantly.

The Chairman of the House Subcommittee on ——— is in my District. It is much easier to deal with him than with other congressmen and senators because he knows the law and operations of our agency. Therefore, the cases he calls about are generally better screened, and eligibility for the benefit sought is established. For this reason, it is easier to work cases he has expressed an interest in because his staff has already done the preliminary work and has all the required information available to us. It may appear that cases he has expressed an interest in are given priority over other congressional office interests because there is generally quicker action on his cases. The quicker action, whether approval or denial, is really the result of better documentation rather than us giving his cases preferential treatment.

6.4. Can Congressional Intervention Backfire?

There is another aspect of equity that requires attention: the possibility that casework intervention might actually hurt, rather than help, the constituent. "I think that sending a case to us, and our sending it to the Civil Service Commission,'' said one House staffer, ''actually slows down the process. When a person wants to have a civil service rating expedited, I tell them to go to the agency, not us.'' Agency personnel corroborate these experiences. According to an INS official: ''The net effect on cases is to expedite them; it takes the case out of the pile. But many times it works just the opposite. A case may be ready for a decision next week; but by taking it out of the lineup in order to respond to a congressional, the case gets delayed for several weeks.'' Especially in situations where a government payment is involved, a check may be delayed when a case is pulled out of the pile. That is why so many administrators believe that constituents often would get quicker answers if they contacted the bureaucrats directly rather than through their congressmen.

A second drawback stems from a sense of resentment. ''Certain agencies on certain levels of issues,'' according to an aide to former Cong. Robert Drinan (D., Mass.), ''really resent congressional involvement, particularly on technical issues where a Member of Congress has no expertise at all.''[19] According to one administrator, ''We resent that sort of attempted intimidation.'' Worst of all may be a situation in which a congressional intervention succeeds. According to a former Republican member of the House: ''We had a lot of clout to get speedy action and an answer: but we couldn't change the substantive decisions. And it can be counterproductive. If you get Washington to override a local bureaucrat, the guy would get ticked off and you'd be in trouble next time.''

Another problem is ''bureaucratic revenge.'' The armed services, despite vigorous denials by some of their liaison officers, have a reputation for getting even. According to a Senate aide, ''I often hesitate to process a case, because I know that the poor soldier is going to catch hell from his sergeant.'' More generally, several agency people take pride in dealing slowly and negatively with cases and projects submitted by what they take to be excessively demanding or obnoxious congressmen and staffs, or by constituents who insist that their congressmen press worthless cases. Bureaucratic hearts, in other words, may be hardened, not sensitized, by congressional intervention. Said one Labor Department official: ''Some of our district offices become hardened to congressional inquiries. They'll tell a person, 'I don't give a damn if you write your congressman.' It's a dilemma: congressional inquiries fill a real need, but they can backfire by aggravating our field people.''

Caseworkers, too, develop negative attitudes. Several aides confessed that working on cases had made them rather cynical and distrustful, leading them to approach certain cases more skeptically and to pursue them with less enthusiasm and diligence—and therefore, perhaps, with less success.

Vigorous action without proper caution likewise can create problems for some constituents and their congressmen. As one Senate projects specialist explained: "Sometimes you've got to be really careful not to automatically write the usual letter of endorsement or set up a meeting because, if one city gets the grant, another won't—and they're in competition with each other. You've got to watch out or you'll be robbing Peter to pay Paul." An independent regulatory commission official provided basically the same story: "Sometimes a caseworker pushes a case or application too hard, trying to get a favorable decision for a constituent. Then we have to inform her that she might not be serving her boss very well because constituents B, C, and D are firmly against the decision. 'Oh, yeah?' they say, 'Thanks.' Then they back off." VA officials occasionally have to remind congressmen seeking to have a constituent admitted to a VA hospital that to do so would mean bypassing one or more of their other constituents. Even vigorous efforts on what seems to be a perfectly legitimate case can backfire. Intervening on behalf of a serviceman at the request of parents or spouse may not be welcome. For example, Cong. Jim Wright recounted the story of a congressman who discovered that a GI was having trouble getting his Japanese war bride into the United States. He dutifully went to bat for the soldier, only to receive a bitter letter from him telling the congressman to keep his nose out of the GI's business. It seems that the soldier already had a wife in the states. Eventually the soldier was court-martialed.[20] Another danger that members are aware of is falsely encouraging constituents to believe that their problems can or will be solved by their representatives. Finally, there may be a problem attendant upon helping constituents with requests from or grievances against local governments. Two students of British politics noted that local elected officials resented intrusions on their "turf" by members of the House of Commons.[21] Congressmen who too readily have their staffers handle purely local cases could run the same risk.

6.5. Summary

Casework intervention, by most accounts, is reasonably successful. Equity seldom is undermined, and the process basically is fair. Congressional offices do not discriminate for or against particular constituents, but they do work a bit harder for VIPs and friends of the congressmen. Although a measure of political clout exists, it is neither widely spread nor frequently invoked. Certain congressmen benefit disproportionately with respect to federal spending and project allocation from specific agencies because of their strategic positions, but such benefits normally do not extend to individual-level casework and are not uniform (with respect to projects) across all agencies. By and large, the nature of congressional influence over cases—and many projects—is less a matter of "clout" than of congressional diligence, caseworker skills, the inherent merit of cases, and clear communication. Whatever concrete advantages one member may enjoy over another because of his or her position are mostly procedural—not substantive. The bottom line of the success story, then, would show relatively little inordinate "influence" per se; some very small amount of substantive favoritism; and a noticeable dash of procedural favoritism, both in Congress and in the executive. Congressmen and their staffs are facilitators, not pushers. Objectively, at least, there are few grounds for believing that service responsiveness works to undermine symbolic responsiveness and institutional legitimacy.

CHAPTER 7

Casework and Policymaking

There are two schools of thought on the effects of casework on the policymaking process. One argues that this particularistic form of representation intrudes upon policy responsiveness and that casework detracts from the primary responsibilities of Congress and the executive. The other disagrees, claiming that there is no better information available on how well laws and programs are working than the feedback provided by constituent complaints and that, therefore, casework is fully compatible with, and conducive to, effective policymaking. The truth lies somewhere in between.

7.1. Congress, Casework, and Policy: The Negative View

Among the most commonly heard indictments of casework are that it wastes the precious time of congressmen and their staffs and directly interferes with the legislative and oversight functions of Congress. Donald R. Matthews years ago paraphrased a typical complaint: "If only the people would leave us alone," say senators, "we could do our job the way it ought to be done."[1] A former member bluntly called casework a "misuse of a congressman's time."

Scholars, too, believe that casework may be time-consuming and dysfunctional. Roger H. Davidson saw casework as detrimental to congressmen's legislative tasks, claiming that "it is at least arguable that ever-more-demanding *ombudsman* functions have helped to erode the legislative and institutional folkways identified by observers in the 1950s and early 1960s—especially the folkways of specialization, apprenticeship, and institutional loyalty. At the very least, it has placed demands on Members' time and energies."[2]

Some critics have gone so far as to suggest that the burden of serving constituents has contributed to the increasing delegation of congressional authority to the executive.[3] Others see casework and constituency service activities as forcing congressmen to focus inordinately on the "electoral" arena and to "get out of the business of legislating,"[4] leading some members to early retirement and discouraging competent state officials from running for the House or Senate.[5] Joseph Cooper believes that "constituency service has [transformed] members into modern versions of old-time ward politicians, [which] undermines concern with policy questions . . . and threatens the House's policy role."[6] Legislation and congressional oversight of the executive, the argument runs, suffer not only because of time pressures, but also because solving constituent problems on an ad hoc basis produces a disincentive for systematic oversight of the administrative bureaucracy.[7] Further, the casework responsibility of congressional offices leads to a misallocation of staff resources.[8]

Some of these criticisms are not susceptible to rigorous analysis. For example, although it is well documented that retirements from Congress have been increasing and have supplanted electoral defeat as the prime cause of congressional turnover, it is not clear precisely what the reasons have been. Age, political vulnerability, and political ambition are common explanations, but there can be no doubt that disaffection with congressional service in general plays a part. Members complain bitterly about the disruption of family life, the frustration of not being influential, and the inability to accomplish their goals. They grumble about the constant demands made on their time by organizations and individuals in their districts. In short, the things that directly block the achievement of their legislative goals and directly take up their own time are causes of their disaffection. But the preponderance of evidence suggests that retirees not only do not cite casework per se as the cause of their leaving Congress, but in fact seem to have fond memories of it.[9]

Similarly, the degree to which anticipated reactions to the burdens of congressional service dissuade potential candidates from seeking congressional office is unclear. The number of candidates running for congressional seats has been growing, not declining, with 41 percent more candidates running for the House in 1976 than in 1960.[10] Some races draw crowds, such as the one for an open seat in Maryland that attracted thirty-one candidates in 1981. And while challengers recognize the difficulty of overcoming the electoral advantages of incumbency that constituency service supposedly brings, they realize that such advantages would be theirs should they win.[11] The question of the extent to which casework and various other "unpleasant" duties are seen as a burden of office and thus a deterrent to tossing one's hat into the ring thus remains unanswered, but there are grounds for skepticism about the explanatory power of this hypothesis.

Participants in the casework process seem dubious of the interference thesis. Asked to agree or disagree with the proposition that casework detracts from other, more important, things that congressmen and their staffs should be doing, well over 80 percent of members, administrative assistants, and staffers in Washington and home offices disagreed, as did over half of the executive officials surveyed. Naturally, duties affect perceptions. Fully one-fourth of senators, representatives, and administrative assistants, whose major responsibilities do not encompass casework, agreed that casework is a distraction, compared to only 5 percent of the staffers located in home offices, whose everyday activity is dominated by constituency service. Moreover, disagreement was three times higher among aides in offices where casework was specialized (done by "caseworkers" only) than among those working in offices where casework was done by staffers who also handled legislative, public relations, or other duties. Occasionally a staffer took the opposite view, complaining that legislative duties interfered with the more important function of casework.

There are two specific ways in which casework might interfere with more important functions of Congress. First, it could force members themselves to devote less time to legislative and oversight duties. Second, and more important, it could force them to make less than optimal staff allocations and drain the time and energy of staff members away from Congress's basic duties. Both possibilities merit careful consideration here.

7.2. Casework and Members' Time Allocations

Before addressing the charge that casework takes up too much of congressmen's time, it is essential to examine just how much time senators and representatives in fact devote to casework, which members spend the most time, and why.

Undoubtedly, in years gone by, senators and representatives personally devoted a good deal of time to casework. Leonard D. White noted that in the nineteenth century "congressmen were more and more oppressed by constituent business." After the Civil War, "more than ever Congressmen were plagued by the necessity of performing errands for their constituents. . . . The life of a congressman was made miserable by this kind of business, but he could not escape."[12] As recently as 1946, a congressional study concluded that members spent between half and two-thirds of their time "running errands and knocking on departmental doors on behalf of constituents."[13]

A more authoritative analysis in 1965 claimed that about 28 percent of House members' time was devoted to constituency affairs, although the time specifically given to handling constituent problems was 5.9 hours per week (8.6 percent of the working day).[14] According to Dartmouth scholars, 18 of 115 representatives in the early 1960s listed casework and "errands" as their major time-consuming activity, with 67 citing them as second.[15]

In 1977 the House Commission on Administrative Review asked members of the House how much time they spent on the seventeen functions listed in table 2.1.[16] Two results are important. First, a majority of members said they spent "a great deal" or at least "some" time on thirteen of the seventeen tasks, with one-quarter or more of the congressmen spending "a great deal" of time on eight of them. On only six functions did as many as 10 percent say they spent "hardly any" time. Apparently, congressmen perceive themselves as very busy. Second, looking at the "great deal of time" responses, although the single most frequently cited activity was getting back to one's district to stay in touch with constituents (which arguably is as much a representational or educational task as it is constituency service), the second- and third-ranked functions (working in subcommittees and working in committees to develop legislation) are clearly legislative. Casework ("helping people in your district who have personal problems with the government") came fourth, with 35 percent saying it took a great deal of, and 32 percent claiming some, time. "Making sure your district gets its fair share of government money and projects" fell into ninth place, with one-quarter of the members saying they spent a great deal of time on it. In short, cases and projects per se apparently are not quite the great time consumers many charge.

One problem with the commission data is their ambiguity (what does "great deal" mean?). Another is their inability to distinguish between the members' time spent on the various tasks while in Washington and the time they spent visiting their districts. The latter takes up a good portion of modern congressmen's time, especially on weekends, but even home visits and fence-mending cannot simply be equated with constituency service. A third problem is that members may have an incentive to be ambiguous and to exaggerate—certainly they cannot spend as much time on as many activities as their responses imply. Clearly, better measures are needed.

Among the Obey Commission's activities was a time-use study of House members undertaken in the late spring and early summer of 1977. Out of an eleven-hour work day, members spent an average of three hours and nineteen minutes in their offices; about four and one-half hours on the floor and in committee; two hours elsewhere in Washington (including nine minutes with constituents in the Capitol); and one hour and forty minutes on miscellaneous activities.[17] Assuming that half the time spent with constituents and organized groups, one-third of the time spent on the phone and handling mail, and a quarter of all time spent with staff involve cases and projects, the total amount of daily effort devoted to casework in Washington would be fifty-five minutes — about four and one-half hours weekly. These assumptions are quite generous, but even they do not indicate an excessive Washington time commitment to running interference for constituents with the federal bureaucracy.

A second measure comes from a mail survey of 123 House offices conducted by Robert Klonoff. Klonoff found that 46 percent of the representatives were reported by their aides to spend less than 5 percent of their own time on casework, and another 36 percent to give from 5 to 15 percent of their time. Fewer than one member in twenty were said to devote more than a quarter of their personal time to casework.[18]

As part of the research for this book, members and staffs were asked how much time they (or, in the case of staff respondents, their employers) spent on cases and projects *while in Washington*. Table 7.1 presents the data, which, although probably containing inaccuracies, represent decent approximations of reality. Note that the data are consistent with other recent estimates and those calculated from the Obey Commission studies above. Senators, naturally, spend less time than do members of the lower chamber, but the differences are not staggering. By 1982, representatives' time commitments appeared to have decreased considerably, but the small sample suggests caution in any such interpretation. Both time estimates are quite low, much below comparable estimates for legislators in American states and in parliaments around the world.[19] More interesting than the averages are the ranges: from absolutely no time given to casework to ten hours in the Senate and an incredible thirteen (in 1982) to twenty-seven hours (in 1977–78) in the House. Senators, it appears, are more constrained than representatives. Beyond devoting a couple of hours a week to cases and projects, few senators can spare much time.

The bulk of senators' and representatives' personal involvement in casework occurs when they are back home in direct contact with their constituents. And for some members, especially those living close to Washington and commuting daily, such activity can be considerable. Cong. William A. Barrett (D., Pa.), for example, claimed in 1971 to have spent only three nights in six years in Washington. Each evening he held office hours for constituents from 9:00 to 11:00 in his home district.[20] At such times these members serve as casework "intake" agents, passing names, addresses, and problems on to the relevant staffers. In Washington, a surprisingly large number of congressmen and senators at least sample the letters from constituents; and there still remain several members who read virtually all incoming letters. Many read and sign all, or a good proportion, of the outgoing mail both to constituents and to departments and agencies.

Table 7.1: Estimates of Time Senators and Representatives
Spend on Casework When in Washington

Amount of Time (Hrs.) per Week Spent on Casework and Federal Projects	Responding Offices		
	Senators	Representatives	
		95th	97th
None, virtually none (0–2 hours)	55%	49%	60%
Little; seldom (3–4 hours)	22	20	9
Moderate, somewhat (5–8 hours)	12	14	26
Heavy; great deal (over 8 hours)	8	17	6
(N)	(49)	(136)	(47)
Mean number of hours	3.7	5.9	3.0
Median number of hours	2.9	3.0	1.4
Range of hours	0–10	0–27	0–13
(N)	(31)	(98)	(47)

NOTE: The *Ns* in the upper and lower portions of the table differ. Those in the four general categories include nonnumerical responses which were specific enough to code, such as: "hardly at all," "only a little time," "quite often," and "a lot." "Coding of such responses was a subjective undertaking, and thus the figures presented in the table must be read with caution. Figures in the lower portion were actual hour figures furnished by respondents.

SOURCE: Author's interviews and questionnaires. Based on responses to the open-ended questions: "On the average, how many hours per week did (do) you personally spend on cases and projects when you were (are) in Washington?" and "When he is in Washington, how often does the Congressman/Senator get involved in cases and projects?" Figures in the table are those provided by the most authoritative source for each senator and representative, in the following order: (1) the member himself/herself; (2) the administrative assistant or personal secretary; (3) caseworkers or other staff. When two or more caseworkers provided estimates, their estimates were averaged.

Beyond such passive involvement, members engage in three other types of casework activity. First, some congressmen frequently, and most occasionally, meet with their case and project staffs for briefings and discussions on how to handle particular problems. Second, a few members personally talk to constituents on the phone or when they visit the Capitol. As one aide put it: "You know how it is; some constituents just won't talk to us staff people." Another aide offered a different reason: "When we get good results, the boss sometimes likes to pick up the phone and call the person directly. He likes the gratification—but also the effect it has on the guy on the other end of the line." And a couple of staffers said that their bosses would even "talk to the nuts" who call. Finally, members occasionally make personal contact with the agency involved in a case, but such involvement—rather common in the past—is infrequent today. A veteran reminisced about how "I used to accompany constituents to see the FCC or the RFC. We all used to do it—we really took care of our constituents."[21] Still, some members do become dramatically entangled in constituents' affairs. Cong. George Hansen (R., Idaho) flew to Bolivia to obtain the release of a constituent jailed on drug charges, and later made a trip to Iran to try his hand at negotiating the release of Americans held as hostages there during 1979–80.[22] And few Americans will easily forget the murder of Cong. Leo J. Ryan (D., Cal.), who was ambushed while investigating the Jonestown religious cult in Central America, of which one of his constituents was said to be a member.

The most common reason for members' personal involvement is simple need: when a staffer believes that progress on a case has been stalled because of bureaucratic runaround or resistance—when it appears that the member's personal clout could help—the aide will take the case to the senator or representative for his personal attention. "If I'm getting nowhere," said one aide in a typical comment, "all I have to do is go into him and he'll pick up the phone. I don't like to do it, but if needed, I will."

The type of case often determines the level of involvement. It is not uncommon for members to spend three or four hours a week on major items, especially federal projects, while devoting only several minutes to individual cases. Said one representative: "Get involved personally? If I get time and if the case is important—especially when it affects a municipality or lots of people." That theme was repeated time and time again. One aide said of her boss: "She'll get involved when a group is getting hurt. For example, O. E. cut off funds for [the member's state] under the Guaranteed Student Loan Program due to a high default rate. She called." There seems to be a distinct tendency for representatives from rural areas, which unlike cities do not have their own grant application experts, to get personally involved in projects.

Federal projects and group cases are not the only cases which may command special attention. As one former member explained: "The case was interesting. For example, I strongly opposed the Vietnam war, and the number of dishonorable discharges for young men in my district got me mad. So, often I'd take on one of those myself." Similarly, it is common for members to take a direct interest in cases that raise policy questions or have potential for legislative remedies.

A third reason for direct intervention is similarly understandable. When members are involved in a case from the outset—perhaps they first heard the constituent's complaint when visiting the district—or subsequently were brought in, they tend to stay involved. Such involvement, however, often takes the form of "looking over the shoulder" of the caseworker and inquiring about the status of the case from time to time. Closely related to this reason is particular member knowledge of a problem. One midwestern Democratic congressman's caseworker explained: "There was this ski resort in trouble, and [the congressman] knows the owner and all the details of the situation. He knows more than we ever could find out; so he took over."

Finally, one in six respondents indicated that congressmen handle cases personally when the constituent is important: a relative, friend, or local VIP. Often, such VIPs refuse to deal with staff assistants. But even in these cases, member involvement comes mainly at the outset and at the end, with everything else usually handled by staff—unless, of course, personal intervention is needed to make the required impression on executive officials. One aide to an "opportunistic" (her word) congressman explained her situation: "He gets into cases for anybody with influence—labor leaders, business or community leaders. Otherwise I don't go to him. Even immigration cases—normally, if the case isn't justified I won't push it to him. But this particular case I'm doing now; it's a big contributor, and the guy is giving me a hard time. To cover myself, I'll call [the member] and let him take over."

Staffers cite three reasons for not wanting to ask for help. One is that they feel that the members are busy on legislative matters. A second is that they believe themselves to be competent and therefore able to do their jobs without assistance. Finally, as one put it, "We don't want to cheapen the currency; if we asked him to call regularly, it would lose its effect."

If soliciting cases and allocating staff resources are somewhat systematically determined, so might be congressmen's decisions on how much of their own time to devote to casework and projects. A simple model resembling those used earlier of time spent in 1977–78 is presented in table 7.2.

With other factors held constant, senators from the West Coast spent more time on cases and projects. They probably return home less frequently than their colleagues nearer to Washington and thus have more Washington time to give to constituents. (Similarly, the coefficient for the western region variable is positive, but not statistically significant, in the House.) In the lower chamber the decision to spend time on casework is affected by both personal and constituency factors. Although the coefficient is not significant (due to the presence of the leadership variable), seniority is inversely related to casework time. Indeed, two-thirds of the representatives elected in 1970 or earlier devoted virtually no

Table 7.2: Congressmen's Personal Time Allocation
to Casework When in Washington, 95th Congress

Independent Variables	Senators B [*Beta*]	Representatives B [*Beta*]
Electoral Margin	−.004 [−.017]	.056 [.135]
Seniority	.051 [.124]	−.120 [−.121]
Leadership status	— —	−3.175** [−.171]
Conservatism	−.001 [−.006]	.036* [.171]
Constituency median education	−1.342 [−.292]	−1.786** [−.232]
Casework load	.004** [.521]	−.0004 [−.006]
East	−1.363 [−.107]	4.298** [.297]
Midwest	.094 [.013]	−.995 [−.071]
South	.212 [.029]	−.005 [−.000]
West	3.141* [.474]	1.360 [.082]
CONSTANT	17.178	23.573
(*N*)	(27)	(82)
R-squared	.39	.21
Adjusted *R*-squared	.07	.10

NOTE: Electoral margin = percent of vote won in 1970–76 for representatives; percent won in previous election for senators. Standardized regression coefficients in brackets: *$p < .10$; **$p < .05$.

time to casework, compared to 41 percent of first- and second-term members. Conversely, a third of the most junior members, versus one in five of their colleagues, were reported to spend five or more hours each week on this aspect of constituency service. Holding a leadership position clearly detracts from time for casework, even when controlling for seniority.[23] Two very senior and powerful committee chairmen commented: "As chairman, I didn't have time to do those sorts of things." "Get involved personally? When I was younger, sure; but as I moved up in the pecking order? Almost never. I was too busy doing other things." A former Republican member agreed: "Just no time — my ranking minority status on the ———— Committee kept me too busy. Maybe freshmen have time, but when you become senior, you have too many responsibilities."

Surprisingly, the equations offer no support for the "electoral connection" thesis,[24] but conservatives in the House do seem more inclined to give of themselves. Interestingly, the higher the district median education levels, the less time members devote to casework — perhaps reflecting greater pressures in such districts for policy-related activities. Finally, there appears to be something about the East — probably its political culture and traditions — that inclines its congressmen to spend more of their own time on constituent problems.

Overall, the two equations do not explain much of the variance in time allocations, no doubt because decisions to use precious time for constituent affairs are intensely personal choices. Some members simply value casework and enjoy it, devoting much greater than average amounts of their own time (and assigning greater staff resources) to it for seemingly inexplicable reasons. As a former Republican congressman put it:

It's hard to generalize. It depends on the personality of the person. Some congressmen are perfectly at home with their constituents — a perfect match. They don't like Washington and prefer to be back home or, when in Washington, to be dealing with constituents. For them, it's perfectly natural and comfortable to do casework — they like it. But the other type who like Washington and never go home — like ————, whose only home is in my district and who drives into his district to give a speech — for them, casework probably is a pain. They don't like it. It's a very personal sort of thing.

One of the sharpest critics of the constituency service function has been Thomas E. Cavanagh, who has used Obey Commission data to explore the relationship between "electoral arena" and "institutional arena" activities.[25] His conclusion is that, particularly for junior members of the House, the electoral imperative of servicing constituents does in fact detract from legislative and oversight tasks. He cites as evidence that half of the commission's responding congressmen indicated that constituent demands of one sort or another—including ceremonial functions and stumping for reelection—account for the major differences between how they actually have to spend their time and what they ideally would prefer to devote time and energy to.[26] And, after comparing how many members reported spending a "great deal" of time on each of the seventeen congressional functions in the commission's study to how many believed each function to be "very important," Cavanagh notes that the gaps between time and importance are largest in the institutional arena (policymaking) and smallest in the electoral arena (functions concerning constituents, such as visits home, speeches, keeping in touch, casework, and so on). Congressmen, he argues, must sacrifice institutional time for constituency time. In its broad outline it is a powerful and undoubtedly true indictment.

The evidence, however, does not necessarily prove the charge against *cases and federal projects work*. First, congressmen and senators do not in fact spend all that much time on casework when they are in Washington (and, perhaps, not even when they are back home).[27] As one former representative explained, "There's plenty of time to do both constituency and policy work." Second, there is little or no relationship between the two measures of legislative activism employed earlier (the number of bills sponsored or cosponsored and the number of floor appearances) and time devoted to casework. Were casework as serious a distraction as is claimed, and to the extent that these two factors genuinely represent policy involvement, a rather strongly negative correlation might be apparent—unless, of course, casework takes time away only from committee activities and private study and research, not from floor activity or the introduction of legislation. Analysis of the Obey data corroborates this view. As indicated in table 7.3, when an additive index of time spent on policy-related functions is arrayed against indicators of time spent on cases and projects, the expected negative correlations simply do not appear.[28] (Nor do controls for seniority bring them forth for any particular cohort.) As one might predict, there are positive associations between time dedicated to case and projects work, on the one hand, and time given to other constituency service tasks. But they are not, for the most part, very robust relationships. Rather surprisingly, the relationships between case and project time, on the one hand, and time spent on various policy-related duties, on the other, also are positive, with only a couple of weak exceptions. These are not the sorts of results one would expect if congressmen were being forced to trade off constituency duties for "institutional" ones. The reason for such phenomena is that congressmen have large enough staffs to attend to constituency duties. According to one congressman, "There's a difference between what I do and what my staff does; [casework] causes no big problem."

Table 7.3: Effects of Time Spent on Cases and Projects on Policy Activities

Index of Time Spent on Seven Policy-Related Congressional Activities	Time Spent on:					
	Cases			Projects		
	Hardly Any, Little Time	Some Time	Great Deal Of Time	Hardly Any Time	Some Time	Great Deal Of Time
Hardly Any, A Little Time	22%	20%	12%	20%	16%	17%
Some Time	66	69	79	70	79	60
Great Deal of Time	12	11	10	10	5	22
(N)	(45)	(46)	(49)	(45)	(46)	(49)
	tau_b = .07; N.S.			tau_b = .08; N.S.		

SOURCE: House Commission on Administrative Review, 1977.

NOTE: Index based on the following items: studying and doing basic research on proposed legislation, debating and voting on legislation on the floor of the House, keeping track of the way government agencies are administering laws, working in full committee to develop legislation, working in committee or subcommittee on oversight activities, and working informally with other members to build support for legislation about which the member was personally concerned.

Other evidence is available. If one uses Cavanagh's measurement of the gaps between the time and importance members assign to various tasks but includes not only their responses of a "great deal" of time and their judgments that a task is "very important," but also responses of "some" time and "fairly" important, the gaps are reduced in thirteen of seventeen activities. And the discrepancies between time and importance for constituency service duties and those for legislative functions become virtually identical. Only for congressional oversight of executive agencies does the difference remain substantial, and that probably has nothing to do with time pressures.

Moreover, analysis of the House Commission data shows virtually no relationship between what congressmen say they feel they are *expected* to do (constituency service) and the time they reportedly devote to cases and projects. If critics are correct, one would expect to see a strong and positive correlation. One also would expect to hear congressmen complain that casework interferes with the House's ability to do its job. The commission asked members what they thought were the two most important roles for the House, and then what obstacles "stand in the way of the House in doing a better job" on those two tasks. The results are interesting. On the first mention, ninety-eight of the responding members cited legislative, oversight, constitutional, or checks and balance roles as important, and twelve mentioned the ombudsman or the representational roles. Of the ninety-eight, only sixteen cited district demands as interfering with the policy-related duties; twenty-two blamed inertia, ten the executive, and nineteen the committee structure. Of the twelve who identified constituent activities as a key role, four thought that district demands were obstacles to successful performance—twice as many, proportionally, as blamed constituents for interfering with the policy role. Given a second response, sixty-six members mentioned legislation, oversight, and other institutional or policy duties, and twenty-three mentioned the ombudsman or representational roles. This time, only two of the sixty-six members blamed district demands for interfering with policymaking. Again, if the critics are correct, one would expect to see many more members faulting constituent concerns than actually do.

Finally, the commission asked its sample of congressmen what they thought were the two or three biggest obstacles encountered in trying to do their jobs the way they felt they ought to be done—''the things which frustrate you the most.'' Eighty percent of the complaints cited a lack of time, and of these, only 3 percent were connected to casework. Another 6 percent specifically mentioned casework as a frustration. The conclusion is that casework and projects at least—and maybe most other constituent-related activities—cannot be blamed so readily if congressmen fail to devote their entire working days to intensive study of legislation and oversight of federal programs. Of course, in a purely time-accounting sense, time spent talking to and working for constituents is time not available for studying a committee report. And members do spend a fantastic amount of time in their districts, both serving constituents' needs and conducting permanent electoral campaigns. There *are* only twenty-four hours in a day. But to blame constituency service for inadequate or defective legislative performance overlooks far too much and overly simplifies a complex phenomenon—not to say reduces democratic government to a one-dimensional (policymaking) enterprise.

7.3. Casework and Staff Allocations

Since members themselves spend little time on cases and projects, that task falls to their staffs. Not only are casework staffs growing (see chapter 4) but the amount of time they spend on casework seems to be on the rise. In the early 1960s, John S. Saloma's careful study of a sample of House offices concluded that a quarter of personal office staff time went to constituency service (19 percent to casework specifically), with another 41 percent dedicated to correspondence and only 14 percent to legislative matters.[29] Klonoff's 1977 study found that in one-third of 123 House offices, half or more of staff time was taken up by casework, and in another 38 percent of those offices, staffers gave one-quarter or more of their time to that activity.[30] Is that too much time? Does casework force members to divert valuable staff resources away from policy matters? In a simple sense, the answer has to be in the afirmative. Surely, if casework were to cease today, most legislators would use a much greater portion of their staff allowances for legislative research than they now do. But just as surely, they would put some staffers to work on other constituency-related or public relations business; and some would decide not to spend the excess funds at all. In truth, the situation is complex. As one House aide mused: "Casework detracts from staffers' time, but it isn't necessarily a substantive distraction—it's neutral or even helpful."

First, much if not most of the drive for larger personal staffs since World War II has been the result, not the cause, of constituent demands (some of which are stimulated by Congress). Without casework pressures, what is the likelihood that Congress would have enlarged personal office staff budgets as much as has been done? And what, specifically, are the chances that such budgets would have been earmarked for legislative and oversight staffs? Second, the fact that the growth in congressional staff has occurred at the committee and subcommittee levels as much as (or more than) in personal offices suggests both that alternative staffing arrangements can be made for legislative work and that congressmen take their policy responsibilities seriously and are prepared to take the necessary measures (in terms of staffing) to carry them out.[31] Indeed, given the way Congress handles policy matters—in committees—that is where most legislative staffing *must* be located.

Third, personal offices apparently are not particularly understaffed, even for legislative work. Most senators have a half-dozen or more legislative researchers, and the average House office has two or three. Only one-quarter of the members in the Obey Commission's survey, and 15 percent of their administrative assistants, believed that the limiting of House staffs to eighteen members (subsequently increased slightly) was a "major problem." Over half of the AAs believed that they were adequately or more than adequately staffed in the area of legislative research, with only 42 percent complaining about understaffing.[32] Obey Commission data on staffing patterns allow a crude test of the forced tradeoff between legislative and constituency service staffs. If such tradeoffs had occurred, one would expect that offices with more caseworkers would have fewer legislative researchers and vice versa. That is in fact the case: the correlation between caseworkers and legislative aides is negative, but barely ($r = -.14$). Since not all members employ a full complement of staff, it is appropriate to compare the proportions of legislative and casework staffs (as percentages of the entire staffs) working for each congressman. The result again shows a negative correlation ($r = -.29$), suggesting that there is some degree of tradeoff. As one would expect, the tradeoff is the sharpest for first- and second-term congressmen.[33] The reason, of course, is that as representatives become more senior, they move into subcommittee and committee leadership positions that carry access to legislative staffing, thus releasing their personal staffs for constituency service. Recall that, other things being equal, leaders in 1977–78 had, on average, one additional staffer assigned to casework.

In short, having to tend to casework and projects poses only a relatively minor staffing problem in terms of pressure on staffers who *might otherwise realistically be assigned to legislation*. For juniors, the problem is more serious. Perhaps the size of House personal office staffs should vary inversely with seniority. Currently, junior senators and members of key House committees (Appropriations, Budget) are assigned additional staff to help them with this committee work.

7.4. Casework as Congressional Oversight

Given that handling constituent complaints and requests drains some time and energy from purely legislative tasks, a balanced judgment requires consideration of casework's potential for enhancing a member's policy responsiveness and for augmenting Congress's capabilities in the areas of legislative initiative and supervision of executive agency programs and operations. Using a reasonably broad definition that incorporates "latent" as well as "manifest" oversight,[34] it is easy to see that casework fits the standard purposes of oversight:

To determine whether legislative policies are being faithfully carried out. . . . To determine whether legislative programs are accomplishing their desired objectives, and if further legislation is needed. . . . To ascertain that the laws are being administered in the public interest, and to encourage diligence on the part of administrative officers. . . . To check on the systems of internal management and control. . . . To hold responsible executive officials accountable.[35]

The vital question, of course, is not whether casework counts as oversight but how often, how well, and under what conditions it positively contributes to the legislative and oversight functions. Predictably, scholars are in disagreement on this question, with some dismissing casework virtually out of hand[36] and others claiming that casework "may constitute the most pervasive and fundamental form of legislative oversight."[37]

If casework and federal projects efforts are helpful for legislative and oversight purposes (the two are considered together here), they could be so in any of four ways. The first is informational: cases can contribute to a general awareness of problems and can provide "feedback" to Congress. Second, such awareness, if properly channeled, may lead directly either to more formal oversight techniques, such as hearings or investigations, or to the introduction of remedial legislation. Third, when successful in resolving a case, correcting an error, or catching an abuse of power, congressmen and their staffs can achieve, albeit partially, some of the objectives of systematic oversight. Such "narrow-gauge" casework[38] is a shortcut of sorts to, or substitute for, other techniques. Finally, as a result of incoming congressional complaints and requests, departments and agencies might change regulations or procedures, conduct their own internal oversight, or, at the least, become more aware of problems and be more careful when similar cases arise. The process of dealing with "congressionals," moreover, might help sensitize bureaucrats to the human consequences of their rules, regulations, and operations. Challenges to bureaucratic decisions, especially when accompanied by complaints about specific personnel or particular agency procedures, could lead to oversight via the agency's anticipated reaction to congressional interference. Trying to measure or quantify such effects is difficult, because the only source available to the investigator is soft, interview-type data. And much depends on who is interviewed. One study sought the views of Senate committee staff members, who were asked to rank the effectiveness of casework as a method of oversight. Responses placed casework second (of sixteen techniques) in frequency of use, but only eleventh in effectiveness. Routine staff communication with agencies, hearings and meetings, and staff investigations—all frequently employed—were considered the three most effective tools of oversight.[39] Presumably, similar results would be obtained for the House. But if one turns from committee to personal office staffs, a somewhat different picture emerges.

A precondition to oversight or legislative activity is the knowledge that problems exist in the administration of public policy. Given busy congressional schedules, members and staffs have relatively few opportunities to explore agency behavior. Thus any and all feedback or information sources are valuable. According to the vast majority of members and staffers interviewed, case and project work provides low-cost, generally accurate intelligence, along with a good dose of motivation. It periodically stimulates a dialogue about problems of mutual interest to Congress and the executive branch. As one former Republican congressman explained, congressmen live a sheltered life; it takes "real people's problems to get them to pay attention to how government affects the country." Other comments from members and staffs were similar:

Oh yes; you can find out what is working out—why a USDA regulation or program will fit on the plains but not in Arizona.

Casework brings a lot of policy matters to our attention—not lots in terms of volume but rather in terms of importance.

You find out what's happening in the agencies. We don't have time to read the *Federal Register,* so cases tell us what's going on. Even one case can open up a whole world.

If we didn't have cases and projects, we'd have more time for legislation; but we wouldn't know how well the legislation works.[40]

In short, casework constitutes Congress's "antennae" for oversight.

If casework is to lead regularly to the introduction of remedial legislation or to formal congressional oversight, several conditions would seem beneficial, if not necessary. Ideally: (1) records of cases would be searched periodically and systematically—or at least cases pointing to problems about which something might be done would be duly noted; (2) attempts would be made to generalize from individual cases to the underlying programs and administrative problems that caused them; (3) some sort of oversight action would be recommended to explore and correct the underlying problem; and (4) the appropriate member, committee, or other unit would be contacted. While few of these conditions consistently hold, enough of them do with sufficient frequency to allow for considerable casework utility.

Although almost all offices claimed to keep careful records, there was little evidence that those records were searched systematically to uncover underlying and recurrent problems. Only a half-dozen offices indicated that such searches were undertaken primarily for the purpose of oversight. A growing number of offices, however, do keep a count of cases by type of problem or by agency, and they seem to find some marginal oversight benefits in that practice. (These offices often search casework files to prepare members for problems they might confront in particular areas they plan to visit.) Systematic searches, however, are not necessary. In most offices, aides insist that it is easy to pick up patterns of administrative flaws and abuses. Caseworkers say that they "just know" when a problem goes beyond the instant case. "It's easy to recognize a pattern," said one; "you don't need to dig through your files." Another wrote:

Although no specific records are kept to identify recurring problems, such problems do come in "bunches," it seems, and we have been able to pretty much deal with these problems as a whole, usually by seeking relief through changes in agency regulations and/or policy. In addition, caseworkers develop good memories for recognizing repeat situations and can check files to see if administrative change is necessary. Keeping records by agency, type of case, etc., would probably be helpful, but would require additional time and staff not available to us if we want to keep up with the workload we already have.

One aide who does make a systematic search every six months said that these produce little more than "what I find intuitively."

Members and staffs were asked if they made "any attempts to generalize about problems discovered in constituency service operations so that some remedial action, such as introduction of legislation, might be taken." Two-thirds of 346 respondents, including 77 percent of the members responding but only half of the administrative assistants, answered affirmatively. As one House aide put it, "Yes, I'm always looking. That's what casework is all about. I try to be conscientious, and it frequently happens. It should happen more."

Respondents were asked whether, when they discovered underlying weaknesses in laws, regulations, or agency operations, they did anything to correct them other than merely attending to the case at hand. One-quarter of 306 members and staffers indicated that they had recommended remedial legislation, 14 percent claimed to have taken some sort of oversight action (contacted the relevant committees, suggested a GAO inquiry, prepared questions for hearings), and another 39 percent indicated that they had done both. One in ten gave an unspecified affirmative answer. If the responses are even remotely accurate, it appears that staffers who perform the casework function, those who supervise them, and congressmen themselves do make efforts to spot and remedy statutory and bureaucratic deficiencies. As a Republican member of the House explained, "One reason I try to stay on top of case matters is that many times I have come across errors in the way executive agencies are interpreting or carrying out the laws; and they can be dealt with by legislation or oversight." Some examples (based on the recollection of members and aides) of casework-inspired bills that were at least introduced include the Pension Benefits Reform Act; the Equal Pay for Women Act; the Forgotten Widows Bill; the Truth in Mailing Act; the Pregnancy Disability Act; the Social Security Recipients' Fairness Act; the Medical Freedom of Choice Act; and the Veterans Judicial Review Act. Another former member cited Food Stamp legislation and laws mandating the compulsory inspection of poultry and the training of teachers for exceptional children. Members and staffs mentioned numerous other measures.[41]

Two points should be apparent. First, these legislative efforts are remedial; they seldom deal with sweeping changes or major innovations in public policy. Second, a good many concern agencies and programs that involve large numbers of citizens and / or are particularly clientele-oriented: Social Security, Veterans Administration, Housing and Urban Development, and the military. Casework-inspired legislation, in other words, is highly people-oriented.

At times the stimulus for remedial legislation comes directly from agency personnel. A caseworker explained: "Sometimes the agency will reply, 'Under the law we can't help.' So I'll call or write the agency asking if a statutory change is needed. Sometimes they say yes, and even make suggestions." Some agency officials view congressionals as an opportunity to "end-run" their immediate superiors and to apply pressure to change programs and policies that they do not like.

The results of casework are used for other legislative tasks. Several representatives and staffers, for example, commented that casework — and unusually good or bad experiences with agencies on cases — had affected floor voting on bills and decisions to cosponsor. Said one senator: "Casework can sometimes affect how I'd vote on amendments. For example, the Post Office lobbyists came to me to point out amendments that, if passed, would eliminate some of the problems which we'd had lots of complaints on. The same with Amtrak." A House aide elaborated on what she thought was a common situation: "When a matter is brought to the floor that would have a direct effect on recurring problems brought to the congressman's attention through casework, the staff provides him with the input. If one of the LAs or caseworkers knows of a bill providing relief for, let us say, a problem of social security regulations, the cases which brought that problem to light are brought to his attention. Also, this is done when he is asked by another member to cosponsor a bill."

Testimony by members during legislative hearings commonly includes references to casework. One caseworker said that her boss used casework experiences five or six times per year. According to a Republican congressman, "On these [pension] matters, I'd call the constituent to see if I could use his case in giving testimony before the committee. We did it a lot on product liability insurance legislation, too."

Casework seldom leads *directly* to oversight hearings or formal staff investigations, but it does happen.[42] An influx of citizen complaints about the Minority Business Enterprise Office, for example, allegedly led to hearings on that program, and hearings on the Office of Workers' Compensation supposedly were triggered by constituent dissatisfaction.[43] One senator, pestered by constituents about federal education programs in his state, pressed the General

Accounting Office to investigate, and the results of the GAO effort led to changes in agency practices. A House subcommittee chairman whose constituents complained about military housing held hearings. And Congressmen G. William Whitehurst and Robert W. Daniel, among others, in 1976 inspired a GAO study of the hearing loss compensation program in OWCP. Apparently, calling on the GAO for such casework-inspired investigations is not uncommon.[44]

Nonstatutory controls can derive from casework. One House staffer explained: "In the agricultural area, we saw that farmers weren't getting good treatment from the FmHA. It's a vicious cycle: a farmer doesn't have enough money to qualify for a loan; no loan means no investment, leading to low income. Low income means no loan. Anyhow, we pulled out all the cases on this that we'd had over the last two years, then interviewed FmHA people, bankers, interest group staffs, and the ASCS committees; and we developed a report which we're using subtly to get the system changed."

Less dramatic than these overt uses of casework are the "incidental" ones. Asking questions of witnesses during legislative or appropriations hearings—questions based on case experiences—is a common but important aspect of "latent" oversight. One House aide felt that "if you find there's an abuse [concerning housing programs] in one town, you can generalize. We use cases during hearings. Your focus is on the problem and the statutory vagueness."[45] Other oversight uses of casework include speeches on the floor of the House and Senate, press releases, interviews, introduction of constituent complaints into the *Congressional Record,* and—probably the most important of all oversight tools—personal or telephone contacts with agency representatives.[46]

Perhaps the critical question is: Precisely how often do such legislative and oversight consequences of casework occur? Most commentators clearly do not see it happening often, especially not on major matters.[47] Unfortunately, no single question to probe the frequency of oversight application was included in this study, but several questions can shed some light. Asked how often legislation was introduced as a result of cases, five of twenty-six Washington offices answered "often" or "frequently"; and ten replied "occasionally."

The last round of questionnaires sent to home offices included three items relevant to the oversight function. Staffers were asked to indicate: how often they and their coworkers recommended to their Washington offices that their members sponsor legislation to correct problems uncovered during casework; how often they recommended that Washington at least "look into" the problems; and how often they personally tried to rectify such general problems by contacting agency supervisers directly. Table 7.4 provides the results.

Considering that the chances to become involved in genuine legal or adminis-

Table 7.4: Frequency with Which House and Senate Home Staffs Undertake Remedial Action to Correct Statutory or Administrative Problems, 95th Congress

Type of Remedial Action Undertaken	Reported Frequency with Which Remedial Action Is Undertaken							
	Always; When Needed	Regularly; Frequently; Often; More than 6 Times per Year	Sometimes; Occasionally; 2–6 Times per year	Rarely; Seldom; Infrequently; Not Often; Once or Twice per Year	Never	0–5% of the Time	5–10% of the Time	Over 10% of the Time
Recommend to Washington that member sponsor legislation	15	22	17	23	14	1	0	0
Recommend that Washington "look into" problem	7	19	2	15	13	1	0	5
Take direct action with agency supervisors	14	19	18	17	14	1	3	1
Total $N = 43$								

SOURCE: Author's interviews and questionnaires. Based on the following open-ended questions: (1) "Having identified underlying and recurring problems (in casework), how often does your office recommend to the Washington office that the senator/representative sponsor legislation to correct the problem?" (2) "How often do you recommend that the Washington office at least 'look into' the problem?" (3) "How often do you try to rectify general program weaknesses, underlying problems, and/or patterns of bureaucratic difficulties by contacting agency supervisors to inform them of the need to reexamine agency regulations or to check the behavior of their staffs?"

trative problems arising from cases are limited, the data suggest that concerted efforts in fact are made quite often, albeit unsystematically, to use casework information as a source for legislative initiatives and various forms of oversight. As one aide put it, "To me it's checks and balances at the gut level."

The 1982 survey raised several oversight-related issues. Asked whether the representatives for whom they worked discussed cases with their staffs for legislative or oversight purposes, about a third of the respondents said that their bosses did so regularly; fewer than one in five said that such discussion occurred "never or rarely." Twenty-two percent indicated that their members regularly referred to cases during hearings, committee meetings, or floor debates, and 46 percent thought that they did so "occasionally." Sixty percent claimed that their congressmen examined statistical breakdowns of cases at least on occasion, and two of three said that their bosses contacted agencies on the policy implications of cases regularly or occasionally.

Another approach to "measuring" the utility of casework for oversight is simply to ask members and staffs for their opinions. Thirteen percent of the members, 9 percent of House administrative assistants, and 25 percent of other House and Senate aides believed that casework was very effective for providing ideas and incentives for legislation, while about one-quarter of members and staffers deemed it rarely effective. Fully 60 percent of the 350 respondents considered casework "somewhat" effective. They gave slightly more positive answers to the question of how valuable casework is "for providing ideas and incentives for oversight."[48] Taken together, these responses hardly constitute proof that casework is a vital cog in Congress's oversight machinery, but they do indicate quite clearly that it *sometimes* is. Put negatively, they argue forcefully against the view that casework is not very useful.

7.5. The Executive, Casework, and Policy: The Negative View

A familiar criticism of casework is that it interferes with the administrative process without making any long-run difference in policies or procedures. Most participants disagree. Congressional and executive branch officials were asked their responses to the statement that "congressional inquiries on behalf of constituents disrupt the efficient running of the executive agency or office and detract from more important things agency employees should be doing." Only 22 percent of administrators believed that casework is an interference; 63 percent of the 216 disagreed, as did four-fifths of congressmen and their staffs.

Insofar as casework is disruptive of the administrator's job, how much and how often is it so? Is it a problem? How? Those questions were put to the executive officials in the mail sample. Asked the extent to which casework interfered with their jobs, 45 percent responded that it was "no problem." Nineteen percent saw it as a minimal interference. Nearly one-fifth each cited minimal, moderate, and serious disruption. Asked point-blank if they saw casework as a problem, 61 percent said no; 32 percent said yes; and 6 percent responded "sometimes."

In answer to the question of how and why responding to congressionals constituted a problem, the most frequently mentioned reasons (63 of 141) were that casework is unproductive, that it diverts manpower, that it costs money, or that it ties up operations. Another 29 cited the waste of time. As one complained, "For the staff, it is disruptive. Here are staff people who are very busy with stacks of very important things to do; then in comes this congressional that forces them to set all this work aside to deal with something that doesn't seem as important." "One senator," wrote an Energy Department official, "sends us so many inquiries that it is equivalent to the workload of one full-time employee for one week per month."

A number of administrators furnished estimated or actual time and cost data for congressionals, ranging from five minutes for a phone call, twenty for a letter, and $3.00 per case to three hours and $30 per case. The highest figure came from one of the military services: "In 1976," said the liaison officer, "it cost us $180 per congressional case." An Agriculture Department official recalled that it took two hundred man-hours for one case that went to the assistant secretary.

A half-dozen respondents expressed the belief that a "successful" congressional intervention creates disrespect for and short-circuits the executive administrative process. One administrator explained that if a constituent seeks congressional help and if the case is resolved in his favor, he "ends up having less regard for the government worker, whose competence, de facto, has been questioned." Another believed that successful casework encourages people to bypass normal channels. It creates, the administrator said, a double workload problem: "Instead of coming to us, people go to their congressmen, and if they 'win,' they think the congressmen did it for them. So next time they have a problem, instead of coming to us, they go back to their congressmen, creating extra work again. We can't deal with them."

Another adverse effect of casework concerns morale within agencies. At one level, staff morale is undermined by the sheer boredom of dealing with congressional inquiries. An extreme example was offered by an administrator in an area office of the Labor Department:

After a while, you just get numb answering "congressionals." The whole process becomes so automatic and routine. There was a case, for example, of a woman in New York, whose husband worked for Workman's Comp. She wrote to her senator complaining that her husband's OWCP office was understaffed. The letter got bucked to Washington, which processed it back to the OWCP office in New York, where the husband's staff prepared the usual answer and took it to him to sign. He did. A couple of days later his wife showed it to him — it was a complete surprise.

More devastating to morale is the danger that agency officials might perceive their legitimate authority being undercut, as one immigration officer explained: "It is very upsetting to a conscientious government employee to be contacted by a congressman's office to set a case forward or to give representation to an illegal alien — more representation than a U.S. citizen receives. Immigration law passed by Congress protects aliens and congressmen should be able to check this closely. However, they should not bend and abuse the law for special interests." A few bureaucrats pointed to another cost of doing casework: having to tell staffers, and sometimes congressmen themselves, that "some of the laws we operate under don't make any sense. Obviously, they tend to disagree."

Despite the very real negative consequences of added work, disruption, and challenges to morale, agency personnel tended to be willing to pay the price, with several volunteering the notion that this sort of disruption is necessary. An HEW liaison officer admitted that there was interference "at some levels," but added that "the purpose of government is to deliver services well" — implying that casework can foster that goal. Another liaison specialist agreed: "Sure, it interferes and causes someone to put aside one case and pick up another; but sometimes that's needed." A Labor Department official summed it up: "I look at Congress as our 'Board of Directors.' They are entitled to know how we operate; it's a check on the bureaucrats, and we should be responsive."

7.6. Casework as Internal Executive Oversight

Just as casework occasionally bolsters congressional supervision of executive operations, it can strengthen the agencies' own efforts to correct weak procedures, supervise personnel, and improve programs. Such effects take the forms of feedback and "political heat" — or at least repetitious pestering — to do something about recurring problems. "The congressional inquiry," said one administrator, "is a way of seeing the outside; it is important in showing what's actually going on — a fail-safe mechanism." The interesting questions have to do with whether agencies actually get such input, how they get it, how often, and with what results.

Each administrator was asked if his/her agency, bureau, or office "attempts systematically to use congressional inquiries to discern general problems or patterns of problems in its operations.'' Of 212 who answered, 35 percent responded affirmatively, and 3 percent indicated that it occasionally occurred. Various techniques are used, ranging from regular computer searches to centralizing in one official the job of clearing all responses to Congress.

A related question asked respondents whether, if no *systematic* attempt is made to use congressional inquiries, such inquiries ''help to point out weaknesses or difficulties. That is, do congressional inquiries help in any way to highlight problems?'' Two-thirds answered with a clear ''yes,'' and 16 percent said ''sometimes'' or ''occasionally.'' The majority saw cases as instruments for helping them accomplish their tasks. ''Casework,'' volunteered an HEW administrator, ''helps in serving people who may not have been served or did not know that they could ask us for help.'' Only 17 percent of the sample answered negatively. As one would expect, the higher the official's rank (GS rating), the more likely he or she was to respond affirmatively.

The preponderance of positive answers to this question, of course, hardly proves the point. It could be that a ''yes'' answer really means ''yes, but rarely,'' or, as in the case of one SBA official, ''yes, but it's no different than if citizens themselves complain.'' Respondents accordingly were asked how often programs or operating weaknesses were detected or highlighted as a result of congressional inquiries. Five percent answered ''frequently'' (once a month), but 23 percent said virtually ''never'' (once or twice in memory). Most responses fell into the ''rarely'' (once a year) or ''occasionally'' (several times a year) categories. Even that, however, is significant, given the overwhelming number of routine, noncontroversial congressionals flooding agency offices. Overall, three-quarters said that at least once a year congressional inquiries pointed out basic problems—many of which would not have been noticed as soon or with the same intensity of concern.

To argue that congressional cases help administrators spot program weaknesses and personnel problems is not to claim that cases are the exclusive sources of information. As one bureaucrat explained, ''Most of the time I know about the problem before we get a congressional.'' But he went on to point out, as did numerous others, that receiving complaints adds to the total picture that gradually emerges when difficulties arise. According to another official: ''Many congressionals are our first indicator that something is wrong. Occasionally they do tip us off to new problems, but most often they confirm what we already knew.'' Most administrators also mentioned that casework generates a greater—though not necessarily ''great'' in absolute terms—sense of urgency and seriousness. Awareness is heightened.[49] On rare occasions, administrators at the local level only learn about policy or program changes when some congressional staffer calls about a case. And it may be that only through casework will one agency learn of contradictory rules or regulations in another. When feedback is thus obtained from congressional casework, administrators were asked what typically happens: ''In what ways are such inquiries useful? (For example, has remedial legislation been recommended? Rules or regulations changed? Personnel changed? More care given to the problem the next time it arose?).''

Responses covered all conceivable actions. While, in the words of one administrator, ''most changes are simple internal adjustments on procedures,'' a noticeable proportion involve substantial change. Nine percent of responses mentioned legislative proposals, such as an INS bill on the adoption of alien children (of course, not all became law). Ten percent pointed to changes in rules or regulations, with another 7 percent saying that rules were rewritten, reexamined, or reinterpreted, and 13 percent mentioning studies, investigations, meetings to discuss the problem, and / or referring the issues to higher authority. Both congressional and agency personnel were asked for specific examples of such rules changes, and they reported a good number.[50] An EPA spokesman furnished one example: ''Sure, EPA had regulations on electroplating, which causes pollution. We got lots of complaints, including a good number from congressmen. We reviewed them and learned that nobody in EPA realized that most of these electroplating operations were 'mom and pop' types that couldn't afford antipollution equipment. So we reconsidered the requirements to see if they were cost-effective.''

A common response (cited by one in six) to inquiries is to increase supervision over the individuals or offices against whom congressional complaints have been lodged. A Farmer's Home Administration regional office director explained that ''congressionals give us insight into personnel problems we have — a very useful tool. We try to find out what will alleviate the problem without taking drastic action. So we give our people some extra training or just have a good long talk with the guy who's the object of the complaint.''

One frequently mentioned remedial action is the most obvious. As one administrator put it: ''When we start getting a series of complaints about the same problem, we of course take a good look at it. And we make sure that the next time the same situation develops, our people handle it the right way.'' Fifteen percent of respondents pointed to this use, and another 12 percent simply said that modes of operating and procedures are changed.

It is hard to say how consistently and in precisely what manner concrete remedies are sought and effected. An SBA administrator described the process as ''indirect.'' Others referred to it in terms of anticipated reactions: when lower-level bureaucrats know that their bosses are listening to congressional complaints (or any complaints, for that matter), they are less apt to make the same mistake twice. According to a liaison officer in HEW: "When someone in the bowels of this organization knows that someone upstairs is concerned, that's good. The program people ought to notice problems themselves but they're the ones who [screwed] up in the first place."

Not only do congressionals provide feedback and help to correct potential wrongs, but, as a case described by a military liaison officer illustrated, they occasionally save some money: "We had a guy who was trying to make colonel. The law lets you out of the service after six months in grade, but the army had a two-year rule. The guy wanted out in order to get a civilian job he had lined up. The army denied his application, which would mean at least one, and maybe two, transfers, at significant cost to the army. We intervened after hearing from the guy's congressman's office; and we won, saving the army a bundle and helping the guy to get his job."

A complementary, though no less subjective, picture can be had by examining the answers to two closed-end questions asking how useful casework is for generating ideas and incentives for agency legislative recommendations and for spurring changes in rules, regulations, and practices.

While only 6 percent of 210 administrators deemed cases and congressionals to be very helpful to executive agencies for generating ideas or incentives for legislative proposals, and although 45 percent dismissed them as rarely or not at all effective (with a third saying the same with respect to rules or operations changes), fully half of the respondents deemed casework "somewhat effective" for both purposes. A more positive assessment was given to the utility of casework as a means of making agencies more sensitive to people's problems: only 17 percent of administrators perceived casework to be rarely or not at all effective, while one in three agency officials saw cases as "very" effective.

One final benefit of constituency service to the executive branch deserves mention: the accumulated experience of congressional caseworkers. In his first year in office, President Carter commissioned studies by the Office of Management and Budget of agency performance in a number of areas. During the summer of 1977 an OMB study team under Richard Pettigrew (Assistant to the President for Reorganization) surveyed congressional offices for their judgments—based on casework experience—of which federal programs constituents thought were administered least efficiently, which were most confusing, which were thought to be least successful, which resulted in excessive paperwork, and which were most responsive. The results were tabulated and sent to some fifteen agencies, all of which, according to an OMB official, said they were "happy" to hear about their weaknesses. The survey focused on some "awful" problems and helped direct attention to some internal management flaws. According to a news report, some agencies used the data for extensive internal oversight efforts. Others were not so diligent.[51] As one OMB official argued, "Some agencies may be thankful for a slow, inefficient bureaucracy, since it tends to slow down their expenditures while giving the appearance of activity and it gives department heads someone to blame for their poor records."

7.7. The Effective Use of Casework for Oversight

In his study of committee oversight, Ogul identified a series of "opportunity factors" which both make possible and, if not taken advantage of, limit committee oversight of the executive.[52] The same reasoning applies for using casework to enhance supervision and control. The opportunity factors are: (1) case loads and case type; (2) staff (adequacy, location, structure, procedure, and motivation); (3) member characteristics (motivation, committee assignment, and status); and (4) agency motivation and procedures.

The utility of casework for oversight is dependent on the incoming cases. At first glance, the relatively large case loads described in chapter 3 seem to present abundant opportunities for discovering program inadequacies and bureaucratic errors and abuse. But such is not necessarily the case, for several reasons. First, excessive workloads may restrict oversight. Offices flooded with cases and projects must either allocate additional staff resources to casework just to cope with the workload, or they must cut corners somewhere else. Such corner-cutting often means that staffers do *not* pay attention to the oversight and legislative possibilities inherent in cases. "Look at this desk," said one caseworker; "I'm lucky if I can just keep up with the mail, let alone give each case the attention it deserves." Another complained that "if only I had more time, I could do more in the way of looking for general solutions to these problems."

Second, the vast majority of cases and projects—estimates range up to 90 percent and beyond—are strictly routine and raise no serious questions that lead to oversight. A social security or veteran's check that was delayed (perhaps through the fault of the constituent) or a request for special immigrant status for a relative usually would not raise significant questions to potential overseers of administrative behavior. One aide who said she "really can't think of any legislative utility" explained that "I just don't get those kinds of cases." Many other case requests are without merit or even fraudulent. Thus the key to casework may be the volume of *nonroutine, nontrivial* cases. Since all offices probably receive roughly the same proportion of "useless" complaints, it may be that, other things being equal, the greater the volume of cases, the greater the oversight potential. Offices that receive a relatively low number of cases and which might therefore have the time to follow up more thoroughly have a more limited field in which to do so. Analysis of staffers' responses to several questions about oversight in fact indicates positive, albeit inconsistent, relationships between the total case load in a given office and that office staff's propensity to say that they use cases for legislation and oversight and to rate casework as very effective as a technique. Presumably there is an optimal volume—large enough to bring interesting cases but small enough to allow aides time to search for underlying causes.

Third, limits on usefulness are imposed by the types of cases received. Social security, veterans, military transfers, treatment of military personnel, and Labor Department cases are most common. But few cases relating to foreign or defense policy, energy, environment, education, or transportation matters reach congressional offices, thus effectively eliminating whole areas of public policy—and a good number of departments and agencies—from casework-related oversight and legislative activity. Moreover, cases dealing with independent regulatory agencies are dealt with gingerly, usually in a pro forma, arm's-length fashion that precludes further investigation and follow-up.

Finally, as described previously, the types of cases received by different offices vary greatly according to the nature of the districts and states and according to the "nature of the times" (what is "hot" in a given week or month). Thus, the range of some members' oversight and legislative use of constituency service is limited by the types of cases received. This problem becomes important when related to those members' committee assignments; frequently, a member whose cases tend to be of one or two particular types sits on the "wrong" legislative committee and cannot make use of those cases as readily as he could if he sat on a different committee. Moreover, the likelihood of legislative or oversight action on a particular problem may also depend on the number of congressional offices being contacted by constituents on that problem at a given time. A groundswell of activity on a specific matter—such as social security disability reviews in 1981–82—may be the best guarantee that Congress will move on it.

Staff size and adequacy may be crucial. A small and overworked staff is unlikely to have time to pursue the oversight implication of cases. Common responses to the question, "What are the biggest problems you face in doing casework?" were "not enough time" and "we're understaffed." However, analysis of the relationship between staff sizes in various offices and responses to the questions about the use and value of casework for legislation and oversight yields little in the way of concrete evidence. Generally, larger staff sizes were positively linked with the use of casework and with a favorable view of its utility for legislation and oversight, but almost all such relationships were very weak.

Certain characteristics of caseworkers might affect the degree to which they look for legislative or oversight implications in casework or projects. Aides with the highest education levels seemed slightly more likely to try to extrapolate from their case experiences, but again the linkage was weak. Overall, the most and the least experienced caseworkers claimed to do so more than those in between. Younger staff members seemed just a bit more inclined than older ones to use casework for legislation and oversight. On the other hand, older caseworkers were somewhat more likely to believe that casework is a very effective technique for oversight.

Caseworkers' very positioning as boundary-spanning agents oriented, by and large, to constituents (not to legislation and oversight) probably explains some of the weak linkages, as does a lack of familiarity with legislative issues. Caseworkers and other congressional personal office aides seldom know agency programs and the statutory provisions under which constituents are complaining, and this lack of knowledge interferes with attempts to look beyond the instant case, with communication with the executive, and with efficiency.

Staff location may affect the chances of using cases for oversight. Caseworkers located in state or district offices may not be, or feel, in close enough contact with the senators and representatives or with legislative assistants in Washington to allow or encourage them to look for oversight possibilities. Certainly, a common complaint from field offices was that AAs and LAs in Washington paid little heed to their insights and warnings. Coordination and communication may suffer. Said one home-based caseworker for a midwestern Democratic senator, "Unfortunately, no one in this organization bothers to ask the right questions of staff working in the field offices." Conversely, some Washington offices do not rely on field offices because, as one AA commented, "the home office doesn't feed us legislative ideas as often because they're not as experienced at catching them." Nonetheless, the survey data calls even this explanation into question, since a slightly greater proportion of those in field offices said that they tried to correct program flaws than did those working on Capitol Hill.

Another important staffing variable for converting cases into oversight or legislation is the way casework is structured. Other things (such as experience and motivation) being equal, where case and project workers are specialists, their primary orientation would be to deal with the cases on their merits and to "win" for the constituents. Oversight considerations would take a back seat. But when other aides, especially LAs or those particularly close to the senators and representatives, handle cases and projects, their professional inclinations and their sense of what their bosses are concerned with would alert them to be on the lookout for oversight and legislative potential in constituency service. As one assistant who does both case and legislative work explained, "Casework gives me an insight I wouldn't otherwise get." Unfortunately, data gathered in this study are not appropriate to testing this theory formally. Given the increased tendency, by 1982, to structure casework in this latter fashion, prospects for the use of cases for policymaking and oversight would appear brighter—unless, of course, the alternate view comes to dominate, namely, that casework is a "make-work" function somehow beneath the dignity of legislative aides. Given the growing number of well-educated and ambitious legislative assistants on the Hill, this latter view could prevail in the future.

In offices that employ case and project specialists, successful use of casework for oversight requires a free flow of information between caseworkers and the congressmen or their legislative assistants. Given the semi-institutionalization of the casework function and the considerable autonomy under which casework operations are carried out, such access and exchange arrangements do not always exist. As one House caseworker, representing a sizable minority view, complained, "There's almost no contact; I seldom talk to the LA." Obviously, the problem is compounded when caseworkers are isolated in field offices. Many believe that much more coordination could and should be undertaken. To overcome that difficulty, several senators and representatives have located legislative assistants in home offices.

A majority of offices took the opposite view. A rather typical Senate staffer described what she said was "a great deal of interaction between us and the LAs: this office really tries to use casework for legislation." According to one House aide, "Anytime I see anything that needs legislation, I take it to the LA: we're very close in this office." According to another staffer, contact may be initiated by the legislative staff: "Sometimes they'll ask me about my experience on a particular problem." Even sitting at adjacent desks and overhearing each other's phone conversations allegedly contributes to the dialogue. A number of offices have tried to routinize the interaction between constituency service and legislative staffs by scheduling regular meetings between them and by inviting caseworkers to policy meetings with the congressmen. Home-based staffers are brought to Washington at periodic intervals to share their experiences and to participate in the legislative end of things. That sort of incentive is likely to keep caseworkers on their toes and well attuned to the legislative and oversight implications of their jobs.

The structural problems are compounded by staff training and operating patterns. Without at least a rudimentary training or orientation program, few beginning aides are likely to take note of oversight or legislative implications of cases: they have a hard enough time learning whom to call for help in the executive branch. Furthermore, the lack of interoffice cooperation (fewer than half of the respondents reported *any* pooling or sharing of efforts) undoubtedly limits some of the oversight and legislative potential of casework. Except for a few obvious cases, few offices realize that others are getting the same constituent complaints.

Nor do case and projects specialists compensate for the lack of cooperation between offices by maintaining close contacts with other congressional units that would be interested in policy or oversight. About half the interview and survey respondents were asked if they "ever seek help from, or refer casework [or] federal project problems to, congressional committees [or to] any congressional staff agency, such as the GAO, Congressional Research Service, etc." About 90 percent answered affirmatively, but in the vast majority of instances, such contact was sporadic at best, and more often than not the purpose was to ask for information or help. Only seldom do personal staffers, on their own initiative, bring case-related suggestions and issues to committee staffs. Those who do, however, do so with some regularity. One veteran aide, for example, described her boss as not "terribly active legislatively." In order to use casework for oversight and legislation, she said, she has to "feed the information" to one of the subcommittee staffers assigned to the congressman.

Much of the variation in the use of casework for legislation and oversight can be attributed to member and staff motivation or the lack thereof. Clearly, some members and staffs are far more disposed to watch for the policy aspects of casework than others. As one AA said, "It requires a training of the mind and a degree of creativity: we encourage it." According to a veteran House caseworker, "That's what casework is all about, really—remedying the defects in legislation. We really try to be conscious of legislation or of the regulations that are causing the problems we get. We're very, very attuned to legislative implications." Five years later she repeated: "I keep my eye cocked toward the LAs; the congressman expects me to bring legislative ideas to his attention or to the committee counsel." At the opposite extreme was the House aide who complained that "unfortunately, no one in this organization asks the right questions. No one cares." The AA to a southern Democrat described casework as a "second-class citizen." What amounts to the modal response came from an aide to a midwest Republican: "We get ideas once in a while and send them to the committee or talk to the boss. No—no one told us to watch for policy implications, but the congressman and AA are open to it whenever we do." Presumably, staff motivation derives from member motivation. Are congressmen oriented toward oversight? As the Obey Commission data presented in chapter 2 indicate, the answer is "yes—but." Yes, they do rank oversight as important, but not as important as legislation. Yes, some (one in ten, according to the commission's data) feel that they are expected to conduct oversight, but many, many more feel pressure to legislate and to attend to constituency service.

Motives are elusive and varied. Even if one could establish a hierarchy of congressional functions and members' allocation of time, it would be risky to offer judgments about the inclinations specifically to link casework to oversight. While it is unlikely that offices which care little for oversight or for initiating legislation will search cases for their oversight potential, it is not impossible. And it does seem likely that policy-oriented offices, especially those that have enjoyed past success in converting casework into oversight or legislation, would be very much inclined to harbor positive views of the efficacy of casework for legislative and oversight purposes and to report that they try to generalize from individual cases. Data to test this supposition directly are not available. Using the number of bills introduced and floor appearances as a measure of an office's policy orientation yields inconclusive evidence.

What of seniority or other characteristics that have been shown to affect members' propensities to introduce or cosponsor legislation?[53] Fox and Hammond's study of Washington staffs found that offices of members with high, but not the highest, seniority were more inclined to use casework experience for legislation.[54] Data for this study give some credence to their findings. On the whole, aides to representatives with less than ten years' seniority were considerably more inclined to believe that casework is very effective for legislative ideas and incentives than were their colleagues who worked for senior members. Middle seniority representatives (those in their fourth through ninth years) were distinctly more likely than their more junior and senior peers to have assistants who believed that casework was very effective for oversight, for sensitizing bureaucrats, and for forcing them to reevaluate their rules and operations. The implication is that the offices of "up-and-coming" members, many of whom are beginning to move into positions of institutional responsibility and power, may be precisely the ones who most successfully utilize — or seek to utilize — casework for legislative and oversight purposes. For the most junior members, oversight pales in comparison to the electoral attraction of casework, and their staffs tend to be young and inexperienced. Very senior members may be too distracted with committee and other leadership tasks to put much emphasis on casework as a vehicle for oversight or new legislation. Among House offices studied, staffs of backbenchers and subcommittee chairmen more frequently indicated attempts to generalize from specific cases than did those working for full committee chairs. And aides to backbenchers were most likely to judge casework "very effective" (and least likely to judge it rarely effective) for legislation. (Whether this is naive optimism or evidence that juniors need to rely on means other than committees to become involved in policymaking and oversight is unclear.) Staffs of committee chairmen were at the opposite pole.

For formal oversight and successful attempts at remedial legislation, committee involvement is essential. Yet committee involvement in constituency service is rare. Where committee and subcommittee chairmen use committee staff to do all or some of their casework, a natural link may be forged between constituent problems and the legislative and oversight functions—especially if the cases came to the members *because* of their committee assignments and committee-related reputations. Subsequent action depends on the usual factors associated with legislative initiative and committee oversight.[55] But for the vast majority of members, and certainly for all junior ones, the linkage between personal office casework and committee awareness and effort—though indispensable—is difficult to establish. Aides are most able to convert their observations and concern into legislation and oversight if: (1) they can interest their bosses or staff superiors (AAs or LAs); and (2) their congressmen sit on, or, preferably, chair, the relevant committees and subcommittees or are sufficiently important to be able to gain the attention of those members who do. The first condition is a function of staff structure and office motivation, and it does occur more often than commonly thought. The second condition is a matter of accident. Committee assignments and position make possible oversight in certain areas for each member; but, more important, they also severely constrain oversight opportunities in most other areas. As one Senate AA said: "Use casework for oversight? Only if it deals with the Senator's committee. You know how it is around here—if it's not a matter for your own committee, nothing will happen." The same holds in the lower chamber, where one caseworker described her situation: "No—he's on Rules and does little substantive legislating." The process thus requires, first, that the caseworker interest his or her representative in a given problem, and, second, that the member find a colleague on the appropriate committee who will agree to look into the problem—not an easy task, unless the latter is getting similar complaints and problems from constituents.

The final factor lies outside of Congress. Department and agency staffing, motivations, and procedures all affect not only how congressional inquiries are processed but whether or not they have an impact on policies, programs, and people.

Faced with constituent complaints or problems, most caseworkers either contact legislative liaison offices in Washington or go directly to regional or local federal offices that have the constituents' records. In the former instance they deal with liaison officers, whose responsiveness to, knowledge of, and, especially, concern for fundamental problems vary immensely. Typically, legislative liaison units do not possess great clout in departments and agencies. So, for a case or group of cases to have an oversight impact it is necessary that the liaison officers be interested in, and able to generalize from, recurring or significant problems; that they have access to superiors who likewise are concerned with overall agency performance; that these superiors possess some influence over the operating and service-delivery divisions of the agencies (and thus are able to get them to correct problems); that the superiors have access to the top echelons of their departments and agencies (the policymaking core); and that the top-echelon officials themselves be concerned about and able to remedy flaws. When legislative liaison staffs are bureaucratically situated in the offices of legislation—which often are distinct from congressional relations units—their chances of contributing to legislation and internal oversight probably are improved.

Such conditions are not always met. Normally, liaison officials are so busy just coping with cases that they have no time for going beyond the specifics to examine deeper problems or to advocate solutions. On top of these difficulties, one can readily surmise just how impressed most bureau chiefs are when they get complaints and recommendations from congressional liaison offices about their subordinates or about decisions they have made.

There are two closely related situations in which oversight activity is most likely to flow from congressional inquiries. The first occurs when a caseworker or, better yet, a senator or representative calls agency higher-ups directly to complain or to appeal over the heads of liaison people or various program administrators. Such calls are occasioned by serious problems which agencies usually are anxious to solve if they can. The second situation exists when, within an agency or bureau, responses to congressional cases flow across the desks of high-ranking administrators before being sent to the Hill.

On the local office level, for the most part, executive officials are concerned with delivering various services. When congressionals come in that have validity, administrators seem interested in rectifying the underlying problems if these problems adversely affect their local operations and clients. Even if they are inclined toward internal oversight and program improvement, locally based federal administrators often do not get enough cases from which to generalize—although a single case sometimes does trigger agency actions—and they have difficulty pressing their concerns on Washington. They might simply inform the congressional staff that legislation is needed or that, under agency regulations, their hands are tied. That puts the ball back in the congressional court.

Conversely, a few local office officials registered the opposite complaint: too much work. As one area director moaned, "I doubt if [congressionals] help; I for one am too busy grinding out replies to think about them. You get numb; the whole process becomes so automatic and routine."

To make maximum use of congressional inquiries, it would seem agencies ought to develop methods of record-keeping and to undertake regular reviews of such records with an eye to spotting program imperfections.[56] Perhaps the best examples of such systems exist in the military services, which routinely employ case inquiries for purposes of internal supervision. In the air force, for example, every inquiry from a congressional office is entered into a computer, and periodically the liaison heads in the Pentagon examine printouts on a sample of cases to see how fast and how well liaison officers are handling congressionals, what sort of complaints are being sent to Congress by air force personnel, and where—at which air force bases—the complaints are cropping up. Said one military officer: "If problems are spotted, I notify the appropriate agency. I watch very closely; we can take these cases to the assistant secretary if need be." He went on to cite specific regulations that were changed, personnel transferred, and new units created as a result of this record-keeping and search operation.

In short, for congressional inquiries on behalf of aggrieved constituents to cause agencies to consider legislation or to study their regulations, procedures, and personnel, and for them to help sensitize bureaucrats, requires a series of conditions, linkages, and effects that are not easy to piece together.

7.8. Miscellaneous Benefits

In addition to oversight and legislation, and over and above the considerable personal satisfaction derived from casework, congressional and executive branch personnel see other benefits to casework. Thirty percent of all replies to a question about the benefits of prompt and careful handling of congressionals dealt with improving relations with Congress. One HEW official explained that "we think it's really important to keep congressmen happy; it's our job: stroke 'em; be responsive—show 'em we care." An independent regulatory commission spokesman said that such handling "creates an image of responsiveness and concern. When they're voting on matters concerning the [commission] I'd rather have members who know us; it helps counter the emotional congressmen who attack us. Those who know us will go to bat for us." Notions of reciprocity and exchange dominate thinking on this subject, as one Commerce Department liaison official indicated: "A chit's a chit. We do them a favor and they do us a favor. Our most useful service is getting constituents off congressmen's backs. They come to Washington and the member sets up an interview or meeting with us and we explain how to apply for a grant."

Few administrators thought that congressional votes are won specifically by favors rendered in casework; but most believed that votes can be lost if casework is done poorly.[57] The White House perspective, however, appears to be somewhat more optimistic, with a strong majority of former White House Office of Congressional Relations aides believing that access to congressmen was enhanced and votes were influenced by the Office's responsiveness to congressional requests for help.[58]

Another 13 percent of the responses were indirectly related to Congress: some administrators thought that casework educated Congress to agencies' operations and problems: "We make ourselves available to congressmen and their staffs. We see it as a real opportunity to help them understand HUD's programs and rules; it gives us a chance to explain." Others thought that doing a good job of casework helped keep constituents off Congress's back and helped keep Congress off theirs. Just as congressional staffs feed casework-related questions to their bosses before and during hearings, three administrators indicated that they had observed casework data used to prepare for hearings or visits to the Hill. According to a Commerce Department official, "When the secretary or undersecretary is scheduled to visit a congressman or appear at a hearing, we pull the file to see what problems that congressman's constituents are having with us." Moreover, a couple of executives said that if they learned in advance that a congressman was planning to bring in a constituent to testify, the agency would examine any files it had on the constituent's case.

Nearly a quarter of executive branch respondents mentioned that casework helps to provide better service delivery and to improve their programs — which amounts to the "internal oversight" discussed above. Others emphasized that doing a good job on casework "improves credibility." Casework, said one, "is good public relations for our office." It also is a safety valve. Agencies sometimes encourage clients to take their problems to Congress, in hopes of generating pressure for changes they have long advocated, but which Congress has been reluctant to grant. Several also mentioned that because of an influx of cases, their offices had undergone expansion. One agency official explained that, "actually, our backlog and delays in answering congressionals helped us get five hundred additional positions this year, and we're getting more next year."

Educating the public was cited by nine respondents as a benefit. Congressional staffers were even more apt to mention it. "If we can't help," said one Senate aide, "we're concerned to explain why; it's an educational function." Another thought that "casework gives us an opportunity to show constituents how to go about getting a problem solved the next time it occurs." Such an attitude is especially prevalent among aides specializing in federal projects: "We try to show communities why they lost out and what is needed to get a grant." "I've taught college presidents how to apply," boasted one aide.

Several administrators and a surprisingly large number of congressmen and their aides are convinced that casework prevents public cynicism about government. Thirteen of 18 executive officials and 87 percent of 230 congressmen and staffers agreed that ''citizens who receive casework help from their senators and representatives will have a more favorable impression of Congress and of government in general than those who do not.'' Although a caution against self-serving evaluations always is in order, the testimony here is powerful, as these typical comments suggest:

People are so grateful just to hear a response. There's no more important function for a congressional office than to give constituents the feeling that they have access to government.

If democracy is to work, people in general must feel that government is an advocate and that they have an opportunity to be heard and that government will provide the services that have been promised.

People are becoming alienated from government because they feel that it is too large and unresponsive. Any effort we can make to increase responsiveness gives the public more confidence in its government.

Various scholars, it should be noted, seem to have accepted such views, concluding that ''errand-running may be a more noble form of representation than has heretofore been recognized.''[59] The empirical question, naturally, is whether they are correct: does casework alleviate cynicism? Findings of previous studies are ambiguous, in part due to methodological problems.[60] Lacking panel data to determine attitudes toward government before and after exposure to casework, the best that can be done is to compare the attitudes of those who have received casework assistance with the attitudes of those who have not, realizing full well that causality could run either way. That is, casework experience could have an effect on attitudes, or, as suggested in chapter 2, attitudes (cynicism) could affect the propensity to make contact with congressmen and seek assistance and could affect judgments about the quality of that assistance. Cross-tabulating the Michigan CPS index of cynicism used in table 2.2 with various contact variables produces little in the way of meaningful results.

First, comparing those who contacted their congressmen (for any reason) with those who did not, several more of the former than of the latter fell into the ''high'' cynicism category, but the relationship is trivial in magnitude. However, a weak but significant relationship in the expected direction exists when cynicism and satisfaction in 1978 (but not 1980) are correlated: the more satisfied with the congressional response, the less cynical. Second, comparing those who made contact specifically to ask for help on a problem with those who made no contact at all, there again, surprisingly, was a very slight positive association (in 1978) between casework experience and cynicism. But there was a moderate tendency for those who were satisfied with the results to exhibit lower degrees of cynicism than those who were less satisfied. Third, similar analyses were run to compare contact and casework requests in both years with three specific indicators of citizen attitudes: ratings of Congress's performance, trust in Washington, and trust in Congress. Assuming that causality does run from casework experience to trust, there is no evidence of a positive influence of casework contact on trust. There are very weak tendencies for *satisfaction* with case (or contact) experience to correlate negatively with cynicism (positively with trust). What matters, therefore, may be the quality, not the fact, of casework contact. Surely that is what is implied in the efforts of congressional staffers to please their clients. But, again, the caveat is crucial. Causality may run either way—or both ways: less cynical and more trusting constituents may well be inclined to be understanding and thus more satisfied with their casework experiences. And in any case, the relationships are *very* weak indeed.

7.9. Summary

Casework confers certain institutional benefits, not the least of which is its contribution to the legislative and oversight functions of Congress. Several conclusions about oversight seem warranted. First, within the limits imposed by the four opportunity factors, there can be no doubt that a good number of congressional offices do try to use casework for legislative and oversight purposes. Considering how totally stacked the deck seems to be against such use, it is a wonder that it occurs at all and that staffs judge constituency service to be as effective for oversight as they do.

Casework is but one of many facets of oversight, and one which has its own powerful rationale independent of any contribution it can make to oversight or legislation. Moreover, as Keefe and Ogul point out, "oversight inevitably will be partial and selective."[61] Insofar as constituency service is concerned, its impact on oversight *must* be selective: it will be useful for some issues (remedying program flaws) and for certain agencies (especially those operating directly with the public), and it will more likely be employed for oversight in some offices (primarily those of relatively junior, up-and-coming congressmen) by certain caseworkers. Case loads and types, staff characteristics, the motivation and committee status of members, and agency operations all limit casework's utility.

Second, casework constitutes a direct yet informal and relatively "inexpensive" congressional intervention into agency operations, and therefore it is, by itself, a kind of oversight. Individual cases that had been handled erroneously or too slowly are frequently corrected, other kinds of problems solved, and many requests for help filled, obviating the need for extensive and sophisticated congressional examinations of agency programs and administrative behavior.

But casework is a mixed blessing. It does require time and energy of congressional staffers. It is an inefficient way to keep track of agency behavior and programs. It is not particularly well orchestrated. And to the extent that dealing with people's problems one at a time—to their satisfaction—reduces the political pressure to effect major correctives in programs, one might argue that there is a disincentive for conducting formal and systematic oversight. That, however, seems to stretch things too far. Such formal oversight is committee-based—and there is a large gap between what committees do and what goes on in personal offices. Each is a world unto itself. The problem is not so much that doing casework inhibits systematic oversight; rather, there simply is little institutional or individual member incentive for *any* formal oversight at all. Casework may well be highly correlated with a lack of committee oversight, but (1) oversight was just as rare—perhaps more so—before the recent rise in casework loads, and (2) correlation need not imply causation.

Third, and maybe most important, casework is a genuine, though limited, contributor to internal agency supervision and self-correction. One need not claim any miracles or exaggerate the argument, but legislative liaison specialists, program-level administrators, and caseworkers on the Hill do see congressional inquiries as a tool to be used for profit administratively, and they can cite numerous examples. Certainly the potential is there. It may well be, therefore, that those who denigrate constituency service as a technique of oversight are focusing on the wrong area. Rather than look for new bills or oversight hearings, perhaps judgments should be based upon internal agency remedial actions.

In short, a balanced assessment of the interaction between casework and policymaking (between service and policy responsiveness) *has* to be mixed. In such instances, ultimate judgments turn on other factors: how much one values an institution that can redress grievances at little cost to the constituent versus, perhaps, how much casework undermines policy accountability by substituting one rationale for casting a vote at election time for another. The next chapter addresses that question.

CHAPTER 8

Casework and Votes

Incumbent congressmen tend to be reelected over and over again, usually with substantial victory margins. According to the best available studies, incumbents win because they are recognized by voters, are popular and well liked, are evaluated quite favorably on their job performance by their constituents, and run well-financed campaigns.[1] Such advantages do not operate in a vacuum: challengers are less well recognized, less well liked, and less often and less favorably evaluated. Voters prefer incumbents over challengers and vote accordingly.

The burning question, however, is, Why are incumbents recognized, popular, highly evaluated, and therefore preferred? No one has been able to say for certain, but tentative answers include: (1) the inherent visibility of officeholders; (2) the perquisites of office that allow congressmen to make contact with constituents and to control the flow of information in order to claim credit, advertise, take positions,[2] stress desirable personal traits (such as personality, loyalty, power, experience), and demonstrate their concerns for constituents; and (3) incumbents' considerable responsiveness to constituents. Morris P. Fiorina, in particular, has focused on service and allocation responsiveness, arguing that the constituency service function is the key to the puzzle. By helping his district secure federal grants and projects and, especially, by becoming a "monopoly supplier of bureaucratic unsticking devices for his district," the congressman secures enough good will, and thereby votes, to move his district into the "safe seat" column.[3] Whereas taking positions on controversial issues can harm a congressman, serving the district cannot: "Pork barrelling and casework," asserts Fiorina, "are basically pure profit."[4]

8.1. The Casework Hypothesis

We had a high recognition factor. And of all the things said about me, none of them said, "He's a conservative or a liberal" or "He votes this way on such and such an issue." None of them said that at all. There were two things said. One, "He works hard." Two, "He works for us." Nothing more than that. So we made it our theme. "O'Connor gets things done;" and we emphasized the dams, the highways, the buildings, and the casework. . . . The biggest part of getting reelected is casework. . . . Financially, my strong support comes from the Chamber of Commerce types, business and professional people. They finance my campaigns. But if you are talking about grassroots support, the most loyal followers are the people for whom we have done casework.[5]

This view of an exchange of votes for favors now has become the basis of conventional wisdom, in part because it is intuitively attractive and in part because it is so difficult to subject to empirical scrutiny. The list of citations of congressmen, staffers, political journalists, party officials, political activists, and scholars who have affirmed its validity literally runs pages in length. And there is considerable evidence, albeit mostly circumstantial, in its favor. It has been shown, for example, that constituents' evaluations of their representatives, as opposed to their judgments of Congress as an institution, are heavily influenced by their views of congressmen's personal characteristics and constituency service.[6] A CBS–*New York Times* poll found that more people believed it important for a congressman to "help people in his district who have a problem with the government" than felt it important for him to "work in Congress on bills of national interest."[7] Analysis of the Obey Commission's 1977 survey reveals that of those respondents who personally had requested help from their congressmen, 76 percent gave their representatives an "excellent" or "pretty good" rating, compared to 63 percent of those who had not sought help. And of those who had sought out assistance, 36 percent rated their congressmen's performance as "better" than the performance of other representatives. Only 20 percent of those who had not asked for help did so. Similarly, the 1978 CPS Election Study data showed that while 78 percent of those who had contacted their congressmen gave them a "very good" or "good" rating, only 61 percent of those who had not asked for assistance did so. In 1980, nine of ten who had been assisted by their representatives with problems they were having with the government approved of the way those members were handling their jobs, compared to only 54 percent of those who had not received casework help. (Of course, a major problem with such figures is that it might have been the favorable job rating that stimulated the constituent to seek help in the first place, rather than the other way around, or that either could be caused by other factors.)

Still other evidence is available. A Roper poll in 1978 asked respondents: "In voting for congressmen, will you vote for a candidate more because of what you think he can do for this community, or more because of his stand on national issues, or more because you respect him as a person?" Fully 47 percent said that the congressman's efforts for the community would be primary, followed by 36 percent citing his stand on issues. Apparently, the number of voters mentioning constituency service as the basis for their evaluation has grown.[8] Relying on a measure of district office "capability" to advertise the congressman's name and claim credit for various benefits and services, Cranor and Westphal found a moderately strong correlation between district office capabilities in 1975–76 and the percent of electoral improvement in 1976 over 1974 for nonurban incumbents who were marginal in 1974 and who fared better in 1976.[9] And a recent study suggests that mailings of various documents to constituents enhances a representative's recognition and evaluations among them—at least in the short run— and adds to the likelihood that the recipients would vote for the incumbent.[10] More formal analyses purport to show that constituents' ability to recognize and favorably rate congressmen is positively affected by having contacted them and having been satisfied with such contacts.[11] And the work of several political scientists indicates that various measures of congressmen's attentiveness to their constituents (usually measured by the amount of time spent in their districts) correlate positively with election results.[12] Finally, two scholars have tried to demonstrate directly that votes for incumbents are influenced by satisfaction with casework.[13]

In short, the argument is that strategic time and staff allocations, attentiveness, and, in particular, individual and "high-level" casework (federal projects) make recipients grateful or at least create a feeling that "the congressman cares about us." Such feelings produce favorable evaluations and trust, and they contribute to a good reputation, which, in turn, scares off challengers, affects the views of potential donors to campaigns, and thus directly and indirectly translates into votes. As one former senator explained: "It has been my experience that little, almost trivial things bring more gratitude than monumental things. As a general rule, good service helps at election time." That is precisely the conclusion to which congressmen, staffers, and agency bureaucrats have come after dealing with casework. Four out of five senators and representatives, the same proportion of agency administrators, and 85 percent of House and Senate staffers in the 1977–78 sample agreed or strongly agreed that "citizens who receive help from their congressmen are likely to vote for them at the next election." One-tenth of the members, 3 percent of their aides, and one in twenty bureaucrats disagreed. Asked to rate the effectiveness of casework for strengthening congressmen's electoral bases, equal proportions of members (42 percent) deemed it somewhat and very effective. Fifty-nine percent of the staffers thought casework very effective (compared to 75 percent of administrators), and 35 percent (20 percent among agency officials) saw it as somewhat effective. Could they be wrong?

Several pieces of evidence suggest that they might be, or at least that these views oversimplify reality. Fenno, after all, discovered a variety of "homestyles," only a few of which depended heavily upon constituency service. Cranor and Westphal found no correlation between actual district office creditclaiming activities—as opposed to capabilities—and improvement in incumbents' electoral fortunes. An analysis of the growth in "safe" seats in the House showed that marginal districts began to vanish in the 1920s—well before the recent explosion of government programs that gave rise to the casework empires of today. [14] A recent study by Jon Bond found little evidence of impact by various types of "advertising" (newsletters, questionnaires, trips home, newspaper columns, and radio and television shows) on the competitiveness of districts. [15] And Richard Born could not find any relationship between the number of district offices, district staffers, or specially designated "communications" aides, on the one hand, and electoral margins, on the other. [16] More important, Thomas E. Mann noted that in one district he was able to study intensely, voters who had received help or communications from the incumbent were no more likely to vote for him than those who had not. [17] And of those surveyed in the 1978 CPS study, there was no difference in ratings of their congressmen between those who had made contact specifically to request casework help and those who had done so for other reasons. Thus the picture is anything but clear. Methodological problems and disputes over whether "casework" or some other aspect of constituency service is important make difficult the task of bringing clarity out of confusion.

Before dealing with these questions empirically, it may be useful to explore the ways in which casework (and service more generally) can be and is exploited to produce the electoral effect that, thus far, has been so difficult to pin down.

8.2. Translating Casework into Votes

How do congressmen and their staffers go about trying to generate votes from casework? Members and staffs in 1977–78 were asked: "What 'political use,' if any, is [was] made of casework and projects assistance?" Respondents were offered six answers, along with an open-ended "other" choice. In 1982 the question was rephrased: "Are casework or case records used in your office for other (informational or political) purposes?" Although there is reason to be suspicious of the responses, table 8.1 presents the results. [18]

About three-quarters of all offices surveyed in 1977–78 indicated some political or public relations use of case and project results. Commonly, successes are mentioned in speeches, campaign literature, newsletters, and radio or television ads. One New England senator, for instance, swore that a casework film used in his last reelection bid won the election for him. In his 1978 reelection campaign, Cong. Henry Reuss (D., Wis.) used a large fold-out brochure that included numerous pictures of constituents praising him for his helpfulness: "Heaven knows how many months we would have been without income without Congressman Reuss''; and "With the help of Congressman Reuss we got in touch with the president of a major oil company. We were able to get [our] product within 4 days." A House staffer recounted how his "good letter file" (especially warm thank-you letters) and newspaper clipping file were searched for good quotations to be used in campaign brochures.

Such testimonials are not often sought out. Rather, when a constituent who received help directly suggests such a tribute, the offer is accepted. As one aide explained, "We don't use casework as such, but if someone writes and volunteers help, we tell him to write a letter to the local newspaper's editor." Staffers sometimes leak accounts of favorable cases to reporters as well. The use of voluntary testimonials is reasonably widespread, and they are believed to be potent. Indeed, House Majority Leader Jim Wright (D., Tex.) in the summer of 1978 wrote a "Dear Colleague" letter urging Democrats to seek out such visible praise and spelling out techniques for so doing. He even went so far as to suggest a method whereby the constituent would not appear to be reading from a script. He concluded: "Get about 20 of these little testimonials, schedule them for saturation broadcast in the days immediately prior to the election and it will sound as if the Congressman has personally helped virtually everybody in town."[19]

A somewhat more imaginative and dramatic use of casework was employed by a former representative who had her own weekly television show. A feature of that program was the reading of letters from constituents who had sought her assistance. The congresswoman proceeded to explain what her office had done to correct the problem, often launching into a discussion of broader legislative efforts made to remedy the situation.

Adding names of casework recipients to mailing lists is a standard procedure in many offices, and it is automatic when requested by constituents. Often, congressmen and senators want to do a mailing addressing a single issue, such as education or veterans' policy, to a particular group. Constituents who have requested casework on those matters are logical targets for such mailings.[20] Whether the purpose is merely to keep the congressman's name before potential voters or to keep interested constituents up-to-date on policy matters, the effect is the same.

Table 8.1: Political Use of Casework Results

Ways in Which Casework Is Used	Senators 95th	Reps. 95th	Representatives (97th)	
			Done Routinely	Done If Constituent Volunteers
Campaign literature or speeches (1978); campaign materials, public appearances, speeches, ads at election time (1982)	35%	29%	27%	17%
Newletters; TV or radio appearances or advertisements (1978); newsletters or other nonelection communications to constituents (1982)	32	31	30	19
Only special cases or federal projects mentioned; not individual cases	16	14	NA	NA
Names of recipients added to political or campaign mailing lists	3	7	NA	NA
Recipients urged to write their newspapers about help they received	NA	NA	0	20
Recipients urged to "spread the word" about help they received	NA	NA	4	21

continued

Table 8.1: *continued*

Ways in Which Casework Is Used	Senators 95th	Reps. 95th	Representatives (97th)	
			Done Routinely	Done If Constituent Volunteers
Names of recipients added to general or specific mailing lists (1978); names added to nonpolitical mailing lists (1982)	13	27	40	20
Recipients contacted for campaign help or donations (1978); asked to work in or contribute to election campaigns, or their names forwarded to campaign committee (1982)	10	1	2	58
Only general references to casework are made (1978)	10	1	NA	NA
No political use of casework at all	26	24	a	a
(N)	(31)	(95)	(134)	(134)

NOTE: Percentages do not total to 100 because multiple responses were coded. N = the number of senators and representatives whose offices gave the indicated response. Data from all respondents (member and staffers) for a given congressman or senator are combined to yield a single response per member. In 1982, respondents were asked whether a given activity was done routinely or only if the constituent volunteered to help in some way. NA = Question Not Asked.

[a] Combining the two response categories, 18 percent undertook no activity at all, either routinely or if the constituent volunteered.

In three Senate and seven House offices, staffers in 1977 and 1978 indicated that casework was used directly for soliciting electoral help. One assistant bluntly admitted that "if successful, we make out a duplicate three-by-five card that we send to the campaign committee headquarters. At election time a letter is sent soliciting campaign help and money." Another aide explained that "we put their name on a campaign list if we figure they owe us a favor." Other offices were more circumspect: "If the constituent says, 'Thanks, can I do anything?' we'll make out a card." Another said that his office would do so only in extreme emergencies: "We only did it in 1972—a really tough race—when we needed every bit of help." Most staffers keep a "good letter" file of constituents who have expressed gratitude. How much campaign help and money result from these efforts is unclear, but studies suggest that it might be substantial.[21] Six of ten offices in 1982 indicated that they would send names of constituents to the campaign committee, tell constituents to contact the committee, or urge the committee to contact the constituents *only* if the casework recipients volunteered to help their benefactors.

While many offices are reticent about the results of casework, very few hesitate to claim credit for obtaining federal projects. One aide described his office's activity as "generating a certain amount of puff on successful projects." Congressional offices are anxious to make announcements concerning contracts, grants, and the like, and they exert considerable pressure on the agencies to keep them informed. Such credit is claimed in newsletters and campaign literature, of course, but even better is the publicity that can be had from newspaper headlines. Thus offices stay on their toes to provide the media with press releases concerning newly released federal largesse for their districts.

One-fourth of the offices studied in 1977–78 reported doing nothing to take political advantage of casework and projects. By 1982 that figure had dropped to 18 percent. Using a narrower definition of "political use" (including only the routine use of casework in campaigning, soliciting recipients to help at election time, and encouraging constituents to write to newspapers or otherwise to spread the word), only 28 percent of House offices admitted to overt use of casework for political gain. Most, of course, welcome voluntary assistance that arises out of casework. In several instances, senators and representatives explicitly overruled their campaign managers. Four reasons account for their behavior. First, a few congressmen simply do not need whatever electoral help casework might bring: "No, we don't need it," said an aide to a very senior southern senator. An administrative assistant to a representative from a state with an almost legendary senator spoke of gaining credit for projects: "If someone contacts the senator, we simply coordinate with his office. No problem in credit claiming. We know we're competent and don't worry about the senator upstaging us. We're safe."

A second, quite prevalent, reason is more personal. "It would be a miserable thing to do," commented the Washington caseworker for a powerful western senator. "I don't like to exploit people's problems," said a staffer to an eastern senator; "we try to protect constituents as much as possible. To use casework for political reasons is reprehensible." "Mr. ———— is a modest man," said his caseworker; "he won't brag about casework and won't use it for political benefit." Most offices go to great lengths to distance themselves from their campaign committees. But as one aide explained: "Many people come to us and begin by saying, "I'd really like to help you in your campaign. I've got this problem. . . ." So we tell them, "Look, you don't have to say that." If they persist and really want to help, we keep their names and send them to the election committee."

Third, regardless of how they really feel, a good number of members and aides are afraid to use casework because constituents might resent it and / or it could cause legal or ethical problems. Using official mailing lists for campaign purposes was prohibited by a ruling of the House Administration Committee in 1978, and campaign activity by staffers is illegal. "It could backfire," thought one former member. "We wouldn't dare advertise it," insisted a Senate aide. Constituents, many claim, would not tolerate it. In a number of House offices, the resistance to using casework politically was overwhelming. For example, one staffer told how, when the member's campaign committee prepared mailing lists at election time, she insisted on examining them and removing all names of constituents who had received casework aid. Routinely, of course, checks sent by constituents to the congressmen in gratitude for service rendered are returned.

Finally, among both those who do and those who do not exploit casework, there is the belief that the biggest political payoff comes not from overt publicity but rather from word-of-mouth advertising by satisfied constituents. Only 14 percent of congressmen and staffers believed that casework was "very valuable and effective" in generating publicity, compared to over half who thought it very effective in strengthening their electoral bases. Said one House aide: "We don't use it politically. In the past I did use it in campaign advertising, but generally word-of-mouth advertising is best. You don't have to blow a bugle." According to another: "The best and most effective political use is to do the casework well—no sense screwing up a good effort by claiming special credit." There is a firm conviction among caseworkers that the results of good work for constituents will spread quickly without advertising. Matthews years ago quoted a senator's assistant: "When you get somebody $25.00 from the Social Security Administration, he talks to his friends and neighbors about it. After a while the story grows until you've single-handedly obtained $2,500 for a constituent who was on the brink of starvation."[22] At the most, staffers will merely remind the constituent "not to forget us."

For most offices, it is an absolute rule to convey the impression that the congressman—not the caseworker—is really at work on the constituent's problem. The casework manual used in one representative's office has this advice: "The caseworker should remember that he is acting for Congressman ———, rather than for himself. Thus, a caseworker's attitude toward the constituent should not be, 'I am helping you,' rather, it should be, 'Congressman ——— is helping you.'" If, as occurs in several House offices, the congressman himself can telephone the constituent with the good news on a case, so much the better. Conventional wisdom has it that the constituent will have told all his relatives by the next morning.

A plausible hypothesis is that congressmen and senators representing marginal districts, or those whose most recent election victories were close, would be more likely to try to use casework results for political purposes. So might junior members. Findings from earlier chapters might imply that eastern congressmen also would be more likely to try to advertise or otherwise use casework results or records for such purposes. A multivariate (PROBIT) test of these hypotheses yields the maximum likelihood estimates in table 8.2. As is apparent, there is no support for either the electoral or the seniority hypotheses, but several other results are interesting. Easterners and representatives from districts characterized by low education levels seemed more inclined to try to translate casework into political benefit. Democrats and party and committee leaders, on the other hand, did not.[23] Presumably, eastern representatives are used to operating in a highly politicized and traditional environment where credit-claiming is the norm. Leaders are less in need of such publicity. Congressmen from low education districts may believe that their constituents are more susceptible to being impressed by casework; several of the findings of previous chapters tend to support such a view. It may be, too, that members whose seats are precarious fear taking the risk that might attend being "caught" trying to make political capital out of people's problems. One cannot be certain, however, and the relatively small number of congressmen included in the analysis should give reason to pause before proclaiming a definitive judgment.

Using the data on case loads described in chapter 3, the author and a colleague, in an article published in 1981, tested the hypothesis that congressmen who do a good deal of casework derive electoral benefits.[24] Specifically, the test was whether case loads in 1977–78 would affect the 1978 election results. Employing various baseline measures against which the impact of casework could be measured (the 1976 election, party identification in the district, and the aver-

Table 8.2: Use of Casework Results for Political Purposes, 95th Congress

Independent Variable	PROBIT Maximum Likelihood Estimates	Standard Error
East	1.027*	(.545)
Democrat	−1.492**	(.681)
Leader	− .954*	(.570)
Conservatism Scores	− .016	(.011)
Seniority (Years)	.001	(.042)
Electoral Trend 1970–1976	−.007	(.016)
Activism (Bills)	−.005*	(.003)
Activism (Floor)	.001	(.008)
Median Years Education	−2.098**	(.768)
Median Income	.0003*	(.0002)
CONSTANT	26.028	(9.2425)
(N)	(77)	
Estimated R-squared	.62	

$*p < .10; **p < .05; ***p < .01.$

age vote for the incumbent or his party's candidate in the three previous elections), and controlling for important factors (the incumbent's party, seniority, and legislative activism, his ideological distance from his constituents, and the median education level of his district), the analysis produced surprising results. While a congressman's previous vote margins, party (there was a pro-Republican national trend in 1978), activism (visibility), and ideological compatibility or lack thereof, and the constituency's education, partisanship, and previous voting habits proved to be solid predictors of the vote margin, casework loads did not. Doing large amounts of casework had no independent effect on the percentage of vote won in 1978. The analysis was not technically a test of the general constituency service hypothesis since it did not address the effectiveness of an incumbent's pork-barrel successes or ability to fulfill constituents' noncasework (information and small favors) requests. Nor did it test explicitly for the effects of various advertising, position-taking, and credit-claiming techniques, such as newsletters, speeches, and time spent in the district. (The positive findings concerning legislative activism — floor appearances and the introduction of legislation — imply that these dimensions of position-taking and advertising are somewhat important.) But the findings on casework clearly run counter to expectations.

8.3. An Individual-Level Analysis

Before accepting the aggregate-level analysis as proof that casework does not pay off electorally, corroboration from individual-level analysis would seem appropriate, if not strictly necessary. The 1978 and 1980 CPS National Election Studies make possible such a check. The model to be used resembles the one used for the aggregate data, and the variables include: the incumbent's party (to measure any national electoral trend) and seniority; the voter's partisanship (whether or not the same as the incumbent) and education; a measure of the ideological discrepancy between voter and incumbent; a variable to take account of voters who, having no ideological orientation, could hardly cast a ballot on the basis of ideological discrepancy; and, of course, casework contact (having sought help from the incumbent and received an answer).[25]

The CPS data contain no exact analogue for the measures of bills introduced and floor appearances used in the aggregate analysis, but other measures of congressmen's salience are available: whether the respondent has personally met the congressman, has heard him speak at a meeting, has talked to someone on his staff, has received mail from the him, has read about him, has heard him on the radio, or has seen him on television. The dependent variable is whether or not the respondent voted for the congressional incumbent in 1978 or 1980.

The results, shown in the first two columns of table 8.3, are quite consistent with the aggregate analysis. Party identification had a powerful effect on voting behavior, as did ideological compatibility. It can be estimated from the PROBIT statistics that if a Republican had a .50 probability of voting for a given Democratic incumbent in 1978, an otherwise identical Democrat would have a .964 probability of voting for the same incumbent. If a 1978 liberal respondent had a .90 probability of voting for a given liberal incumbent, an otherwise identical conservative respondent would exhibit only a .754 probability of doing likewise. Approximately the same impact was evident in 1980. Voters apparently used a rather simple liberal-conservative continuum to judge incumbents' policy orientations. The variables for a Democratic incumbent and the voter's education level show the expected signs, but only education in 1978 can be deemed statistically different from zero (and then only by using very generous significance levels).

Of the ways in which constituents may receive information about their repre-

Table 8.3: Determinants of the Congressional Vote

| Independent Variables | PROBIT Maximum Likelihood Estimates | | | |
	(1) 1978	(2) 1980	(3) 1978	(4) 1980
Member is Democrat	−.107	−.161	−.090	−.042
Same party	1.801***	1.497***	1.755***	1.311***
Member's seniority	.096	−.018	.001	−.109
Constituent's education	−.224*	.010	−.214	.033
Ideological discrepancy	−.594***	−.537***	−.494**	−.409**
Party-issues voting	—	—	−.657**	−1.291***
Challenger spending	—	—	−.116***	−.178***
No ideology	−.171	.197	−.105	.223
Met incumbent	.049	−.097	—	—
Meeting with incumbent	.248*	−.032	—	—
Staff contact	−.087	.449**	—	—
Received mail	.114	.186**	—	—
Heard on radio	−.228*	−.027	—	—
Saw on TV	−.067	.067	—	—
Read about incumbent	.488***	.270**	.453***	.320***
Casework	.281	.445*	.247	.272
Information	—	—	.214	.548**
Pork barrel	—	—	.384**	.341*
Summary contact	—	—	.004	.076*
CONSTANT	−.207	−.031	.638	1.219
(N)	(750)	(772)	(750)	(772)
Est. R-squared	.41	.36	.44	.46

NOTE: One-tailed test of significance required for all variables except for Democrat, Seniority, and No Ideology: * $p < .10$; ** $p < .05$; *** $p < .01$.

sentative, only reading about him clearly seemed important in 1978. (In 1980 other factors — mail and staff contact — mattered, as will be explained below.) If one's probability of voting for the incumbent in 1978 was .50, having read about him in a newspaper or magazine increased that probability by about .19. In 1980, newspaper coverage was important, but less so.

As was the case with the aggregate data, the coefficient for casework failed to achieve the usually accepted .05 level of statistical significance, but in 1980 it came close. The magnitude, in any case, was rather small. Specifically, if one's probability of voting for the incumbent in 1978 was .50, receiving the benefits of casework would increase that probability by .111. Of course, not all voters are positioned near a .50 probability of voting for the incumbent. More are near .90, where the payoff from casework is .041, and many are positioned above .90, where the payoff is even less. Could this constitute a substantively important effect?

One can take all the respondents in the 1978 survey who lived in a congressional district where the incumbent was running for reelection with opposition and use the coefficients in table 8.3 to estimate the probability of each respondent's voting for the incumbent in the absence of casework. Similarly, the probability that a respondent will vote for the incumbent if he or she received the benefits of casework can be estimated. The mean difference in these probabilities across all respondents is .061. That is, the expected increase in the probability that a randomly drawn constituent would vote for the incumbent after benefiting from casework is .061. But this has to be discounted, since many casework recipients will not vote. One House staffer, asked if casework produces votes, responded: "We strongly suspect that our cases didn't help. I checked our 'active' cases, and most people weren't even registered." According to Obey Commission data, of those who themselves asked for help from their congressmen, at least 22 percent had not voted in 1974; and of those who said someone in their family had sought assistance, 42 percent had cast no ballot. Performing the same simulation using only those who claimed to have voted (a figure that substantially exceeded actual turnout) yields a much lower (.028) probability. Since most who submit case requests share the incumbent's party affiliation, and thus are more likely to support him, the effect of casework has to be discounted even further. Finally, the higher socioeconomic-status respondents, who are most likely to vote, are least likely to be swayed by casework. The payoff from casework, it appears, came close to being nil in 1978. That both the aggregate- and individual-level analyses reach this conclusion is noteworthy, especially in connection with the problem of the direction of causality that might be raised against the analysis. It is reasonably plausible to argue that a congressman might step up his casework efforts in response to perceived electoral weakness, thus causing casework and votes to be simultaneously determined. (Were that the case, a positive effect of casework on vote totals might be counterbalanced by a negative effect of vote totals on case loads). However, it is most implausible to suggest that an individual voter who dislikes and does not expect to vote for an incumbent might therefore submit a request for casework assistance. The reverse is more likely true. And if so, then the extremely modest estimate of casework effect is inflated, and the real effect of casework is even smaller than the coefficients suggest.

Several objections might be raised. Perhaps the definition used here is too narrow. Providing information to inquiring constituents, sending them documents, pointing them to agency offices, and so on are forms of constituency service: should they not be included in the analysis? It is virtually impossible to obtain estimates of some of these variables for an aggregate analysis, but (thanks to the CPS survey) they can be included in an individual-level study. Similarly, what about the effects of the pork barrel and of federal grants and projects? Again, for an aggregate analysis, this factor would prove extraordinarily difficult to measure; but it can be used in an individual-level study. Finally, perhaps the focus should be on casework success rates. Maybe only *successful* casework wins votes. Recall from chapter 6 that congressional staffers believe themselves to be quite successful and that they make every effort to be polite and helpful even when unable to ''win'' for constituents. Does success matter? Limits on the nature of the data preclude a direct answer, but when the reported success rates of 180 individual House caseworkers are correlated with the 1978 electoral margins of their employers, the resulting correlation is nil ($r = -.03$).

Another pair of equations (the third and fourth in table 8.3) can be generated to meet some of these objections and to incorporate other important factors. In the earlier model, the contact items (meetings with member or staff, mail, news media exposure) are replaced with a single contact variable produced by summing together the omitted variables. The use of this index allows a test of the hypothesis that total cumulative contact with the incumbent increases the likelihood that a citizen will vote for him. One would expect this index to be more reliable than any individual item, and therefore perhaps capable of producing a significant coefficient where no individual item could.

A dummy variable indicating that the respondent was aware of some specific instance of the incumbent's ''bringing home the bacon'' is added.[26] Among voters in the sample, 10.4 percent were able to recall a specific example of something the incumbent had done for the district. Another dummy variable is set equal to 1 for respondents who had asked their congressman for noncasework information and had received an answer. Together, the variables for casework, recollection of pork barreling, and information requests come close to exhausting the types of particularized favors which incumbents can provide to constituents.

To generate a more complete picture, an additional element of issue voting needs to be added. Erikson found that in placing their congressmen on the CPS issue scales, voters were not influenced by the congressmen's actual voting records.[27] However, voters tended to place Democrats on the liberal end of the various issue scales, and Republicans on the conservative side, regardless of their individual voting records. This suggests that voters may not cue on the positions of particular candidates in particular races but rather on the relative positions of the two parties. Given the scarcity of information about individual candidates, and since Democrats in Congress are more liberal and Republicans more conservative, this would be a highly rational strategy. To explore this possibility, a "party-based issue voting" measure, based on voters' positions on five specific issues, was devised to test whether voters key on the perceived positions of parties rather than on incumbents' ideologies.[28] A negative coefficient would reflect the tendency of those whose ideologies or issue positions differ from those of the incumbent's party to defect to the opposition.

It seems likely that some challenger characteristics might be relevant, and the most important of them would be a challenger's election spending. Therefore, the natural log of the challenger's campaign spending in thousands of dollars is added to the model. Since better-financed candidates also tend to be "higher quality" candidates,[29] this variable should proxy the general seriousness of the opposition the incumbent faces.

The results of the second pair of equations in table 8.3 differ little from those of the first two. The new party-based issue voting variable has a statistically significant effect, and its inclusion in the model only slightly reduces the estimated effect of the ideological discrepancy variable. Thus, two independent and significant issue-related processes are at work. Voters key on the ideology of the incumbent and punish him if he is not ideologically congruent. Additionally, those with liberal positions on the issues are more likely to vote for Democrats, relative to those with conservative positions.

As expected, the more the challengers spent, the worse the incumbents fared. The coefficients for recalling something the incumbent did for the district are positive (as expected) and statistically significant. If the simulation used above to estimate the payoff from casework is repeated, the coefficient for 1978 pork barreling implies a mean payoff among all voters in the sample of .074, suggesting that a congressman whose ability to be perceived as "bringing home the bacon" was at an average level (10.4 percent) would gain 0.77 percent of the vote if he could double the level of perception of his having been successful in bringing federal programs and dollars to his district. Given the low level of attention most voters accord to the Congress, it is doubtful that more than a tiny handful of congressmen ever gain any significant electoral advantage through this process—unless they do so indirectly by attracting campaign support from district elites sufficient in quantity and quality to scare off potentially strong challengers.[30] Note, too, that pork barreling may backfire: a grant obtained by one city in a state may mean that another gets nothing; support for a waterways project could alienate truckers and railroad constituents; a dam may anger farmers; and a subsidy for a highway may offend environmentalists. Furthermore, looking at the current status of grant programs and projecting it into the future suggests that proportionately less and less federal money will become available by means of discretionary funding.

At this point, a closer look at the 1980 analysis is in order. Since 1980 was a presidential election year in which both the economy and the incumbent president were key issues, it seems appropriate to include those factors in any analysis of the voting. Thus three new variables are included in the model. First, there is a scale representing the respondent's assessment of President Carter's performance in office. It is based upon CPS questions which asked voters to rate the president's handling of five issues: inflation, unemployment, the hostage crisis, the energy crisis, and the situation in Afghanistan.[31] Two variables in the model test for voting based on the performance of the economy. "Personal finances" tests for whether voters' assessments of their own economic situations influenced their votes. It is based on the CPS question asking respondents whether their *personal* finances had "gotten better," "stayed about the same," or "gotten worse" during the past year.[32] "National economy" tests for "public-regarding" economic voting. It is based on the CPS question asking respondents: "Would you say that over the past year the nation's economy has gotten better, stayed the same, or gotten worse."[33]

The results of the analysis (equation 1 in table 8.4) confirm those in the previous equations and emphasize the substantial degree of partisan and issue voting. Voters' assessments of President Carter's performance in office and of their own personal financial situations mattered, with negative judgments costing Democratic House incumbents a good number of votes. Surprisingly, the maximum likelihood estimate for voters' views on the health of the national economy, though very large and carrying the expected sign, was not statistically significant at the standard .05 level. In actuality, assessments of the national economy probably did enter into the House election. Their effects, it can be shown, were indirect, through the evaluations of the president. Moreover, it is likely that the status of the economy (and of the president) played a big role in enticing strong challengers and substantial campaign funds into the race.[34] Again, challengers' spending and voters' exposure to news about incumbents played important roles in the casting of ballots. Casework, however, did not; the coefficient was neither large nor statistically different from zero. But recalling specific pork-barrel activities of the incumbent and having received information

Table 8.4: Determinants of the Congressional Vote, 1980

Independent Variables	PROBIT Maximum Likelihood Estimates	
	(1)	(2)
Member is Democrat	.393	—
Same party	1.211***	1.260***
Member's seniority	−.112	—
Constituent's education	.019	—
Ideological discrepancy	−.353**	−.404***
Issues-party voting	−1.205***	−1.142***
Challenger spending	−.179***	−.173***
No ideology	.176	.209*
Staff contact (no service)	—	.576**
Received mail	—	.234**
Read about incumbent	.327***	.283**
Casework	.336	—
Information	.462*	—
Pork barrel	.354*	.360*
Summary contact	.078*	—
Summary service	—	.648***
Personal finances	−.257**	−.268**
National economy	−.355*	−.017
Carter evaluation	−.097**	−.093**
CONSTANT	1.621	1.359
(N)	(772)	(772)
Estimated R-squared	.48	.49

NOTE: One-tailed test of significance required for all variables except for Democrat, Seniority, and No Ideology: * $p < .10$; ** $p < .05$; *** $p < .01$.

from him may have affected the outcome (the maximum likelihood estimates are moderately strong and are significant at the .10 level). The combined contact variable also yields an "almost significant" coefficient, although its magnitude is very small.

Since the casework variable in 1980 is of moderate size and, at least in table 8.3, comes close to achieving acceptable significance levels, since the variable representing contact with the incumbent's staff was rather substantial and significant, and since staff contact may result from casework (the two are correlated quite strongly in 1980), it is instructive to attempt a sorting out of their effects on the vote. When three new variables—representing constituents who had received casework and had had staff contact, constituents who reported casework but no staff contact, and those who reported contact with the incumbents' staffs but not casework—were entered into the first model of table 8.4, the results were confusing. The equation suggests that the effects of receipt of mail, casework, and staff contact—but, strangely, not casework for constituents who also reported staff contact—were real. The only plausible explanations for such strange findings are sampling error or the possibility that constituents reporting both casework and staff contact were those whose cases were difficult (thus requiring repeated contacts with staffs) and unsatisfactorily resolved. But there is no evidence in the data that these respondents were particularly dissatisfied with their experiences. The results remain a puzzle.

One last equation is needed to meet the argument that casework and information requests really ought to be combined into a single constituency service variable to assess their impact. The equation resembles the previous one, except that it omits several variables that are substantially intercorrelated with other important variables and / or that, in the previous analyses, have been shown to have no independent effect on the vote. When the equation is "cleaned up," the effects of several key variables are more likely to be apparent. The model isolates staff contact, receipt of mail, newspaper coverage, pork barreling, and service (casework or information) as the crucial techniques of influencing the vote. Equation 2 in table 8.4 reports the results.

Not surprisingly, partisanship and issues—measures of voters' ideological differences with the incumbents and measures of economic retrospective voting—stand out, as does challenger spending. Voters appear to be quite responsible. It also would appear that mail, pork barreling, service, and staff contacts all influenced voters' electoral decisions in 1980. Could it be that Fiorina was correct about casework or that, as Jacobson put it, "everything incumbents do appears to help them win support"?[35] Clearly, if the 1980 data are accepted in preference to those of two years earlier, the answer has to be yes. (Of course, there could be sampling error in either of the CPS surveys; or perhaps in difficult economic times, such as 1980, casework requests are of a different type than in more favorable circumstances; or it may be that there is something about a presidential election that changes voters' expectations.) But even if the 1980 data are preferred over those of 1978, the affirmation needs qualifications. Not only do some congressional gambits (meeting constituents, speeches, and radio and television appearances) have no impact, but even those that do show an effect that is both small absolutely and very small relative to the effects of partisanship and ideological or issue voting. A comparison of the probabilities of voting for the incumbent after having received service (casework or information) from him and voting for him without having had such service yields a difference of only .013. In other words, aggregating across the electorate, all the *individualized* constituency service performed by 1980 incumbents netted them about 1.33 percent of the vote. A comparable analysis for mailings, by contrast, suggests that the incumbents' use of postal privileges may have accounted for about 3.3 percent of the vote. In a half-dozen House races in 1980 the winning incumbents beat their closest rivals by less than 1.3 percent, and in eleven contests the victory margin for incumbents fell below 3.3 percent. The analysis is of course limited: there are no congressmen who do no casework, who refuse to provide information when requested, or who do not send at least occasional mailings to their districts. Casework per se, it should be noted, does not seem to provide any particularly strong electoral advantage. Estimates (in both tables) for the separate effects of casework and information produce the interesting finding that providing information has an electoral payoff as great as, or greater than, that produced by intervening with the bureaucracy on behalf of constituents. Moreover, staff contact in the absence of service seemed in 1980 to have almost as much influence on the vote as did the combined service variable. From an incumbent's perspective, receiving a lot of (presumably favorable) press coverage may be more beneficial than rendering service. Although the coefficients suggest that service has a greater impact on the individual voter, six times as many constituents in 1980 read about their congressman as asked him for help, and eleven times as many did so as sought information. Given that even under the best of conditions, the number of constituents who would seek information or casework is inherently limited, the effects of these activities will inevitably be marginal.

There remains one other possibility. Maybe what counts most is how constituents *perceive* congressional casework efforts. Fenno quotes one congressman as saying: "People feel they can talk to me. When they are talking, they feel that I'm listening to what they have to say. . . . They feel that if they come to me with a problem, I'll do everything I can to help them."[36]

And certainly a congressman's reputation for service and for paying attention does seem to enhance his popularity and his vote.[37] Thus real or imagined satisfaction with constituency service, as well as the expectation that the congressman would help if called upon, may be the keys to the electoral advantage of casework. Certainly, most constituents are satisfied. A 1973 Louis Harris poll found that, of those U.S. citizens who had gone to the federal government for help with some problem, 46 percent said they were highly satisfied with their experience, and only 24 percent said they were not at all satisfied. Fully 61 percent of respondents in the 1977 Obey Commission's poll indicated that they were very satisfied with the help offered by their congressmen (or staffs), and another 7 percent declared themselves mostly satisfied (23 percent, however, were not at all satisfied).[38] In the CPS 1978 survey, of those who had contacted their representatives, 65 percent were very satisfied, and 24 percent said they were somewhat satisfied. Comparable figures two years later were 62 percent and 21 percent. Only 15 of 171 said they were not at all happy. As table 8.5 indicates, people who are satisfied tend to support their incumbent. Similarly, people overwhelmingly believe that their congressmen would help them if asked; and the more helpful they believe their representatives would be, the higher they rank them.

The problem with both these explanations is that causality could run either way: people who rate their congressmen highly (and would therefore vote for them) naturally would report being more satisfied with their contacts with, and casework help from, their representatives; and they would be most likely to believe that their congressmen would be very helpful if they were to ask for help. Attempts to measure the effects of satisfaction or expectations on the vote have not been very successful.[39]

Casework fails to produce a significant effect on the vote for several reasons. There are not that many people who receive casework; and most of those who do either were already inclined to support their congressmen or simply do not vote at all. More important, voters are ingrates: they fully expect their congressmen to render services. As noted in chapter 2, there is no doubt that such expectations are real and overwhelming. Meeting such expectations, which all members of the House seem to do at last passably well, generates little or no support for the congressman over and above what would be given on partisan, ideological, issue orientation, name recognition, or other grounds. When everyone expects to be served (by whoever happens to be the incumbent), there is no particular gain in providing that service. As long ago as 1969, Lewis Anthony Dexter observed that "case service . . . is generally a retail matter. It is only rarely that it can be dramatized or publicized so that a large group of voters appreciates the Congressman who provides it. And although many of the recipients may be grateful enough, on the whole, people who want this sort of case service are not the kind of people who organize voters *en masse,* bring them to the polls, etc."[40] More recently, a congressman who won in the "Watergate" election of 1974 but lost in 1978, Cong. Edward W. Pattison (D., N.Y.), complained: "After four years of high visibility congressional services, people have come to expect them. . . . If you're a Republican, you're going to say this guy [the Republican candidate] is as capable of doing the same thing as Pattison, so why not vote for the Republican?"[41] Interviews in 1982 turned up a surprisingly large number of casework

Table 8.5: Casework Satisfaction and Ratings of Incumbents

	Level of Satisfaction with Casework Experience			
Ratings of Own Congressman	Not at All Satisfied	Only Somewhat Satisfied	Mostly Satisfied	Very Satisfied
Obey Commission [a]				
Poor	24%	8%	0%	4%
Only Fair	35	0	21	19
Pretty Good	35	49	44	43
Excellent	7	44	35	35
(N)	(38)	(12)	(15)	(108)
		$tau_b = .25; p < .01$		
Worse than Others	12	7	0	1
Same as Others	69	28	41	51
Better than Others	19	65	59	48
(N)	(40)	(13)	(15)	(102)
		$tau_c = .16; p < .01$		
1978 National Electional Survey[b]				
Very Poor	11	0	0	0
Poor	22	0	0	0
Fair	22	80	37	5
Good	33	20	40	48
Very Good	11	0	23	48
(N)	(9)	(5)	(30)	(101)
		$tau_c = .30; p < .01$		
Feeling Thermometer				
Low (0–70)	90	100	55	25
Medium (71–90)	10	0	39	31
High (91–100)	0	0	6	44
(N)	(10)	(5)	(31)	(103)
		$tau_c = .36; p < .01$		

continued

Table 8.5: *continued*

Ratings of Own Congressman	Level of Satisfaction with Casework Experience			
	Not at All Satisfied	Only Somewhat Satisfied	Mostly Satisfied	Very Satisfied
1980 National Election Survey[b]				
Strongly Disapprove	14	0	0	0
Disapprove	0	13	6	0
Approve	57	75	33	15
Strongly Approve	29	13	61	85
(N)	(7)	(8)	(18)	(65)

$$tau_b = .46; p < .01$$

[a] Based on satisfaction levels reported by those who responded affirmatively to the question: "Have you, or has anyone in your immediate family, ever requested any kind of help or assistance from a Member of Congress or his staff?" As noted in chap. 2, this question included some respondents who had contacted Congress on other than strictly casework grounds. Eliminating those respondents reduced the number on the table to 123, but served only to strengthen the relationship reported. For the more limited samples, *tau* = .33 and .26, respectively.

[b] Based on those who reported contacting congressmen only to get help on a problem. An almost identical relationship holds when all respondents who contacted their congressmen for any reason at all are included in the analysis.

aides who had come to share these skeptical notions about the efficacy of casework. Whereas some years ago doing yeoman's service on casework might have marked a congressman as somewhat out of the ordinary, it no longer does—at least not for constituents who matter. One recalls the question a voter is supposed to have put to Alben Barkley, "What have you done for me lately?" Certainly there is evidence that the positive effects of mailings wear off over time;[42] perhaps it is the fact that mailings, newspaper coverage, and even simple information requests—unlike casework—are likely to be repetitive that explains their greater effects in the statistical analyses above.

Logically, therefore, seeking out ever more cases (from first-time requesters) makes little sense. According to staffers, active solicitation produces weak cases, largely from nonvoting and overexpectant constituents. If generating larger and larger numbers of cases ties up scarce staff resources, leading to delays and less satisfactory casework services, and if a decline in the quality of casework service and in "customer satisfaction" inclines voters to believe that the congressman has not met the expectations for casework, stimulating additional casework might actually backfire. Scholars who have examined casework satisfaction seem to agree that doing casework poorly can hurt.[43] As one former congressman put it, "Contrary to popular belief, the electoral 'rewards' of casework can be negative, since you cannot always be successful; and those you cannot help never forget, while those you help feel that's why they elected you." Another former House member described three ways in which casework could prove counterproductive. If it is sloppily handled, the representative is likely to gain a reputation of not caring; if the load is such that the backlog of cases prevents quick action, constituents, who may care more about speedy, sincere efforts than actual results, will probably become angry; and if the member tries to exploit it in a district where prominent constituents—those who do the fund raising, campaigning, and influencing of others—expect their representative to do casework without taking credit for it and/or are primarily issue-oriented, those constituents may well reject him as a self-serving opportunist. "Especially in a district like mine," he went on, "people expect service. If I went to a town meeting or the Chamber of Commerce and started telling them about how much I had done for them, they'd say, 'What kind of a nut is he?' It just isn't that useful. You can't win votes, but you can lose them."

Therefore, a rational congressman would avoid excessive stimulation of casework requests so that scarce staff resources could be used to insure satisfactory handling of those cases which come in as a matter of course or to handle other tasks that are more important. A handful of congressmen clearly do *not* go out of their way to seek cases. This is very much the minority position in Congress, but it may be the correct one. There simply are too many congressmen who did all they could on casework but lost their jobs in subsequent elections. That seemed to be the case in the 1980 elections. Cong. Andrew Maguire (D., N.J.) had been viewed as the perfect model for congressmen who were ideologically out of touch with their constituencies but who survived by virtue of excellent constituency service. He lost. So did Cong. Bob Carr (D., Mich.), whose "chief strategist" in the election, John Swain, complained that "doing all this stuff [constituency service] keeps your head above water, is all. . . . I guess they didn't care about our constituent service record." As Cong. Thomas J. Downey (D., N.Y.) put it, "I had the first mobile office on Long Island, but now everybody has one. . . . All these frills can be quickly forgotten."[44] Even in 1978, a one-term midwestern Democrat who had done infinitely more casework and had brought his district twenty-five times as much federal money as his predecessor lost his bid for reelection.

It should be noted that a rational voter, whether or not grateful for casework actually performed, might vote for an incumbent (especially a senior one) on the grounds that increasing seniority correlates with power and that power would bring about successful intervention with the bureaucracy if the constituent were ever to need it. But in such a case it is not the actual doing of casework, or even successful or satisfactory casework, that directly triggers the vote. Soliciting more cases in such a situation would be irrelevant. Finally, leaving expectations and all else aside, the evidence suggests, as noted above, that constituents who contact their congressmen for casework assistance (or for any other reason) already are inclined to vote for them—or at least not vote against them (if they vote at all)—for the very reasons that lead them to make contact in the first place: generalized affect, member visibility, and partisan and ideological compatibility.

8.4. Summary and Conclusion

Congressmen and staffs believe in the electoral efficacy of casework and other forms of constituency service, but if the analyses here are correct, they are somewhat mistaken, at least insofar as casework per se is concerned. Voters cannot be bought cheaply (by casework alone), or, if they can be—by casework, mailings, pork barreling, or anything else—they do not *stay* bought. Perhaps some combination of members' district attentiveness and "home styles"—trips home, staff resources allocated to the district, mailings, favorable news coverage, member visibility, and the like, along with successful pork barreling—explains the incumbency advantage. Perhaps not. Undoubtedly, such explanations apply even less appropriately to Senate elections, which are more visible and, probably, more susceptible to partisan swings and policy voting. Members and staffs interviewed were virtually unanimous on that score, and a good deal of political science research agrees.

It is impossible to say, of course, whether or how much policy responsiveness suffers from service responsiveness. Congressmen may in fact court their constituents assiduously precisely in order to gain leeway to do what they want in Washington. But what this chapter has argued is that, if they fail to represent their districts, sooner or later they will be caught.

CHAPTER 9

Improving Casework Operations

Complaints about the quality of casework and accompanying recommendations for improvement come from all quarters. While on the whole overwhelmingly satisfied with the service they receive, constituents have some complaints. In the survey of the House Commission on Administrative Review in 1977, for example, 7 percent of the respondents felt that the congressmen whom they had contacted (or their staffs) could have exerted more influence or pursued their cases more strongly. Another 7 percent believed that their representatives could have spent more time and investigated their claims more thoroughly, while 5 percent wanted to receive more than one letter from Washington or wanted more personal interest, and 1 percent thought that they had not not been treated with sufficient politeness and consideration. Eight percent claimed that their congressmen had done nothing at all to help, but fully 65 percent believed that everything that could have been done had been done.[1]

Scholars who have studied constituency service and members and staffers who have commented about it likewise have registered dissatisfaction with the process. Their complaints, and thus proposed solutions, focus on four areas. First, like some constituents, they believe that the speed, quality, and efficiency of service can be improved. Accordingly, they propose such remedies as larger and better-trained staffs, more intensive use of computers, centralized processing of cases, closer legislative-executive interaction, and greater efforts to educate constituents. Some seek greater outreach efforts. A second category of problems concerns the equity question. Reformers propose removing the casework function from Congress altogether, instituting more stringent ethics codes, or increasing professionalism. A third group seeks to remove the "burden" of casework from congressmen and their staffs, usually by creating another institution to handle casework. A small minority would eliminate the function outright. Finally, a good number of critics seek to link cases and projects more closely to the legislative and oversight functions. Their recommendations encompass various techniques to centralize and coordinate constituency service operations within and across congressional offices. As one HEW official explained, "As a management tool, you'd have to centralize it."

9.1. An Ombudsman for the United States?

One of the most commonly proposed remedies for the alleged deficiencies of congressional casework and projects operations—and of course for the general inability of citizens to complain effectively of mistreatment—is the creation of a national ombudsman like those found in many countries throughout the world. According to a recent count, which did not include subnational ombudsman offices, in the late 1970s there were fourteen such ombudsmen.[2] The defining characteristics of an ombudsman are that the individual (or individuals) filling the post is (are): constitutionally or legally independent from other political institutions; impartial; expert in government affairs; universally accessible to all citizens (with respect to those problems falling within its jurisdiction); and empowered to recommend solutions to specific grievances, to suggest administrative and sometimes legislative changes, and to publicize instances of maladministration.[3] Normally, ombudsmen enjoy complete authority to investigate citizen complaints, including the power to gain access to internal executive branch documents and correspondence;[4] and many ombudsmen are granted the right to make the final determination when the merits of a case are in dispute. Rarely, however, can they require an administrative agency to change a decision, and most are confined to dealing with written complaints. Some are allowed to initiate disciplinary proceedings against government officials.

Such characteristics are quite different from those of congressional casework practices. And they are totally unrelated to the advocacy and service orientation of other congressional activities, such as providing routine information and non-casework favors and pursuing federal projects. Nevertheless, the establishment of a national ombudsman has appealed to many as an attractive idea. In all likelihood, it would remove at least some of the burden on congressional offices, might provide more effective intervention with the bureaucracy, might produce more equitable, evenhanded service to all citizens, and could serve oversight and remedial legislative goals more efficiently. Experience elsewhere suggests that both legislators and administrators have adjusted to the ombudsman and hold the office in reasonably high esteem, perceiving it as placing no inordinate burden on their own operations.[5]

Respondents in this study were asked whether a European-style national ombudsman should be established to deal with citizen grievances. Only 8 percent of senators and representatives and 8 percent of staffers in home offices, along with fewer than one in five administrative assistants, thought it would be a good idea. Twenty-eight percent of Washington-based aides liked the notion. Only among the 206 executive officials did less than a clear majority disagree with the concept—and then the figure was 48 percent. In short, little support exists for the establishment of an ombudsman. Among members, Republicans and conservatives were most strongly opposed.

Arguments against such an institution cover a host of issues. Perhaps uppermost in the minds of critics is the idea that an ombudsman would become just another bureaucracy, causing a loss of the "personal touch." Members and staffs believe that one-to-one contact with constituents is essential for handling their problems. As one Senate staffer argued, "No—you need either the political incentive or empathy; and you don't get either in a bureaucracy." Remarked another: "What—another 10,000-person bureaucracy? Then you'd need caseworkers just to interface with the ombudsman. Face it—we have a messy bureaucratic system."

Surprisingly, a plurality of bureaucrats themselves disagreed with the ombudsman idea. One Labor Department liaison official supported the view above: "I don't like the idea. I prefer the 50/50 political and humanitarian motivation of a congressman. I have trouble with people's altruism—as you would have in an ombudsman agency. I don't know where they're coming from, but self-interest—the political motivation—is reliable. And it produces better, more predictable results."

Some members and staffers, viewing casework and projects from a legislative or oversight perspective, also thought that members would too easily lose touch with their districts and with the "real world." "No," commented one caseworker, the ombudsman "wouldn't give the congressmen a chance to see people's problems in their districts."

Such negative comments not only indicate a lack of support for a national ombudsman—no one seriously believes such a proposal could be enacted—but also point out the real weaknesses such an institution would have, especially in a country as large as the United States. It is no accident that the four states that have established similar offices—Alaska, Hawaii, Nebraska, and Iowa—are quite small and relatively homogeneous in population. There are other drawbacks.

What sort of jurisdiction would a national ombudsman have? Congressmen are not confined to dealing only with federal problems, but most ombudsmen in other lands are limited to national issues.[6] How would projects be handled? Is there any guarantee that constituents would avoid taking their problems to their congressmen, who would have every incentive to attempt to find solutions themselves? And if they failed, could the ombudsman succeed? As one New Zealand M.P. put it, "If I can't get something for a constituent, I'm damn sure the ombudsman can't."[7] Conversely, if the ombudsman did not produce satisfactory results, the aggrieved citizen no doubt would appeal to his representative or senator, thus merely compounding the paperwork. No doubt, many citizens would seek help from both the ombudsman *and* their congressmen. (Certainly, Anagnoson's study of members of New Zealand's Parliament indicates heavy casework involvement.) Duplication would run rampant. Nor, if the experience of other countries is any indication, would an ombudsman necessarily produce more or better recommendations for legislative or administrative policy changes. Moreover, if Congress holds the purse strings for the office, would the ombudsman be, or be perceived as being, independent? Bureaucrats express concern that an ombudsman would ruin their relationships with their clients. As one administrator explained: "I think the ombudsman idea is excellent, but I would not want it to be a barrier to citizens' direct communications with agencies. It should be available when agencies don't respond to help determine if they were responding properly or if the citizen is not satisfied. Yet what would a citizen likely do for future grievances if, on a given case, he or she had received favorable help from the ombudsman?" Nor is there any evidence that, case for case, an ombudsman would "interfere" less with the administrative process. Studies of national ombudsmen indicate a wide variation on that score.

Finally, since ombudsmen rarely undertake the sort of outreach efforts that are common in Congress and since they often are allowed to deal only with written grievances and with cases of maladministration, turning over the complaint process to such an institution would result in restricting casework services — probably to the more educated and politically efficacious. Equity and equal access would suffer, as appears to have occurred in New Zealand.[8]

The closest the national government has come to creating an ombudsman was a bill (S. 90 – 1195) introduced by Sen. Edward V. Long (D., Mo.) on March 7, 1967. The measure would have established the office of Administrative Ombudsman, which would have possessed many of the traditional ombudsmanic powers, receiving directly from citizens their complaints against the Social Security Administration, Veterans Administration, Internal Revenue Service, Bureau of Prisons, and (by an amendment the senator offered in February,

1968) the Selective Service System.[9] At the hearings held on the bill in 1968, the executive agencies registered firm disagreement with the Long proposal. The bill was not reported. Subsequently, similar proposals were offered, but none was enacted.[10] In recent years, however, several federal agencies, and of course state and local governments, have on their own adopted modified versions of the ''executive ombudsman.'' But on the national level, no proposal for a genuine ombudsman has been seriously considered. Moreover, even if such a proposal were to be given careful study, chances are nil that it would be enacted. Not only is the idea itself fraught with problems, especially given the size of the country, but institution-building is a risky and time-consuming undertaking that as often as not carries numerous unforeseen and harmful consequences.

9.2. Centralizing Congressional Constituency Service

Testifying to the recognition that no national ombudsman will be established, various proposals have been made to solve Congress's constituency service problems directly by centralizing some or all of the casework function. Suggestions cover a wide range of possibilities.

At least four times during the 1960s, Cong. Henry S. Reuss (D., Wis.) introduced legislation to establish an office to handle grievance-related congressional casework. The proposed Office of Administrative Counsel (later designated the Congressional Ombudsman) would have been a creature of the Congress— roughly akin to today's Congressional Budget Office or the House and Senate Offices of Legislative Counsel (Congress's bill-drafting services)—receiving citizen complaints only by referral from House and Senate offices, processing them, and then reporting back to Congress.[11] The basic idea was that, by filtering citizen complaints through the congressional offices, the number of complaints to be dealt with by this central office would be kept at a manageable level and, more important, senators and representatives still would be able to take the credit for any success. The ombudsman would be appointed by the Speaker of the House and president pro tem of the Senate and would have the same investigatory powers as congressional committees. Reuss's idea did get a hearing, but it never emerged from committee.[12] Moreover, the Joint Committee on the Organization of Congress also recommended against it.[13] In essence, members objected on the grounds that creation of such an agency would unduly separate them from their constituents and remove an important function from their control. Some witnesses hesitated to embark on such an unusual journey without first having studied similar operations elsewhere. Still others feared the costs.

Similar proposals have been introduced by others over the years. For example, Sen. Vance Hartke (D., Ind.), along with a number of cosponsors, in 1971 and 1973 proposed the creation of an Office of Constituent Assistance,[14] which would have served as an intermediary between congressional offices (which still would receive and process constituent complaints) and executive agencies. As in the Reuss plan, the linkage between congressmen and constituents would remain intact. The proposed office also would have had the responsibilities of analyzing in a systematic fashion the patterns of grievances and of considering appropriate legislative solutions. Thus were wedded three reformist strains: improving the efficiency of casework operations, removing some of the burden from House and Senate offices, and enhancing the legislative and oversight potential of constituency service. Hartke's plan, however, got nowhere, even though the idea—or something similar to it—keeps popping up each year.

A less formal plan was proposed by Cong. Les Aspin (D., Wis.) in 1972. Aspin sought to provide a special staff member, designated as an "ombudsman," for each congressional district. In addition, an "Ombudsman Center" would be established as a training, resource, and evaluative institute. The center would receive annual reports from each congressman's district ombudsman.[15] The proposal made no headway in the House.

Institutions comparable to the Reuss-Hartke offices do exist elsewhere. In 1967, the Parliamentary Commissioner began operating in Great Britain, receiving complaints concerning maladministration from members of the House of Commons, who, accordingly, have two options for casework: acting directly with administrative offices and working through the commissioner. Six years later the office of *Mediateur* was established in France to assist members of the National Assembly and the Senate in their efforts to help constituents with grievances against executive agencies. The latter has a considerably broader jurisdiction than its British counterpart, but in other respects is more limited, being able to consider complaints only after they have been taken to the appropriate government authorities.[16] In neither case may citizens take their problems directly to the ombudsman.

Members, staffs, and administrators surveyed for this study were asked their judgments on the advisability of establishing a "Congressional Office for Casework which would receive referrals from congressional offices, do the needed investigating, and report the results back to the originating office for action." Of 260 congressional respondents, only 12 percent approved, with three-quarters in disagreement. Among administrators the responses were similar: 14 percent agreed but 66 percent disagreed. Generally, those who saw casework as disruptive of either congressional or executive processes, those who believed it to be unfair, and those administrators who thought that congressional offices should not intervene with the executive on behalf of constituents exhibited tendencies to believe that this office ought to be established.

Arguments against such an office resemble those cited above for the ombudsman. "You need the personalized approach," argued the House aide; "the danger with a separate congressional office is that it, too, would become a bureaucracy." Workload would become a problem. The existence of the British Parliamentary Commissioner apparently has increased the casework burden on executive departments.[17] According to the most authoritative study, the Parliamentary Commissioner at first instilled considerable fear and indecision in the British executive, and it tended to weaken morale. It also slowed down the casework process, not only because of the middleman's role but also because bureaucrats became much more cautious in their responses.[18]

There are yet other problems. Would the office have genuine power to rule definitely on a case? If so, how would the bureaucracy react? Would there be constitutional problems? Would members freely use the office, or would they continue to take constituent grievances directly to agencies? Would they reject negative recommendations from the office, thereby merely duplicating efforts as they pressed cases on administrators? What about federal projects? Who would hire and fire the staff? How could it be guaranteed that the office would faithfully serve all congressmen and senators equally? Would it pursue cases fairly and aggressively? Would it be independent? If so, would it seek as much favorable publicity as it could garner? Would public relations thus direct its energies? And if the office were to strive to analyze cases for legislative and oversight implications, would it be any more effective than individual congressmen now are in converting casework to rules changes or statutory modifications? The answer to the latter question would depend, of course, on what cases individual congressmen and committees or subcommittees sent to the central office and what they did with the office's reports and recommendations — as is largely true of the situation that now exists. Under the Aspin plan, there would be no assurance that cases handled by staffers other than the district ombudsmen would be reported to the Ombudsmen Center for evaluation; and the Reuss plan would not further the goals of oversight and remedial legislation unless the ombudsman received all, or at least a representative sample, of cases from every congressional office and had a strong legal and institutional interest in — and authority for — so doing.[19] The clear temptation would be for senators and representatives to send only trivial or routine cases — which would alleviate only slightly the amount of work handled by personal office staffs, since they would want to stay in contact with constituents. Conversely, doing so would not contribute to the offices' ability to use cases for oversight.

That the French and British experiments, on the whole, have worked quite well is no guarantee that the same would be true in the American context.[20] The two political systems simply are different. As a rule, one would expect that such an office in a parliamentary system (with its more unified legislature and the built-in linkages between legislators and government ministers and thus ministries) would fare better than in the fragmented system of this country. Still, were one forced to choose between a national ombudsman and a congressional casework office, the latter would make more sense.

Those with a centralizing instinct might recommend the creation of single committee in each house of Congress (or, simply, one joint committee) to handle casework. The advantages presumably would be a shift of the casework burden from individual offices to the committee, greater specialization, neutrality, enhanced oversight potential, and perhaps greater clout vis à vis the administrators. Such a committee exists in Kuwait and apparently works reasonably well.[21] But Kuwait is not the United States. Interestingly, the authors of the 1946 Legislative Reorganization Act, looking to the oversight potential of casework, wanted more of the casework task channeled to and through the standing committees of Congress;[22] and that has, to a slight degree, happened. Members and staffs do take cases to committees, both to secure advice and assistance in helping constituents and for legislative and oversight purposes. As indicated in previous chapters, however, they do so only when *they* perceive it to be advantageous.

The objections to such a committee, again, are obvious. Who would want to serve on it? Members of the Kuwait Assembly, apparently, are not enthralled at the prospect. Who would staff it? Would members rely on it, or would they act independently in contacting executive units? Would it function in a partisan or bipartisan manner? Undoubtedly, were such a committee to be created, were its members to take their jobs seriously, and were it properly used by all others, it might work nicely. But the odds against these conditions are overwhelming.

Without creating any new institutions, it is possible to increase efficiency, to improve the oversight potential of casework, and perhaps, to alleviate some of the duplication, and thus some of the burden, inherent in constituency service. That coordination is needed is apparent from the number of agency officials complaining about receiving the same case from several House and Senate offices, a situation that often leads to delays. Further evidence comes from the three-to-two majority of congressional aides agreeing that "cooperative arrangements among members of Congress or of state delegations should be established to deal more effectively with constituency service." Two sorts of cooperation are possible. The first concerns the intake function. Greater efforts should and could be made for members of state delegations in the House to set up joint offices with senators—especially those of the same party. As already seems to be happening in scattered locations around the country, such offices might include representatives of state or local legislatures as well. Thus constituents would be discouraged from using the ''shotgun'' approach on their Washington representatives, and House and Senate offices might divide up some of the labor, perhaps even saving some time and money in the process. Less congressional time would be spent on state and local cases and projects.

Second, and more important, coordination should be increased during and after the processing of cases. Not only might House and Senate offices from the same state work more closely together—almost any efforts in this direction would be a major improvement over the current situation—but communication should be increased among House and Senate offices across the board. After studying Senate offices, Susan Webb Hammond concluded that ''there is an information vacuum among Senate offices regarding organization and services. Too often, offices are afraid to share problems with each other, . . . yet common interest and activities as well as common problems are present. The creation of regular and institutionalized opportunities for objective discussion and exchange of information would increase the effectiveness of each office and of the Senate as a whole.''[23]

Cooperation in the House, and across the House-Senate boundaries, is as bad as or worse than in the Senate. Solutions are not hard to devise. Breslin, for example, has proposed an informal coordinating council from House, Senate, and agency offices dealing with a given set of programs.[24] Such a unit would facilitate interoffice communication and gather oversight-relevant data based on case and project experiences. An alternative would be some form of reporting system, perhaps centrally coordinated, so that offices would be better informed of what others are doing. Some form of computerized tabulation, resulting in a monthly newsletter-type document, might work.

Three forces inhibit greater cooperation. One is the tendency of each office to want whatever political benefits might accrue from dealings with constituents. The second is the belief, held by a surprisingly large number of aides, that by working independently, offices guarantee constituents a fail-safe mechanism. If one office does not render satisfactory assistance, another in the state delegation might. Finally, many staffers simply do not see the need for statistical compilations of case types or frequencies in order to raise issues for oversight or legislative purposes. A flood of similar cases gets the message across without an accurate count, and even a single case can lead to action.

A growing number of congressional offices—7 percent of all House offices in 1977[25] and about 40 percent in 1982—file their case (and sometimes projects) records on the computer. At the touch of a button, staffers can generate statistical breakdowns of casework activities. Two widely used devices are "Information Systems for Congress," an in-house minicomputer system, and DIALCOM, an on-line connection to an outside computer. Introduced in the early 1970s, they have become quite popular for tracking cases. And since almost all House and Senate offices have some type of computer system, there is no good reason why this capability should not be extended. The advantages are potentially substantial. First, as already is being done in some offices, a sound computerized record-keeping and electronic mail system would link Washington and home offices, allowing both to have access to a common case and projects file, thus eliminating some duplication of effort and perhaps speeding up response time. Such computer systems could be shared by several congressmen and senators. Assuming a way around Privacy Act restrictions, a staffer could, before processing a case, check to see if it was being handled in an office of another member of the state delegation. Second, if executive branch information on the status of pending cases and projects were available in such congressional data banks, a good deal of time could be saved, since many cases are nothing more than requests for status checks. Rather than calling or writing to the executive agency, the congressional caseworker might be able to satisfy a constituent merely by tapping the appropriate keys on his or her computer terminal to see where the case or project stood. Electronic mail systems also would allow more efficient transmittal of case requests to agencies and quicker responses to Congress. Messages could be sent more quickly than by regular mail and without the delays that often occur when trying to track down one's counterparts in the agencies (or on the Hill) by telephone. A few experiments with this sort of capability already are being conducted.[26] Third, the computer could be programmed—as some offices have done—to kick out all cases and projects on which agency responses were overdue, or on which constituents had not yet submitted necessary documentation. An automatic reminder could be sent to the agency and a letter to the constituent. Constituents interested in certain cases and projects or in legislation dealing with problems identified through casework could be sent information with a minimum of staff effort.[27] Fourth, office supervisors could call up case records to monitor the effectiveness and efficiency of caseworkers.

Finally, and most important, if the data from each congressional office were merged into a centralized file, assuming a uniform reporting scheme and, of course, anonymity of the constituent, congressmen and committees interested in oversight or legislation would have at their fingertips complete statistical breakdowns of constituent complaints. Such data might be used by individual members, appropriate committees, or the GAO to initiate investigations and bolster arguments on behalf of legislative or oversight recommendations.[28] They also would be of use to executive agencies and, perhaps, the Executive Office of the President. Conversely, if congressional computer systems could tap into agency casework files, executive records could be used by congressional investigators. There has been some experimentation at the state level with this sort of data collection and processing scheme, and it seems to have been reasonably successful.[29] To those concerned with Congress's weaknesses in oversight and remedial legislation, creation of such a centralized data bank might constitute a dream come true. Could such increased computerization be accomplished? When asked in 1977–78 if cases and projects should be computerized, forty-four staffers said yes, thirty-five no, and twenty-eight were uncertain. The major objections were that it would be too costly and time-consuming and that it would jeopardize the "personal" touch which congressmen treasure. Further, constitutional objections (separation of powers) could be raised to the proposal that Congress have some sort of access to executive files; and the danger that congressmen might go on "fishing expeditions" in agency records is very real.

Although there is little demand for larger staffs to handle cases and projects, there certainly is a great need for recruitment of skilled personnel and for training. Members should recognize that they need to develop a greater sense of professional competence among their caseworkers. Freshman members ought to recruit experienced constituency service staffs to complement staff newcomers. If they wish to emphasize the legislative and oversight aspects of casework, congressmen and senators should seek out young, well-educated, legislatively oriented aides for such work, paying them better salaries than their current status (as little more than clerks) is perceived to justify.

More formal training courses should be implemented. As one staffer remarked, "While I was learning, our constituents got hurt." Indeed, over half of the administrative assistants surveyed by the Obey Commission believed that some sort of formal training program would be "very helpful" for caseworkers.[30] Perhaps experienced case and projects specialists could conduct periodic seminars and prepare up-to-date casework manuals. Some of this already is occurring, but much more could be done.[31]

Casework should be more closely integrated with other congressional activities, particularly legislative and oversight tasks of individual member offices and of committees. The key is to bring casework experiences to the awareness of members, administrative assistants, and, especially, legislative assistants in personal offices and, even more important, to committee staffs. At least two mechanisms are available. One is to blend case and project work with legislative tasks by assigning a share of casework to the legislative assistants in offices.

There appears to be a growing trend in this direction. Another approach is to guarantee case and project staffers access to the congressmen and policy-oriented staff, perhaps by means of weekly meetings at which summaries of the preceding week's cases and projects could be presented and discussion of oversight and legislative implications could ensue. Such ideas are not novel. A Senate subcommittee in 1976 made quite similar recommendations.[32]

The problem of isolation of field staffs—and the accompanying loss of morale—might be alleviated, and oversight clearly enhanced, by efforts to link home-based aides and Washington office operations more closely. Perhaps regular staff exchanges between home and Capitol Hill are in order.

None of these matters is difficult, but all require a substantially greater commitment to casework, and to using casework for policy purposes, than now exists. Of course, the perennial lament of congressional scholars, and of members themselves, is that incentives to perform oversight and to undertake the drudgery of remedial legislative work simply are lacking. If there were a will, the way is clear.

A related suggestion for improving the executive side of casework operations came from several administrators. Caseworkers, they believe, should exercise greater discretion in sending cases to agencies. They ought to screen out the obviously weak and unmeritorious grievances and requests—ought to have the courage to say no—so that agency liaison and program-level staffs could avoid wasting valuable time and could give better attention to worthy cases. Congressional reluctance to alienate potential voters and the belief that even "crazy" cases may turn out to be valid, however, incline caseworkers to buck just about everything "downtown."

Executive and congressional personnel both agree that more should and could be done to educate constituents, but they disagree concerning the purposes of such education. On the one hand, some caseworkers think that citizens are not sufficiently aware of the services they can receive from their senators and representatives. Thus, recommended one aide, "newspapers should educate constituents," and more citizens should be encouraged to write their congressmen. Indeed, legislation once was introduced to allow constituents to write their congressmen postage-free (H.R. 91-15576), and there is talk of linking constituents who have their own home computers to Congress.[33]

On the other hand, a more common view is that citizens expect too much and must be taught the limits of congressional intervention. "Constituents," lamented one House staffer, "need to realize that it is not the member's choice [about what can be done on a case] or that he or she has little ability to make effective changes in government organizations. Constituents think that writing is tantamount to success.'' Better public education—perhaps via newsletters—might forestall useless cases, alleviate some duplication via multiple requests, and reduce the incidence of excessive follow-up calls and letters occasioned by constituents' ignorance-induced impatience. Agency operations could be improved as well. To the extent that there is concern about a lack of equity on partisan grounds, one reform would be to make sure that all liaison officers were career civil servants. On the other hand, if the political incentive is valued, and if bureaucrats are distrusted, liaison staffs should be partisan political (Schedule C) appointees. In the best of all worlds, they would be former congressional aides. A formal exchange program between the two branches might be the ideal solution. As one agency official explained, ''The people in the program offices and our district offices—the bureaucrats—just don't understand Congress at all.'' Precisely the same can be said of many case and project aides, whose ignorance of agency rules, regulations, and procedures often is appalling. If such a program should prove impossible, the current system of agency-sponsored tours and seminars should be increased, especially for newly elected congressmen and senators, and for new staffers.

Within agencies, some increased influence for liaison offices might better enable them to use casework experiences for policy purposes. As one bureaucrat argued, ''Each regional office of an agency needs congressional liaison specialists directly responsible to the regional director so he can be aware of what's going on.''

Two final tongue-in-cheek solutions have been suggested. The first is simply to allow citizens to sue their government whenever they feel aggrieved. Cong. Fred Hartley (R., N.J.) once introduced such legislation, labeling it a bill for ''the Emancipation of John Q. Public from Government Bureaucrats.''[34] The other remedy, less facetious, is to forbid Congress to engage in constituency service altogether. Such proposals were made in the 1940s (before the growth in staffs) by congressmen and scholars.[35] It takes little imagination to guess what sort of reaction such an idea would receive today.

In short, there are a number of realistic modifications in legislative and executive structures and procedures that could improve the effectiveness, efficiency, and equity of casework and could enhance its utility for legislation and oversight. In almost every case—excepting those that raise constitutional problems or confront technological barriers—the only roadblocks are a lack of willpower and the prevalent judgment that changes are not worth the effort. Given current heavy workloads, a sometimes-perverse incentive structure, turnover among staffs, the tension between the imperative to handle all cases efficiently and the desire to deal with the meritorious ones (or those raising policy questions) in depth, fears of depersonalizing member-constituent relations, and, not unimportant, the fear of loss of votes and therefore potential loss of tenure, the prospects for substantial improvement in casework operations are not bright. The reforms that do emerge will come incrementally.

9.3. Conclusion

Congress—or, more properly, each individual congressional office—has become the ombudsman of the American political system. Members of the House, especially, seem to have undertaken this intermediary function with particular relish. Constituency service has increased dramatically in the past two decades, and Congress's ability to adapt to the burgeoning demands has been remarkable. The casework function in both Congress and the executive has become more bureaucratized and more professionalized. If the characteristics of institutionalization are distinctive activity, permanency, and independence, the casework enterprise is on its way to achieving that status, although the form it will ultimately take is uncertain. Moreover, the linkage between congressional case and projects staffs and executive administrators is relatively clearly delineated and firmly established. Something approaching a classical ''system,'' or at least ''whirlpool'' or ''subgovernment,'' is emerging, in which elite participants come to share a common set of perceptions and interests. Casework operations now clearly span the whole range of intergovernmental relations. Congressional offices not only aid state and local governments in their efforts to pick up federal funds, but also assist individual constituents who experience problems with subnational governments. Congress has become not only a national ombudsman but a ''federal'' one as well. Indeed, it has become a consumer complaint agency.

Casework by legislators fits the American system of government. Representation—literally a ''re-presentation''—of constituents occurs where it affects them in a most practical fashion. By handling constituent requests and grievances, as burdensome as they can be, congressmen and senators have the opportunity to come into contact with constituents who would not think of writing them on policy-related matters directly. Conceivably, doing casework may open channels of communication to a different group of citizens on a range of issues that otherwise might be excluded from congressional concern. Verba and Nie concluded, concerning legislator-constitutent contacts in general: ''Citizen-initiated contacting brings into the political system a set of concerns roughly as wide as the set of concerns that the citizenry faces.''[36] For many people, asking help on personal problems is their first and only direct contact with Congress.

Although it cannot be demonstrated empirically that casework strengthens citizens' faith in their government (or at least in Congress), the possibility cannot be ruled out. True, diffuse support for a political system may not rest on particular outputs, especially legislative acts.[37] But surely courteous and efficient treatment must leave some favorable impressions, and positive casework results must counteract some of the cynicism that pervades the body politic concerning "those dirty politicians." (Conversely, of course, poor treatment or unsuccessful casework could work in the opposite direction.) A danger is that, as the casework function becomes ever more bureaucratized, an important element of the "personal touch" will be lost. And as constituents come to expect diligent and successful casework as a matter of right, it will be increasingly difficult for Congress to meet their demands, thereby leading to negative judgments on the part of petitioners.

Casework facilitates independent congressional activity on legislation and oversight—not as well as it might, certainly, but nonetheless to a noticeable degree. According to Gray: "Despite abuses of the system by all the participants, and despite the burden placed on administrators, the system operates effectively to bend central administration to meet the desires of individuals, groups, and non-central governments."[38] Legislative, and thus democratic, oversight and control are enhanced, albeit far from perfectly; and the individualistic and localistic concerns that run so deep in American culture are injected into the bureaucratic system.

Casework has drawbacks, some of them very serious. It involves considerable time, money, and staff effort. To an extent it is disruptive. It is not always neutral and equitable—though it usually is. The system needs improvement. Concerning the electoral effect, if in fact casework in and of itself could effectively guarantee a "safe seat" for most members—and thus if it dangerously insulated incumbents from popular control—there would be a real problem. But the electoral impact does not go so far—and it is unlikely to in the future. Nor, apparently, are members' motives concerning casework so exclusively or primarily electoral as to divert them from other responsibilities. Without doubt, members of both houses are overworked and overly inundated with interest group pressures and with constituent expectations of all sorts; and—above all—members are consumed with the desire to be reelected, which leads not only to casework but to a variety of time- and energy-consuming activities. Casework itself does not seem to be the culprit it so often is made out to be. As one of the more visible manifestations of the increasingly hectic congressional life, it frequently draws the blame when harried legislators fail to achieve their goals or when pundits seek to explain why their favored programs have not been enacted.

In the end, the good must be balanced against the bad. Huntington's assessment seems accurate: serving constituents and watching over the bureaucracy "are functions which no other public agency is as well qualified as Congress to perform. Responding to needs unmet elsewhere, Congress plays an increasingly important role as the representative of the interests of unorganized individuals and as the stimulant, monitor, corrector, and overseer of a growing federal bureaucracy."[39] Most congressmen take casework obligations seriously, and not just for electoral reasons. They *want* to help constituents. The concepts of representation and responsiveness are not empty, and they are deeply felt by most members of Congress.

One might even go so far as to agree with Gray's assessment that "congressional interference in administration . . . is one of the best things Congress does."[40] At the very least, casework is a function that should be appreciated and scrutinized more than it has been. American democracy would be much the worse if citizens had no recourse from bureaucratic errors, rigidities, and—occasionally—arrogance.

Data gathering for this study was undertaken in a series of steps. The original design was to examine in depth, via mail questionnaires[1] and personal interviews, the casework operations of 100 randomly chosen members of the House and 30 members of the Senate during the 95th Congress. Additionally, 210 former senators and congressmen who had served during the previous decade were chosen for study. These research plans, however, proved impossible to fulfill by means of a single mailing (including questionnaires and a request for interviews). Accordingly, a more complicated and incremental process was undertaken.

In May and June, 1977, questionnaires were mailed to 52 former senators and 158 former members of the House. Many addresses were outdated; consequently, 21 questionnaires were returned with no hope of being forwarded. Of the 189 that, presumably, reached the intended recipients, 25 (13 percent) were completed and returned: 20 from former representatives and 5 from senators. Letters from 7 others were received indicating their inability or unwillingness to participate.

One year later, questionnaires were mailed to 110 former members in hopes that some would have changed their minds about cooperating. The questionnaires had been sharply reduced in size as an incentive. However, only five completed questionnaires were received.

During the period from June, 1977, through February, 1979, interviews ranging up to one hour were held with two former and current senators, and six current and former members of the House. And among the questionnaires sent to House staffers (below), there were two that were completed by the members themselves. Again, in May, 1979, letters were sent to thirty-one former members living in the Washington, D.C., area, asking for interviews during June. Four were returned unopened, with no forwarding address, and three members indicated that they would not be in Washington during the time requested. Of the remaining twenty-four, two senators and seven congressmen (37.5 percent) granted interviews; and one—who could not be interviewed—completed a questionnaire. Of these interviews, nine were with members who had served in the 95th Congress.

Thus the sample of members of Congress who either were interviewed or responded to questionnaires included twelve senators (of whom five were interviewed and of whom two served in the 95th Congress and seven in the 94th); and thirty-nine members of the House (of whom nine were interviewed and of whom eleven served in the 95th Congress and fifteen in the 94th). Two-thirds were Republicans, and they came from all regions of the country.

Since the primary concern of this study was casework activity of members and staffs during the 95th Congress, questionnaires were mailed in May and June, 1977, to the Washington offices of 30 randomly selected senators and 100 randomly selected members of the House and to their 228 principal home offices as identified in the *Congressional Staff Directory*.[2] The questionnaires sent to the Washington office were abbreviated and slightly different versions of those sent to the home offices. Because a high return rate from Washington was not expected and because certain data were sought from Washington offices that were not appropriate for home offices, additional questionnaires were mailed to 270 randomly chosen House offices and to 50 randomly selected Senate offices. Thus the total for the first mailing was 450 to Washington and 228 to home offices.

Return rates, as anticipated, were low, especially for Washington offices. Accordingly, in July, 1977, a one-page questionnaire was delivered by hand to 35 House and 16 Senate offices in Washington whose home offices had responded, indicating that a significant portion of their casework was handled by Washington staffs. These 51 offices were part of the original 130-office sample. The combined return rates from these two rounds of surveys was 29.4 percent of home offices and 17.7 percent of Washington offices.

In July, 1977, personal interviews ranging from ten to sixty-five minutes in length were conducted with one senator and sixteen aides in fourteen Senate offices and with four congressmen and thirty-two staffers in twenty-eight House offices in Washington. Also during this time, the author obtained some very basic information on casework operations by asking several questions of the receptionists in nine Senate and House offices while distributing the one-page questionnaires. These contacts are not counted as interviews.

In September, 1977, a second round of questionnaires was sent to 90 home offices (62 in the House, 28 for the Senate), seeking certain types of data not included in the earlier surveys as well as some that were. The targeted home offices were those of members whose other home offices or Washington offices had responded earlier. Some were part of the original 130-member sample. The return rate in this survey was excellent: 51 House and 19 Senate staffers replied, for a response rate of 77.8 percent. In May, 1978, a final questionnaire was sent to 220 home offices (160 House, 60 Senate). The purpose was twofold: (1) to complete the data on those senators and representatives for whom replies had been received from some but not all of the offices that handled substantial amounts of their casework; and (2) to generate answers to several new questions that had arisen during the analysis of earlier data. Of the 220 offices surveyed, 14.5 percent responded.

Reasons for the rather low response rate are several. A growing number of congressional offices have instituted rules against responding to mail questionnaires; no fewer than twenty-seven senators and representatives indicated, in letters, that they simply would not complete questionnaires. Some offices receiving questionnaires did no casework. Many, apparently, simply discarded the questionnaires, while others forwarded them to office locations where casework was performed. But many of *those* offices already had received one of the questionnaires, so they completed one and threw the other away. As a result, more offices appear not to have replied than actually was the case. Finally, twenty-five questionnaires from staffers were returned anonymously. It is highly possible that many of these offices were sent second or third questionnaires in the belief that they had not responded when in fact they had. Thus the actual return rates for the second Washington and the second home questionnaires actually may be higher than indicated.

Throughout the period from the late summer of 1977 through the autumn of 1978, personal and telephone interviews were conducted with staffers in both Washington and home offices around the country. Thirteen Senate aides in Washington and four in home offices were interviewed in person, and six in home offices were interviewed over the phone. Twenty House aides on the Hill and five in district offices, plus one former House AA, were personally interviewed by the author; and seven Washington House staffers and twenty-four in home offices were interviewed by telephone.

Thus the data-gathering process was lengthy and multifaceted. Not all questionnaire or interview responses were usable; on the other hand, some useful data were obtained in brief conversations with office receptionists. Moreover, bits and pieces of information were gleaned from other sources. Casework data on one senator, for example, came from a Washington journalist who had spent

Table A.1: Respondents in the Congressional Samples

Type of Respondent	95th Congress		97th Congress	
	N	%	N	%
Senator	11	3	—	—
Representative	37	9	1	*
Senate administrative assistants in Washington	10	2	—	—
Senate caseworker and staff in Washington	22	5	—	—
Senate staff in home offices	74	18	—	—
House administrative assistant in Washington	26	6	30	11
House caseworker and staff in Washington	61	15	60	22
House staff in home offices	161	40	187	67
Total Sample	402	98	278	100

NOTE: Percentages do not add to 100 due to rounding error. Figures include personal and telephone interviews and questionnaire responses. In many cases in the 1982 sample, the same staff member who completed a questionnaire was interviewed as well. The 278 figure represents 278 distinct individuals.

* Less than 1 percent.

considerable time interviewing the staffs of that senator. In 1977, the Office of Management and Budget surveyed House and Senate caseworkers concerning their assessments of how well various federal departments and agencies dealt with the public and with those congressional staffers. Some of the congressional responses contained basic information on staffs, casework loads, and other aspects of casework operations. And in a few instances, letters from members declining to participate in the study furnished valuable information. Finally, a half-dozen aides who are not caseworkers but who are close enough to casework operations to make insightful comments provided both factual information and assessments of their office operations.

In the end, usable (even if partial) responses were obtained from 402 respondents, as seen in columns 1 and 2 of table A.1. Of these respondents, 108 were interviewed in person and 38 over the phone, as indicated in the first three columns of table A.2.

The sum total of these questionnaire and interview responses provided at least some data on the casework operations in the offices of 75 senators and 178 representatives during the 95th Congress and in the offices of 10 senators and 27 congressmen who served in previous years. This is not a strictly random sample. However, of the 30 senators included in the original research design's random sample, some data are available on 26 (86.7 percent); and of the original 100 House offices, at least partial data were gathered on 55 percent. Moreover, these figures do not count anonymous replies, some of which certainly have come from the original sample.

Though not purely random, the sample is quite representative of the 95th Congress. There is no reason to believe that nonrespondents were systematically atypical. Table A.3 illustrates the characteristics of the sample. Discrepancies in the total N result from anonymous replies; discrepancies in the N for a given characteristic result from not having complete data on each respondent. Finally, as part of another project undertaken with a colleague, the author personally interviewed 59 staffers in 53 House offices in Washington and held brief phone interviews with another 16 in June of 1982, repeating several of the questions of

Table A.2: Respondents Interviewed in Person and by Telephone

| | Number and Type of Interview | | | | | |
| | 95th Congress | | | 97th Congress | | |
Type of Respondent	Personal	Phone	Total	Personal	Phone	Total
Senator	5	0	5	—	—	—
Representative	12	1	13	—	—	—
Senate administrative assistant	9	0	9	—	—	—
Senate caseworker and staff	24	6	30	—	—	—
House administrative assistant	14	0	14	13	9	22
House caseworker and staff	44	31	75	46	112	158
Totals	108	38	146	59	121	180

NOTE: Especially in 1982 there is some overlap between staffers interviewed in person and by phone; several follow-up calls had to be made. A substantial number of phone calls had to be made to aides who filled out questionnaires as well.

Table A.3: Comparison of Sample Characteristics
to Characteristics of Full Senate and House

Party Affiliation

	Senate (95th)			House (95th)			House (97th)		
	Dem. (%)	GOP (%)	(*N*)	Dem. (%)	GOP (%)	(*N*)	Dem. (%)	GOP (%)	(*N*)
Sample	63	37	(75)	67	33	(164)	59	41	(137)
Total membership	62	38	(100)	66	34	(435)	56	44	(433)

Region [a]

	East (%)	South (%)	Border (%)	Midwest (%)	West (%)	(*N*)
Senate (95th)						
Sample	12	21	16	28	23	(68)
Full Senate	18	22	12	22	26	(100)
House (95th)						
Sample	27	21	5	27	20	(158)
Full House	24	25	8	26	17	(435)
House (97th)						
Sample	23	24	6	27	16	(137)
Full House	24	25	8	26	17	(433)

continued

the 1977–78 interviews and surveys. Two rounds of one-page questionnaires were sent to every House office in the country. The first yielded 108 signed surveys (and a dozen anonymous ones). The second produced 93 usable questionnaires. Long-distance phone interviews with 105 offices (3 in Washington) followed, in 10 cases bringing questionnaire responses as well. Only preliminary data from the 1982 study of 137 representatives were available at the time of this writing. See tables A.1 and A.2 for details.

Data for executive branch sources were obtained in a fashion similar to that described above. In July, 1977, personal interviews were conducted with 28 department and agency officials in Washington, all of whom were congressional relations specialists. One OMB official was interviewed over the phone. In September, 1978, a mail questionnaire was sent to 390 randomly selected executives in regional and area/district offices around the country. Names and addresses were taken from the *1977–78 United States Government Manual*. In a

Table A.3: *continued*

Seniority, by Years Served in Present Seat, as of 1977

	1–3	4–7	8–11	12–15	16+	(N)
	%	%	%	%	%	
Senate						
Sample	30	22	19	10	19	(73)
Full Senate	29	20	17	9	25	(100)
House						
Sample	46	23	9	11	10	(154)
Full House	37	21	12	13	17	(435)

Ideology

	Conservative Coalition Support Scores [b]		
	Republicans	North. Dems.	South. Dems.
Senate			
Sample	68 (N = 28)	23 (N = 27)	66 (N = 14)
Full Senate	61 (N = 38)	21 (N = 43)	62 (N = 19)
House			
Sample	70 (N = 52)	19 (N = 78)	58 (N = 28)
Full House	72 (N = 148)	23 (N = 94)	59 (N = 193)

continued

[a] East: Connecticut, Maine, Massachusetts, New Hampshire, New Jersey, New York, Pennsylvania, Rhode Island, Vermont;

South: Alabama, Arkansas, Florida, Georgia, Louisiana, Mississippi, North Carolina, South Carolina, Texas, Virginia;

Border: Delaware, Kentucky, Maryland, Missouri, Oklahoma, West Virginia;

Midwest: Illinois, Indiana, Iowa, Kansas, Michigan, Minnesota, Nebraska, North Dakota, Ohio, South Dakota, Wisconsin;

West: Alaska, Arizona, California, Colorado, Hawaii, Idaho, Montana, Nevada, New Mexico, Oregon, Utah, Washington.

[b] *Congressional Quarterly Weekly Report* 36 (December 16, 1978): 3442–46. Scores for the full House and Senate are averages for 1978. Scores for the sample represent the mean of the scores of individual representatives and senators in the sample during the entire 95th Congress. For seven anonymous senators and twelve anonymous House responses, conservative coalition scores were estimated from responses to a question about the member's liberalism and conservatism. Those identified as liberals were assigned a coalition support score of 20; conservatives were given a score of 80; northern moderates received a 40, while southern moderates were scored 60.

Table A.3: *continued*

Safety / Marginality of Seat, by Percentage of Vote Won at Last Election

	0–55%	Over 55%	(N)
Senate			
Sample	43%	57%	(72)
Full Senate	40%	60%	(100)
House			
Sample	28%	72%	(152)
Full House	17%	83%	(435)

Urban / Rural: Percentage of Constituency Living in Standard Metropolitan Statistical Area (SMSA) [c]

	Senate	House
Sample Median	61.1 (N = 73)	70.5 (N = 152)
National Median	68.6	68.6

continued

[c] Computed from the *Congressional District Data Book, 93d Congress* (Washington, D.C.: U.S. Bureau of the Census, 1973).

few instances (for Social Security offices), addresses were taken from the telephone directories in eight major U.S. cities. Responses were received from 186 offices (47.7 percent). In some cases questionnaires were forwarded to other units of the receiving agency for completion — offices which already might have completed the questionnaire or been interviewed. (Since almost all questionnaires were returned anonymously, one cannot be certain of the number and proportion of questionnaires so forwarded; letters from respondents indicate a minimum of eight.) Moreover, during 1977 and 1978, 16 area office officials in nine agencies located in five midwestern cities were interviewed personally, and 12 more by telephone.

Since not all the interviews proved complete enough to record in detail, code, and computerize, the working sample of department and agency personnel included 232 respondents, representing all eleven departments in 1977, eight independent agencies, and three regulatory commissions. Table A.4 describes the sample's characteristics.

Questionnaires sent to congressional staffers and former members allowed

Table A.3: *continued*

	Senate	House
Constituents' Median Education (Years) [d]		
Sample Median	12.1 (*N* = 73)	12.1 (*N* = 152)
National Median	12.1	12.1
Constituents' Median Income Levels [d]		
Sample Median	$9017 (*N* = 73)	$9744 (*N* = 152)
National Median	$9586	$9586
Median Percentage of Constituents Aged 65 and Over [d]		
Sample Median	10.0% (*N* = 73)	9.6% (*N* = 152)
National Median	9.9%	9.9%

NOTE: Data are for 95th Congress, unless otherwise indicated. Data for 97th Congress are as of June, 1982, when interviewing took place.

[d] Figures for the sample represent the median of the medians. That is, for each senator and representative in the sample, median education, income, and age of constituents were recorded. The numbers presented here are the medians of those figures. Data are from the *Congressional District Data Book*.

for, but did not encourage, anonymity. As indicated, however, several respondents did opt to remain anonymous. In a few cases, it was possible to figure out without difficulty who the respondents were, thus reducing the number of *actual* anonymous sources. Survey instruments sent to executive officials, on the other hand, were intended to be returned anonymously, with only the names of the agencies, the respondents' office level (regional or area/district), and their GS ratings provided.

Although the samples are not purely random, they are representative. But there is another, perhaps more serious, problem with the data that must be mentioned. Very few congressional offices, and not many more agency offices, keep reliable statistical data on casework and congressional inquiries. And those that do commonly employ different data-keeping systems and, worse, different definitions of, for example, a "case" or a "success" or a "change in a decision." Some congressional offices include federal projects in "casework," complaints; still others keep records only on those constituent cases that require the opening

Table A.4: Characteristics of Federal Executive Officials and Offices Included in Interview and Questionnaire Sample

TYPE OF RESPONDENT

Cong. Liaison/Cong. Relations Official	11% ($N = 25$)
Program and Administrative Officials	89% ($N = 207$)

REPRESENTATIVENESS OF SAMPLE

Department or Agency	Number of Respondents
Agriculture (incl. FmHA; Forest Service; Agric. Stabilization and Conservation Service)	12
Commerce (incl. EDA)	6
Defense (incl. Army, Navy, Air Force)	4
HEW (incl. Social Security, Food and Drug, Health Care Financing, Child Support Enforcement, Human Development)	29
HUD (incl. Federal Disaster Admin.)	27
Interior (incl. Bureaus of Indian Affairs, Land Management, Reclamation)	18
Justice (incl. Bureau of Prisons, Immigration and Naturalization, Law Enforcement Assistance Admin.)	20
Labor (incl. Workers' Compensation, Employment and Training, Occupational Safety and Health Admin., Wages and Hours Division)	19
State (incl. Passport Office)	5
Transportation (incl. Federal Highway, Federal Railroad, Urban Mass Transit Administrations)	9
Treasury (incl. Customs and Internal Revenue Services)	9
Civil Service Commission	4
Community Services Administration	3

continued

Table A.4: *continued*

Department or Agency	Number of Respondents
Environmental Protection Agency	4
Postal Service	1
Small Business Administration	21
Veterans Administration	15
Independent Regulatory Commissions (FCC, FMA, ICC)	6
Miscellaneous or Anonymous/Unidentified	20

Location of Respondents

Washington	25 (10.8%)
Regional Offices	103 (44.4%)
Area/District Offices	89 (38.4%)
Unknown	15 (6.5%)

Respondents' GS Ratings

GS-18	1 (0.4%)
GS-17	3 (1.3%)
GS-16	14 (6.0%)
GS-15	58 (25.0%)
GS-14	47 (20.3%)
GS-13	22 (9.5%)
GS-12	22 (9.5%)
GS-11	7 (3.0%)
GS-10 and below	7 (3.0%)
Unknown	51 (22.0%)

of a file and a good deal of paperwork. Accordingly, much of the data used in this study had to be generated from scratch, often relying on staff estimates based on definitions supplied by the author. Unfortunately, especially on mail question-naire responses, there is no guarantee that staffers heeded the definitions and directions printed on the questionnaires. Nor is there assurance that, for example, the Washington offices of congressmen counted only cases that came directly to them from constituents, rather than including cases referred to them by their state and district offices. (The second and third rounds of questionnaires provided for this contingency by rephrasing this and other questions.) In short, the numbers used herein can be challenged on several grounds. There are three defenses to such challenges. First, there is little reason to believe that there are *systematic* biases or imbalances in the data; if they are in error, they are consistently so. Thus differences that appear among offices are likely to be real differences. Second, reliance on staff estimates (given the author's definitions) is not unreasonable in the absence of hard data and commonly agreed upon definitions. Third, in many cases, estimates were received from more than one source for each Senate and House office. Questions were phrased to elicit data for each of the several office locations handling casework for a given congressman as well as to get estimates of his/her total casework operations in all locations. And in some instances, more than one staffer in a given office location responded. The result is that certain important variables used in this study are products of more than one esti-mate, and thus they are more likely to be accurate than if they relied on only one respondent for judgments concerning, say, a senator's total casework load or the percentage of casework done in Washington. Therefore, while no claim can be made that the quantitative data used here are without error, there is good reason to believe that they are quite accurate. It is certain that there are no better data available.

NOTES

Chapter 1

1. Quoted in Joe L. Evins, *Understanding Congress* (New York: Clarkson N. Potter, 1963), p. 18.
2. One useful definition of "pork-barrel" expenditures (or legislation) is "expenditures that are not justifiable on strict economic grounds." See John A. Ferejohn, *Pork Barrel Politics: Rivers and Harbors Legislation, 1947–1968* (Stanford: Stanford University Press, 1974), pp. 232–52.
3. Definitions of casework vary from author to author. See Walter Kravitz, "Casework by Members of Congress: A Survey of the Literature" (Washington, D.C.: The Legislative Reference Service, Library of Congress, 1968), pp. 4–5.
4. Ibid., pp. 1, 38.
5. Heinz Eulau and Paul D. Karps, "The Puzzle of Representation: Specifying Components of Responsiveness," *Legislative Studies Quarterly* 2 (August 1977): 233–54. For an application, see Malcolm E. Jewell, *Representation in State Legislatures* (Lexington: University Press of Kentucky, 1982).
6. Robert Weissberg, "Collective vs. Dyadic Representation in Congress," *American Political Science Review* 72 (June 1978): 535–47; and Patricia A. Hurley, "Collective Representation Reappraised," *Legislative Studies Quarterly* 7 (February 1982): 119–36.
7. Quoted in Charles L. Clapp, *The Congressman: His Work as He Sees It* (Garden City, N.Y.: Doubleday & Co., Anchor Books, 1963), p. 57.

Chapter 2

1. Roger H. Davidson, *The Role of the Congressman* (New York: Pegasus, 1969), p. 198; and Joel D. Aberbach and Bert A. Rockman, "The Overlapping Worlds of American Federal Executives and Congressmen," *British Journal of Political Science* 7 (January 1977): note 39.
2. U.S. Congress, House of Representatives, Commission on Administrative Review (Obey Commission), *Final Report*, 95th Cong., 1st sess., 1977, H. Doc. 95-272, vol. 2, pp. 865–67 (hereafter cited as House Commission, *Final Report*). The figures that follow in the text are taken from pp. 879–82 and from the author's analysis of commission data.
3. Richard C. Elling, "The Utility of State Legislative Casework as a Means of Oversight," *Legislative Studies Quarterly* 4 (August 1979): 357; Edward I. Sidlow, "Professionalism in a State Legislature: The Case of Ohio" (Ph.D. diss., The Ohio State University, 1979) cited in Herbert B. Asher, "The Unintended Consequences of Legislative Professionalism," paper prepared for delivery at the annual meeting of the American Political Science Association, New York, August 1978, p. 17; Herbert Weisberg, Thomas Boyd, Marshall Goodman, and Debra Gross, "Reelection and Constituency Service as State Legislator Goals: It's Just Part of the Job," paper prepared for delivery at the annual meeting of the American Political Science Association, Denver, September 1982, p. 7; and Malcolm E. Jewell, *Representation in State Legislatures,* chap. 6.
4. See Lawrence Le Duc, Jr., and Walter L. White, "The Role of Opposition in a One-Party Dominant System: The Case of Ontario," *Canadian Journal of Political Science* 7 (March 1974): 86–100; Richard G. Price, Harold D. Clarke, and Robert M. Krause, "The Socialization of Freshman Legislators: The Case of Canadian M.P.'s," in Jon H. Pammett and Michael S. Wittington, eds., *Foundations of Political Culture: Political Socialization in Canada* (Toronto: Macmillan, 1976), pp. 211–38; Manindra Kumar Mohapatra, "The Ombudsmanic Role of Legislators in an Indian State," *Legislative Studies Quarterly* 1 (August 1976): 302; M. C. Kumbhat and Y. M. Marican, "Constituent Orientations among Malaysian State Legislators," ibid.: 398; and Iqbal Narain and Lata Puri, "Legislators in an Indian State: A Study of Role Images and the Pattern of Constituency Linkages," ibid.: 319.
5. Contrary to Davidson's finding (*Role of the Congressman*, p. 123), members' representational focus was unrelated to views on casework. Self-identified district-oriented representatives were only marginally, and not significantly, more likely than nationally oriented ones to mention the ombudsman role of the House and to value casework and fund-seeking as personally important. It should be noted that, since the Obey Commission's survey of members was not strictly random, many of the usual statistics employed in such research do not apply. However, they will be used to

provide a better feeling as to the generalizability of the findings. Note, however, that no committee chairmen were included in its sample, which probably biased some findings.

6. Those who did dichotomize, however, exhibited predictable attitudes toward casework and projects. The handful of legislators more oriented toward constituency-related than policy activities considered casework and projects to be relatively important, while those stressing the importance of legislation and oversight tended not to. These conclusions were reached by constructing simple additive indexes from the policy-related and the constituency-related (except casework and projects) items in table 2.1, and cross-tabulating one against the other. Each index was then cross-tabulated with three variables measuring orientations toward casework: (1) whether or not members cited the ombudsman role as one of the two most important functions of the House: (2) the importance they attached to helping constituents who had problems with the government; and (3) their judgment of the importance of getting a fair share of federal funds and projects for their districts.

7. Mohapatra, "Ombudsmanic Role," p. 297; Rounaq Jahan, "Members of Parliament in Bangladesh," *Legislative Studies Quarterly* 1 (August 1976): 355–70.

8. *Comparative Legislatures* (Englewood Cliffs, N.J.: Prentice-Hall, 1973), p. 94.

9. Narain and Puri, "Legislators in an Indian State," p. 320.

10. Mohapatra, "Ombudsmanic Role," pp. 298, 302; and John E. Schwarz and L. Earl Shaw, *The United States Congress in Comparative Perspective* (Hillsdale, Ill.: Dryden Press, 1976), p. 284.

11. Anthony Barker and Michael Bush, "Members' Postbags," in Dick Leonard and Valentine Herman, eds., *The Backbencher and Parliament: A Reader* (London: Macmillan, 1972), p. 33. See also Bruce E. Cain, John A. Ferejohn, and Morris P. Fiorina, "The House Is Not a Home: British MPs in Their Constituencies," *Legislative Studies Quarterly* 4 (November 1979): 501–23.

12. Schwarz and Shaw, *United States Congress*, p. 284.

13. All quotations, unless otherwise attributed, are from the author's interviews with members and staffs of Congress or officials in executive agencies, or are their written responses to questions contained in the mail questionnaires. In the case of interviews, the author transcribed respondents' remarks as nearly verbatim as possible within minutes of the interviews. Notes were taken during the interviews to facilitate accurate transcription.

14. Quoted in Thomas E. Cavanagh, "The Two Arenas of Congress," in Joseph Cooper and G. Calvin Mackenzie, eds., *The House at Work* (Austin: University of Texas Press, 1981), p. 69.

15. Robert Klonoff, "The Congressman as a Mediator Between Citizens and Government Agencies: Problems and Prospects," *Harvard Journal on Legislation* 16 (1979): 710.

16. Compare Davidson's findings (*Role of the Congressman*, p. 112) to those of the Obey Commission (*Final Report,* pp. 887, 890).

17. Richard Fenno, *Home Style: House Members in Their Districts* (Boston: Little, Brown and Co., 1978), pp. 157, 199. John A. Ferejohn makes the same point in his *Pork Barrel Politics*, p. 54.

18. Roger H. Davidson, "Our Two Congresses: Where Have They Been? Where Are They Going?" in William J. Crotty, ed., *Paths to Political Reform* (Lexington, Mass.: D. C. Heath & Co., Lexington Books, 1980), p. 298.

19. House Commission, *Final Report,* pp. 822–23. Thirty-five percent answered that it was most important for a congressman "to represent the people in his district and vote according to their wishes"; 12 percent said members should find out what the people need, want, and think; and 10 percent each said that members should attend congressional sessions regularly, be honest and fair, and work to improve the economy.

20. Ibid., pp. 823–24.

21. Ibid., pp. 828–30.

22. Others who disproportionately expected helpfulness were constituents raised in rural or small-town areas, those from New England or border states, those who were government employees or conservative in their political outlook, and those who rated Congress and their congressmen highly. Multiple regression analysis—holding various of these traits constant while assessing the independent impact of others upon the expectation of helpfulness—weakens most of these relationships.

Using a different statistical technique, Morris P. Fiorina has presented data showing that the expectation of helpfulness is linked to name recognition, various forms of direct and indirect contact with incumbents, recollection of the congressman's service for his district, shared partisanship with the representative, agreement with the congressman's voting record, great satisfaction with casework experiences, and reports of very satisfactory casework experiences from acquaintances. See his "Some Problems in Studying the Effects of Resource Allocation in Congressional Elections," *American Journal of Political Science* 25 (August 1981): 563. Such analyses cannot answer questions of causality; the relationships may be simultaneously determined. For exmple, while it may be true that agreement with the congressman's voting record could cause the constituent to believe that his representative would be helpful if called upon, the reverse could just as easily be true. Being very satisfied with previous casework experiences and thinking one's congressman would be helpful might be projections onto the congressman deriving from generalized affect. Expectation of helpfulness (however caused) might *lead* one to make contact, to go to a meeting where the congressman was speaking, or even to listen to or recall his radio advertisements during a campaign. And to show that name recognition is associated with an expectation of helpfulness is to beg the question: what are the antecedents of such recognition? Do they, rather than the recognition, lead to the expectation?

23. Glenn R. Parker and Robert H. Davidson, ''Why Do Americans Love Their Congressmen So Much More Than Their Congress,'' *Legislative Studies Quarterly* 4 (February 1979): 53–61.

24. House Commission, *Final Report,* pp. 874–75.

25. Larry B. Hill, *The Model Ombudsman: Institutionalizing New Zealand's Democratic Experiment* (Princeton: Princeton University Press, 1976), pp. 93–94.

26. For reproductions of actual letters, see Don Radler, *How Congress Works, with a Foreword by the Hon. Jack Brooks* (New York: New American Library, Signet Books, 1976), pp. 59–62.

27. In 1977–78, 37 Senate offices reported that an average (mean) of 73.2 percent (median of 74.6 percent) of all cases came from individuals; 11.2 percent (median of 9.9 percent) from state and local governments; and the remainder from businesses, private organizations, and so on. The 144 House offices responding indicated that an average (mean and median) of 80 percent were from individuals; 8.9 percent from governments; and the rest from businesses and other organizations. In 1982 (see table 3.1) respondents were asked separately for estimates of cases and of projects. These findings are in line with those of other studies. See, for example, Walter Gellhorn, *When Americans Complain: Governmental Grievance Procedures* (Cambridge: Harvard University Press, 1966), p. 66, n. 15; Kenneth E. Gray, ''Congressional Interference in Administration,'' in Daniel J. Elazar et al., eds., *Cooperation and Conflict: Readings in American Federalism* (Itasca, Ill.: F. E. Peacock Publishers, 1969), pp. 530–33.

28. House Commission, *Final Report,* p. 830.

29. Quoted in *Congressional Quarterly Weekly Report* 35 (October 29, 1977), p. 2317.

30. *Milwaukee Journal,* Local News Section, June 13, 1982, pp. 1, 5.

31. Bruce E. Cain, John A. Ferejohn, and Morris P. Fiorina. ''The Electoral Incentive in Comparative Perspective: Constituency Service in Great Britain and the U.S.,'' paper delivered at the annual meeting of the Midwest Political Science Association, Cincinnati, March 1981, p. 12.

32. *Washington Post,* May 29, 1976, pp. A-1, A-6.

33. *Milwaukee Journal,* April 9, 1978, pp. 1, 19; November 11, 1977, p. 3.

34. U.S. Senate, Committee on Government Operations, Subcommittee on Intergovernmental Relations, *Confidence and Concern: Citizens View American Government, A Survey of Public Attitudes,* 93rd Cong., 1st Sess., 1973, Committee Print, pt. 1, p. 256; Sidney Verba and Norman H. Nie, *Participation in America: Political Democracy and Social Equality* (New York: Harper & Row, 1972), p. 31; Daniel Katz, Barbara A. Gutek, Robert L. Kahn, and Eugenia Barton, *Bureaucratic Encounters* (Ann Arbor: Institute for Social Research, 1975), p. 20.

35. House Commission, *Final Report,* p. 830.

36. Verba and Nie, *Participation,* chap. 8; Karl A. Friedman, *Complaining: Compara-*

tive Aspects of Complaint Behavior and Attitudes toward Complaining in Canada and Britain (Beverly Hills, Calif.: Sage Publications, 1974), pp. 10–49; David R. Mayhew, *Congress: The Electoral Connection* (New Haven: Yale University Press, 1974), p. 109. For example, the 1978 CPS data indicate that, while only 6.5 percent of the respondents with a grade-school education ever contacted their congressmen, fully 20 percent of those with at least some college education did so. See also Elaine B. Sharp, "Citizen-Initiated Contacting of Government Officials and Socioeconomic Status: Determining the Relationship and Accounting for It," *American Political Science Review* 76 (March 1982): 109–15.

37. Arnold Vedlitz, James A. Dyer, and Roger Durand, "Citizen Contacts with Local Governments: A Comparative View," *American Journal of Political Science* 24 (February 1980): 50–67.

38. Bryan D. Jones, Saadia R. Greenberg, Clifford Kaufman, and Joseph Drew, "Bureaucratic Response to Citizen-Initiated Contacts: Environmental Enforcement in Detroit," *American Political Science Review* 71 (March 1977): 148–65; and Paul M. Sniderman and Richard A. Brody, "Coping: The Ethic of Self-Reliance," *American Journal of Political Science* 21 (August 1977): 501–21. For a model of "clientele participation" that combines perceived needs, citizen concerns, and socioeconomic status, see John Clayton Thomas, "Citizen-initiated Contacts with Government Agencies: A Test of Three Theories," *American Journal of Political Science* 26 (August 1982): 504–22.

39. Among Obey Commission respondents who reported requesting help from their representatives, nearly one out of five were coded as having done so to express opinions, seek information, or obtain military academy appointments. In addition, 40 percent of those seeking help were coded as seeking assistance for indeterminate purposes — and thus could have been contacting their representatives for noncasework purposes. See House Commission, *Final Report*, p. 830.

40. See Diana Evans Yiannakis, "The Grateful Electorate: Casework and Congressional Elections," *American Journal of Political Science* 25 (August 1981): 574–75. Using discriminant analysis, she, too, found relatively minor effects of education and income on case requests.

41. Verba and Nie, *Participation*, p. 135.

42. PROBIT coefficients (maximum likelihood estimates) are interpreted as probabilities: a value of zero suggests that altering the independent variable will not affect the existing probabilities of the occurrence of an event (in this example, requesting help from a congressman). A coefficient value of 1 implies that a unit change in the independent variable will lead to an increase of one standard deviation (assuming a normal curve distribution) in the existing probabilities that an event will occur (that the dependent variable will change) — assuming all else is held equal. See D. J. Finney, *Probit*

Analysis, 3rd ed. (Cambridge: Cambridge University Press, 1971); William Zavoina and Richard McKelvey, ''A Statistical Model for the Analysis of Legislative Voting Behavior,'' paper delivered at the annual meeting of the American Political Science Association, New York, August, 1969; Eric A. Hanushek and John E. Jackson *Statistical Methods for Social Scientists* (New York: Academic Press, 1977), chap. 7.

43. See John C. McAdams and John R. Johannes, ''Does Casework Matter? A Reply to Professor Fiorina,'' *American Journal of Political Science* 25 (August 1981): 581–604. When these variables are included in the equations, they usually produce large, positive coefficients and, naturally, strengthen the explanatory power of the equations. For example, it turns out that having had contact with the congressman is independently associated both with case requesting and (in 1980) with opinion expressing. Believing that one's congressman would be *very* helpful if asked for help likewise is strongly related to asking for help and, to a lesser degree, to expressing opinions. Interestingly, believing that the congressman would *not* be very helpful still is positively correlated with requesting help.

Chapter 3

1. According to the Obey Commission, 51 percent of the House administrative assistants surveyed indicated that staff members maintain records on the number of cases. House Commission, *Final Report,* p. 1068.

2. See Kravitz, ''Casework by Members of Congress: A Survey of the Literature,'' pp. 7–12; Gellhorn, *When Americans Complain,* pp. 63–65; John D. Macartney, ''Political Staffing: A View from the District'' (Ph.D. diss., University of California at Los Angeles, 1975), p. 15; and David Kovenock's ''Influence in the U.S. House of Representatives: A Statistical Analysis of Communication,'' *American Politics Quarterly* 1 (October 1973): 431–32.

3. Bruce E. Cain, John A. Ferejohn, and Morris P. Fiorina, ''The Demand for Constituency Service in Great Britain and the United States,'' paper delivered at the annual meeting of the Western Political Science Association, San Francisco, March, 1980, p. 6.

4. House Commission, *Final Report,* p. 890.

5. Four factors account for the differences. First, almost all previous attempts to tabulate casework loads used broader definitions than those used here; thus some of those earlier efforts produced larger figures. Second, the commission's data came from congressmen themselves, who, frankly, know less about casework in their offices than do their staffs (and who might have a tendency to exaggerate). Third, many of the figures collected by others are from a bygone era when case loads were lower. Finally,

Cain et al. apparently obtained estimates only from one staff aide in the Washington offices of their 100-member sample, thus probably missing some casework done in district offices.

6. U.S. Congress, Senate Committee on Appropriations, *Legislative Branch Appropriations for Fiscal Year 1979, Hearings,* 95th Cong., 2d sess., 1978, p. 149; House Committee on Appropriations, *Legislative Branch Appropriations,* 95th Cong., 2d sess., 1978, p. 96.

7. Richard C. Elling, "The Utility of State Legislative Casework as a Means of Oversight," p. 359; Cain, Ferejohn, and Fiorina, "The House Is Not a Home," p. 518. For comparable data in countries using an ombudsman to handle complaints, see Frank Stacey, *Ombudsmen Compared* (Oxford: Clarendon Press, 1978), pp. 7, 13, 20, 29, 48, 56, 101, 129, 207.

8. Morris P. Fiorina, *Congress: The Keystone of the Washington Establishment* (New Haven: Yale University Press, 1977).

9. Kenneth E. Gray, "Congressional Interference in Administration," p. 540.

10. Similar expectations develop in Britain. See Bruce E. Cain and David B. Ritchie, "Assessing Constituency Involvement: The Hemel Hempstead Experience," *Parliamentary Affairs* 35 (Winter 1982): 80.

11. William S. Cohen and Kenneth Lasson, *Getting the Most Out of Washington: Using Congress to Move the Federal Bureaucracy* (Washington, D.C.: Facts on File, 1982).

12. Outreach efforts are common among legislators in other settings. See Cain, Ferejohn, and Fiorina, "The Demand for Constituency Service"; Hill, *The Model Ombudsman,* p. 270; and Steven A. Peterson and William H. Dutton, "Errand-Boy Behavior and Local Elections," paper delivered at the annual meeting of the Midwest Political Science Association, Cincinnati, March, 1981, table 1.

13. House Commission, *Final Report,* pp. 879, 877.

14. Fenno, *Home Style,* p. 33; Cain, Ferejohn, and Fiorina, "The Demand for Constituency Service," p. 11. The one factor that best explained the rising number of trips home was the increased travel allowance. Glenn R. Parker, "Sources of Change in Congressional District Attentiveness," *American Journal of Political Science* 24 (February 1980): 115–24.

15. Quoted in Larry Light, "Pressing the Flesh: For Many Incumbents, Running for Re-election Is Now a Full-time Job," *Congressional Quarterly Weekly Report* 37 (July 7, 1979): 1356; David M. Alpern, with Henry W. Hubbard, "Tending to the Home Folks," *Newsweek,* April 25, 1977, p. 26.

16. Alpern and Hubbard, "Tending to the Home Folks," p. 26

17. Another survey produced identical results for the House. See Cain, Ferejohn, and Fiorina, "Demand for Constituency Service," p. 13; and their "Electoral Incentive in Comparative Perspective," p. 10.

18. For evidence of the electoral margin connection, see Fiorina, "Some Problems," pp. 16–19; Albert D. Cover, "Contacting Congressional Constituents: Some Patterns of Perquisite Use," *American Journal of Political Science* 24 (February 1980): 125–35; Cain, Ferejohn, and Fiorina, "Electoral Incentive" pp. 14–22; John D. Cranor and Joseph W. Westphal, "Congressional District Offices, Federal Programs, and Electoral Benefits: Some Observations on the Passing of the Marginal Representative, 1974–1976," paper delivered at the annual meeting of the Midwest Political Science Association, Chicago, April, 1978, p. 22; Davidson, "Our Two Congresses," p. 4; Lynda W. Powell, "Constituency Service and Electoral Margins in Congress," paper delivered at the annual meeting of the American Political Science Association, Denver, September, 1982; and Barry S. Rundquist and Lyman A. Kellstedt, "Congressional Interaction with Constituents: A Career Perspective," paper delivered at the annual meeting of the American Political Science Association, Denver, September, 1982. For a partial dissent, see Fenno, *Home Style,* pp. 40–43; Peterson and Dutton "Errand-Boy Behavior," p. 6; Jon R. Bond, "Dimensions of District Attention Over Time," paper delivered at the annual meeting of the Midwest Political Science Association, Chicago, April, 1983, pp. 16, 19, 23; J. Theodore Anagnoson, "Home Style in New Zealand," *Legislative Studies Quarterly* 8 (May 1983): 157–75; and Lawrence W. Miller and Robert D. Wrinkle, "Errand-Boy or Constituency Service: A Multi-State Study of Municipal Legislators," paper delivered at the annual meeting of the Midwest Political Science Association, Chicago, April, 1983, p. 10.

On the generally mixed evidence for the effect of seniority, see Fenno, *Home Style,* p. 209; Bond, "Dimensions of District Attention," pp. 17, 19, 22; Anagnoson, "Home Style," p. 166; Powell, "Constituency Service," pp. 5–6; Diane Evans Yiannakis, "House Members' Communication Styles: Newsletters and Press Releases," paper delivered at the annual meeting of the Midwest Political Science Association, Chicago, April, 1979, pp. 33–34; Richard Born, "Perquisite Employment in the U.S. House of Representatives, 1960–1976: The Influence of Generational Change," *American Politics Quarterly* 10 (July 1982): 347–62; and Glenn R. Parker and Suzanne L. Parker, "The Causes and Consequences of Congressional District Attention," paper delivered at the annual meeting of the American Political Science Association, Denver, September, 1982; Parker, "Sources of Change," p. 122; Mohapatra, "Ombudsmanic Role," pp. 295–314; and Kumbhat and Marican, "Constituent Orientations among Malaysian State Legislators," pp. 389–404.

19. Cain, Ferejohn, and Fiorina, "Demand for Constituency Service," p. 24. According to Bond's study ("Dimensions of District Attention," pp. 17, 19, 23), party leaders and members of the three "power" committees in the House (Rules, Appropriations, and Ways and Means) seem to devote less effort to district-related activities than do

their colleagues. Anagnoson ("Home Style," p. 162) found that New Zealand MPs who held ministerial status spent less time in their constituencies.

20. Bond, "Dimensions of District Attention," pp. 18–19; Powell, "Constituency Service," pp. 5–6; Kenneth Greene, "Policy and Service Representation by Municipal Legislators," paper delivered at the annual meeting of the Midwest Political Science Association, Chicago, April, 1983, p. 7; Harold D. Clarke, "Determinants of Provincial Constituency Service Behaviour: A Multivariate Analysis," *Legislative Studies Quarterly* 3 (November 1978): 601–28; Yiannakis, "House Members' Communication Styles," pp. 23–29; Cain, Ferejohn, and Fiorina, "The Demand for Constituency Service," p. 23, and "Electoral Incentive," p. 17; Harold D. Clarke, Richard G. Price, and Robert Krause, "Constituency Service among Canadian Provincial Legislators: Basic Findings and a Test of Three Hypotheses," *Canadian Journal of Political Science* 8 (December 1975): 530, 533; LeDuc and White, "The Role of Opposition," pp. 94–96; R. E. Dowse, "The MP and His Surgery," in Leonard and Herman, *The Backbencher and Parliament*, p. 56; Mohapatra, "Ombudsmanic Role," pp. 303–306; Peterson and Dutton, "Errand-Boy Behavior," p. 6; Kumbhat and Marican, "Constituent Orientation," p. 401.

21. James L. Payne, "The Personal Electoral Advantage of House Incumbents, 1936–1974," paper delivered at the annual meeting of the Southern Political Science Association, Gatlinburg, Tennessee, November, 1979, pp. 11–12. In abbreviated form the paper was published in the *American Politics Quarterly* 8 (October 1980): 465–82.

22. Davidson, *The Role of the Congressman*, pp. 78–85.

23. Daniel J. Elazar, *American Federalism: A View From The States*, 2d ed. (New York: Thomas Y. Crowell Company, 1972), pp. 93–119.

24. Demographic and political data used here and throughout the book are taken from two sources: *Congressional District Data Book, 93rd Congress* (Washington, D.C.: U.S. Bureau of the Census, 1973) and the 1974, 1976, and 1978 editions of Michael Barone, Grant Ujifusa, and Douglas Matthews, *The Almanac of American Politics* (New York: E. P. Dutton, 1975, 1977, 1979).

25. This finding contrasts with that of Cain, Ferejohn, and Fiorina, who found that 1976 election results did predict the decision to solicit or not to solicit cases in 1977. See their "Electoral Incentive," p. 16. Still, when the dependent variable here was coded to reflect "some" or "no" casework stimulation (as Cain et al. had done), no relationships of any magnitude (let alone statistical significance) emerged between the decision to solicit or not to solicit cases, on the one hand, and the percentages of the vote won in either 1976 or over the 1970–76 period, on the other. Nor was any relationship at all apparent using a bivariate (cross-tabulation) test. The discrepancy in findings could be due to sampling differences or sample size (102 versus 132). It also could be due to the way in which data were collected. See note 5 above.

26. Both party and ideology need to be included, despite their strong intercorrelation. Not only are the signs different, but when the equations were run with only one of them, the coefficient for that variable failed to reach acceptable levels of statistical significance. Cain, Ferejohn, and Fiorina (ibid.) also found that Republicans are more apt to engage in entrepreneurial activities.

27. The same equations were run using other indicators of need: percent of the elderly (over sixty-five) in the districts and states, and percent of urban residents (those living in standard metropolitan statistical areas). In neither case were the coefficients large or statistically significant. In the Senate, population also proved unrelated to case-work entrepreneurship.

28. Quoted in Danny Wilks, "Congressional Resources for the Grant Seeker," *Grantsmanship Center NEWS*, January / February, 1980, p. 31.

29. See New York Senator James Buckley's testimony, and that of several others, in U.S. Congress, Senate Committee on Appropriations, *Legislative Branch Appropriations for Fiscal Year 1974, Hearings before a Subcommittee of the Committee on Appropriations on HR 6691*, 93rd Congress, 1st sess., 1973, p. 687. Democratic Study Group staff director Richard Conlon agreed; see *Inside Congress* (Washington: Congressional Quarterly, Inc., 1976), p.31.

30. Labour MPs in Britain have twice the case loads of Tories, and Liberals receive many cases from (presumably Liberal) constituents of Conservative and Labour members. Cain, Ferejohn, and Fiorina, "The House Is Not a Home," p. 37; Barker and Rush, "Members' Postbags," p. 34; Cain, Ferejohn, and Fiorina, "Demand for Constituency Service," pp. 22–24.

31. Donald R. Matthews has offered an alternate hypothesis, based on a "compensation theory." One senator's responsiveness to case mail may affect the load borne by the other senator from the same state, either causing him to compensate for his colleague's deficiencies or allowing him to coast along on his colleague's hard work. A test of the theory using case loads for fourteen pairs of senators proved inconclusive (*U.S. Senators and Their World* [Chapel Hill: University of North Carolina Press, 1960], pp. 224–25).

32. Given the total lack of association between constituents' personal income and the propensity to request help shown in chap. 2, this is puzzling. Of course, it is true that there need not be a relationship between individual-level and aggregate-level findings: people of low or average income in well-to-do districts may be slightly more apt to seek help than their peers in less affluent districts, and vice versa. Moreover, very small individual-level relationships can produce marked aggregate ones.

33. *Milwaukee Journal*, August 31, 1977, p. 3.

Chapter 4

1. The framework described here borrows heavily from Joseph A. Pika, "White House Boundary Roles: Linking Advisory Systems and Presidential Publics," paper delivered at the annual meeting of the American Political Science Association, Washington, D.C., August, 1979, especially pp. 1–6.

2. Macartney, "Political Staffing," p. 87.

3. Nelson W. Polsby, "The Institutionalization of the U.S. House of Representatives," *American Political Science Review* 62 (March 1968): 145; Samuel P. Huntington, "Political Development and Political Democracy," *World Politics* 17 (April 1965): 394–401. For an application of institutionalization principles to the ombudsman office, see Hill, *The Model Ombudsman,* especially pp. 22–36.

4. House Commission, *Final Report,* p. 1026.

5. See Cain, Ferejohn, and Fiorina, "Electoral Incentive" and "Demand for Constituency Service"; and Thomas E. Cavanagh, "Rational Allocation of Congressional Resources: Member Time and Staff Use in the House," in Douglas W. Rae and Theodore J. Eismeier, eds., *Public Policy and Public Choice* (Beverly Hills: Sage Publications, 1979).

6. An objection might be raised that the relationship between electoral margin and either size or decentralization of casework staffs is reciprocal. That is, if having large staffs or putting them in one's district or state offices *causes* one to win by larger vote margins, the equations are simultaneously determined. Thus one must be careful about interpretations. The equations were run without the electoral variable, yielding virtually no changes in the coefficients for the other independent variables.

7. One might object to this analysis on simultaneity grounds: locating staffers in the district offices might tend to generate more cases, rather than vice versa. However, replicating the analysis of case loads (in chap. 3) using the percentage of casework done in the home district or the number or percentage of staffers located there as independent variables resulted in weak and insignificant coefficients in the House. Removing the workload variable in table 4.2 makes no difference in the other coefficients in the House equation and, in the Senate, serves only to strengthen several of them. But no major changes occurred.

8. For a general discussion of staff allocation, see: Marc Yacker, "Congressional Office Operations: Aspects of Staff Organization in Washington and the Congressional District," (Washington, D.C.: Congressional Research Service, Library of Congress, 1976), pp. 11–14; and Janet Breslin, "Constituent Service," in U.S. Congress, Senate, Commission on the Operation of the Senate, *Senators: Offices, Ethics, and Pressures,* 94th Cong., 2d sess., 1977, Committee Print, p. 24.

9. See also Harrison W. Fox, Jr., and Susan Webb Hammond, *Congressional Staffs:*

The Invisible Force in American Lawmaking (New York: The Free Press, 1977), p. 76; Macartney, "Political Staffing," p. 144. Analysis of Obey Commission data indicates that representatives who place the largest proportion of their caseworkers in home offices are significantly more likely to complain of limits in staff size. They want more aides but, presumably, don't want them in Washington.

10. Fenno, *Home Style,* p. 48.

11. House Commission, *Final Report,* p. 943, 1003, 1043.

12. Ibid., pp. 943, 1003, 1043, 1053.

13. U.S. Congress, House Commission on Administrative Review, *Administrative Reorganization and Legislative Management,* 95th Cong., 1st sess., 1977, H. Doc. 95-232, p. 8. Fox and Hammond, *Congressional Staffs,* p. 173.

14. Women constitute 22 percent of administrative assistants, 32 percent of press secretaries, 46 percent of legislative assistants, 69 percent of legislative aides, and 86 percent of office managers (House Commission, *Final Report,* p. 93).

15. Mike Causey, "The Federal Diary," *Washington Post,* November 14, 1982, p. B-2. For comparison, see House Commission, *Administrative Reorganization,* pp. 86–97.

16. On staff turnover, see Robert H. Salisbury and Kenneth A. Shepsle, "Congressional Staff Turnover and the Ties-That-Bind," *American Political Science Review* 75 (June 1981): 318–96.

17. House Commission, *Final Report,* pp. 1002, 1032.

18. Social work professionals who, like congressional caseworkers, find themselves in ambiguous and conflicting roles, experience such problems frequently. See David Harrison, "Role Strain and Burnout in Child Protective Service Workers," *Social Science Review* 64 (March 1980): 31–44.

19. In some respects, the congressional caseworker–constituent relationship resembles the social worker–client or therapist-patient relationship. Often certain myths grow up out of such linkages: that the workers/therapists love their clients, that they are endowed with magical powers, and that the clients-patients will be eternally grateful and kind to the providers. See Dean Briggs, "The Trainee and the Borderline Client: Countertransference Pitfalls," *Clinical Social Work Journal* 30 (Summer 1979): 133–46. One former caseworker, reading Briggs's article, immediately saw the connection: "From my own experience," she said, "these myths could be applied to the congressional caseworkers and their relationships to constituents. Setting limits on what a congressman is capable of actually doing for a constituent and communicating them to the constituent seems important to me."

20. Macartney found that 60 of 125 field office staff members he interviewed said that power was a paramount attraction of their job ("Political Staffing," p. 91).

21. *Congressional Staffs,* pp. 188–89 and chap. 6.

22. Ibid., p. 186.

23. See the series of articles by Stephen Isaacs in the *Washington Post,* Feb. 16–21, 1975, which detail many of the abuses of committee staffs.

24. Kenneth Kofmehl, *Professional Staffs of Congress* (West Lafayette, Ind.: Purdue University Press, 1962), p. 128.

25. Ibid.; Dale Vinyard, "Congressmen as Washington Agents of Constituents," *Business and Government Review* 8 (September–October 1967): 12–25.

26. *Congressional Staffs,* p. 193.

27. This may underestimate the situation. However, a 1978 study by the Congressional Management Foundation found about the same results, namely, that 39 percent of the offices in its sample reported having at least one grants specialist. Wilks, "Congressional Resources," p. 28.

28. Fox and Hammond, *Congressional Staffs,* p. 92.

29. Cain, Ferejohn, and Fiorina, "Demand for Constituency Service," p. 5.

30. Wilks, "Congressional Resources," p. 35.

31. For a discussion, see James A. Robinson, *Congress and Foreign Policy-Making: A Study in Legislative Influence and Initiative,* rev. ed. (Homewood, Ill.: The Dorsey Press, 1967), chaps. 4, 5; Abraham Holtzman, *Legislative Liaison: Executive Leadership in Congress* (Chicago: Rand McNally, 1970); G. Russell Pipe, "Congressional Liaison: The Executive Branch Consolidates Its Relations with Congress," *Public Administration Review* 26 (March 1966): 14–24; and Edward de Grazia, "Congressional Liaison: An Inquiry into its Meaning for Congress," in Alfred de Grazia, ed., *Congress: The First Branch of Government* (Garden City, N.Y.: Doubleday & Co., Anchor Books, 1967), pp. 281–322.

32. Bill Keller, "Executive Agency Lobbying: Mastering the Difficult Art of Congressional Liaison," *Congressional Quarterly Weekly Report* 39 (December 1981): 2389.

33. Pete Earley, "Providing Grist for the Hill's Decision Mill," *Washington Post,* June 24, 1982, p. A-21.

34. James Burnham, "Some Administrators' Unkindly View of Congress," in Robert T. Golembiewski, Frank Gibson, and Geoffrey Y. Cornog, eds., *Public Administration: Readings in Institutions, Processes, Behavior, Policy,* 3d ed. (Chicago: Rand McNally, 1976), pp. 127–34.

35. This is not entirely surprising. See Aberbach and Rockman, "Overlapping Worlds," pp. 23–47. For a state-level analysis, see Richard C. Elling, "State Legislative Casework and State Administrative Performance," *Administration and Society* 12 (November 1980): 327–56. Similarly, bureaucrats in India have a generally positive attitude toward casework. See Mohapatra, "The Ombudsmanic Role of Legislators in an Indian State."

36. See John R. Johannes, "Congress, the Bureaucracy, and Casework," *Administration and Society,* forthcoming.

Chapter 5

1. Bonnie Brown, Patricia Valentine, Barbara Means, and Maureen Reynolds, "Congressional Casework Manual," National Republican Congressional Committee (n.d.: mimeograph). Similar lists of "do's and don'ts" can be found in many office casework manuals. For two published versions, see Donald G. Tacheron and Morris K. Udall, *The Job of the Congressman,* 2d ed. (Indianapolis: Bobbs-Merrill, 1970), pp. 70–82; and Cohen and Lasson, *Getting the Most Out of Washington.* For a general overview of the casework process, see T. Edward Westen, "The Constituent Needs Help: Casework in the House of Representatives," in Sven Groennings and Jonathan P. Hawley, eds., *To Be a Congressman: The Promise and the Power* (Washington, D.C.: Acropolis Books, 1973), pp. 53–72.

2. Riva Lee, "Grantsmanship" (Washington, D.C.: Congressional Management Foundation, 1977), p. 15.

3. Peter Blau, *Exchange and Power in Social Life* (New York: John Wiley Sons, 1964), and R. L. Curry and L. L. Wade, *A Theory of Political Exchange* (Englewood Cliffs, N.J.: Prentice-Hall, 1968).

4. These figures are from a survey conducted as part of the Carter administration's study of executive branch reorganization. For an explanation, see the *Federal Register* 42 (July 7, 1977):34958–59. Responses from congressional offices were made available to the author by the Office of Management and Budget, which conducted the study.

5. See J. Theodore Anagnoson, "Bureaucratic Reactions to Political Pressure—The Case of Federal Community Development Grants," paper delivered at the annual meeting of the American Political Science Association, Washington, D.C., September, 1979.

6. Quoted in Wilks, "Congressional Resources," p. 33.

7. Mary Thornton, "Rep. Lott Forcefully Presents His Views to the Justice Department," *Washington Post,* February 19, 1982, p. A-2.

8. "Heavy Pressure on HEW," *Milwaukee Journal,* Dec. 10, 1979, pt. 1, p. 10.

9. Irwin B. Arieff, "Todd Shipyard Seeks Assistance of Congressman in Claim Against Navy," *Congressional Quarterly Weekly Report* 36 (October 28, 1978): 3151–54.

10. Edmund Beard and Stephen Horn, *Congressional Ethics: The View from the House* (Washington, D.C.: The Brookings Institution, 1975), p. 75.

11. *Pork Barrel Politics,* pp. 61–66, especially p. 65. Former Cong. Frank E. Smith (D., Miss.) recounts a tale concerning the Weather Bureau. By working with a friend who

chaired the key appropriations subcommittee, he got the bureau to undertake some experiments in weather forecasting in his constituency (*Congressman from Mississippi: An Autobiography* [New York: Capricorn Books, 1964], p. 243).

12. *Washington Post,* April 25, 1977, p. C-23.

13. The Obey Commission's survey of members and legislative assistants also uncovered complaints about the bureaucracy's cooperation on cases and projects, with most comments focusing on the problems of inadequate information and tardiness, especially in providing information concerning grants available to their districts. House Commission, *Final Report,* pp. 974–79, 1096–99.

14. When OMB surveyed congressional offices in the summer of 1977 (note 7 above), Labor's Office of Workers' Compensation Programs ranked at the top of the list of most obnoxious agencies. See David S. Broder, "Little Labor Dept. Agency High on Public Gripe List," *Washington Post,* August 15, 1977, p. A-1; Jack Anderson and Les Whitten, "Irritating Bureaucrats Face Curbs," *Washington Post,* October 1, 1977, p. E-39; Frank A. Aukofer, "Agencies Take Their Time," *Milwaukee Journal,* September 13, 1977, p. 4. Almost all agencies came in for criticism, and the results of the White House survey did not match exactly those of the one undertaken here. But there was general agreement on most agencies.

Chapter 6

1. Elihu Katz and Brenda Danet, "Introduction: Bureaucracy as a Problem for Sociology and Society," in Katz and Danet, eds., *Bureaucracy and the Public: A Reader in Official-Client Relations* (New York: Basic Books, 1973), pp. 4–5. Charges of unfair treatment are not peculiar to the U.S. system of legislative casework. See Shiram Mahashwari, "Constituency Linkage of National Legislators in India," *Legislative Studies Quarterly* 1 (August 1976): 346–51.

2. *Congressman from Mississippi,* p. 239.

3. Gellhorn, *When Americans Complain,* p. 72. Former Cong. John Lindsay agreed. See his testimony in U.S. Congress, Joint Committee on the Organization of Congress, *Organization of Congress, Hearings Pursuant to S. Con. Res. 2,* 89th Cong., 1st sess., 1965, pt. 3, p. 444.

4. Gellhorn, *When Americans Complain,* p. 78.

5. *Congressional Record* 108, pt. 13, 87th Cong., 2d sess., August 28, 1962, p. 17875.

6. Quoted in Richard L. Lyons, "Lobby Unit Walks Out of Sikes Inquiry," *Washington Post,* May 7, 1976, p. A-2.

7. Alan Berlow, "Federal Grand Jury, IRS Probing Former Rep. Frank Clark," *Washington Post,* September 8, 1977, p. A-2.

8. Jack Anderson, "The Congressman and the Builder," *Washington Post,* November 25, 1978, p. C-16.

9. *Congressional Record* 116, 91st Cong., 2d sess., January 26, 1978, p. 1078. In 1951 the Subcommittee on Ethical Standards in Government of the Senate Labor and Public Welfare Committee issued a committee print on the subject. In addition, the "Government in the Sunshine Act" (PL 94-409) includes a section on *ex parte* communications with the executive. See Thomas B. Ripy, "Congressional Communication with Administrative Agencies" (Washington, D.C.: Congressional Research Service, Library of Congress, 1977). For a broader discussion of ethical issues, see Robert S. Getz, *Congressional Ethics: The Conflct of Interest Issues* (Princeton, N.J.: Van Nostrand, 1966), chap. 4.

10. This figure is higher than several other estimates. See Gellhorn, *When Americans Complain,* pp. 78–79; Clapp, *The Congressman: His Job as He Sees It,* pp. 87–88. John D. Macartney's finding of an 80 percent success rate included the speeding up of cases as well as the substantive changes ("Political Staffing," p. 173).

11. Dean Mann, *The Citizen and the Bureaucracy: Complain Handling Procedures of Three California Legislators* (Berkeley: Institute of Governmental Studies, University of California, 1968), pp. 19, 41. Hill, *The Model Ombudsman,* pp. 187, 239; Stacey, *Ombudsmen Compared,* pp. 30, 38, 77, 101. One reason for the lower ombudsman figures (8 to 29 percent) could be that they all are taken from "hard" sources—the ombudsmen's records. The caseworker success rates are estimates. For an informative comparative study, see Philip Norton, " 'Dear Minister'—The Importance of MP-to-Minister Correspondence," *Parliamentary Affairs* 35 (Winter 1982): 59–72, especially 64–65.

12. Members also give high ratings to their general performance. Of the 35 congressmen in the Obey Commission's survey who believed that the ombudsman role was one of those the House should play, 42 percent thought that the House was very effective, and an additional one third said it was fairly effective. The same seems to be true in state legislatures. See Alan Rosenthal, *Legislative Performance in the States: Explorations of Committee Behavior* (New York: The Free Press, 1974), p. 12.

13. See Gellhorn, *When Americans Complain,* pp. 70, 71, 78; Macartney, "Political Staffing," pp. 173–74. For state level results, see Mann, *Citizen and Bureaucracy,* p. 19, and Elling, "Utility of Casework," p. 372.

14. Technical Assistance Research Programs, Inc., "Feasibility Study to Improve Handling of Consumer Complaints: Evaluation Report," unpublished report pursuant to contract No. HEW-OS-74-292 (Washington, D.C., December, 1976), pp. 12–13.

15. Federal grants come in various forms: categorical grants, block grants, formula grants, and discretionary grants. Some have matching requirements, and others come as loans. A basic distinction is between formula grants, wherein Congress rigidly

defines the eligibility criteria, and discretionary project grants, wherein the administrative agency must decide which applications are most meritorious. See Lee, "Grantsmanship," pp. 4–8; R. Douglas Arnold, *Congress and the Bureaucracy: A Theory of Influence* (New Haven: Yale University Press, 1979), pp. 4–6; and two works of J. Theodore Anagnoson: "Selecting Federal Projects: A Bureaucratic Perspective," paper delivered at the annual meeting of the Midwest Political Science Association, Chicago, April, 1978; and "Bureaucratic Reactions to Political Pressure."

16. See Charles R. Plott, "Some Organizational Influences on Urban Renewal Decisions," *American Economic Review* 58 (May 1968): 306–21; Leonard G. Ritt, "Committee Position, Seniority, and the Distribution of Government Expenditures," *Public Policy* 24 (Fall 1976): 463–89; Ferejohn, *Pork Barrel,* pp. 133–39, 175–84, 234; and Carol F. Goss, "House Committee Characteristics and Distributive Politics," paper delivered at the annual meeting of the American Political Science Association, San Francisco, August, 1975.

17. *Congress and the Bureaucracy.* This is the best of the studies investigating the link between congressional position and the distribution of federal programs. In addition to developing and testing a coalition theory of influence, alluded to below, Arnold provides a detailed critique of the other major studies in the field.

See also Bruce A. Ray, "Investigating the Myth of Congressional Influence: The Geographic Distribution of Federal Spending," paper delivered at the annual meeting of the American Political Science Association, Chicago, August, 1976. Ray concludes that congressmen are protectors, not promoters, of their district interests. In a subsequent piece, however, he finds that members of congressional committees are no better able to protect their districts from cutbacks by agencies over which their committees have jurisdiction than non–committee member congressmen ("Congressional Losers in the U.S. Federal Spending Process," *Legislative Studies Quarterly* 5 [August 1980]: 359–72).

18. J. Theodore Anagnoson found that in election years the processing of HUD grants was faster for congressmen on two key committees and that congressmen of the administration's party were given the edge in announcing grants. See his "Federal Grant Agencies and Congressional Election Campaigns," *American Journal of Political Science* 26 (August 1982): 549–61.

19. Quoted in Wilks, "Congressional Resources," p. 32.

20. *You and Your Congressman* (New York: G. P. Putnam's Sons, Capricorn Books, 1976) p. 38. See also p. 46.

21. Cain and Ritchie, "Assessing Constituency Involvement."

Chapter 7

1. *U.S. Senators and Their World*, p. 225. Half of the congressmen studied in the early 1960s deemed constituency service a problem. See Roger H. Davidson, David M. Kovenock, and Michael K. O'Leary, *Congress in Crisis: Politics and Congressional Reform* (Belmont, Calif.: Wadsworth Publishing Company, 1966), p. 77.

2. "Our Two Congresses"; see also Warren Weaver, Jr., *Both Your Houses: The Truth About Congress* (New York: Praeger, 1972), p. 178; Philip Donham and Robert J. Fahey, *Congress Needs Help* (New York: Random House, 1966), pp. 33–34; and Robert Klonoff, "The Congressman as Mediator," pp. 701–34.

3. Estes Kefauver and Jack Levin, with a Foreword by Robert M. La Follette, Jr., *A Twentieth-Century Congress* (New York: Duell, Sloan and Pearce, Essential Books, 1947), p. 195.

4. See Thomas E. Cavanagh, "The Two Arenas of Congress: Electoral and Institutional Incentives for Performance," paper prepared for delivery the annual meeting of the American Political Science Association, New York, August, 1978, p. 36. An abbreviated version, not containing this quotation, appears in Cooper and Mackenzie, *House at Work*, pp. 56–77. For a similar argument, see Roger H. Davidson, "Our Changing Congress: The Inside (and Outside) Story," paper delivered at the Conference on Congress and the Presidency, Austin, Texas, November, 1977, p. 22.

5. Christopher Buchanan, "The Non-Candidates: Why They Didn't Run," *Congressional Quarterly Weekly Report* 36 (April 15, 1978): 892.

6. Joseph Cooper, "Organization and Innovation in the House of Representatives," in Cooper and Mackenzie, *The House at Work*, p. 348.

7. Morris P. Ogul, *Congress Oversees the Bureaucracy: Studies in Legislative Supervision* (Pittsburgh: University of Pittsburgh Press, 1976), p. 168; Gellhorn, *When Americans Complain*, p. 82.

8. *O Congress* (New York: Popular Library, 1972), p. 177.

9. John R. Hibbing, "Voluntary Retirement from the U.S. House: The Cost of Congressional Service," *Legislative Studies Quarterly* 7 (February 1982): 62–63.

10. Warden Moxley, "More People Than Ever Are Campaigning for the House," *Congressional Quarterly Weekly Report* 36 (September 30, 1978): 2678–79.

11. Thomas A. Kazee, "The Decision to Run for the U.S. Congress: Challenger Attitudes in the 1970s," *Legislative Studies Quarterly* 5 (February 1980): 79–100.

12. *The Jacksonians: A Study in Administrative History, 1829–1861* (New York: Macmillan, 1954), pp. 144–45; *The Republican Era: 1869–1901* (New York: Macmillan, 1958), pp. 70–73.

13. Warren H. Butler, "Administering Congress: The Role of the Staff," *Public Administration Review* 26 (March 1966): 6. For other estimates, see Walter Kravitz, "Case-

260

work," pp. 16–17; Radler, *How Congress Works*, p. 55; and Stephen K. Bailey, *Congress in the Seventies* (New York: St. Martin's Press, 1970), p. 10.

14. John S. Saloma III, *Congress and the New Politics* (Boston: Little, Brown and Co., 1969), p. 184.

15. U.S. Congress, Joint Committee on the Organization of Congress, *Organization of Congress, Hearings Pursuant To S. Con. Res. 2*, 89th Cong., 1st sess., 1965, pt. 5, p. 775.

16. House Commission, *Final Report*, pp. 877–79.

17. U.S. Congress, House of Representatives, Commission of Administrative Review, *Administrative Reorganization and Legislative Management*, 95th Cong., 1st sess., 1977, H. Doc. 95–232, vol. 2, pp. 16–20.

18. "Congressman as Mediator" p. 708.

19. Chong Lim Kim and Seong-Tong Pai, "Constituency Service among Korean National Assemblymen: A Study of Leadership Responsiveness," in Chong Lim Kim, ed., *Political Participation in Korea* (Santa Barbara, Calif.: CLIO Books, 1980), pp. 181–204; LeDuc and White, "The Role of Opposition," p. 91; Clarke, Price, and Krause, "Constituency Service among Canadian Provincial Legislators," p. 529; Schwarz and Shaw, *The United States Congress in Comparative Perspective*, pp. 283–84; Herbert Asher, "The Unintended Consequences of Legislative Professionalism," paper delivered at the annual meeting of the American Political Science Association, New York, August, 1978, pp. 16–17; Elling, "The Utility of State Legislative Casework," p. 357. In most instances, the differences are striking. At least two reasons can be cited. On the one hand, no other legislators in the world enjoy the staff resources of American senators and representatives. Accordingly, they must attend to constituent problems themselves—or at best with the aid of one or more party agents and personal secretaries (Britain) or a couple of staffers (U.S. states). On the other hand, in many countries, legislating per se is only a peripheral activity, given the existence of strong, often authoritarian, executives.

20. Fox and Hammond, *Congressional Staffs*, p. 77.

21. See former Senator Paul H. Douglas, *In the Fullness of Time* (New York: Harcourt Brace Jovanovich, 1971), p. 186. For other examples, see Kravitz, "Casework" pp. 21–22.

22. *Milwaukee Journal*, November 27, 1979, pt. 1, p. 3.

23. Using Obey Commission data on time spent with constituents and answering the mail when in Washington, and time spent in their districts, Thomas J. O'Donnell concluded that subcommittee chairmen, at least, do not differ significantly from non-chairmen. Two problems with his conclusions are that other leaders are omitted from the sample and that, since he used a bivariate statistical technique, he cannot isolate the effects of leadership from those of other factors (O'Donnell, "The Effects of

Electoral Shifts and Legislative Responsibilities on the Allocation of Time by Congressmen,'' paper delivered at the annual meeting of the Midwest Political Science Association, Milwaukee, April, 1982).

24. Nor do other definitions of marginality (1976 results or the difference between the 1976 results and the 1970–1974 average) produce any relationship. O'Donnell found no significant relationship between electoral situations and a variety of constituency service measures. The sole exception was time spent in members' districts on weekends (ibid.). Cain, Ferejohn, and Fiorina, however, did find a relationship between electoral marginality and time devoted to casework; but their sample included only 55 members, and they failed to control for regional, leadership, or constituency factors (''Electoral Incentive''). One study of local government officials found little effect of electoral marginality on constituency service. See Kenneth R. Greene, ''The Impact of Electoral Competition on Service Representation by Municipal Legislators,'' paper delivered at the annual meeting of the Southern Political Science Association, Memphis, November, 1981.

25. ''Rational Allocation'' and ''Two Arenas.''

26. House Commission, *Final Report,* p. 875.

27. Cain, Ferejohn, and Fiorina, ''Electoral Incentive,'' agree (p. 7).

28. The index is analogous to that described in note 6, chapter 2. See the footnote to table 7.3. A study of 230 New Jersey City council members similarly found no negative trade-off between the policy and service roles; see Greene, ''Policy and Service Representation,'' p. 6.

29. *Congress and the New Politics,* p. 185.

30. ''Congressman as Mediator,'' p. 708. See also Joint Committee on the Organization of Congress, *Organization of Congress,* pt. 1, p. 282; Radler, *How Congress Works,* p. 55; Weaver, *Both Your Houses,* p. 179.

31. In the House, the growth in the number of committee staff since 1946 has considerably exceeded that of personal office staff, whereas in the Senate the two sets of aides have grown approximately at the same pace. However, as Fox and Hammond note, there ''has been a large increase in the number of aides performing legislative work in Senate personal offices.'' Fox and Hammond, *Congressional Staffs,* pp. 25, 171.

32. House Commission, *Final Report,* pp. 1003, 1043, 1053.

33. The correlations are $r = -.41$ and $-.39$, respectively. It is in the offices of these junior members that administrative assistants are most likely to believe that their workload is heaviest in the area of legislative research.

34. The terms are borrowed from Ogul, *Congress Oversees the Bureaucracy.*

35. Joseph P. Harris, *Congressional Control of Administration* (Garden City, N.Y.: Doubleday & Co., Anchor Books, 1964), pp. 1–2.

36. See, for example, Ogul, *Congress Oversees the Bureaucracy,* p. 175; Gellhorn,

When Americans Complain, pp. 125–29; Cavanagh, "Two Arenas," p. 34; and Klonoff, "Congressman as Mediator."

37. Malcolm E. Jewell and Samuel C. Patterson, *The Legislative Process In the United States,* 3d ed. (New York: Random House, 1977), p. 445. See also Fox and Hammond, *Congressional Staffs,* p. 91; Clapp, *The Congressman,* pp. 88–89; and Samuel P. Huntington, "Congressional Responses to the Twentieth Century," in David B. Truman, ed., *The Congress and America's Future,* 2d ed. (Englewood Cliffs, N.J.: Prentice-Hall, 1973), p. 32.

38. Elling, "Utility of Casework."

39. Susan Webb Hammond, Harrison W. Fox, Jr., Richard Moraski, and Jeanne B. Nicholson, "Senate Oversight Activities," in U.S. Congress, Senate Commission on the Operation of the Senate, *Techniques and Procedures for Analysis and Evaluation,* 94th Cong., 2d sess., 1977, Committee Print, pp. 93–94.

40. See similar remarks in Cavanagh, "Two Arenas"; Clapp, *The Congressman,* pp. 88–89; Douglas, *Fullness of Time,* p. 153; Evins, *Understanding Congress,* p. 42; Fred B. Harris, *Potomac Fever* (New York: W. W. Norton, 1977), p. 56. A Senate document of 1976 recognized caseworkers' utility: "Casework and Projects: Oversight in the Member's Office," in U.S. Congress, Senate Committee on Government Operations, Subcommittee on Oversight Procedures, *Congressional Oversight: Methods and Techniques,* 94th Cong., 2d sess., 1976, Committee Print, pp. 67–70. See also Kravitz, "Casework," pp. 31–32.

41. Among them were bills dealing with: protection of job opportunities for military reservists (H.R. 95-7847); preventing reductions in veterans' pensions when Social Security benefits rose (H.R. 95-10173); water sewerage disposal; altering limits on earnings for Social Security recipients; changes in tax provisions concerning capital gains for land owners forced to sell to the government for federal projects; providing federal conservation to states and counties in which there are national wildlife refuge systems; health planning; tax status for Social Security recipients of interest earned on NOW accounts; setting up a VA hospital in a state that had none; payment to nurses and similar aides under Medicare; grain weighing and grain elevator cleanliness; use of FAA funds for airport facilities repairs; proportionate state and federal responsibilities to compensate someone whose property was jeopardized by federal water projects; the funding procedures of the Federal Disaster Assistance Agency for rural cooperatives; limits on BATF regulations; HUD requirements that intrastate realtors must comply with interstate regulations; the Veterans Administration's payment schedule for veterans enrolled in colleges; fraudulent military recruiting practices; product liability; the timing of Social Security payments; freezing the cost of Medicare deductibles; IRS policies on tips earned by waitresses; adverse tax effects on persons who erroneously received money from the government; the Black Lung program; provisions omitting benefits for dependent orphans; the cost of term insurance

for elderly veterans; Social Security benefits for homemakers; Railroad Retirement benefits for divorced wives and widows; other Railroad Retirement provisions; cost-of-living increases for lighthouse operators excluded from certain Civil Service salary computation formulae; adverse effects on Social Security benefits when other government benefits are increased; animal protection; allowing immediate lump-sum Social Security payments for certain medical devices; allowing governors to order utilities in their states to purchase coal from companies within their states despite pollution problems caused by high sulfur content; inclusion of mobile homes in an HUD housing assistance program; changes in the "exclusive use" provision in laws governing private home child-care facilities; allowing Social Security examiners to waive requirements (which previously required written documentation); tax deductions for travel by national guardsmen; an extension of diplomatic immunity protection; and allowing continued payment of Social Security benefits while changes in a recipient's disability status were being appealed. Ogul, *Congress Oversees,* pp. 170–71, found eleven instances in which congressmen introduced legislation because of casework. See also Gellhorn, *When Americans Complain,* pp. 72–73, for examples.

42. Ogul, *Congress Oversees,* p. 168.

43. U.S. Congress, House Committee on Education and Labor, Subcommittee on Manpower Compensation, and Health and Safety, *Hearings on HR 9431,* 94th Cong., 2d sess., 1976.

44. Senate Committee on Government Operations, "Casework and Projects," pp. 67–68.

45. For two examples, see U.S. Congress, House Committee on Appropriations, *Department of Housing and Urban Development–Independent Agencies Appropriations for 1978, Hearings,* 95th Cong., 1st sess., 1977, pt. 3, p. 109, and pt. 6, p. 330. Apparently casework in England also pays off in such oversight. See R. E. Dowse, "The MP and His Surgery," in Leonard and Herman, *The Backbencher and Parliament,* p. 56.

46. See, for example, the *Congressional Record* (daily ed.) 117 (July 12, 1977): E4358. See also Ogul, *Congress Oversees,* p. 166.

47. Ogul, *Congress Oversees,* pp. 170–71; Gellhorn, *When Americans Complain,* p. 73. Interestingly, Ogul (pp. 168–69) asked congressional staffers how often casework leads to investigations or legislation, and nine of thirty-three (27 percent) said "frequently" or "normally," with another 4 responding "from time to time."

48. Klonoff's 1977 surveys support these views. Eighty-three percent of his responses agreed that by handling cases, Congress can learn of patterns of agency misconduct; and 79 percent agreed that problems discovered via casework often form the basis of legislation to effect administrative reform. See his "Congressman as Mediator," p. 712, n. 43.

49. Elling found that two-thirds of the Minnesota and half of the Kentucky administrators

he interviewed agreed that casework alerted them to problems, serving a "red flag" function ("Utility of Casework," p. 366).

50. Congressmen and their staffs cited casework-induced changes in: military regulations concerning killed-in-action cases: military recruitment procedures; VA rules concerning the number of flight hours required by the FAA for a pilot's license the VA would pay for; air force regulations concerning Vietnam personnel who were eligible for combat-zone pay (a problem of medical team members stationed in the Philippines); air force purchasing policies; Civil Aeronautics Board regulations on beacon finders; FCC rules on public radio stations; VA rules on the timing of payments of student benefits which had adverse effects on summer school students; FDA rules as applied to a particular port's unloading and storage operations; the use of food stamps to buy food for seeing eye dogs; regulations requiring public buildings (libraries in very small towns) to have wheelchair ramps; and regulations restricting appeals in Social Security cases. Agency personnel responses included: delaying the required use of metric highway signs; an FCC lawsuit against a radio station; altering rules governing the transfer of an FM station from one town to another; the reversal of the TRIS ban for small businesses; a change in air force recruitment policies, providing the option of leaving the service if certain promises are broken; allowing juvenile felons to enlist in the army; and delaying an IRS tax ruling pending the introduction and enactment of legislation.

51. Haynes Johnson, "Agencies Wade through Flood of Gripes from Hill," *Washington Post,* December 7, 1977, p. A-3.

52. Ogul, *Congress Oversees,* pp. 13–21.

53. See Jack L. Walker, "Setting the Agenda in the U.S. Senate: A Theory of Problem Selection," *British Journal of Political Science* 7 (October 1977): 423–45; Stephen Frantzich, "Who Makes Our Laws? The Legislative Effectiveness of Members of the U.S. Congress," *Legislative Studies Quarterly* 4 (August 1979): 409–28; and James Campbell, "Cosponsoring Legislation in the U.S. Congress," *Legislative Studies Quarterly* 7 (August 1982): 415–22.

54. *Congressional Staffs,* p. 85.

55. Seymour Scher, "Conditions for Legislative Control," *Journal of Politics* 25 (August 1963): 526–51; John F. Bibby, "Committee Characteristics and Legislative Oversight of Administration," *Midwest Journal of Political Science* 10 (February 1966): 78–98; Joel D. Aberbach, "The Development of Oversight in the United States Congress: Concepts and Analysis," in Senate Commission, *Techniques and Procedures,* pp. 53–69; and John R. Johannes, *Policy Innovation in Congress* (Morristown, N.J.: General Learning Press, 1972), pp. 16–24.

56. This also was the recommendation of a study commissioned by the Department of Health, Education, and Welfare: Technical Assistance Research Programs, Inc.,

"Feasibility Study to Improve Handling of Consumer Complaints: Evaluation Report," unpublished report pursuant to contract no. HEW-OS-74-292 (Washington, D.C.: December, 1976), p. ES-12.

57. Abraham Holtzman reached an identical conclusion; *Legislative Liaison*, pp. 177, 190–91. See also the discussion of the State Department's liaison office in Robinson, *Congress and Foreign Policy-Making*, chaps. 4–5; and Gellhorn, *When Americans Complain*, p. 81.

58. Joseph A. Pika, "White House Office of Congressional Relations: A Longitudinal Analysis," paper delivered at the annual meeting of the Midwest Political Science Association, Chicago, April, 1978.

59. Norman C. Thomas and Karl A. Lamb, *Congress: Politics and Practice* (New York: Random House, 1964), p. 46.

60. Sniderman and Brody, "Coping," pp. 501–22, especially 517, 520; Michael L. Mezey, "Constituency Demands and Legislative Support: An Experiment," *Legislative Studies Quarterly* 1 (February 1976): 124; Allan Kornberg, Harold D. Clarke, and Lawrence LeDuc, "Some Correlates of Regime Support in Canada," *British Journal of Political Science* 2 (April 1978): 208–9; and Arthur H. Miller, "The Institutional Focus of Political Distrust," paper delivered at the annual meeting of the American Political Science Association, Washington, D.C., August, 1979, pp. 41–43.

61. William J. Keefe and Morris S. Ogul, *The American Legislative Process: Congress and the States*, 4th ed. (Englewood Cliffs, N.J.: Prentice-Hall, 1977), p. 390.

Chapter 8

1. The literature simply is too voluminous to cite. For summaries and citations, see Barbara Hinckley, *Congressional Elections* (Washington, D.C.: Congressional Quarterly Press, 1981), especially chap. 3; Gary C. Jacobson, *The Politics of Congressional Elections* (Boston: Little, Brown and Co., 1983), especially chap. 3; and John R. Johannes and John C. McAdams, "The Congressional Incumbency Effect: Is It Casework, Policy Compatibility, or Something Else? An Examination of the 1978 Election," *American Journal of Political Science* 25 (August 1981): 512–42.

2. Mayhew, *The Electoral Connection*, pp. 52–57.

3. *Congress: Keystone of the Washington Establishment*, p. 43.

4. Ibid., p. 45.

5. Quoted in Fenno, *Home Style*, pp. 107–8.

6. Parker and Davidson, "Why Do Americans Love Their Congressmen So Much More Than Their Congress?"

7. Cited in *Public Opinion* 1 (November/December 1978): 22.
8. Ibid. A Republican Congressional Campaign Committee poll reportedly found that 33 percent of the public votes for a congressional candidate because "he can help solve my problems," compared to 5 percent who do so because "I agree with his views" (*Washington Post,* June 18, 1977, p. A-3). For the increase, see Glenn R. Parker, "Can Congress Ever be a Popular Institution?" in Cooper and MacKenzie, *House at Work,* pp. 42–43.
9. Cranor and Westphal, "Congressional District Offices."
10. Albert Cover and Bruce S. Brumberg, "Baby Books and Ballots: The Impact of Congressional Mail on Constituent Opinion," *American Political Science Review,* 76 (June 1982): 347–59.
11. Bruce E. Cain, John A. Ferejohn, and Morris P. Fiorina, "What Makes Legislators in Great Britain and the United States Popular?" paper prepared for the Harvard Political Behavior Seminar, March 31, 1980.
12. Parker and Parker, "Causes and Consequences"; and Powell, "Constituency Service and Electoral Margin." For a study emphasizing staffing (a dubious measure of casework or even constituency orientation), see Laurily K. Epstein and Kathleen A. Frankovic, "Casework and Electoral Margins: Insurance is Prudent," *Policy* 14 (Summer 1982): 691–700.
13. Gary C. Jacobson, "Incumbents' Advantages in the 1978 U.S. Congressional Election," *Legislative Studies Quarterly* 6 (May 1981): 183–200; and Diana Evans Yiannakis, "The Grateful Electorate." The latter's analysis, however, omits some important variables and, like that of Cain, Ferejohn, and Fiorina, includes several that are endogenous, thus raising problems of model misspecification.
14. Donald A. Gross and James C. Garand, "The Vanishing Marginals," paper delivered at the annual meeting of the Midwest Political Science Association, Milwaukee, April, 1982. See also Cranor and Westphal, "Congressional District Offices."
15. "A Paradox of Representation: Diversity, Competition, Perks, and the Decline of Policy Making in the U.S. House," paper delivered at the annual meeting of the American Political Science Association, New York, September, 1981, p. 15.
16. Born, "Perquisite Employment," pp. 347–62.
17. *Unsafe at Any Margin* (Washington, D.C.: American Enterprise Institute, 1978), p. 72. See also Smith, *Congressman from Mississippi,* p. 236.
18. The format of this question has changed slightly between the second and third round of mailings and interviews. In the fall of 1977 respondents were asked: "For example, are favorable results mentioned in newsletters? In speeches or during re-election campaigns? Are names of constituents who have been helped added to mailing lists for newsletters, polls, campaign fund solicitation, etc.?" In spring of 1978 the question specifically included these choices: Publicize success in newsletters? Publicize it

in campaign materials? Seek campaign help from those you helped? Mention it while campaigning? Add names of people you helped to "political" mailing lists? Add names of people you helped to general mailing lists? Other? Accordingly, the results reported in table 8.1 may not be perfectly accurate.

19. Mary Russell, "Campaigning Tip: Get Testimonials by Constituents," *Washington Post*, June 2, 1978, p. A-11.

20. For a superb insider account of such mailings, see William Haydon, "Confessions of a High-Tech Politico: Mr. Wang Goes to Washington," *Washington Monthly* 12 (May 1980): 43–47. See also Walter Pincus, "Dear Constituent: Hill Plugs into Computer Age," *Washington Post*, Dec. 10, 1977, p. A-2.

21. Macartney, "Political Staffing," pp. 206, 213; Lynda W. Powell, "A Study of Financial Contributors in Congressional Elections," paper delivered at the annual meeting of the American Political Science Association, Washington, D.C., August, 1979; and Matthews, *U.S. Senators*, pp. 221–26. The 1977 Obey Commission data also show a significant relationship between having donated to a campaign and having requested casework. Again, however, the direction of causality is unclear, and the relationship may be spurious.

22. Matthews, *U.S. Senators*, p. 226.

23. These findings generally agree with those of three other scholars who studied congressmen in 1978 to see whether they did or did not publicize casework results. However, unlike the results reported here, they also found no results for partisanship. See Cain, Ferejohn, and Fiorina, "Electoral Incentive."

24. The author is extremely indebted to his colleague John C. McAdams, who played a major role in developing the model and undertook most of the data analysis that follows. For a more detailed analysis of the argument, a thorough explanation of the assumptions, and a defense of the variables used in both the aggregate- and individual-level analyses here, see Johannes and McAdams, "The Congressional Incumbency Effect." A critique of the analysis is offered by Morris P. Fiorina, "Some Problems"; the authors' rejoinder is McAdams and Johannes, "Does Casework Matter? A Reply to Professor Fiorina."

25. The variables were coded as follows: party identification was coded 1 if the respondent identified with the party of the incumbent, .5 if the respondent was an independent, and 0 if the respondent identified with the opposite party; the incumbent's party equaled 1 if the incumbent was a Democrat; casework was set equal to 1 if the respondent or a family member had ever asked the incumbent for "help on a problem" and had received a response; seniority was the natural log of the number of years the incumbent had served as of 1978 (the electoral advantage of incumbency would come early in one's career); and the respondent's education was coded 0 if the respondent had only a grade school education, .5 if high school, and 1 for at least some college.

Ideological discrepancy was a three-point scale (0, .5, 1) based on the difference between congressmen's ADA scores and respondents' self-placed liberalism or conservatism (see Johannes and McAdams, "Congressional Incumbency Effect"). For respondents who could not or did not classify themselves ideologically, discrepancy equals 0.

26. The CPS asked respondents if they remembered anything the incumbent had done for their district or for its people. If the respondent answered affirmatively, the interviewer asked, "What was that?" Those who mentioned keeping defense contracts, keeping jobs, bringing in federal grants, projects, or revenue sharing, bringing in flood or disaster relief funds or aid for schools, roads, or other local projects were coded 1. General and vague asnwers were not counted.

27. Robert S. Erickson, "Public Opinion and Congressional Representation: Evidence from 1978 CPS Election Data," paper delivered at the annual meeting of the Western Political Science Association, San Francisco, March, 1980.

28. Five of the CPS issue scales (minorities, women's roles, rights of the accused, health care, and government job guarantees) were used. A liberal response was scored 1, a conservative response 0, and a moderate response or no opinion .5. Taking the mean of these five items yields an issues scale which ranges between 0 and 1. Where the incumbent was a Republican, liberals were expected to be more likely to defect to the challenger than were conservatives. Therefore, for a respondent with a Republican incumbent, the value of this "party-based issue voting" variable equals that of the issues scale. Where the incumbent was a Democrat, conservative voters should be more likely to oppose him. Thus, for a voter with a Democrat representative, the value of the variable would be 1 minus the issues scale.

29. Gary C. Jacobson and Samuel Kernell, *Strategy and Choice in Congressional Elections* (New Haven: Yale University Press, 1981).

30. Cranor and Westphal, "Congressional District Offices"; Stephen P. Brown, Beth C. Fuchs, and John F. Hoadley, "Congressional Perquisites and Vanishing Marginals: The Case of the Class of '74," paper delivered at the annual meeting of the American Political Science Association, Washington, August, 1979.

31. For each of these questions approval of Carter's performance was coded as a 1, disapproval was coded 5, and "don't know" or "no opinion" responses received a 3. The mean of these five questions became the "Carter assessment" for respondents with Democratic congressmen. A negative sign for the coefficient indicates that increasingly negative assessments led to fewer votes for Democratic incumbents. For Republican incumbents, increasingly negative assessments of Carter would lead to more votes. Thus for voters with Republican congressmen, the scale was reflected by subtracting it from 6.

32. Respondents who reported improved personal finances during the year were coded 0

if their incumbent House members were Democrats, and 1 if Republicans. Respondents whose finances had deteriorated were coded as 1 if the incumbents were Democrats and 0 if Republicans. Where no change was reported, the variable was set equal to .5. A negative coefficient for the variable thus would indicate that unfavorable personal economic changes harmed Democratic incumbents and helped Republicans.

33. Respondents who felt the economy had improved during the year were coded 1 where the incumbent was a Republican and 0 where the incumbent was a Democrat. Where the voter felt the economy had deteriorated, this coding scheme was reversed, and those who felt there was no change were coded with a value of .5. A negative coefficient would be expected, with perceptions of declining economy hurting Democratic incumbents and helping Republicans.

34. Jacobson and Kernell, *Strategy and Choice*.

35. Jacobsen, "Incumbents' Advantages," p. 189.

36. *Home Style,* p. 65.

37. Glenn R. Parker, "The Advantage of Incumbency in House Elections," *American Politics Quarterly* 8 (October 1980): 449–64; Thomas E. Mann and Raymond E. Wolfinger, "Candidates and Parties in Congressional Elections," *American Political Science Review* 74 (September 1980): 628–29.

38. U.S. Congress, Senate Committee on Government Operations, *Confidence and Concern: Citizens View American Government: A Survey of Public Attitudes* by the Subcommittee on Intergovernmental Relations, 93rd Cong., 1st sess., 1973, Committee Print, p. 293; House Commission, *Final Report,* p. 831.

39. The two major efforts have been Yiannakis, "The Grateful Electorate," and Fiorina, "Some Problems." For a critique of the approach taken by Yiannakis and Fiorina, see McAdams and Johannes, "Does Casework Matter?"

40. *The Sociology and Politics of Congress* (Chicago: Rand McNally, 1969), p. 111.

41. Quoted in "Some Surprises for the Class of 1974," *Congressional Quarterly Weekly Report* 36 (November 18, 1978): 3295.

42. Cover and Brumberg, "Baby Books."

43. A problem in analyzing casework dissatisfaction is that there are so few respondents who were not at all satisfied (see table 8.5). See also Yiannakis, "The Grateful Electorate"; Fiorina, "Some Problems"; and McAdams and Johannes, "Does Casework Matter?"

44. Quoted in Larry Light, "Crack 'Outreach' Programs No Longer Ensure Reelection," *Congressional Quarterly Weekly Report* 39 (February 14, 1981): 317.

Chapter 9

1. House Commission, *Final Report*, p. 831.
2. Kent M. Weeks, *Ombudsmen around the World: A Comparative Chart,* 2d ed. (Berkeley: Institute for Governmental Studies, University of California, 1978). A number of state governments have established internal executive ombudsmen and several large cities have instituted ombudsman offices. See Stacey, *Ombudsmen Compared*, p. 229.
3. Stanley V. Anderson, *Ombudsman Papers: American Experience and Proposals* (Berkeley: Institute for Governmental Studies, University of California, 1969), p. 3. For an alternate, yet similar, definition, see Hill, *The Model Ombudsman*, p. 12. See also Stacey, *Ombudsmen Compared*; and Mikael Hiden, *The Ombudsman in Finland: The First Fifty Years,* trans. Aaron Bell, ed. Donald C. Rowat (Berkeley: Institute for Governmental Studies, University of California, 1973).
4. Stacey, *Ombudsmen Compared*, pp. 223–28; Hill, *The Model Ombudsman*, p. 276.
5. Hiden, *Ombudsman*, p. 33; Hill, *The Model Ombudsman*, pp. 265–310.
6. Roy Gregory and Peter Hutchesson, *The Parliamentary Ombudsman: A Study in the Control of Administrative Action* (London: George Allen & Unwin, 1975), pp. 623, 626.
7. Quoted in Hill, *The Model Ombudsman*, p. 278. Hill found that most New Zealand MPs bring constituent problems directly to the appropriate government offices rather than merely forwarding them to the ombudsman. For an examination of how the MPs handle casework, see Anagnoson, "Home Style."
8. Hill, *The Model Ombudsman*, pp. 239–40. See also Hill, "The Citizen Participation-Representation Roles of American Ombudsmen," *Administration and Society* 13 (February 1982): 405–33.
9. The proposal followed hearings in March, 1966. See U.S. Congress, Senate, Committee on the Judiciary, Subcommittee on Administrative Practice and Procedure, *Ombudsman Hearings,* 89th Cong., 2d sess., 1966; and *U.S. Congressional Record,* 113, 90th Cong., 1st sess., 1967, pp. 5578–80. See Anderson, *Ombudsman Papers,* pp. 20–21.
10. U.S. Congress, Senate, Committee on the Judiciary, Subcommittee on Administrative Practice and Procedure, *Administrative Ombudsman Hearings,* 90th Cong., 2d sess., 1968. For a brief description and legislative history, complete with citations, see Anderson, *Ombudsman Papers,* pp. 21–22. Senator Jacob Javits (R., N.Y.) proposed legislation (S. 92-2200) to experiment with the administrative ombudsman concept. In the House, two Wisconsin congressmen, Democrat Henry Reuss and Republican William Steiger, sponsored an identical bill, H.R. 92-9562.
11. The bills were H.R. 88-7593, H.R. 89-4273, H.R. 90-3388, and H.R. 91-8017. For a nontechnical explanation, see Henry S. Reuss and Everard Munsey, "The United

States," in Donald C. Rowat, ed., *The Ombudsman: Citizen's Defender*, 2d ed. (London: George Allen & Unwin, 1968), pp. 194–200. In the same volume, see the article by Henry J. Abraham, "The Need for Ombudsmen in the United States," pp. 234–40, for a supporting view. For a modified version see Klonoff, "Congressman as Mediator," pp. 724–33. His proposal to establish two separate units (for case-processing and monitoring) falls victim to most of the objections he raises to the Reuss and Aspin plans (below).

12. The story is traced in Anderson, *Ombudsman Papers*, pp. 14–19. Scholars have differed on the proposal. Among those in favor was Kenneth G. Olson, "The Service Function of the United States Congress," in de Grazia, *The First Branch*, pp. 323–64. In opposition were Gellhorn, *When Americans Complain*, pp. 86–94, and Butler, "Administering Congress," pp. 8–10.

13. U.S. Congress, Joint Committee on the Organization of the Congress, *Organization of Congress: Final Report*, S. Report 89-2424, 89th Cong., 2d sess., 1966, p. 36.

14. The measures were S. 92-2134, S. 93-2500, H.R. 93-3692, H.R. 93-7680, and H.R. 93-11257. See *U.S. Congressional Record*, 117, 92d Cong., 1st sess., pp. 21539, 21543, 22043, 44214.

15. H.R. 92-13742; H.R. 93-11257; H.R. 94-3198. See *U.S. Congressional Record*, 118, 92d Cong., 2d sess., 1972, p. 8100.

16. See Stacey, *Ombudsmen Compared*, chaps. 6, 7, 10; Gregory and Hutchesson, *Parliamentary Ombudsman*.

17. Gregory and Hutchesson, *Parliamentary Ombudsman*, pp. 362–69.

18. Ibid., pp. 369–78.

19. For an analysis, see Klonoff, "Congressman as Mediator," pp. 719–24.

20. See Gregory and Hutchesson, *Parliamentary Ombudsman*, chaps. 10, 14. For a somewhat more critical evaluation, see William B. Gwyn, "The Ombudsman in Britain: A Qualified Success in Government Reform," *Public Administration* 60 (Summer 1982): 177–98.

21. Abdo I. Baaklini, "The Kuwaiti Legislature as Ombudsman: The Legislative Committee on Petitions and Complaints," *Legislative Studies Quarterly* 3 (May 1978): 293–307.

22. George B. Galloway, *The Legislative Process in Congress* (New York: Thomas Y. Crowell Co., 1955), p. 665.

23. "The Operation of Senators' Offices," in U.S. Congress, Senate, Commission on the Operation of the Senate, *Senators: Offices, Ethics, and Pressures*, 94th Cong., 2d sess., 1977, Committee Print, p. 10. Interestingly, Hammond concluded that no increase in staff size was called for. Klonoff found that about as many staffers disagreed as agreed that their offices were well aware of the kinds and numbers of cases received by other offices ("Congressman as Mediator," p. 714).

24. Breslin, "Constituent Service," p. 35.

272

25. House Commission, *Final Report,* p. 1072.
26. Stephen E. Frantzich, "Computers in Congress: Policy-Making in the Age of Information Technology," paper delivered at the annual meeting of the American Political Science Association, Denver, September, 1982, p. 12.
27. See, for example, Stephen E. Frantzich, "Computerized Information Technology in the U.S. House of Representatives," *Legislative Studies Quarterly* 4 (May 1979): 262–63; Breslin, "Constituent Service," p. 35; House Commission, *Administrative Reorganization and Legislative Management,* vol. 1, p. 120; and Irwin B. Arieff, "Computers and Direct Mail Are Being Married on the Hill to Keep Incumbents in Office," *Congressional Quarterly Weekly Report* 36 (July 21, 1979): 1445–52.
28. The Commission on the Operation of the Senate in 1976 recommended just this sort of centralized data collection system. See the commission's final report, *Toward a Modern Senate,* 94th Cong., 2d sess., 1976, S. Doc. 94-278, p. 50.
29. John A. Worthly and Jack C. Overstreet, "Modern Technology Applied to Traditional Political Functions: The Florida State Ombudsman Program," *Polity* 11 (Winter 1978): 280–89.
30. House Commission, *Final Report,* p. 1052.
31. For a listing, see Janet Breslin, "Orientation and Training," in Senate Commission, *Senators: Offices, Ethics, and Pressures,* pp. 47–52.
32. Senate Committee, *Congressional Oversight: Methods and Techniques,* p. 68.
33. Frantzich, "Computers in Congress," p. 12.
34. Volta Torrey, *You and Your Congress* (New York: William Morrow & Co., 1944), pp. 139–40.
35. Galloway, *Legislative Process,* p. 204; Breslin, "Constituent Service," pp. 31–32.
36. Verba and Nie, *Participation,* p. 107.
37. John C. Wahlke, "Policy Demands and System Support: The Role of the Represented," in Gerhard Loewenberg, ed., *Modern Parliaments: Change or Decline?* (Chicago: Aldine-Atherton, 1971), p. 155.
38. Gray, "Congressional Interference," p. 541.
39. Huntington, "Congressional Responses," p. 32.
40. "Congressional Interference," p. 542.

Appendix

1. Mail questionnaires have both limitations and advantages. For examples of previous research efforts relying on mail survey instruments, see Jeff Fishel, *Party and Opposition: Challengers in American Politics* (New York: David McKay, 1973); Robert Huckshorn and Robert C. Spencer, *The Politics of Defeat: Campaigning for*

Congress (Amherst, Mass.: University of Massachusetts Press, 1971); and, for a study similar to this, Cranor and Westphal, "Congressional District Offices."

2. Charles B. Brownson, *1977 Congressional Staff Directory* (Mt. Vernon, Va.: 1977).

SELECTED BIBLIOGRAPHY

Published Materials

Aberbach, Joel D., and Rockman, Bert A. "The Overlapping Worlds of American Federal Executives and Congressmen." *British Journal of Political Science* 7 (January 1977): 23–47.

Abney, Glenn, and Lauth, Thomas P. "Councilmen's Intervention in Municipal Administration." *Administration and Society* 13 (February 1982): 435–56.

Abraham, Henry J. "The Need for Ombudsmen in the United States." In *The Ombudsman,* edited by Donald C. Rowat, pp. 234–40. London: George Allen & Unwin, 1965.

Alpern, David M., and Hubbard, Henry W. "Tending to the Home Folks." *Newsweek,* April 25, 1977, pp. 26–28.

Anagnoson, J. Theodore. "Federal Grant Agencies and Congressional Election Campaigns." *American Journal of Political Science* 26 (August 1982): 549–61.

———. "Home Style in New Zealand." *Legislative Studies Quarterly* 8 (May 1983): 157–75.

Anderson, Stanley V. *Ombudsman Papers: American Experience and Proposals.* Berkeley: Institute of Governmental Studies, University of California, 1969.

Arieff, Irwin B. "Computers and Direct Mail Are Being Married on the Hill to Keep Incumbents in Office." *Congressional Quarterly Weekly Report* 36 (July 21, 1979): 1445–52.

Arnold, R. Douglas. *Congress and the Bureaucracy: A Theory of Influence.* New Haven: Yale University Press, 1979.

Baaklini, Abdo I. "The Kuwaiti Legislature as Ombudsman: The Legislative Committee on Petitions and Complaints." *Legislative Studies Quarterly* 3 (May 1978): 293–307.

Barker, Anthony, and Bush, Michael. "Members' Postbags." In *The Backbencher and Parliament: A Reader,* edited by Dick Leonard and Valentine Herman, pp. 29–45. London: Macmillan, 1972.

Beard, Edmund, and Horn, Stephen. *Congressional Ethics: The View from the House.* Washington, D.C.: The Brookings Institution, 1975.

Boehlert, Sherwood. "Telling the Congressman's Story." In *The Voice of Government,* edited by Ray Eldon Hiebert and Carlton E. Spitzer, pp. 127–40. New York: John Wiley and Sons, 1968.

Born, Richard. "Perquisite Employment in the U.S. House of Representatives, 1960–1976." *American Politics Quarterly* 10 (July 1982): 347–62.

Briggs, Dean. "The Trainee and the Borderline Client: Countertransference Pitfalls." *Clinical Social Work Journal* 30 (Summer 1979): 133–46.

Buchanan, Christopher. "The Non-Candidates: Why They Didn't Run." *Congressional Quarterly Weekly Report* 36 (April 15, 1978): 891–94.

———. "Some Surprises for the Class of 1974." *Congressional Quarterly Weekly Report* 36 (November 18, 1978): 3295–97.

Burnham, James. "Some Administrators' Unkindly View of Congress." In *Public Administration: Readings in Institutions, Processes, Behavior, Policy,* edited by Robert T. Golembiewski, Frank Gibson, and Geoffrey Y. Cornog, pp. 127–34. 3d ed. Chicago: Rand McNally College Publishing Company, 1976.

Butler, Warren H. "Administering Congress: The Role of the Staff." *Public Administration Review* 26 (March 1966): 3–13.

Cain, Bruce E., and Ritchie, David B. "Assessing Constituency Involvement: The Hemel Hempstead Experience." *Parliamentary Affairs* 35 (Winter 1982): 73–83.

Cain, Bruce E.; Ferejohn, John A.; and Fiorina, Morris P. "The House Is Not a Home: British MPs in Their Constituencies." *Legislative Studies Quarterly* 4 (November 1979): 501–23.

Campbell, James E. "Cosponsoring Legislation in the U.S. Congress." *Legislative Studies Quarterly* 7 (August 1982): 415–22.

Cavanagh, Thomas E. "Rational Allocation of Congressional Resources: Member Time and Staff Use in the House." In *Public Policy and Public Choice,* edited by Douglas W. Rae and Theodore J. Eismeier, pp. 209–47. Beverly Hills: Sage Publications, 1979.

———. "The Two Arenas of Congress." In *The House At Work,* edited by Joseph Cooper and G. Calvin Mackenzie, pp. 56–77. Austin: University of Texas Press, 1981.

Clapp, Charles L. *The Congressman: His Work as He Sees It.* Garden City, N.Y.: Doubleday & Co., Anchor Books, 1963.

Clarke, Harold D. "Determinants of Provincial Constituency Service Behavior: A Multivariate Analysis." *Legislative Studies Quarterly* 3 (November 1978): 601–28.

Clarke, Harold D.; Price, Richard G.; and Krause, Robert. "Constituency Service among

Canadian Provincial Legislators: Basic Findings and a Test of Three Hypotheses." *Canadian Journal of Political Science* 8 (December 1975): 520–42.

Cohen, William S., and Lasson, Kenneth. *Getting the Most Out of Washington: Using Congress to Move the Federal Bureaucracy.* Washington, D.C.: Facts on File, 1982.

Cover, Albert D. "Contacting Congressional Constituents: Some Patterns of Perquisite Use." *American Journal of Political Science* 24 (February 1980): 125–35.

Cover, Albert D., and Brumberg, Bruce S. "Baby Books and Ballots: The Impact of Congressional Mail on Constituent Opinion." *American Political Science Review* 76 (June 1982): 347–59.

Davidson, Roger H. *The Role of the Congressman.* New York: Pegasus, 1969.

———. "Our Two Congresses: Where Have They Been; Where Are They Going?" In *Paths to Political Reform,* edited by William J. Crotty, pp. 283–306. Lexington, Mass.: D.C. Heath & Co., Lexington Books, 1980.

Davidson, Roger H.; Kovenock, David M.; and O'Leary, Michael K. *Congress in Crisis: Politics and Congressional Reform.* Belmont, Calif.: Wadsworth Publishing Co., 1966.

De Grazia, Edward. "Congressional Liaison: An Inquiry into Its Meaning for Congress." In *Congress: The First Branch of Government,* edited by Alfred de Grazia, pp. 281–322. Garden City, N.Y.: Doubleday & Co., Anchor Books, 1967.

Donham, Philip, and Fahey, Robert J. *Congress Needs Help.* Foreword by David Brinkley. New York: Random House, 1966.

Douglas, Paul H. *In the Fullness of Time.* New York: Harcourt Brace Jovanovich, 1971.

Dowse, R. E. "The MP and His Surgery." In *The Backbencher and Parliament: A Reader,* edited by Dick Leonard and Valentine Herman, pp. 46–60. London: Macmillan, 1972.

Elazar, Daniel J. *American Federalism: A View from the States.* 2d ed. New York: Thomas Y. Crowell Co., 1972.

Elling, Richard C. "State Legislative Casework and State Administrative Performance." *Administration and Society* 12 (November 1980): 327–56.

———. "The Utility of State Legislative Casework as a Means of Oversight." *Legislative Studies Quarterly* 4 (August 1979): 353–80.

Epstein, Laurily K., and Frankovic, Kathleen A. "Casework and Electoral Margins: Insurance Is Prudent." *Polity* 14 (Summer 1982): 691–700.

Eulau, Heinz, and Karps, Paul D. "The Puzzle of Representation: Specifying Components of Responsiveness." *Legislative Studies Quarterly* 2 (August 1977): 233–54.

Evins, Joe L. *Understanding Congress.* New York: Clarkson N. Potter, 1973.

Fenno, Richard F. *Home Style: House Members in Their Districts.* Boston: Little, Brown and Co., 1978.

Ferejohn, John A. *Pork Barrel Politics: Rivers and Harbors Legislation, 1947–1968.*

278

Stanford: Stanford University Press, 1974.

Fiorina, Morris P. *Congress: Keystone of the Washington Establishment.* New Haven: Yale University Press, 1977.

————. "Some Problems in Studying the Effects of Resource Allocation in Congressional Elections." *American Journal of Political Science* 25 (August 1981): 543–67.

Fox, Harrison W., Jr., and Hammond, Susan Webb. *Congressional Staffs: The Invisible Force in American Lawmaking.* New York: The Free Press, 1977.

Frantzich, Stephen E. "Computerized Information Technology in the U.S. House of Representatives." *Legislative Studies Quarterly* 4 (May 1979): 255–80.

Friedman, Karl A. *Complaining: Comparative Aspects of Complaint Behavior and Attitudes toward Complaining in Canada and Britain.* Beverly Hills: Sage Publications, 1974.

Gellhorn, Walter. *When Americans Complain: Governmental Grievance Procedures.* Cambridge: Harvard University Press, 1966.

Getz, Robert S. *Congressional Ethics: The Conflict of Interest Issues.* Princeton: D. Van-Nostrand and Co., 1966.

Gray, Kenneth E. "Congressional Interference in Administration." In *Cooperation and Conflct: Readings in American Federalism,* edited by Daniel J. Elazar, R. Bruce Carroll, E. Lester Levine, and Douglas St. Agnelo, pp. 521–42. Itasca, Ill.: F. E. Peacock Publishers, 1969.

Gregory, Roy, and Hutchesson, Peter. *The Parliamentary Ombudsman: A Study in the Control of Administrative Action.* London: George Allen & Unwin, Royal Institute of Public Administration, 1975.

Gwyn, William B. "The Ombudsman in Britain: A Qualified Success in Government Reform." *Public Administration* 60 (Summer 1982): 177–98.

Harris, Fred B. *Potomac Fever.* New York: W. W. Norton, 1977.

Harris, Joseph P. *Congressional Control of Administration.* Garden City, N.Y.: Doubleday & Co., Anchor Books, 1964.

Harrison, David. "Role Strain and Burnout in Child Protective Service Workers." *Social Science Review* 64 (March 1980): 31–44.

Hartke, Vance. *You and Your Senator.* New York: Coward-McCann, 1970.

Haydon, William. "Confessions of a High-Tech Politico: Mr. Wang Goes to Washington." *Washington Monthly* 12 (May 1980): 43–47.

Hibbing, John R. "Voluntary Retirement from the U.S. House: The Cost of Congressional Service." *Legislative Studies Quarterly* 7 (February 1982): 57–74.

Hiden, Mikael. *The Ombudsman in Finland.* Translated by Aaron Bell. Edited by Donald C. Rowat. Berkeley: Institute for Governmental Studies, University of California, 1973.

Hill, Larry B. "The Citizen Participation–Representation Roles of American Ombudsmen." *Administration and Society* 13 (February 1982): 405–33.

————. *The Model Ombudsman: Institutionalizing New Zealand's Democratic Experiment*. Princeton: Princeton University Press, 1976.

Hinckley, Barbara. *Congressional Elections*. Washington, D.C.: Congressional Quarterly Press, 1981.

Holtzman, Abraham. *Legislative Liaison: Executive Leadership in Congress*. Chicago: Rand McNally, 1970.

Huntington, Samuel P. "Congressional Responses to the Twentieth Century." In *The Congress and America's Future*, edited by David B. Truman, pp. 6–38. 2d ed. Englewood Cliffs, N.J.: Prentice-Hall, 1973.

Jacobson, Gary C. "Incumbents' Advantages in the 1978 U.S. Congressional Election." *Legislative Studies Quarterly* 6 (May 1981): 183–200.

————. *The Politics of Congressional Elections*. Boston: Little, Brown and Co., 1983.

Jacobson, Gary C., and Kernell, Samuel. *Strategy and Choice in Congressional Elections*. New Haven: Yale University Press, 1981.

Jahan, Rounaq. "Members of Parliament in Bangladesh." *Legislative Studies Quarterly* 1 (August 1976): 355–70.

Jewell, Malcolm E. *Representation in State Legislatures*. Lexington: University Press of Kentucky, 1982.

Johannes, John R. "Congress, the Bureaucracy, and Casework." *Administration and Society* (forthcoming, 1983).

Johannes, John R. and McAdams, John C. "The Congressional Incumbency Effect: Is It Casework, Policy Compatibility, or Something Else? An Examination of the 1978 Election." *American Journal of Political Science* 25 (August 1981): 512–42.

Jones, Bryan D.; Greenberg, Saadia R.; Kaufman, Clifford; and Drew, Joseph. "Bureaucratic Response to Citizen-Initiated Contacts: Environmental Enforcement in Detroit." *American Political Science Review* 71 (March 1977): 148–65.

Katz, Daniel; Gutek, Barbara E.; Kahn, Robert L.; and Barton, Eugenia. *Bureaucratic Encounters*. Ann Arbor: Institute for Social Research, 1975.

Katz, Elihu, and Danet, Brenda. *Bureaucracy and the Public: A Reader in Official-Client Relations*. New York: Basic Books, 1973.

Kazee, Thomas A. "The Decision to Run for the U.S. Congress: Challenger Attitudes in the 1970s." *Legislative Studies Quarterly* 5 (February 1980): 79–100.

Keefe, William J., and Ogul, Morris S. *The American Legislative Process: Congress and the States*. 4th ed. Englewood Cliffs, N.J.: Prentice-Hall, 1977.

Kefauver, Estes, and Levin, Jack. *A Twentieth-Century Congress*. Foreword by Robert M. LaFollette, Jr. New York: Duell, Sloan and Pearce, 1947.

Keller, Bill. "Executive Agency Lobbying: Mastering the Difficult Art of Congressional Liaison." *Congressional Quarterly Weekly Report* 39 (December 1981): 2387–92.

Kim, Chong Lim, and Pai, Seong-Tong. "Constituency Service among Korean National Assemblymen: A Study of Leadership Responsiveness." In *Political Participation in*

Korea, edited by Chong Lim Kim, pp. 181–204. Santa Barbara, Calif.: CLIO Books, 1980.

Klonoff, Robert. "The Congressman as a Mediator between Citizens and Government Agencies: Problems and Prospects." *Harvard Journal on Legislation* 16 (1979): 701–34.

Kofmehl, Kenneth. *Professional Staffs of Congress.* West Lafayette, Ind.: Purdue University Press, 1962.

Kornberg, Allan; Clarke, Harold D.; and LeDuc, Lawrence. "Some Correlates of Regime Support in Canada." *British Journal of Political Science* 2 (April 1978): 199–216.

Kumbhat, M. C., and Marican, Y. M. "Constituent Orientation among Malaysian State Legislators." *Legislative Studies Quarterly* 1 (August 1976): 389–404.

LeDuc, Lawrence, Jr., and White, Walter L. "The Role of Opposition in a One-Party Dominant System: The Case of Ontario." *Canadian Journal of Political Science* 7 (March 1974): 86–100.

Light, Larry. "Crack 'Outreach' Programs No Longer Ensure Reelection." *Congressional Quarterly Weekly Report* 39 (February 14, 1981): 316–18.

———. "Pressing the Flesh: For Many Incumbents, Running for Re-election Is Now a Full-time Job." *Congressional Quarterly Weekly Report* 37 (July 7, 1979): 1350–57.

McAdams, John C., and Johannes, John R. "Does Casework Matter? A Reply to Professor Fiorina." *American Journal of Political Science* 25 (August 1981): 581–604.

Maheshwari, Shriram. "Constituency Linkage of National Legislators in India." *Legislative Studies Quarterly* 1 (August 1976): 331–54.

Mann, Dean. *The Citizen and the Bureaucracy: Complaint-Handling Procedures of Three California Legislators.* Berkeley: Institute of Governmental Studies, University of California, 1968.

Mann, Thomas E. *Unsafe at Any Margin.* Washington, D.C.: American Enterprise Institute, 1978.

Mann, Thomas E., and Wolfinger, Raymond E. "Candidates and Parties in Congressional Elections." *American Political Science Review* 74 (September 1980): 617–32.

Matthews, Donald R. *U.S. Senators and Their World.* Chapel Hill: University of North Carolina Press, 1960.

Mayhew, David R. *Congress: The Electoral Connection.* New Haven: Yale University Press, 1974.

Mezey, Michael L. "Constituency Demands and Legislative Support: An Experiment." *Legislative Studies Quarterly* 1 (February 1976): 101–28.

Milwaukee Journal. August 31, September 13, November 11, 1977; April 9, 1978; December 10, 1979; June 13, 1982.

Mohapatra, Manindra Kumar. "The Ombudsmanic Role of Legislators in an Indian State." *Legislative Studies Quarterly* 1 (August 1976): 295–314.

Narain, Iqbal, and Puri, Lata. "Legislators in an Indian State: A Study of Role Images and the Pattern of Constituency Linkages." *Legislative Studies Quarterly* 1 (August 1976): 314–31.

Norton, Philip. " 'Dear Minister' — The Importance of MP-To-Minister Correspondence." *Parliamentary Affairs* 35 (Winter 1982): 59–72.

Ogul, Morris S. *Congress Oversees the Bureaucracy: Studies in Legislative Supervision.* Pittsburgh: University of Pittsburgh Press, 1976.

Olson, Kenneth G. "The Service Function of the United States Congress." In *Congress: The First Branch of Government,* edited by Alfred de Grazia, pp. 323–64. Garden City, N.Y.: Doubleday & Co., Anchor Books, 1967.

Parker, Glenn R. "Can Congress Ever Be a Popular Institution?" In *The House at Work,* edited by Joseph Cooper and G. Calvin Mackenzie, pp. 31–55. Austin: University of Texas Press, 1981.

————. "Sources of Change in Congressional District Attentiveness." *American Journal of Political Science* 24 (February 1980): 115–24.

————. "The Advantages of Incumbency in House Elections." *American Politics Quarterly* 8 (October 1980): 449–64.

Parker, Glenn R., and Davidson, Roger H. "Why Do Americans Love Their Congressmen So Much More Than Their Congress?" *Legislative Studies Quarterly* 4 (February 1979): 53–61.

Patterson, Samuel C.; Hedlund, Ronald D.; and Boynton, Robert G. *Representatives and Represented: Bases of Public Support for the American Legislatures.* New York: John Wiley & Sons, 1975.

Payne, James L. "The Personal Electoral Advantages of House Incumbents, 1936–1976." *American Politics Quarterly* 8 (October 1980): 465–82.

Pipe, C. Russell. "Congressional Liaison: The Executive Branch Consolidates Its Relations with Congress." *Public Administration Review* 26 (March 1966): 14–24.

Plott, Charles R. "Some Organizational Influences on Urban Renewal Decisions." *American Economic Review* 58 (May 1968): 306–21.

Price, Richard G.; Clarke, Harold D.; and Krause, Robert M. "The Socialization of Freshman Legislators: The Case of Canadian M.P.'s." In *Foundations of Political Culture: Political Socialization in Canada,* edited by John H. Pammett and Michael S. Whittington, pp. 211–38. Toronto: Macmillan of Canada, 1976.

Radler, Don. *How Congress Works.* New York: New American Library, Signet Books, 1976.

Ray, Bruce A. "Congressional Losers in the U.S. Federal Spending Process." *Legislative Studies Quarterly* 5 (August 1980): 359–72.

Reuss, Henry S., and Munsey, Everard. "The United States." In *The Ombudsman,* edited by Donald C. Rowat, pp. 194–200. London: George Allen & Unwin, 1965.

Riegle, Donald, with Trevor Armbrister. *O Congress.* New York: Popular Library, 1972.

Rieselbach, LeRoy N. *Congressional Politics*. New York: McGraw-Hill, 1973.

Ritt, Leonard G. "Committee Position, Seniority, and the Distribution of Government Expenditures." *Public Policy* 24 (Fall 1976): 463–89.

Robinson, James A. *Congress and Foreign Policy-Making: A Study in Legislative Influence and Initiative*. Rev. ed. Homewood, Ill.: The Dorsey Press, 1967.

Rosenthal, Alan. *Legislative Performance in the States: Explorations of Committee Behavior*. New York: The Free Press, 1974.

Rowat, Donald C., ed. *The Ombudsman: Citizen's Defender*. 2d ed. London: George Allen & Unwin, 1968.

Salisbury, Robert H., and Shepsle, Kenneth A. "Congressional Staff Turnover and the Ties-That-Bind." *American Political Science Review* 75 (June 1981): 381–96.

Saloma, John S., III. *Congress and the New Politics*. Boston: Little, Brown and Co., 1969.

Schwarz, John E., and Shaw, L. Earl. *The United States Congress in Comparative Perspective*. Hillsdale, Ill.: The Dryden Press, 1976.

Sharp, Elaine B. "Citizen-Initiated Contacting of Government Officials and Socioeconomic Status: Determining the Relationship and Accounting for It." *American Political Science Review* 76 (March 1982): 109–15.

Smith, Frank E. *Congressman from Mississippi: An Autobiography*. New York: Capricorn Books, 1964.

Sniderman, Paul M., and Brody, Richard A. "Coping: The Ethic of Self-Reliance." *American Journal of Political Science* 21 (August 1977): 501–22.

Stacey, Frank. *Ombudsmen Compared*. Oxford: Clarendon Press, 1978.

Tacheron, Donald G., and Udall, Morris K. *The Job of the Congressman*. 2d ed. Indianapois: Bobbs-Merrill, 1970.

Thomas, John Clayton. "Citizen-Initiated Contacts with Government Agencies." *American Journal of Political Science* 26 (August 1982): 504–22.

Thomas, Norman C., and Lamb, Karl A. *Congress: Politics and Practice*. New York: Random House, 1964.

Vedlitz, Arnold; Dyer, James A.; and Durand, Roger. "Citizen Contacts with Local Governments: A Comparative View." *American Journal of Political Science* 24 (February 1980): 50–67.

Verba, Sidney, and Nie, Norman H. *Participation in America: Political Democracy and Social Equality*. New York: Harper & Row, 1972.

Vinyard, Dale. "Congressmen as Washington Agents for Constituents." *Business and Government Review* 8 (September–October 1967): 19–25.

Washington Post. February 16–21, 1975; May 7, 29, 1976; April 25, June 18, August 15, September 8, October 1, December 7, 10, 1977; June 2, November 25, 1978; February 19, June 24, November 14, 1982.

Weaver, Warren, Jr. *Both Your Houses*. New York: Praeger, 1972.

Weeks, Kent M. *Ombudsmen around the World: A Comparative Chart*. 2d ed. Berkeley: Institute for Governmental Affairs, University of California, 1978.

Westen, T. Edward. "The Constituent Needs Help: Casework in the House of Representatives." In *To Be a Congressman: The Promise and the Power,* edited by Sven Groennings and Jonathan P. Hawley, pp. 53–72. Washington, D.C.: Acropolis Books, 1973.

Wilks, Danny. "Congressional Resources for the Grant Seeker." *Grantsmanship Center News,* January/February, 1980, pp. 27–37.

Worthly, John A., and Overstreet, Jack C. "Modern Technology Applied to Traditional Political Functions: The Florida State Ombudsman Program." *Polity* II (Winter 1978): 280–89.

Wright, Jim. *You and Your Congressman*. New York: G. P. Putnam's Sons, Capricorn Books, 1976.

Yiannakis, Diane Evans. "The Grateful Electorate: Casework and Congressional Elections." *American Journal of Political Science* 25 (August 1981): 568–80.

Government Documents

Aberbach, Joel D. "The Development of Oversight in the U.S. Congress: Concepts and Analysis." In *Techniques and Procedures for Analysis and Evaluation,* U.S. Congress, Senate, Commission on the Operation of the Senate. 94th Cong., 2d sess., 1977, Committee Print, pp. 53–69.

Breslin, Janet. "Constituent Service." In *Senators: Offices, Ethics, and Pressures,* U.S. Congress, Senate, Commission on the Operation of the Senate. 94th Cong., 2d sess., 1977, Committee Print, pp. 19–36.

———. "Orientation and Training." In *Senators: Offices, Ethics, and Pressures,* U.S. Congress, Senate, Commission on the Operation of the Senate. 94th Cong., 2d sess., 1977, Committee Print, pp. 47–58.

Brown, Bonnie; Valentine, Patricia; Means, Barbara; and Reynolds, Maureen. "Congressional Casework Manual." Washington, D.C.: Republican National Committee, n.d.

Carlile, Judy. "Casework in a Congressional Office." Washington, D.C.: Congressional Research Service, Library of Congress, 1981.

Hammond, Susan Webb. "The Operation of Senators' Offices." In *Senators: Offices, Ethics, and Pressures,* U.S. Congress, Senate, Commission on the Operation of the Senate. 94th Cong., 2d sess., 1977, Committee Print, pp. 4–18.

Hammond, Susan Webb; Moraski, Richard; and Nicholson, Jeanne B. "Senate Oversight Activities." In *Techniques and Procedures for Analysis and Evaluation,* U.S. Congress, Senate, Commission on the Operation of the Senate. 94th Cong., 2d sess., 1977, Committee Print, pp. 70–105.

Kravitz, Walter. "Casework by Members of Congress: A Survey of the Literature." Washington, D.C.: Legislative Reference Services, Library of Congress, 1968.

Lee, Riva. "Grantsmanship." Washington, D.C.: Congressional Management Foundation, 1977.

Ripy, Thomas B. "Congressional Communication with Administrative Agencies." Washington, D.C.: Congressional Research Service, Library of Congress, 1977.

U.S. Congress. *Congressional Record.* 87th Cong., 1st sess., 1961–97th Cong., 2d sess., 1982.

U.S. Congress. House of Representatives. Commission on Administrative Review. *Administrative Reorganization and Legislative Management.* 95th Cong., 1st sess., 1977. H. Doc. 232.

———. *Final Report.* 95th Cong., 1st sess., 1977. H. Doc. 272, vols. 1–2.

U.S. Congress. Joint Committee on the Organization of Congress. *Organization of Congress: Final Report.* 89th Cong., 2d sess., 1966. S. Report 2424.

———. *Organization of Congress, Hearings* pursuant to S. Con. Res. 2. 89th Cong., 1st sess., 1965, pts. 3, 5.

U.S. Congress. Senate. Commission on the Operation of the Senate. *Toward a Modern Senate.* 94th Cong., 2d sess., 1976. Final Report, S. Doc. 278.

U.S. Congress. Senate. Committee on Government Operations. Subcommittee on Intergovernmental Relations. *Confidence and Concern: Citizens View American Government: A Survey of Public Attitudes.* 93d Cong., 1st sess., 1973. Committee Print, pt. 1.

———. Subcommittee on Oversight Procedures. *Congressional Oversight: Methods and Techniques.* 94th Cong., 2d sess., 1976. Committee Print.

U.S. Congress. Senate. Committee on the Judiciary. *Administrative Ombudsman Hearings* before the Subcommittee on Administrative Practices and Procedures. 90th Cong., 1st sess., 1967.

———. *Ombudsman Hearings* before the Subcommittee on Administrative Practices and Procedures pursuant to S. Res. 190. 89th Cong., 2d sess., 1966, March 7, 1966.

———. *Regional Ombudsman Proposal, Hearings* before the Subcommittee on Administrative Practices and Procedures, pursuant to S. Res. 232. 90th Cong., 2d sess., March 27, 28; May 10, 1968, p. 209.

U.S. Department of Health, Education, and Welfare. "Feasibility Study to Improve Handling of Consumer Complaints: Evaluation Report." Unpublished report prepared by Technical Assistance Research Programs, Inc., pursuant to contract no. HEW-OS-74-292. Washington, D.C., 1976.

Yacker, Marc. "Congressional Office Operations: Aspects of Staff Organization in

Washington and the Congressional District." Washington, D.C.: Congressional Research Service, Library of Congress, 1976.

Unpublished Materials

Anagnoson, J. Theodore. "Bureaucratic Reactions to Political Pressure—The Case of Federal Community Development Grants." Paper delivered at the annual meeting of the American Political Science Association, Washington, D.C., August 31–September 3, 1979.
————. "Selecting Federal Projects: A Bureaucratic Perspective." Paper delivered at the annual meeting of the Midwest Political Science Association, Chicago, April 20–22, 1978.
Asher, Herbert. "The Unintended Consequences of Legislative Professionalism." Paper delivered at the annual meeting of the American Political Science Association, New York, August 31–September 3, 1978.
Bond, Jon. "A Paradox of Representation: Diversity, Competition, Perks, and the Decline of Policy Making in the U.S. House." Paper delivered at the annual meeting of the American Political Science Association, New York, September 3–6, 1981.
————. "Dimensions of District Attention Over Time." Paper delivered at the annual meeting of the Midwest Political Science Association, Chicago, April, 1983.
Brown, Stephen P.; Fuchs, Beth C.; and Hoadley, John F. "Congressional Perquisites and Vanishing Marginals: The Case of the Class of '74." Paper delivered at the annual meeting of the American Political Science Association, Washington, D.C., August 31–September 3, 1979.
Cain, Bruce E.; Ferejohn, John A.; and Fiorina, Morris P. "The Demand for Constituency Service in Great Britain and the United States." Paper delivered at the annual meeting of the Western Political Science Association, San Francisco, March 27–29, 1980.
————. "The Electoral Incentive in Comparative Perspective." Paper delivered at the annual meeting of the Midwest Political Science Association, Cincinnati, March 16–18, 1981.
————. "What Makes Legislators in Great Britain and the United States Popular?" Paper prepared for the Harvard Political Behavior Seminar, March 31, 1980.
Cavanagh, Thomas E. "The Two Arenas of Congress: Electoral and Institutional Incentives for Performance." Paper delivered at the annual meeting of the American Political Science Association, New York, August 31–September 3, 1978.
Cranor, John D., and Westphal, Joseph W. "Congressional District Offices, Federal Programs and Electoral Benefits: Some Observations on the Passing of the Marginal Representative, 1974–1976." Paper delivered at the annual meeting of the Midwest

Political Science Association, Chicago, April 20–22, 1978.

Davidson, Roger H. "Our Changing Congress: The Inside (and Outside) Story." Paper delivered at the Conference on Congress and the Presidency, Lyndon Baines Johnson Library: Austin, Texas; November 14–17, 1977.

———. "Our Two Congresses: Where Have They Been; Where Are They Going?" Paper delivered at the annual meeting of the Southern Political Science Association, New Orleans, November 3–5, 1977.

Frantzich, Stephen E. "Computers in Congress: Policy-Making in the Age of Information Technology." Paper delivered at the annual meeting of the American Political Science Association, Denver, September 2–5, 1982.

Goss, Carol F. "House Committee Characteristics and Distributive Politics." Paper delivered at the annual meeting of the American Political Science Association, San Francisco, September 2–5, 1975.

Greene, Kenneth R. "The Impact of Electoral Competition on Service Representation by Municipal Legislators." Paper delivered at the annual meeting of the Southern Political Science Association, Memphis, Tennessee, November 5–7, 1981.

———. "Policy and Service Representation by Municipal Legislators." Paper delivered at the annual meeting of the Midwest Political Science Association, Chicago, April, 1983.

Gross, Donald A., and Garand, James C. "The Vanishing Marginals." Paper delivered at the annual meeting of the Midwest Political Science Association, Milwaukee, April 29–May 1, 1982.

Macartney, John David. "Political Staffing: A View From the District," Ph. D. diss., University of California at Los Angeles, 1975.

Miller, Arthur H. "The Institutional Focus of Political Distrust." Paper delivered at the annual meeting of the American Political Science Association, Washington, D.C., August 31–September 3, 1979.

Miller, Lawrence W., and Wrinkle, Robert D. "Errand-Boy or Constituency Service: A Multi-State Study of Municipal Legislators." Paper delivered at the annual meeting of the Midwest Political Science Association, Chicago, April, 1983.

O'Donnell, Thomas J. "The Effects of Electoral Shifts and Legislative Responsibilities on the Allocation of Time by Congressmen." Paper delivered at the annual meeting of the Midwest Political Science Association, Milwaukee, April 29–May 1, 1982.

Parker, Glenn R., and Parker, Suzanne L. "The Causes and Consequences of Congressional District Attention." Paper delivered at the annual meeting of the American Political Science Association, Denver, September 2–5, 1982.

Payne, James L. "The Personal Electoral Advantages of House Incumbents, 1936–1974." Paper delivered at the annual meeting of the Southern Political Science Association, Gatlinburg, Tennessee, November 1–3, 1979.

Peterson, Steven A., and Dutton, William H. "Errand-Boy Behavior and Local Elections." Paper delivered at the annual meeting of the Midwest Political Science Association, Cincinnati, March 16–18, 1981.

Pika, Joseph A. "White House Boundary Roles: Linking Advisory Systems and Presidential Publics." Paper delivered at the annual meeting of the American Political Science Association, Washington, D.C., August 31–September 3, 1979.

———. "White House Office of Congressional Relations: A Longitudinal Analysis." Paper delivered at the annual meeting of the Midwest Political Science Association, Chicago, April 20–22, 1978.

Powell, Lynda W. "A Study of Financial Contributors in Congressional Elections." Paper delivered at the annual meeting of the American Political Science Association, Washington, D.C., August 31–September 3, 1979.

———. "Constituency Service and Electoral Margins in Congress." Paper delivered at the annual meeting of the American Political Science Association, Denver, September 2–5, 1982.

Ray, Bruce A. "Investigating the Myth of Congressional Influence: The Geographic Distribution of Federal Spending." Paper delivered at the annual meeting of the American Political Science Association, Chicago, September 2–5, 1976.

Rundquist, Barry S., and Kellstedt, Lyman A. "Congressional Interaction with Constituents: A Career Perspective." Paper delivered at the annual meeting of the American Political Science Association, Denver, September 2–5, 1982.

Weisberg, Herbert; Boyd, Thomas; Goodman, Marshall; and Gross, Debra. "Reelection and Constituency Service as State Legislator Goals: It's Just Part of the Job." Paper delivered at the annual meeting of the American Political Science Association, Denver, September 2–5, 1982.

Yiannakis, Diana Evans. "House Members' Communication Styles: Newsletters and Press Releases." Paper delivered at the annual meeting of the Midwest Political Science Association, Chicago, April 19–21, 1979.

INDEX

Abourezk, Sen. James, 86
Administration, House Committee on, 195
Administrative Counsel, Office of, 216
Administrative Ombudsman, Office of, 215
Administrative Review, House Commission on, 6, 8–11, 14, 18, 25–26, 30, 34–35, 40, 54, 62–63, 71–72, 74, 150–51, 156–60, 178, 188, 200, 207–9, 222
Advertising by congressmen, 44
Agricultural Stabilization and Conservation Service (ASCS), 166
Agriculture, Department of, 87, 122, 169
Air Force. *See* Military
Anagnoson, J. Theodore, 215
Army. *See* Military
Army Corps of Engineers, 21
Arnold, R. Douglas, 139–40
Aspin, Cong. Les, 217–18

Badham, Cong. Robert, 48
Baker, Sen. Howard, 86, 108
Barkley, Alben, 209
Barrett, Cong. William, 151
Bartlett, Sen. Dewey, 86
Bellmon, Sen. Henry, 86

Black Caucus, 82
Black lung disease, 20, 116
Blondel, J., 12
Bond, Jon, 190
Born, Richard, 190
Boundary-spanning agents, 58–59, 76, 92, 176. *See also* Casework staffs
Boundary-spanning structures, 57–58
Breslin, Janet, 220
Brock, Sen. Bill, 86
Brooke, Sen. Edward, 85
Bureaucrats: and casework loads, 50, 52; attitudes toward congressional casework staffs, 102–3, 112–13; casework requests by, 26, 31; congressional caseworkers' attitudes toward, 78–79, 115. *See also* Casework staffs (executive); Legislative-executive relations
Bureau of Prisons, 19, 215

Cain, Bruce E., 34
Campaign spending, 202–3
Carr, Cong. Bob, 210
Carter, Pres. Jimmy: and administrative responsiveness, 173; voters' assessments of, and electoral behavior, 203
Case loads, 34–35, 247 n. 5; and case-